Settele
Tutoring

When it comes to your scores,
don't settle for less…

Settele for more!

SAT® Math Packets

Practice Materials and Study Guide for the SAT Math Sections

by Mike Settele

Los Angeles, CA

www.setteletutoring.com

2022–2023 edition

Settele
Tutoring

Published by Settele Tutoring
For permissions and other inquiries, contact by email at materials@setteletutoring.com

The SAT® is a trademark registered by the College Board, which is not affiliated with, and does not endorse, this product.

Note: All Khan Academy content is available for free at (www.khanacademy.org). Khan Academy is not affiliated with, and does not endorse, this product.

This publication is designed to help students improve on the SAT. However, nothing in this publication should be construed as a guarantee of score improvement.

ISBN-13: 979-8761578753

Thank you for purchasing!

I strongly believe that everyone should be able to achieve their best scores, and the cost of test prep should not limit any student's potential. I'm grateful that you've chosen Settele Tutoring to help you reach your goals.

If you received this copy of the SAT Math Packets from a friend or other source, please consider purchasing your own copy at:

www.setteletutoring.com/materials

Purchasing this book supports a small business and helps me produce more practice materials, most of which are free. In addition to the Settele Tutoring website, you can find more SAT resources on social media. Please follow and subscribe!

YouTube.com/SetteleTutoring

Reddit.com/r/Settele_Tutoring

Instagram @SetteleTutoring

Twitter @SetteleTutoring

Facebook @SetteleTutoring

If you have questions, comments, or criticisms, feel free to reach out via social media or email Settele Tutoring directly. If you're a tutor interested in using the SAT Packets Study Guides with your students, please email for information about bulk pricing:

materials@setteletutoring.com

Author's Note

Dear Hardworking Student,

Thanks for buying my book! I hope it helps you improve your scores, not only by teaching you the topics tested on the SAT, but also by boosting your confidence in yourself.

I've been an SAT and ACT tutor since 2006, and I consistently find that students tend to be overwhelmed and intimidated by the standardized testing process. The scope of the exams is massive, and the pressure to succeed is intense. Maybe it's the stress, maybe it's the wording of the questions, but something about the SAT makes students doubt themselves. They feel like there's just too much that they don't know. But let me be clear — **you're smarter than you think you are**.

In fact, this book wasn't designed to teach you anything new. Instead, it's meant to remind you of what you already know. Still, I've included several test-taking strategies to help you apply your knowledge to the weird world of the SAT. This test is absolutely trying to trick you. But once you learn to see through their traps and disguises, you'll be able to solve and answer with confidence.

I also recommend purchasing *The Official SAT Study Guide* and registering for free SAT prep on the *Khan Academy website*. Both are great resources, but they can be just as overwhelming and intimidating as the SAT itself if you don't know where to start. Read the "How do you use this book?" chapter for advice on taking practice tests and using additional resources.

But the single best place to find more practice is the **Library on the Settele Tutoring website**. You'll find links to all of the video lessons — including walkthroughs for several of the packets in this study guide — and training tools that will help you develop new habits to implement the SAT-specific strategies. You'll also get quick access to the Settele Tutoring social media sites, where you can subscribe for free daily practice questions. My goal is to create a single site that can help you learn every strategy and practice every topic on the SAT. New features are added all the time, so check back frequently!

Once again, thank you for purchasing this book. If you found it helpful, please consider leaving a review so that others can benefit as well. I wish you the best of luck in your studying and on the test!

Sincerely,

Mike Settele
Settele Tutoring
mike@setteletutoring.com
www.setteletutoring.com

Table of Contents

packet checklist

Answers & Explanations

the right column tells you the
answer page for each packet

⬆

If you found this book helpful, please review it on Amazon.
It helps others find this study guide, and the support is greatly appreciated!

How do you use this book?

This study guide is a little different than other practice materials, so don't just dive in. Take a few minutes to read this introduction so that you know what you're getting into. It's better to have a plan!

What are "packets"?

how do you use this book?

The Basics

Think of this book as a collection of tiny "packets" of SAT Math information. Each packet is designed to be a miniature lesson on one very specific math topic. You'll notice that each packet follows the same basic structure:

1. **The Basics** — There are certain fundamental ideas that are central to each packet. This section shows you easy-to-medium level questions from this topic so that you can get a sense for what's expected. These first Examples should refresh your memory on the most important definitions and formulas. There typically won't be very many trap answer choices. In fact, Basic questions should be very similar to what you see in your Math class in school.

2. **The Twists** — Of course, the SAT is more than just a knowledge test. They're testing your problem-solving skills. They like to take the "basic" ideas that you're comfortable with and "twist" them up so that you have a much harder time recognizing what they're even asking. They know the mistakes that you're likely to make, and they put those wrong answers as trap choices to force an error. But don't panic! The Twists section shows you how the SAT makes each packet more difficult so that you can prepare for the traps.

3. **Exercise** — Learning a packet isn't just about memorizing facts. You also need to learn new habits that help you "untwist" the difficult questions and avoid trap answers. The SAT-specific strategies will help too. The Exercises let you practice in a controlled setting. You can NARROW YOUR FOCUS to just one packet at a time so that you aren't distracted by the dozens of other topics that pop up in each Math section. Make a conscious effort to try the Exercise using the new methods from the Examples: **change your strategy, change your score.**

The Twists

In some ways, the packets in this book are similar to the chapters that you'd find in any other test prep guide — they break the test down into more manageable pieces. However, there are two key differences between this book and most others:

1. **Much Less Reading** — Most test prep guides have a lot of text, which can be overwhelming. These packets only have a few sentences of guidance before the Examples. That's because you need to get in the habit of trusting yourself. You're smarter than you think you are! Through math class in school, you've already learned pretty much everything you need for the SAT, so use the Examples to see how much you remember. These are just practice questions, so don't be afraid to try something and fail. Many students struggle with the SAT because they have a bad habit of giving up on questions without really trying them. These packets are designed to help you form the good habit of trying something — anything! — on questions that seem confusing.

2. **Much Less Math** — As you practice, you'll discover that you're better at math than you thought you were. Still, some questions are just hard. If you struggled with a topic when you first learned it in school, you'll probably struggle with it again on the SAT. Most study guides just repeat the same-old, complicated, mathematical explanations that you've already heard from your teachers. This book understands that you need alternatives. **The first section of this guide covers five SAT-specific strategies** that will make many of the questions easier. The explanations in the back of the book will tell you when a question is more easily solved using one of the strategies.

The Packets

free points	**grph**	read the graph
	chrt	charts & probability
	COP	collection of points
arithmetic	**arith**	basic arithmetic
	ratio	ratios & units
	perc	percentages
	stat	statistics
algebra	**CAM**	common algebra mistakes
	rad	radicals
	exp	exponent rules
	abs	absolute value
	MBT	must be true
	POI	point of intersection
	alg+	advanced algebra
	div	dividing polynomials
	imag	imaginary numbers
properties	**LP**	linear properties
	QP	quadratic properties
	FP	function properties
	CP	circle properties
models	**LM**	linear models
	QV	quantity & value
	GM	geometry models
	XM	exponential models
	RAF	rearrange formulas
	WTF	"unusual" models
geometry	**ang**	angle rules
	SCT	similar & congruent triangles
	cyl	cylinders & more
	POW	part over whole
	trig	trigonometry
	geo+	advanced geometry

Typical SAT

No two SATs will be exactly the same, but there are still general trends. The chart below represents the average breakdown of the 58 questions on the Math portion of the SAT.

As you can see, some packets are more important than others. Still, **each question is worth about 10 points**, so even the minor topics can add up. For example, if you study the Circle Properties (CP) questions enough that you always get them right, you're essentially guaranteeing yourself those 10 points on every SAT. That's how you improve your scores — one question at a time!

Math	grph	grph	grph	chrt
ratio	ratio	arith	COP	COP	chrt
ratio	perc	perc	perc	stat	stat
CAM	CAM	CAM	CAM	stat	stat
CAM	rad/ exp	abs/ MBT	POI	POI	POI
LP	LP	LP	div/ imag	alg+	alg+
LP	LP	LP	QP	QP	QP
LM	LM	LM	CP	FP	FP
QV	GM	XM	XM	RAF	WTF
geo+	trig	cyl/ POW	ang/ SCT	WTF	WTF

Study Plans
how do you use this book?

The Basics

In short, there isn't really a wrong way to go through the packets. If you've been practicing for a while already, you probably have a good sense of your weaknesses, so feel free to jump right to those topics. Though, I recommend that **everyone begin with the chapter on SAT-specific strategies** so that you can start seeing the test in a new way. This book repeatedly references the SAT-specific strategies in both the packets and the explanations.

The answer keys are purposely separated from the packets so that you aren't tempted to give up too quickly. You really need to get in the habit of pushing through your confusion to <u>try something</u> on every question. When you're ready to check your work, **use the Table of Contents to find the answers and explanations** for each packet.

It might also be helpful to flip back and forth between the packet and the answers so that you can learn from your mistakes as you go. Here's how that would look for the majority of packets in this book:

1. **Do "The Basics" examples.** Use only your own knowledge and the guidance text on the page.

2. **Check your answers for "The Basics".** Read the explanations. Was there a better way to solve the questions?

3. **Do "The Twists" examples.** Use what you learned from "The Basics" to avoid traps. Don't give up if you're confused. Pick something no matter what!

4. **Check your answers for "The Twists".** Read the explanations. Did you fall for any traps? How would you get past any confusion next time?

5. **Do the entire Exercise.** Flip back to the examples if necessary, but try not to.

6. **Check your answers.** Read the explanations. Make a note to revisit this packet if you found it difficult.

The Twists

The longer answer for how to use this book depends on your study preferences and how much time you have until your SAT test day. If you're a typical high school student, who has minimal SAT experience and lots of other things going on in your life, then you can probably stick to the recommended schedule:

The 2 to 3 Plan

intensity	time	flexibility
low	~10 weeks	high

But if you know what you want and/or have a limited timeframe before the test, then you can choose from one of these specialized study plans to fit your personality. **Details about all study plans, including week-by-week schedules, are on the next few pages.**

The Robot

intensity	time	flexibility
medium	5+ weeks	low

The Collector

intensity	time	flexibility
high	15 weeks	medium

The Procrastinator

intensity	time	flexibility
high	2 weeks	low

The Free Spirit

intensity	time	flexibility
medium	8 weeks	high

The 2 to 3 Plan

The Basics

This is the recommended schedule for most students who have never tested or prepped before. It gets its name from its main principles:

- Start practicing 2 to 3 months before test day.
- Take a practice test every 2 to 3 weeks.
- Work on an additional 2 to 3 packets per week.

The first two weeks give you exposure to the format of the test and an overview of the main strategies. The remaining weeks alternate between targeted practice and big picture reviews. This study plan does not overwhelm you with time-consuming practice tests. In fact, the non-test weeks are relatively light. You can easily follow this plan during the school year when you already have a busy schedule.

The Twists

The non-test weeks may be light, but they should not be taken lightly. It's essential that you choose packets that cover your weaknesses. The goal is to fill in knowledge gaps and learn from mistakes.

As you review your tests, use the **Test Categorization Charts** (page 43) to identify the topics that you struggled with the most. Work through those packets first. On the next test, your goal is to get a higher percentage of those packet questions correct.

If you have more than 10 weeks, continue to repeat the pattern, alternating between a timed test and 2 to 3 packets that correspond to questions that you missed.

intensity	time	flexibility
low	~10 weeks	high

Week	Goal	Complete
1	Lesson 1 — Avoid Algebra	☐
	Lesson 2 — Textbook Math	☐
2	Untimed SAT #1 (standard review)	☐
3	Choose 2-3 packets: ___ ___ ___	☐
4	Timed SAT #5 (standard review)	☐
5	Choose 2-3 packets: ___ ___ ___	☐
6	Timed SAT #6 (standard review)	☐
7	Choose 2-3 packets: ___ ___ ___	☐
8	Choose 2-3 packets: ___ ___ ___	☐
9	Timed SAT #10 (standard review)	☐
10	Choose 2-3 packets: ___ ___ ___	☐

The Robot

The Basics

It's not always bad to be a robot. Robots like structure, order, and predictability. These are excellent qualities when you need to follow a consistent study schedule. The suggested lessons tell you exactly which topics to work on and how to move between the examples, exercises, and practice tests. There are 12 total lessons in this book, and they cover all of the 37 packets, so you can easily adjust this study plan to fit your needs.

The Twists

Practice test reviews are a little different for students who are working through the suggested lessons using this study plan. Instead of reviewing the entire test immediately after taking it, you review the questions based on the packets covered by the next set of lessons. For example, the review of SAT #10 would stretch over Weeks 4 and 5. Here's a more detailed breakdown:

- **Week 4**
  - take SAT #10
  - review test questions covered by Lesson 6 (ratio, POI)

- **Week 5**
  - review test questions covered by Lesson 7 (stat, abs, exp, imag)
  - review test questions covered by Lesson 8 (cyl, ang, SCT)
  - review test questions from past lesson packets
    - Lesson 3 (LP, LM)
    - Lesson 4 (CAM, rad, RAF)
    - Lesson 5 (grph, chrt, perc, XM)
  - review any remaining test questions

This may seem complicated, but it actually makes it easier to learn from your mistakes because you're NARROWING YOUR FOCUS to packets that have something in common, making it easier to recognize patterns and improve. And remember, you're a robot! You love patterns!

intensity	time	flexibility
medium	5+ weeks	low

Week	Goal	Complete
1	Lesson 1 — Avoid Algebra	☐
	Lesson 2 — Textbook Math	☐
	Untimed SAT #1 (standard review)	☐
2	Timed SAT #5 (review with lesson)	☐
	Lesson 3 — The Most Important Equation	☐
3	Lesson 4 — Algebra Crash Course	☐
	Lesson 5 — Avoid Traps	☐
4	Timed SAT #10 (review with lesson)	☐
	Lesson 6 — Stay Organized	☐
5	Lesson 7 — Memorize Math Vocab	☐
	Lesson 8 — Geometry Crash Course	☐

The Collector

The Basics

Some people absolutely hate leaving a box unchecked or a page unread. This study plan will have you answer every single question in this book and complete every single practice test in *The Official SAT Study Guide*. It's a big undertaking!

The Twists

Don't rush through it, especially the reviews. Even though you're signing up for the study plan with the greatest amount of work, you still need to follow the principle that quality is better than quantity. If you do a thousand questions but never pause to learn from your mistakes, then you'll still get the same score, as if you never practiced at all. Change your strategy, change your score!

Another problem that you might face is memory loss. For example, you'll be working through the Statistics packet during Week 5, which is more than two months before your actual SAT. That's a long time! It's likely that you'll forget a definition or some obscure fact, like "margin of error". It's okay! You're not superhuman. There's only so much information that any of us can pack into our brains. That's why each chapter includes an **Important Ideas** page, which summarizes the key formulas, strategies, definitions, etc. You should look these pages over before your practice tests to refresh your memory. They're especially helpful in the weeks leading up to the real test. Some ideas are tested very rarely (like margin of error), so it's possible that you haven't seen a question about a specific fact for a long time before your SAT. Even seeing it just one more time before the exam can help you get those points if the fact happens to show up in a question.

You may also decide to retake the SAT at some point, but you'll have used up your books, making it harder to study the second time around. Well, you should still review the packets in this study guide. You won't remember every single question. But you should also check the Settele Tutoring online library and social media platforms for links to additional resources and practice tests.

intensity	time	flexibility
high	15 weeks	medium

Week	Goal	Complete
1	Lesson 1 — Avoid Algebra	☐
	Lesson 2 — Textbook Math	☐
2	Untimed SAT #1 (standard review)	☐
3	all Free Points packets	☐
4	Timed SAT #3 (standard review)	☐
5	all Arithmetic packets	☐
6	Timed SAT #5 (standard review)	☐
7	all Algebra packets	☐
8	Timed SAT #6 (standard review)	☐
9	all Properties packets	☐
10	Timed SAT #7 (standard review)	☐
11	all Models packets	☐
12	Timed SAT #8 (standard review)	☐
13	all Geometry packets	☐
14	Timed SAT #9 (standard review)	☐
15	Timed SAT #10 (standard review)	☐

The Procrastinator

The Basics

Oh, boy… what have you done to get to this point? Well, there's nothing you can do about it now except roll up your sleeves and get to work. You can make a lot of progress in a short amount of time if you are open-minded about new strategies.

Nevertheless, this is a two-week study plan, not a two-day study plan. You should not cram all of this work into just a few days. Spread it out. You need to give the strategies and lessons time to absorb into your brain.

The Twists

If you're already short on time, it's going to be tempting to skip the Timed SATs, but you cannot do that. No exceptions. Find a time in your schedule when you can set aside the 3 ½ hours to take the entire test in one sitting. You need the experience, and a timed exam is an indispensable opportunity to build your endurance.

Similarly, do not skimp on the review. You need to do more than simply check your answers. Use the Settele Tutoring video explanations to understand your mistakes. You will choose packets based on those mistakes, but there will be other topics that you do not have time to cover thoroughly. Reviewing the one Imaginary Numbers question from SAT #1, for example, might be enough to get you the Imaginary Numbers points on the real test.

And perhaps most important, whatever happens on this SAT, please plan out your study schedule better for the next SAT! You should start practicing at least 2 months before test day. You'll definitely notice the difference.

intensity	time	flexibility
high	2 weeks	low

Week	Goal	Complete
1	Lesson 1 — Avoid Algebra	☐
	Lesson 2 — Textbook Math	☐
	Untimed SAT #1 (standard review)	☐
	Lesson 3 — The Most Important Equation	☐
	Timed SAT #5 (standard review)	☐
2	Choose 6 packets: (see note below):	☐
	___ ___ ___	
	___ ___ ___	
	Timed SAT #10 (standard review)	☐

Note: Choose 2 packets from each category, based on your weaknesses from the last practice test.

Short	Medium	Long
Read the Graph	Ratios & Units	Statistics
Charts & Probability	Percentages	Common Algebra Mistakes
Collection of Points	Point of Intersection	Quadratic Properties
Rearrange Formulas	Exponential Models	Function Properties
Angle Rules	Trigonometry	WTF Models

The Free Spirit

The Basics

Some people like charting their own course… marching to the beat of their own drum… playing by their own rules. Cool beans, dude. You do you. Ride those SAT vibes.

But you <u>must</u> start with the first two lessons! No exceptions! This entire book frequently refers back to those strategies, and they are an essential tool for improving your scores. You can "vibe" all you want <u>after</u> you've learned the fundamental ideas.

The Twists

This study plan might be good for students who suffer from **test anxiety**. It doesn't have timed practice tests until you're halfway through the schedule, which gives you plenty of time to ease into the format of the SAT. If you're not worried about your pacing, you can focus instead on learning new strategies and ideas. You can also pick the lessons that match your concerns about the test. The lessons themselves will still provide some structure, but you can jump around without feeling like you're missing anything. Even though the lessons are presented in an order that prioritizes the most important topics and ideas, each lesson is still designed to be self-contained. In other words, do what you feel like doing.

This study plan also uses the tests as "break weeks" to lower the stress. Of course, a 3 ½ hour test doesn't feel like a break while you're taking it. But saving the reviews for the following week gives you time to decompress. Even the final test during Week 7 can be reviewed during Week 8 if you prefer. Remember, you're the free spirit! You don't need to conform to checklists and rules (except the rule that you must do Lessons 1 and 2 first). It's okay if you adjust this plan to suit your schedule and your needs. Just don't let your studying get skipped until the last minute. You don't want to become the Procrastinator!

	intensity	time	flexibility
	medium	8 weeks	high

Week	Goal	Complete
1	Lesson 1 — Avoid Algebra	☐
	Lesson 2 — Textbook Math	☐
2	Untimed SAT #1 (review with lesson)	☐
	Pick a lesson:	☐
	_____	
3	Untimed SAT #5 (review with lesson)	☐
	Pick 2 lessons:	☐
4	_____	
	_____	☐
5	Timed SAT #10 (review with lesson)	☐
	Pick 2 lessons:	
6	_____	☐
	_____	☐
7	Timed SAT #9 (standard review)	☐
	Choose 3 packets:	
8	_____	☐
	____ ____ ____	

Suggested Lessons

how do you use this book?

The Basics

If you choose to follow one of the study plans, you'll be directed to these suggested lessons. The packets have been grouped in ways that emphasize big picture ideas and link key formulas and facts. The lessons are in order of relative importance.

No matter which study plan you choose or how you intend to work through this book, **everyone should start with Lesson 1 and Lesson 2**. These two lessons introduce the most important SAT-specific strategies. The rest of this study guide will make much more sense if you learn these strategies first.

The Twists

The study plans and lessons are meant to help you organize your SAT prep. At times, it might feel a bit disorganized as you flip between different packets and tests, but trust the process.

Following a plan is much better than blindly doing a series of practice tests without any guidance. The packets let you NARROW YOUR FOCUS to just a handful of topics and ideas at a time. Use the checkboxes to keep track of what you've done for each lesson.

Narrow Your Focus

In fact, this is a big picture idea that serves as a guiding principle for this entire study guide and all of the Settele Tutoring resources. The SAT tests dozens of topics in virtually limitless ways. If you try to tackle all of these topics at once, you won't absorb the information. It's too overwhelming.

But if you NARROW YOUR FOCUS to just one idea at a time — a single packet of information — then you're much more likely to learn. You'll notice the patterns that unify each topic. Repetition makes it more likely that you'll turn strategies and skills into habits.

Lesson Format

Each lesson has a few key components that you should be familiar with:

Big Picture Ideas

As you work through "The Plan" checklist, you'll be briefly directed to the 3 or 4 "Big Picture Ideas" in the righthand column. Read these paragraphs and keep the ideas in mind as you continue through the lesson. These ideas can help you understand the patterns that unify the packets in each lesson.

Review Worksheet

For some study plans, you won't immediately review a practice test after you take it. You'll use the lessons to organize your review instead. There are two ways to review tests:

Standard Review — This is what you'd probably do if you were studying completely on your own. Go in order through the sections, reviewing any questions that you got wrong or starred (see pages 42-43). You should do this before you move on to the next step in your study plan.

Review with Lesson — After you take the test, you can score your results, but you should wait to review the wrong answers and starred questions. For the upcoming lessons, use the Test Categorization Charts (page 43) to identify the packets for the questions that you got wrong or starred, and fill out the Review Worksheets. The lessons will instruct you to review all questions from each packet at once, which helps you notice patterns and learn from mistakes. As best you can, identify the reason that you got the question wrong or struggled with it. Before the next practice test, make sure that you review any additional questions that were not covered by these lessons.

Lesson Contents

The first two lessons cover strategies that apply to every single topic on the test. The table to the right represents the approximate number of questions covered by the other lessons. You can see why Lesson 3 is so important — those 9 questions represent more than 15% of the entire Math portion of the SAT!

1. Avoid Algebra
   - Guess & Check
   - Arithmetize
   - Plug Points Into Equations
2. Textbook Math
   - Memorize Formulas
   - Get Back to Basics
3. The Most Important Equation
4. Algebra Crash Course
5. Avoid Traps
6. Stay Organized
7. Memorize Math Vocab
8. Geometry Crash Course
9. Use the Strategies
10. Structures of Equations
11. Sorting Through Stories
12. Untwisting Geometry

Reasons for Wrong Answers

The "Review Worksheet" includes a place for you to identify the reason that you might have had trouble with a question. Hopefully, you'll see patterns that will help you understand your scores and ways to improve them. But this isn't an exact science. Plus, there might be multiple reasons involved!

Math	LP	LP	LP	LP	
CAM [4]	LM	LM	LM	LP [3]	LP
CAM	CAM	CAM	CAM	RAF	rad / exp
grph	grph	grph [5]	chrt	stat [7]	abs/ imag
perc	perc	perc	chrt	stat	stat
XM	XM	ratio	ratio [6]	ratio	stat
COP	COP [9]	POI	POI	POI	ang/ SCT [8]
MBT/ div	alg+	alg+	GM	arith	cyl / POW
QP	QP [10]	QP	WTF	QV [11]	trig [12]
FP	FP	CP	WTF	WTF	geo+

Reason	Symbol	Possible Remedy
carelessness — losing a negative; multiplying wrong; misreading a question	C	**Show Your Work** — do every step on the page; underline key words; note your frequent mistakes
fell for a trap — question led you to a trick answer; caught being lazy	T	**Sense the Difficulty** — hard questions won't have easy answers; know the SAT's favorite traps
should have used a strategy — algebra mistake; gave up on the question	S	**Avoid Algebra** — when a question is hard, try Guess & Check, Arithmetize, or Plug Points Into Equations
need to memorize a rule/formula — did not know a relevant fact	M	**Memorize Formulas** — go to the corresponding packet; review the "Important Ideas" pages
just a hard question — too hard, too confusing, or takes too long to solve	H	**Prioritize** — improve on easier questions to free up time for the hard ones; Get Back to Basics

#1 — Avoid Algebra

Guess & Check (55-56), Arithmetize (57-58)
Plug Points Into Equations (59-60)

The Basics

The most important thing you can do for your score is incorporate these strategies into your process. They're new tools that let you answer more questions, reduce careless mistakes, avoid trap answers, and work more efficiently.

The Twists

The exercises for these packets will help you see the strategies in action on a wide variety of topics. But the real SAT isn't so nicely organized. At first, you won't be sure when these strategies will work. It takes practice to learn the patterns.

The chart on the next page can help you identify questions that might use the strategies. You can also use the interactive version of the trainer tool on the Settele Tutoring website. Better yet, scan the code to the right to access a video walkthrough for this lesson. It's really good!

The Plan

1. **Learn Something New**
   - ☐ Big Picture #1 — Know Yourself
   - ☐ Guess & Check examples
   - ☐ Big Picture #2 — Trap Answers
   - ☐ Arithmetize examples
   - ☐ Plug Points Into Equations examples
   - ☐ Big Picture #3 — Don't Be Smart
   - ☐ Guess & Check exercise
   - ☐ Arithmetize exercise
   - ☐ Plug Points Into Equations exercise
   - ☐ Do the examples and exercises for Lesson 2
2. **Practice**
   - ☐ Untimed practice sections
3. **Improve**
   - ☐ *If you have the Settele Tutoring "SAT Reading & Writing Packets" study guide, you should complete Lessons 1 and 2 in that book too.*
   - ☐ Timed practice SAT (or do whatever is next in your chosen study plan)

Online Lessons and Tools

Avoid Algebra Lesson

SetteleTutoring.com/math

Math Strategy Trainer

SetteleTutoring.com/trainer/math

Big Picture Ideas

#1 — Know Yourself

Look at the first question for Guess & Check. *How does it make you feel? How confident are you that you can flawlessly work through all of the algebra steps?* As you learn the strategies, this gut reaction to questions is an important clue, telling you when to avoid algebra and try a strategy instead.

#2 — Trap Answers

For all of the Guess & Check examples, there were trap answers that often get picked when students use traditional algebra to solve (C, A and B, respectively). The Arithmetize examples have them too. This is why the strategies are better, even when you know the "textbook" way to solve. You may not make algebra mistakes often, but when you do, you will fall for an SAT trap without knowing it.

#3 — Don't Be Smart

Of all the SAT-specific strategies, Plug Points Into Equations is the easiest to implement. Don't think too hard about this. If you have points and equations, just plug the points into the equations. Don't worry whether it will work. Trust the process!

Math Strategy Trainer Tool

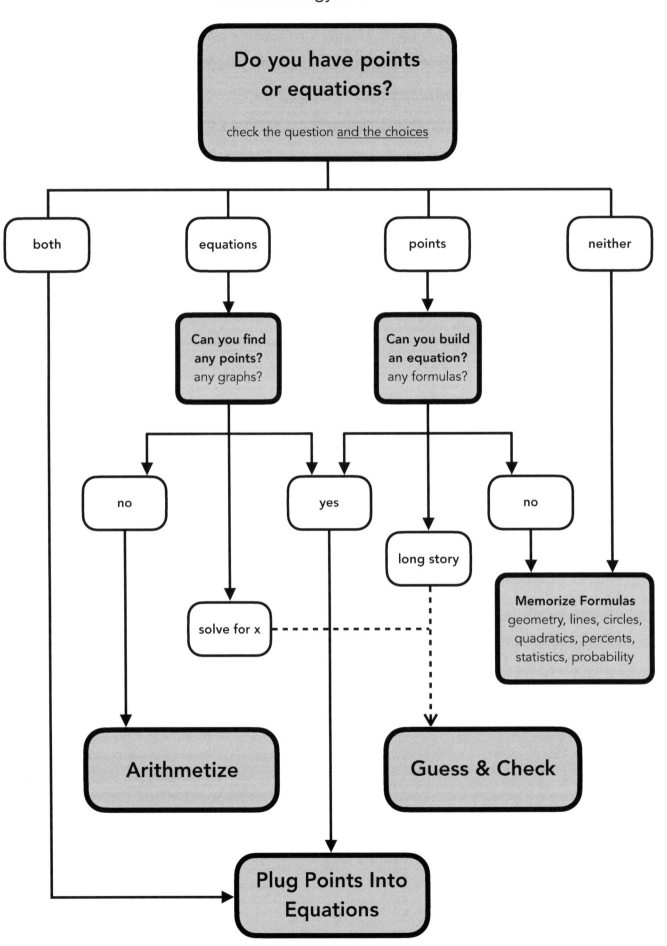

Do you have points or equations?

check the question <u>and the choices</u>

both · equations · points · neither

Can you find any points? any graphs?

Can you build an equation? any formulas?

no · yes · long story · no

solve for x

Memorize Formulas geometry, lines, circles, quadratics, percents, statistics, probability

Arithmetize

Guess & Check

Plug Points Into Equations

18

#2 — Textbook Math

Memorize Formulas (61-62)
Get Back to Basics (63-66)

The Basics

This is the Math section of the SAT, so it shouldn't be surprising that you need to know Math. Generally, by the time you take the SAT (in junior year of high school), you will have learned all or most of the topics that could appear on the test. Of course, you may have forgotten some of them. The packets in this study guide will remind you.

The Twists

Even if you've memorize every single fact and formula, you will likely still encounter SAT questions that stump you. That's because the SAT is very good at "twisting" familiar topics into unfamiliar shapes. Your job is to **Get Back to Basics** so that you can apply your knowledge. That's definitely easier said than done!

The strategies in Lesson 1 (Guess & Check, Arithmetize, and Plug Points Into Equations) are powerful tools that can untwist hard questions, but you'll also need the confidence to try your ideas. For now, don't be afraid to take risks.

The Plan

1. **Learn Something New**
    - [ ] Do the examples and exercises for Lesson 1
    - [ ] Memorize Formulas examples
    - [ ] Big Picture #1 — Know Yourself
    - [ ] Memorize Formulas exercise
    - [ ] Get Back to Basics examples
    - [ ] Big Picture #2 — Keep It Simple
    - [ ] Get Back to Basics exercise
2. **Practice**
    - [ ] Big Picture #3 — Prioritize
    - [ ] Untimed practice sections
3. **Improve**
    - [ ] *If you have the Settele Tutoring "SAT Reading & Writing Packets" study guide, you should complete Lessons 1 and 2 in that book too.*
    - [ ] Timed practice SAT (or do whatever is next in your chosen study plan)

Big Picture Ideas

#1 — Know Yourself

Is your mind a library, organizing and storing information for a long time? Or is it a grocery store, stocking the shelves with popular products, but throwing them out once they pass their expiration date? Many of us (understandably) forget rules and formulas that we're not using on a regular basis. In school, once we take the test, we toss whatever we don't need to make room in our brains for the next chapter or topic. Unfortunately, the SAT covers multiple years of math, so you may have thrown away some stuff that you're going to need. The Memorize Formulas exercise tests some of the more obscure topics that appear on the SAT. You've probably learned them before, but pay attention to how well you remember them. It's important to be honest with yourself about how good your memory is. That way, you can also be honest about how much studying you'll need to re-learn these topics for the SAT.

#2 — Keep It Simple

The SAT can "twist" up topics so that they become extremely confusing. But somewhere in that mess, there's almost always some clue that alerts you to the basic topic. For the Get Back to Basics examples, once we think in terms of $y = mx + b$, the questions quickly become much simpler. Your brain is actually pretty good at noticing the clues, so you have to have the confidence to act on them. If a question gives you an idea, write it down. Start on whatever Step 1 you notice. The odds are good that it's the right Step 1. Don't worry about Step 2 yet. In general, if you <u>can</u> do something, you <u>should</u> do it.

#3 — Prioritize

You won't be able to learn every single formula and fact at once, so don't try. Use the worksheet on the next page to create a personalized list of formulas, rules, definitions, skills, etc. that you need a little help remembering. Include example questions from this book and the practice tests. You're creating your own small study guide!

Memorization Worksheet

Formula / Fact / Definition (include whatever info you'd want the night before the test)	Example (page, question, test, section, etc.)	Formula / Fact / Definition (include whatever info you'd want the night before the test)	Example (page, question, test, section, etc.)

#3 — The Most Important Equation

Linear Properties (127-130),
Linear Models (145-148)

The Basics

A large portion of the SAT involves linear equations, specifically $y = mx + b$. The slope is m. The y-intercept is b. And (x, y) represent all of the points that lie on the line. There are other ways to write linear equations, but you should get back to $y = mx + b$ whenever you can. It's the most helpful and most easily understood version of a line.

The Twists

Lines are so common on the SAT because there are infinite ways to ask questions about them. You won't always immediately recognize that the question involves lines, so you need to train your brain to look for key words, such as "constant rate". Writing $y = mx + b$ on your page will keep you focused. There are a few other important formulas and terms to memorize, but $y = mx + b$ is the centerpiece.

Not all Linear Models stories will need you to think specifically about lines, but doing so can help when you're confused. The same goes for questions that ask about the number of solutions for an equation or two. You could solve these questions algebraically, but picturing lines and thinking about slopes is safer and easier.

The Plan

1. **Learn Something New**
   - ☐ Big Picture #1 — Prioritize
   - ☐ Linear Properties examples
   - ☐ Big Picture #2 — Get Back to Basics
   - ☐ Linear Models examples
2. **Learn from Past Mistakes**
   - ☐ Big Picture #3 — Memorize Formulas
   - ☐ review Linear Properties test questions
   - ☐ review Linear Models test questions
3. **Improve**
   - ☐ Big Picture #4 — Show Your Work
   - ☐ Linear Properties exercise
   - ☐ Linear Models exercise 1

Big Picture Ideas

#1 — Prioritize

If you study only one thing for the entire SAT, this is it! The vast majority of Math questions involve linear equations. Mastering these topics can lock in a large chunk of points. Plus, there isn't actually all that much to memorize for lines. Your biggest challenge will be recognizing <u>when</u> a question involves lines, so focus your mental energy on finding patterns that you'll be able to notice when you take the real test.

#2 — Get Back to Basics

Most SAT stories involve linear relationships. As much as you can, try to bring the story back to $y = mx + b$. Think in terms of slopes and intercepts. Learn the different words that questions use to talk about these concepts. Slopes are often described as rates, increases, decreases, and changes. Y-intercepts are starting points and initial values. You can usually make more sense of the story if you have an equation that condenses the story into mathematical terms.

#3 — Memorize Formulas

As you've seen by now, $y = mx + b$ is essential for a lot of questions. Beyond that, you need to memorize how this formula is affected by other "linear" terms, such as "parallel", "perpendicular", and "no solutions". These terms are a code that gives you secret instructions for the $y = mx + b$ equations that you build. You have to be able to translate quickly.

#4 — Show Your Work

Over time, you'll become so confident with linear equations that you'll start to cut corners when you solve them. Don't! People frequently lose points because they confuse x and y, especially in the slope formula. The confused version will almost certainly be a tempting wrong answer choice. More important, people get stuck on line questions because they don't do the simplest thing and write $y = mx + b$ on their page. Seeing the equation helps your brain think about it.

Review Worksheet

Reasons for wrong answers or confusion:

C = carelessness   **T** = fell for a trap   **S** = should have used a strategy

M = need to memorize a rule/formula   **H** = just a hard question

Linear Properties

Test	Section	Question	Reason
			C T S M H
			C T S M H
			C T S M H
			C T S M H
			C T S M H
			C T S M H
			C T S M H
			C T S M H
			C T S M H
			C T S M H
			C T S M H
			C T S M H
			C T S M H
			C T S M H

Linear Models

Test	Section	Question	Reason
			C T S M H
			C T S M H
			C T S M H
			C T S M H
			C T S M H
			C T S M H
			C T S M H
			C T S M H
			C T S M H
			C T S M H
			C T S M H
			C T S M H
			C T S M H

#4 — Algebra Crash Course

Common Algebra Mistakes (97-106),
Radicals (107-108), Rearrange Formulas (157-158)

The Basics

For better or worse, the SAT is largely an algebra test. If you don't know algebra, you're going to have a hard time improving your score. Practice solving and manipulating equations. Get comfortable working with variables.

The Twists

The SAT likes to take the algebra that you're used to and "twist" it up so that it looks harder. They'll have you solve for groups of variables or add in weird questions and stories. Mostly, these twists are distractions that can be ignored. And sometimes, the twisted questions are actually easier because we can use an SAT strategy to make the algebra go away.

The Plan

1. **Learn Something New**
   - [ ] Common Algebra Mistakes examples 1-5
   - [ ] CAM Distribution examples (6-10)
   - [ ] Big Picture #1 — Trap Answers
   - [ ] CAM Fractions examples (11-14)
   - [ ] CAM Inequalities examples (15-18)
   - [ ] CAM Factor & FOIL examples (19-22)
   - [ ] Radicals examples
   - [ ] Big Picture #2 — Know Yourself
   - [ ] Rearrange Formulas examples
2. **Learn from Past Mistakes**
   - [ ] Big Picture #3 — Show Your Work
   - [ ] review Common Algebra Mistakes test questions
   - [ ] review Radicals test questions
   - [ ] review Rearrange Formulas test questions
   - [ ] Big Picture #4 — Careless Mistakes
3. **Improve**
   - [ ] Essential Algebra exercise
   - [ ] Distribution exercise
   - [ ] Fractions exercise
   - [ ] Inequalities exercise
   - [ ] Factor & FOIL exercise
   - [ ] Radicals exercise
   - [ ] Rearrange Formulas exercise

Big Picture Ideas

#1 — Trap Answers

You should already sense that the wrong answers aren't random — they represent the most common algebra mistakes that everyone makes. Even on the most basic algebra questions, if you lose a negative or distribute incorrectly, your wrong answer is likely to be a choice. *Do you pick your answer immediately after you finish solving?* I recommend inserting a brief pause into your process so that you can hopefully notice if a mistake is leading you into a trap.

#2 — Know Yourself

Are you good at algebra? Be honest with yourself. If you were already struggling with the Fractions examples, then you're going to face some real challenges, especially on the No Calculator section. There are some questions where the SAT strategies are absolutely more efficient than traditional algebra. But there are many questions where you'll have no choice but to solve the traditional way. For the toss-up questions, where the strategies and algebra are equally effective, you need to pick your default move. If you're good at algebra, then stick to what works. If you're not, then the strategies <u>must</u> become your main tool to earn those algebra points. Use the Rearrange Formulas examples to test out your chosen method.

#3 — Show Your Work

As you review your answers, make sure that you find the spot where you went wrong. *Did you show your work for every step?* Doing steps in your head does not save time — it causes mistakes.

#4 — Careless Mistakes

Algebra can get very difficult, and simple rules can be tested in complex ways. But there are definitely times when you make careless errors that could have been easily prevented. You really want to lock in the points on easy questions at the beginning of each section. *How many questions did you get wrong because of careless mistakes?*

Review Worksheet

Reasons for wrong answers or confusion:

C = carelessness   **T** = fell for a trap   **S** = should have used a strategy

M = need to memorize a rule/formula   **H** = just a hard question

Common Algebra Mistakes

Test	Section	Question	Reason				
			C	T	S	M	H
			C	T	S	M	H
			C	T	S	M	H
			C	T	S	M	H
			C	T	S	M	H
			C	T	S	M	H
			C	T	S	M	H
			C	T	S	M	H
			C	T	S	M	H
			C	T	S	M	H
			C	T	S	M	H
			C	T	S	M	H
			C	T	S	M	H
			C	T	S	M	H

Radicals

Test	Section	Question	Reason				
			C	T	S	M	H
			C	T	S	M	H
			C	T	S	M	H
			C	T	S	M	H
			C	T	S	M	H

Rearrange Formulas

Test	Section	Question	Reason				
			C	T	S	M	H
			C	T	S	M	H
			C	T	S	M	H
			C	T	S	M	H
			C	T	S	M	H
			C	T	S	M	H
			C	T	S	M	H
			C	T	S	M	H

#5 — Avoid Traps

Read the Graph (69-70), Charts & Probability (71-74),
Percentages (85-88), Exponential Models (153-156)

The Basics

The College Board would probably strongly protest the labeling of some choices as "traps" or "tricks". But the truth is that the wrong answer choices aren't random — they're purposely chosen based on the mistakes that you're most likely to make. These topics, in particular, involve mistakes that can be hard to notice and correct.

The Twists

The Read the Graph and Charts & Probability questions don't involve much arithmetic, which makes you more likely to jump to your first answer without second guessing. On the other hand, Percentages and Exponential Models do involve arithmetic, but it's often done on the calculator, so you trust the machine too much and don't pause to check your work. In all cases, knowing that the traps exist is the first step to avoiding them.

The Plan

1. **Learn Something New**
    - ☐ Read the Graph examples
    - ☐ Big Picture #1 — Know the Rules
    - ☐ Charts & Probability examples
    - ☐ Big Picture #2 — Memorize Formulas
    - ☐ Percentages examples
    - ☐ Exponential Models examples
2. **Learn from Past Mistakes**
    - ☐ Big Picture #3 — Show Your Work
    - ☐ review Read the Graph test questions
    - ☐ review Charts & Probability test questions
    - ☐ review Percentages test questions
    - ☐ review Exponential Models test questions
3. **Improve**
    - ☐ Big Picture #4 — Trap Answers
    - ☐ Read the Graph exercise
    - ☐ Charts & Probability exercise 1
    - ☐ Percentages exercise 1
    - ☐ Exponential Models exercise 1

Big Picture Ideas

#1 — Know the Rules

Did you fall for any of the traps? Did you forget to check the scale of the graphs? Even if not, you should still look for trap answers so that you can learn to recognize them on future questions. The SAT absolutely loves to create traps by messing with the scale on a graph. If you know that the SAT is playing by this rule, you also know to watch out for it and check the scale every time, no matter what. In the remaining packets, try to learn the SAT's rules so that you can play the same game and avoid the traps.

#2 — Memorize Formulas

There are a lot of percentage formulas out in the world, but the OPEN formula is specifically designed to stop you from falling for SAT traps. It works so well because it keeps you organized and helps on a wider variety of topics than most other percentage formulas. I highly recommend that you memorize all of its variations and integrate them into your process.

#3 — Show Your Work

As always, the more of your ideas that you can put on the page, the better. Graph questions often seem like exceptions that don't require any work, but you still need to do whatever you can to get all of them correct. Even just circling the title, axis labels, and scale can make a big difference if it helps you notice and avoid a potential trap. You know that the traps are coming, so underlining key words and using the OPEN formula are your way of playing defense.

#4 — Trap Answers

Obviously, this is a big picture idea — it's the whole point of this lesson! But many people understand that trap answers exist, but they fail to incorporate that knowledge into their work. You need to be aware of traps every time one of these topics appears on your test. If you remember that the traps exist, you're much less likely to fall for them.

Review Worksheet

Reasons for wrong answers or confusion:

C = carelessness   **T** = fell for a trap   **S** = should have used a strategy

M = need to memorize a rule/formula   **H** = just a hard question

Read the Graph

Test	Section	Question	Reason
			C T S M H
			C T S M H
			C T S M H
			C T S M H
			C T S M H
			C T S M H
			C T S M H

Percentages

Test	Section	Question	Reason
			C T S M H
			C T S M H
			C T S M H
			C T S M H
			C T S M H
			C T S M H
			C T S M H

Charts & Probability

Test	Section	Question	Reason
			C T S M H
			C T S M H
			C T S M H
			C T S M H
			C T S M H
			C T S M H

Exponential Models

Test	Section	Question	Reason
			C T S M H
			C T S M H
			C T S M H
			C T S M H
			C T S M H
			C T S M H

#6 — Stay Organized

Ratios & Units (81-84),
Point of Intersection (117-118)

The Basics

Some SAT questions are hard because the topic is hard (Exponent Rules). Other questions are hard because the stories are confusing (Quantity & Value). But the questions in this lesson are hard because they involve a lot of steps. Each individual step is pretty easy, but together, they can make a frustrating whole. One error in one step can cost you all of the points. Show your work and stay organized to protect those points.

The Twists

There's really no limit to the complexity of these questions. Point of Intersection questions can involve factoring, and even the quadratic formula. Ratios & Units questions can require six or seven conversion steps. Try not to get intimidated into quitting. That said, if you're running short on time, these questions might be good ones to skip. They can be time consuming, and they're not worth more points than any of the other questions. Just make sure that you look at the answer choices first. There might be a way to Guess & Check or eliminate some numbers that don't make sense with the story.

The Plan

1. **Learn Something New**
   - ☐ Big Picture #1 — Show Your Work
   - ☐ Ratios & Units examples
   - ☐ Point of Intersection examples
2. **Learn from Past Mistakes**
   - ☐ Big Picture #2 — Memorize Formulas
   - ☐ Big Picture #3 — Careless Mistakes
   - ☐ Big Picture #4 — Trap Answers
   - ☐ review Ratios & Units test questions
   - ☐ review Point of Intersection test questions
3. **Improve**
   - ☐ Ratios & Units exercise 1
   - ☐ Point of Intersection exercise

Big Picture Ideas

#1 — Show Your Work

Both of these packets involve questions with multiple steps and multiple opportunities for mistakes. And with so many steps and so much time invested in just one question, a little mistake can cost you a lot. Even if you are the greatest mathematician alive, there is still a chance that you could lose a negative or multiply incorrectly. Don't take risks! Every single step should be on your page. Seeing the arithmetic gives you an extra moment to catch a mistake before it gets buried in the rest of the steps. This is especially important with Ratios & Units questions, which almost always require your calculator. But the calculator is only as good as your entries. It's easy to make a mistake by ignoring the order of operations when you enter your calculations. You can catch these mistakes by writing every step on the page, even if you use the calculator to perform the arithmetic. Only doing the work in your head or on the calculator saves you maybe 5 seconds, but it could cost you 10 points!

#2 — Memorize Formulas

As you review your answers, your goal should be to understand why you got these questions wrong. There might not be one single cause. *First, did you not know how to solve these topics?* Hopefully, working through the examples in each packet lets you memorize the process for next time.

#3 — Careless Mistakes

Second, did you make careless arithmetic mistakes? Can you pinpoint the mistake in your work? See if there are steps that repeatedly create errors for you.

#4 — Trap Answers

Finally, the SAT's wrong answers aren't random. *Did you solve for the wrong variable? Did you leave out a part of the question?* Showing work by underlining important information might have saved the points. Try to figure out the reason for your mistakes, and adjust your process to prevent them next time.

Review Worksheet

Ratios & Units

Test	Section	Question	Reason
			C T S M H
			C T S M H
			C T S M H
			C T S M H
			C T S M H
			C T S M H
			C T S M H
			C T S M H
			C T S M H
			C T S M H
			C T S M H
			C T S M H
			C T S M H
			C T S M H

Point of Intersection

Test	Section	Question	Reason
			C T S M H
			C T S M H
			C T S M H
			C T S M H
			C T S M H
			C T S M H
			C T S M H
			C T S M H
			C T S M H
			C T S M H
			C T S M H
			C T S M H
			C T S M H

#7 — Memorize Math Vocab

Statistics (89-94), Exponent Rules (109-112),
Absolute Value (113-114), Imaginary Numbers (123-124)

The Basics

When most people think of SAT vocabulary, they imagine the weird "SAT words" that show up in the Reading section. The older versions of the SAT had a plethora of esoteric and archaic terminology that left students bewildered and vexed. Even though jargon like this is currently less important in the Reading section, vocabulary has become a surprisingly large part of the Math section. The packets in this lesson show questions with very little arithmetic or algebra, where knowing a vocab word or math fact is often enough to earn the points.

The Twists

The packets in this lesson aren't the only ones that are heavy on vocabulary. There are several definitions to memorize for Linear and Quadratic Properties, in particular. But this lesson emphasizes topics where you can't really get the points without the vocabulary. SAT strategies won't help you too much. Learn the words, get the points!

The Plan

1. **Learn Something New**
   - ☐ Big Picture #1 — Memorize Formulas
   - ☐ Statistics examples (1-7)
   - ☐ Absolute Value examples
   - ☐ Big Picture #2 — Prioritize
   - ☐ Exponent Rules examples
   - ☐ Imaginary Numbers examples
2. **Learn from Past Mistakes**
   - ☐ Big Picture #3 — Show Your Work
   - ☐ review Statistics test questions
   - ☐ review Absolute Value test questions
   - ☐ review Exponent Rules test questions
   - ☐ review Imaginary Numbers test questions
3. **Improve**
   - ☐ Statistics exercises (1-15)
   - ☐ Absolute Value exercise
   - ☐ Exponent Rules exercise 1
   - ☐ Imaginary Numbers exercise

Big Picture Ideas

#1 — Memorize Formulas

The line between formulas and vocabulary words is thin. Knowing a formula is about knowing the words that trigger you to use it. Statistics questions might not involve much math, but they still require an understanding of mathematical concepts. In fact, you won't be able to get many of the Statistics questions right without memorizing the relevant facts. There's no way to figure them out in the moment. The same is true of the hardest Exponent Rules and Imaginary Numbers questions, where the math gets too complex to Arithmetize or Guess & Check. You have to solve by memorizing the rules and formulas.

#2 — Prioritize

If you're not great at algebra, then Exponent Rules and Imaginary Numbers questions will probably be hard for you. The SAT-specific strategies don't work very well because exponents and imaginary numbers are weird and unintuitive. Memorize what you can, but also remember that these topics do not make up a large portion of the SAT. There are better places to spend your practice time. Statistics is one of them. It's a big part of the Calculator section, and many of the questions are quick and easy if you've memorized the vocabulary. The brain can only learn and store so much information, so try to memorize the stuff that will get you the most SAT points.

#3 — Show Your Work

Some of the most common Statistics mistakes come from taking shortcuts. If you try to compute an average with your calculator in one entry, it's common to forget parentheses, which would create an arithmetic error. If you rush through finding a median, you could forget to order the terms sequentially or completely ignore the frequencies for each value. *As you review your answers, did you make mistakes because you didn't show work?* This is also true for the other topics, especially Exponent Rules, where it's best to apply the rules one by one on your page.

Review Worksheet

Reasons for wrong answers or confusion:

C = carelessness   **T** = fell for a trap   **S** = should have used a strategy

M = need to memorize a rule/formula   **H** = just a hard question

Statistics

Test	Section	Question	Reason
			C T S M H
			C T S M H
			C T S M H
			C T S M H
			C T S M H
			C T S M H
			C T S M H
			C T S M H
			C T S M H
			C T S M H
			C T S M H
			C T S M H
			C T S M H
			C T S M H

Absolute Value

Test	Section	Question	Reason
			C T S M H
			C T S M H
			C T S M H

Exponent Rules

Test	Section	Question	Reason
			C T S M H
			C T S M H
			C T S M H
			C T S M H

Imaginary Numbers

Test	Section	Question	Reason
			C T S M H
			C T S M H
			C T S M H
			C T S M H

#8 — Geometry Crash Course

Angle Rules (165-166), Similar & Congruent Triangles (167-170),
Cylinders & More (171-172)

The Basics

You spent a year or more learning Geometry in school, but the SAT doesn't test it all that much. Just a handful of rules and formulas show up in the questions, and many of those formulas are given to you in the Reference Chart. Make sure that you learn the basics so that the easy Geometry questions don't get missed.

The Twists

Of course, the SAT will find all sorts of ways to make the basic ideas much harder to spot in the difficult questions. Don't let the wording of the question intimidate you! If a question is about a cylinder, write down the cylinder volume formula. If a question has two triangles, start building ratios. Even the hard questions involve the basic formulas, so putting them down on the page will help you figure out how to "untwist" the question. If you're stuck, look for words that might give additional information, like "isosceles" and "parallel".

The Plan

1. **Learn Something New**
   - [ ] Cylinders & More examples
   - [ ] Big Picture #1 — Memorize Formulas
   - [ ] Angle Rules examples
   - [ ] Similar & Congruent Triangles examples
2. **Learn from Past Mistakes**
   - [ ] Big Picture #2 — Careless Mistakes
   - [ ] review Cylinders & More test questions
   - [ ] review Angle Rules test questions
   - [ ] review Similar & Congruent Triangles test questions
3. **Improve**
   - [ ] Big Picture #3 — Keep It Simple
   - [ ] Cylinders & More exercise
   - [ ] Angle Rules exercise
   - [ ] Similar & Congruent Triangles exercise 1
   - [ ] Big Picture #4 — Prioritize

Big Picture Ideas

#1 — Memorize Formulas

The 3-dimensional shapes are all included in the Reference Chart, so there's not much to memorize. Ironically, it's the simpler shapes and pictures that will require memorization. You need to memorize the relevant vocabulary for angles and triangles, but you also need to be able to recognize when the rules are necessary to solve the question.

#2 — Careless Mistakes

You can memorize all of the formulas but still lose points if you're not careful. The SAT tries to mislead you with certain terms, so pay attention to the difference between diameter and radius or perimeter and area. Be careful that you actually give them the angle or side that they're asking for. Instead of x, label your work with the actual names of angles and sides, such as $\overline{AB}$ or $\angle PQR$.

#3 — Keep It Simple

Geometry questions can look very unique, making it hard to recognize patterns that would help you on every test. But remember that there aren't actually that many shapes or formulas. The combinations may seem endless, but the building blocks are limited. When in doubt, Get Back to Basics and write whatever rules you can remember on the page. Seeing them might help you see the next step.

#4 — Prioritize

If you're still struggling with these topics, don't worry. They're not a large portion of the SAT. You're probably skilled enough to handle the easy and medium level questions. You can afford to let a hard one slip by occasionally, especially since the chance of seeing a hard question from these topics is pretty low. You're better off mastering more frequently tested topics, like Linear Properties and Common Algebra Mistakes.

Review Worksheet

Reasons for wrong answers or confusion:

C = carelessness   **T** = fell for a trap   **S** = should have used a strategy

M = need to memorize a rule/formula   **H** = just a hard question

Cylinders & More

Test	Section	Question	Reason
			C T S M H
			C T S M H
			C T S M H
			C T S M H
			C T S M H
			C T S M H

Angle Rules

Test	Section	Question	Reason
			C T S M H
			C T S M H
			C T S M H
			C T S M H
			C T S M H
			C T S M H
			C T S M H

Similar & Congruent Triangles

Test	Section	Question	Reason
			C T S M H
			C T S M H
			C T S M H
			C T S M H
			C T S M H
			C T S M H
			C T S M H
			C T S M H
			C T S M H
			C T S M H
			C T S M H
			C T S M H
			C T S M H

#9 — Use the Strategies

Collection of Points (75-76), Must Be True (115-116), Advanced Algebra (119-120), Dividing Polynomials (121-122), Geometry Models (151-152)

The Basics

The SAT is going to throw a lot of complicated-looking questions at you. They want to scare you and force you to make mistakes. You can't let them win! SAT questions are as varied as the stars, but you need to recognize patterns that indicate when an SAT-specific strategy is more efficient and effective.

The Twists

One of the most common SAT frustrations is, "I don't know when to use the strategies." This can be hard, but it's essential that you figure it out. Notice that almost all of the questions in this lesson involve algebra that looks hard. That's a big clue that a strategy might save you. Listen to your confusion — it's your brain's way of telling you that your normal methods might not work. And whenever you think a strategy might work, you need to try it, even if you're not completely sure. You won't know unless you try.

The Plan

1. **Learn Something New**
   - ☐ Big Picture #1 — Keep It Simple
   - ☐ Collection of Points examples
   - ☐ Big Picture #2 — Show Your Work
   - ☐ Must Be True examples
   - ☐ Geometry Models examples
   - ☐ Advanced Algebra examples
   - ☐ Dividing Polynomials examples
2. **Learn from Past Mistakes**
   - ☐ Big Picture #3 — Trap Answers
   - ☐ review Collection of Points test questions
   - ☐ review Must Be True test questions
   - ☐ review Geometry Models test questions
   - ☐ review Advanced Algebra test questions
   - ☐ review Dividing Polynomials test questions
3. **Improve**
   - ☐ Collection of Points exercise
   - ☐ Must Be True exercise
   - ☐ Geometry Models exercise
   - ☐ Advanced Algebra exercise
   - ☐ Dividing Polynomials exercise

Big Picture Ideas

#1 — Keep It Simple

The simplest and most useful SAT-specific Math strategy is Plug Points Into Equations. If you have points and you have equations, plug the points into the equations! You don't need to ask any deeper questions. The SAT disguises these situations with elaborate stories or confusing math vocabulary, but your job is to immediately recognize when you have points and equations. Strip the question down to its simplest components.

#2 — Show Your Work

The main reason that people get these question types wrong is that they "think" about them. They use logic and reasoning to choose an answer, but there's no work on their page proving the answer. On the SAT, it's very rare for a question to be definitively solved without some sort of work. Often, the best way to turn a "think" question into a "work" question is to show your reasoning using actual numbers. Arithmetize to give your brain numbers to work with and show the arithmetic on the page.

#3 — Trap Answers

As you review the questions, think about why you chose these wrong answers. *Did an arithmetic mistake lead you astray?* It happens. But more often, people fall for traps on these types of questions because the SAT is purposely trying to lead you away from the right answer. Trap answers are usually very logical, and it's easy to see why someone would pick them based on a quick reading of the question. Unfortunately, this quick logical reasoning almost always leaves out an important fact, and so you fall for the trap. The best way to avoid traps is to use SAT-specific strategies, like Arithmetize, Guess & Check, and Plug Points Into Equations. *Did you confidently pick an answer without showing much work?* You almost certainly fell for the exact trap that the SAT was hoping for.

Review Worksheet

Reasons for wrong answers or confusion:

C = carelessness   **T** = fell for a trap   **S** = should have used a strategy
M = need to memorize a rule/formula   **H** = just a hard question

Collection of Points

Test	Section	Question	Reason
			C T S M H
			C T S M H
			C T S M H

Must Be True

Test	Section	Question	Reason
			C T S M H
			C T S M H
			C T S M H

Geometry Models

Test	Section	Question	Reason
			C T S M H
			C T S M H
			C T S M H
			C T S M H
			C T S M H

Advanced Algebra

Test	Section	Question	Reason
			C T S M H
			C T S M H
			C T S M H
			C T S M H
			C T S M H
			C T S M H
			C T S M H
			C T S M H

Dividing Polynomials

Test	Section	Question	Reason
			C T S M H
			C T S M H
			C T S M H
			C T S M H
			C T S M H

#10 — Structures of Equations

Quadratic Properties (131-136), Function Properties (137-140),
Circle Properties (141-142)

The Basics

Exponents make algebra much more complex, and these packets reflect that. You'll notice that quadratics, polynomials, and circles involve more equations and more vocabulary than the lesson on lines. Prioritize quadratics, but look for patterns that can help you memorize the rest.

The Twists

These packets have a wide range of difficulty. For example, you could get a very easy quadratics question with simple factoring to find the roots, or you could have a difficult, tedious quadratics question that involves quadratic formula. Pay attention to the question number, since easier questions are at the beginning of the sections and harder ones are near the end. You should not be using quadratic formula on question #4!

The Plan

1. **Learn Something New**
   - ☐ Big Picture #1 — Memorize Formulas
   - ☐ Quadratic Properties "The Basics"
   - ☐ Convert Quadratics Exercise
   - ☐ Big Picture #2 — Get Back to Basics
   - ☐ Function Properties examples 1-4
   - ☐ Circle Properties examples
   - ☐ Function Properties examples 5-8
   - ☐ Quadratic Properties "Twists" (examples 2-4)
2. **Learn from Past Mistakes**
   - ☐ Big Picture #3 — Know Yourself
   - ☐ review Quadratic Properties test questions
   - ☐ review Function Properties test questions
   - ☐ review Circle Properties test questions
3. **Improve**
   - ☐ Graphs of Quadratics exercise (QP 1-10)
   - ☐ Functions and Factors exercise (FP 1-4)
   - ☐ Big Picture #4 — Prioritize
   - ☐ Circle Properties exercise
   - ☐ Function Values exercise (FP 5-7)
   - ☐ Special Function Values exercise (FP 8-9)
   - ☐ Advanced Quadratics exercise (QP 11-15)

Big Picture Ideas

#1 — Memorize Formulas

The first page of the Quadratic Properties packet is one of the most helpful in this book. You should review it before every practice test and real SAT that you take. You need to be able to quickly recognize different versions of quadratic equations, which behave like formulas. But you also need to be able to quickly recognize the various vocabulary words associated with quadratics. Many Quadratic Properties questions involve very little math because they test the vocab instead. These are easy points if you've memorized everything on that first page.

#2 — Get Back to Basics

As you learn about functions and circles, look for similarities with quadratics. You'll see that the factors and x-intercepts of higher order functions behave the same way as they do for quadratics. You'll also notice that the circle formula mimics the vertex form of a quadratic in some important ways. In fact, you can think of the vertex as the center of a parabola to help you remember the formula. The packets in this lesson involve a lot of memorization, so finding similarities will help you recall the information later.

#3 — Know Yourself

Are you making algebra mistakes? Did you miss vocabulary questions? Are there specific formulas that you have trouble remembering? Use this review to look for patterns. You want to know your weaknesses so that you can review them before the next test.

#4 — Prioritize

The previous exercises hit the highlights of these packets — the stuff that's likely to come up again in a similar way on the real test. The remaining exercises are more difficult and have a lower probability of showing up on tests. If you're struggling with Math, don't worry as much about these harder topics. There are easier ways to improve your score.

Review Worksheet

Reasons for wrong answers or confusion:

C = carelessness   **T** = fell for a trap   **S** = should have used a strategy

M = need to memorize a rule/formula   **H** = just a hard question

Quadratic Properties

Test	Section	Question	Reason
			C T S M H
			C T S M H
			C T S M H
			C T S M H
			C T S M H
			C T S M H
			C T S M H
			C T S M H
			C T S M H
			C T S M H
			C T S M H
			C T S M H
			C T S M H

Function Properties

Test	Section	Question	Reason
			C T S M H
			C T S M H
			C T S M H
			C T S M H
			C T S M H
			C T S M H
			C T S M H

Circle Properties

Test	Section	Question	Reason
			C T S M H
			C T S M H
			C T S M H
			C T S M H
			C T S M H
			C T S M H

#11 — Sorting Through Stories

Basic Arithmetic (79-80), Quantity & Value (149-150),
WTF Models (159-162)

The Basics

The SAT uses stories to turn simple arithmetic into a confusing mess. Most of the time, the actual math involved in these questions is fairly basic. The challenge is figuring out which operations to perform. Try to use one piece of information at a time, instead of building elaborate equations. If you remember that the underlying math is probably easy, then you won't let the story shake your confidence.

The Twists

The WTF Models packet includes everything that doesn't fit neatly into another category. It's all twists! No matter how much you practice for the SAT, you will still encounter questions that defy categorization, that break the normal patterns that you spent all that time learning. It's okay! You can handle it.

The same strategies that you've been using for all of the other packets will still work when things get weird, so don't let the weirdness intimidate you. As always, it's better to use numbers to understand a story, so look for opportunities to Guess & Check and Arithmetize.

The Plan

1. **Learn Something New**
   - ☐ Big Picture #1 — Know Yourself
   - ☐ Quantity & Value examples
   - ☐ Big Picture #2 — Don't Be Smart
   - ☐ Basic Arithmetic examples
2. **Learn from Past Mistakes**
   - ☐ Big Picture #3 — Work Backwards
   - ☐ review Quantity & Value test questions
   - ☐ review Basic Arithmetic test questions
   - ☐ review WTF Models test questions
3. **Improve**
   - ☐ Quantity & Value exercise
   - ☐ Big Picture #4 — Show Your Work
   - ☐ Basic Arithmetic exercise
   - ☐ all WTF Models packet

Big Picture Ideas

#1 — Know Yourself

If you're confident with algebra, Quantity & Value Models will seem easy because they're so repetitive. There will still be places to watch for mistakes, but you'll likely get over the highest hurdle: generating the equations. However, if you're not great at algebra, these questions can be a minefield. You might create the wrong equations; it's easy to lose negatives or distribute incorrectly; and you could even solve for the wrong variable. It's probably better to Guess & Check. Choose the method that's going to get you the most points.

#2 — Don't Be Smart

High school algebra classes have destroyed your brain. You've been programmed to solve every problem with an equation. But equations have their drawbacks. They force you to incorporate every piece of information perfectly, all at once. And they also obscure important aspects of the question, like rounding and remainders, that might affect your final answer. Use the stories to your advantage. Treat the story like a set of instructions, and use arithmetic to take the information one piece at a time.

#3 — Work Backwards

As you review your answers, keep track of how many questions were more easily solved by starting with the answer choices. It won't always work, but stories are sometimes better understood if you start with the answers. It helps you focus on just one piece of information at a time.

#4 — Show Your Work

Stories can be confusing because they include a lot of information. The arithmetic is often easy, but sorting through everything is hard. Writing your ideas down on the page lets your brain make connections. Don't worry about whether you're doing the right thing. Try your ideas before you dismiss them.

Review Worksheet

Reasons for wrong answers or confusion:

C = carelessness   **T** = fell for a trap   **S** = should have used a strategy

M = need to memorize a rule/formula   **H** = just a hard question

Quantity & Value

Test	Section	Question	Reason				
			C	T	S	M	H
			C	T	S	M	H
			C	T	S	M	H
			C	T	S	M	H
			C	T	S	M	H

Basic Arithmetic

Test	Section	Question	Reason				
			C	T	S	M	H
			C	T	S	M	H
			C	T	S	M	H
			C	T	S	M	H
			C	T	S	M	H
			C	T	S	M	H
			C	T	S	M	H
			C	T	S	M	H

WTF Models

Test	Section	Question	Reason				
			C	T	S	M	H
			C	T	S	M	H
			C	T	S	M	H
			C	T	S	M	H
			C	T	S	M	H
			C	T	S	M	H
			C	T	S	M	H
			C	T	S	M	H
			C	T	S	M	H
			C	T	S	M	H
			C	T	S	M	H
			C	T	S	M	H
			C	T	S	M	H
			C	T	S	M	H

#12 — Untwisting Geometry

Part Over Whole (173-174), Trigonometry (175-176),
Advanced Geometry (177-180)

The Basics

The hardest Geometry questions will test some advanced topics (trigonometry) and some unfamiliar shapes (shaded region). There are a few extra formulas to memorize, like soh-cah-toa, but a lot of these questions can be "untwisted" by thinking about the same simple shapes that show up on the easy questions — triangles, rectangles, and circles. Get Back to Basics!

The Twists

For Part Over Whole and Trigonometry questions, there's a clear "basic" formula that most of the questions will use. Twisted questions will add some more steps, but the formula is still an essential piece of the puzzle. Write it down to organize your thoughts. If soh-cah-toa doesn't work, you might get nervous because there are a lot of trigonometry formulas that you learn in school. But on the SAT, the questions are much more limited. If the "basic" soh-cah-toa doesn't apply, then you're almost certainly going to need the "90 – x" formulas. Essentially, when the basics don't work, you luckily don't have a long list of possible twists to choose from.

The Plan

1. **Learn Something New**
   - ☐ Big Picture #1 — Keep It Simple
   - ☐ Part Over Whole examples
   - ☐ Trigonometry examples
   - ☐ Big Picture #2 — Get Back to Basics
   - ☐ Advanced Geometry examples
2. **Learn from Past Mistakes**
   - ☐ Big Picture #3 — Prioritize
   - ☐ review Part Over Whole test questions
   - ☐ review Trigonometry test questions
   - ☐ review Advanced Algebra test questions
3. **Improve**
   - ☐ Part Over Whole exercise
   - ☐ Trigonometry exercise
   - ☐ Advanced Geometry exercise 1

Big Picture Ideas

#1 — Keep It Simple

Almost everybody hates Geometry. One reason is that you were probably forced to memorize dozens of formulas. Luckily, the SAT gives you many of them, but there are still some gaps, and the less you need to memorize, the better. In school, you probably had to memorize 3 or 4 different formulas for circle sectors, but the Part Over Whole packet condenses them all into one simple idea: make fractions. This is easier to remember and easier to apply, no matter what the picture and question look like. If a question involves a piece of a circle, the odds are very good that you'll use part over whole fractions.

#2 — Get Back to Basics

No matter how complicated the picture looks, it will almost always come down to three shapes: triangles, rectangles, and circles. Think in those terms and get back to those formulas. Also, if you see angle measures of 45, 30, or 60 degrees, then you probably have a special right triangle somewhere, and all of those formulas are given in the Reference Chart. If you are confused and you have a circle, draw a radius or two by connecting any obvious points on the outside to the center. The odds are good that you'll make a triangle. And since all radiuses are the same length, you've probably made an isosceles triangle.

#3 — Prioritize

Overall, Geometry makes up a very small part of the SAT, maybe 5 questions. And about half of those will be very simple, where you only need to use the Reference Chart or a basic fact, like soh-cah-toa. Focus on getting those points first. If you are only missing the complex Geometry questions, don't worry. The hardest Geometry questions aren't a good use of your practice time if you're still struggling with bigger topics, like lines and quadratics. Focus your practice on algebra.

Review Worksheet

Reasons for wrong answers or confusion:

C = carelessness   **T** = fell for a trap   **S** = should have used a strategy

M = need to memorize a rule/formula   **H** = just a hard question

Part Over Whole

Test	Section	Question	Reason
			C T S M H
			C T S M H
			C T S M H
			C T S M H
			C T S M H
			C T S M H

Advanced Geometry

Test	Section	Question	Reason
			C T S M H
			C T S M H
			C T S M H
			C T S M H
			C T S M H
			C T S M H
			C T S M H
			C T S M H
			C T S M H
			C T S M H
			C T S M H
			C T S M H
			C T S M H

Trigonometry

Test	Section	Question	Reason
			C T S M H
			C T S M H
			C T S M H
			C T S M H
			C T S M H
			C T S M H
			C T S M H

Practice Tests
how do you use this book?

The Basics

Full-length practice tests are an essential part of SAT prep. Yes, that means you will need to sit for 3+ hours to take an entire practice test in a single sitting, just like the real SAT exam. It's not fun, but it's extremely important. You need to build your endurance and learn how to pace yourself through each section.

Finding Tests

As of November 2021, the College Board has released 10 official practice exams. However, they are not all found in the same places. Here's where to find each test, as of November 2021:

	Official SAT Study Guide		Online	
Test #	2018 edition	2020 edition	CB website	Khan Academy
1	✔	✔	✔	✔
2	✔			
3	✔	✔	✔	✔
4	✔			
5	✔	✔	✔	✔
6	✔	✔	✔	✔
7	✔	✔	✔	✔
8	✔	✔	✔	✔
9		✔	✔	✔
10		✔	✔	✔

Note: Tests 2 and 4 have been banished by the College Board. For whatever reason, they have been removed from all official practice sites and books. However, you can probably still find digital copies online if you search for them.

Taking Tests

The best way to take a practice SAT is with a **pencil and paper copy of the test**. *The Official SAT Study Guide*, which is the big blue book published by the College Board, contains 8 practice tests that you can take right in the book. If possible, you should purchase a copy of *The Official SAT Study Guide* so that taking tests is as easy as possible.

Alternatively, the tests are also available for free on the College Board website. You could download the PDFs and print them out one at a time. If you are unable to purchase the practice test book, this is the second best option:

www.sat.org/practice

If you can only take the practice tests online, then I recommend using *Khan Academy*. Their platform still allows you to cross off answers and bookmark questions for later. Still, you should have scrap paper with you to **show your work**. Writing your steps down is crucial for avoiding careless mistakes and producing new ideas. It's also essential that you look back at your work as you review your answers later.

If you use the study plans on the previous pages, you'll see that you're occasionally allowed to take a practice test without a timer. But for the most part, **practice tests and sections should be timed so that you can practice your pacing and endurance**.

You can use your own timer or one of the timers on the Settele Tutoring website and YouTube channel:

www.SetteleTutoring.com/timer

www.youtube.com/SetteleTutoring

The *Khan Academy* online platform has a built-in timer. Unfortunately, you cannot pause the timer or turn it off completely to take the section untimed.

Bubbling Answers

The SAT answer form, or "bubble sheet", is a key piece of the test-taking experience and a powerful tool that can actually help improve your scores. If you have *The Official SAT Study Guide*, you can find the bubble sheets at the end of each test (after the no-longer-necessary Essay). **Cut or rip these pages out.** You want to have the bubble sheet right next to you as you take the test, without having to flip between the pages.

Some students only write their practice test answers in the book, without bothering to bubble them on the answer form. This is a bad habit because you <u>must</u> bubble all of your answers on the real test. As dumb as this may sound, **you need to practice bubbling**. I've seen students lose points because they bubble the wrong answer or accidentally skip a question.

Also, do <u>not</u> wait until the end of a section to bubble all of your answers. Doing so is extremely risky because you can mis-bubble and get a dozen questions wrong. The time pressure will make it hard to re-bubble if you make a mistake. Bubble each answer immediately after you circle the choice in your test book. This also lets you use the bubble sheet to keep track of your pacing and progress:

Star questions that you're unsure of so that you remember to go back if you have time.

Draw a line where you ran out of time so that you remember that the remaining questions were random guesses.

Starred questions will come up again during your review of the test, so don't skip this important part of taking the test!

Scoring Tests

The College Board has made this extremely hard for some reason! If you take your test on *Khan Academy*, you will automatically have your test scored once you complete the entire exam, but it's not very easy to see an overview of your answers.

If you use the College Board's PDFs or *The Official SAT Study Guide*, you will need to download the scoring PDFs here:

<u>www.sat.org/scoring</u>

You might find references to the College Board's *Daily Practice for the New SAT* app or the "scan and score" feature. However, this app is no longer supported, and it cannot be downloaded.

The actual scoring PDF instructions are confusing. Open the PDF for your test and do this instead:

1. Use the "Answer Key" tables to check your answers on the bubble sheet. Put a big X next to any question that you got wrong or left blank. Write down the correct answer.

2. Count up your correct answers for:
   - Reading
   - Writing
   - both Math sections added together

3. Use the "Raw Score Conversion" tables to get your actual score. The number of correct answers for each subject determines your score for that section. You will get:
   - Reading score out of 40
   - Writing score out of 40
   - Math score out of 800

4. Add the Reading and Writing scores together. Put a zero at the end. This is your Evidence-Based Reading & Writing score out of 800. Add this to your Math score for your total out of 1600.

If you're curious, you might find some value in the Subscores (Command of Evidence, Words in Context, etc.), but they're not very helpful. Ignore the Cross-Test Scores for history and science. They're completely useless.

The Twists

Once you've calculated your scores, it's easy to measure your improvement from previous tests, including PSATs and real SATs. Just do some subtraction. But understanding what you did wrong and what you can do differently next time is an essential component of your SAT preparation. Simply counting up your right and wrong answers is not enough. You need to learn from your mistakes!

Reviewing Tests

If you're using one of the Study Plans in this book, test reviews will be built into the specific lessons. Use the Review Worksheets to organize your practice test mistakes. The **Test Categorization Charts** to the right give you the packet from this book that corresponds with each Math question from all 10 of the official practice SATs that have been released by the College Board.

These same Test Categorization Charts, as well as video explanations for every single question from all 10 of the official practice SATs, can be found on the Settele Tutoring website:

www.SetteleTutoring.com/tests

Use these videos! They're awesome! Each one includes a detailed walkthrough for the question, and you will always be told if an SAT-specific strategy would have been effective.

The videos will also make it easier to notice your own weaknesses. You'll find out if you fell for a trap, made a careless mistake, or needed to memorize a formula. You'll see these reasons appear on the Review Worksheets for the suggested lessons.

Starred Questions

Don't rush through the test review. Of course, you should watch the video for every question that you got wrong. But just as important, **you should watch the video for any question that you starred during the test**, even if you got it right. If you guessed and got lucky, you still need to learn how to actually answer it. Even if you eventually figured it out during the test, you might still learn that there was an easier way to solve it.

Test Categorization Charts

SAT Practice Test 1

Sect. 3	#	Sect. 4
CAM	1	grph
imag	2	CAM
WTF	3	ang
LM	4	CAM
CAM	5	grph
LM	6	ratio
RAF	7	grph
CAM	8	abs
POI	9	RAF
alg+	10	LM
WTF	11	CAM
LP	12	stat
alg+	13	perc
exp	14	stat
QP	15	LM
CAM	16	LM
SCT	17	FP
POI	18	MBT
trig	19	QV
rad	20	perc
	21	chrt
	22	chrt
	23	ratio
	24	CP
	25	QP
	26	perc
	27	ratio
	28	LP
	29	FP
	30	QP
	31	arith
	32	WTF
	33	grph
	34	arith
	35	cyl
	36	FP
	37	XM
	38	XM

SAT Practice Test 2			SAT Practice Test 3			SAT Practice Test 4		
Sect. 3	#	Sect. 4	Sect. 3	#	Sect. 4	Sect. 3	#	Sect. 4
CAM	1	WTF	WTF	1	grph	abs	1	LM
POI	2	ratio	CAM	2	chrt	alg+	2	LM
LM	3	LM	exp	3	grph	POI	3	ratio
CAM	4	ratio	WTF	4	COP	alg+	4	perc
rad	5	perc	CAM	5	perc	CAM	5	WTF
LP	6	CAM	POI	6	CAM	MBT	6	WTF
exp	7	QP	FP	7	CAM	LM	7	chrt
GM	8	WTF	LP	8	LM	LP	8	LP
LP	9	QV	LP	9	ratio	rad	9	chrt
FP	10	FP	POI	10	LM	CAM	10	grph
imag	11	ratio	ang	11	LM	POI	11	grph
RAF	12	LM	QP	12	FP	WTF	12	FP
QP	13	stat	div	13	RAF	QP	13	XM
XM	14	grph	QP	14	WTF	imag	14	XM
div	15	ratio	LM	15	stat	QP	15	XM
arith	16	chrt	alg+	16	FP	arith	16	WTF
CAM	17	perc	CAM	17	LM	trig	17	LM
SCT	18	stat	ang	18	WTF	alg+	18	cyl
geo+	19	stat	WTF	19	ratio	POI	19	CAM
LP	20	stat	trig	20	grph	ratio	20	XM
	21	WTF		21	XM		21	WTF
	22	RAF		22	WTF		22	perc
	23	RAF		23	trig		23	stat
	24	CP		24	arith		24	POW
	25	LP		25	cyl		25	alg+
	26	FP		26	LP		26	MBT
	27	grph		27	GM		27	LM
	28	LP		28	XM		28	QP
	29	QP		29	WTF		29	stat
	30	geo+		30	alg+		30	FP
	31	ratio		31	arith		31	arith
	32	arith		32	stat		32	LM
	33	QP		33	CAM		33	ratio
	34	WTF		34	POW		34	WTF
	35	LM		35	stat		35	RAF
	36	POW		36	LP		36	POW
	37	WTF		37	WTF		37	XM
	38	WTF		38	WTF		38	XM

Note on Tests 1-4: These were the first four tests released by the College Board ahead of the new SAT in 2016. In my opinion, they are not as perfectly polished as Tests 5-10. Test 4, in particular, has a lot of quirky questions and a highly unusual emphasis on Exponential Models. **If you want to practice taking sections without timing yourself, I recommend using Tests 1-4.**

SAT Practice Test 5				SAT Practice Test 6				SAT Practice Test 7		
Sect. 3	#	Sect. 4		Sect. 3	#	Sect. 4		Sect. 3	#	Sect. 4
LP	1	grph		LM	1	CAM		WTF	1	chrt
POW	2	COP		WTF	2	LM		CAM	2	CAM
QP	3	ratio		imag	3	grph		POI	3	ratio
QP	4	CAM		CAM	4	LM		imag	4	stat
rad	5	arith		LP	5	CAM		alg+	5	COP
CAM	6	QV		CAM	6	perc		LM	6	alg+
QV	7	XM		RAF	7	stat		QP	7	grph
LM	8	CAM		COP	8	chrt		arith	8	grph
POI	9	ratio		rad	9	ratio		QV	9	alg+
CAM	10	RAF		WTF	10	WTF		FP	10	ratio
cyl	11	LP		QP	11	POI		exp	11	QV
exp	12	POI		div	12	grph		QP	12	perc
LM	13	POI		QP	13	LM		div	13	grph
FP	14	chrt		WTF	14	COP		GM	14	ang
WTF	15	stat		CAM	15	COP		alg+	15	ratio
arith	16	LM		exp	16	SCT		CAM	16	CAM
CAM	17	LM		CAM	17	RAF		geo+	17	LM
POI	18	LM		SCT	18	WTF		trig	18	grph
alg+	19	geo+		WTF	19	WTF		LP	19	RAF
ang	20	WTF		POW	20	QP		CAM	20	RAF
	21	MBT			21	stat			21	LM
	22	perc			22	stat			22	stat
	23	COP			23	grph			23	cyl
	24	perc			24	perc			24	QP
	25	WTF			25	LP			25	COP
	26	geo+			26	ratio			26	WTF
	27	stat			27	CP			27	XM
	28	LP			28	abs			28	LP
	29	CP			29	WTF			29	CP
	30	CAM			30	QP			30	perc
	31	ratio			31	arith			31	ratio
	32	ratio			32	CAM			32	LP
	33	GM			33	cyl			33	WTF
	34	alg+			34	POI			34	POW
	35	GM			35	LP			35	POI
	36	geo+			36	stat			36	trig
	37	WTF			37	XM			37	stat
	38	WTF			38	perc			38	chrt

Note on Tests 5-8: These four tests were added to *The Official SAT Study Guide* in 2018. They are actual SAT exams that were given to real students just like you. Those students took these exams under proctored conditions, got official scores, sent those scores to colleges, and received acceptances based on those scores. For that reason, I trust Tests 5-8 more than Tests 1-4. **Save Tests 5-8 for when you need to take full exams under proctored conditions to receive reliable practice scores.**

SAT Practice Test 8

Sect. 3	#	Sect. 4
CAM	1	WTF
LM	2	grph
RAF	3	ratio
ang	4	LM
GM	5	ang
POI	6	QV
rad	7	LP
alg+	8	alg+
CP	9	WTF
QV	10	WTF
FP	11	ratio
CAM	12	QV
LM	13	exp
POI	14	FP
alg+	15	GM
QP	16	chrt
CAM	17	stat
POI	18	grph
LM	19	QP
POW	20	WTF
	21	LM
	22	perc
	23	XM
	24	stat
	25	LM
	26	stat
	27	LP
	28	stat
	29	WTF
	30	FP
	31	ratio
	32	CAM
	33	LP
	34	ratio
	35	POI
	36	trig
	37	COP
	38	XM

SAT Practice Test 9

Sect. 3	#	Sect. 4
POI	1	CAM
CAM	2	ratio
LP	3	CAM
LM	4	rad
LM	5	grph
POW	6	grph
CAM	7	ang
LP	8	LM
POI	9	chrt
alg+	10	arith
CAM	11	ratio
div	12	ratio
QP	13	QV
POI	14	LM
rad	15	LP
GM	16	alg+
CAM	17	POI
FP	18	WTF
trig	19	WTF
LP	20	LM
	21	XM
	22	stat
	23	stat
	24	alg+
	25	trig
	26	QP
	27	FP
	28	QP
	29	LM
	30	LM
	31	CP
	32	LP
	33	chrt
	34	stat
	35	perc
	36	LP
	37	stat
	38	perc

SAT Practice Test 10

Sect. 3	#	Sect. 4
CAM	1	LM
LM	2	grph
COP	3	grph
grph	4	CAM
rad	5	alg+
CAM	6	CAM
FP	7	stat
ang	8	grph
LP	9	alg+
QP	10	stat
CP	11	stat
trig	12	perc
QP	13	grph
alg+	14	ratio
LP	15	geo+
WTF	16	perc
abs	17	RAF
XM	18	chrt
POI	19	QP
CAM	20	stat
	21	WTF
	22	XM
	23	LP
	24	LM
	25	POI
	26	XM
	27	CAM
	28	QP
	29	LM
	30	geo+
	31	arith
	32	ang
	33	stat
	34	CAM
	35	LP
	36	QP
	37	ratio
	38	ratio

Note on Tests 9-10: Like Tests 5-8, these tests were official exams given to students just like you. Since they are the most recent official tests, I believe they are the most representative of the content and difficulty that you're likely to see on your own SAT. **Since I trust Tests 9-10 the most, I recommend saving them for big moments in your test prep schedule, like the halfway point and your final practice test before the real SAT.**

More Practice
how do you use this book?

The Basics

If you've done all of the lessons, there will still be a few bonus exercises for certain packets. These were included because those packets tend to give students the most difficulty. If you need more practice with those topics, review the examples and the first exercise, then try Exercise 2 and Exercise 3. Here's a full list of the extra exercises:

- ☐ Charts & Probability 2
- ☐ Charts & Probability 3

- ☐ Ratios & Units 2
- ☐ Ratios & Units 3

- ☐ Percentages 2
- ☐ Percentages 3

- ☐ Exponent Rules 2
- ☐ Exponent Rules 3

- ☐ Linear Models 2

- ☐ Exponential Models 2
- ☐ Exponential Models 3

- ☐ Similar & Congruent Triangles 2
- ☐ Similar & Congruent Triangles 3

- ☐ Advanced Geometry 2
- ☐ Advanced Geometry 3

Outside of this book, the best place to find more practice is the Settele Tutoring website. You'll find a library with links to video lessons, prep tools, and all of our social media profiles. New resources are released all the time!

Library of Settele Tutoring Resources

scan or visit:

SetteleTutoring.com/library

The Twists

Beyond that, *Khan Academy* is a great free resource for more practice. You can sync your PSAT and practice test scores with your account, and the website will tell you which topics to practice. The exercises will get easier or harder, depending on your skill level.

Unfortunately, *Khan Academy*'s topic categories aren't great. They mix a lot of different kinds of questions together, so it's harder to NARROW YOUR FOCUS to very specific ideas. Also, the questions don't always capture the style of SAT questions. They don't involve as many twists or tricks.

Still, *Khan Academy* is very useful if you need more practice with "The Basics". Sometimes you just need to practice simple things like factoring and FOILing. What follows on the next page is a list of the packets from this book and the *Khan Academy* categories that include similar questions.

Additional Practice Tests

There are plenty of prep books that include more practice tests, but I do <u>not</u> recommend any of them. Test prep companies typically produce practice tests that are poor quality and do not reflect the difficulty of the real SAT.

Every year, the College Board releases a few of the actual SAT exams that are given in the US and internationally. These are called the **QAS exams**, and you can actually pay extra for a copy of the test if you happen to take your SAT on one of the QAS dates. It might be worthwhile if you want to see the specific questions that you got wrong. Regardless, these tests find their way onto the internet, and they're the ideal way to continue your test prep if you've taken all of the official practice tests from *The Official SAT Study Guide*. The <u>r/SAT subreddit</u> has a comprehensive list of QAS exams. That said, stay far away from any pirated SAT exams that you find on the internet. They are often littered with typos, and using them can invalidate your actual SAT scores!

Khan Academy Categories

- ## <u>Free Points</u>
  - **read the graph**
    - Scatterplots
  - **charts & probability**
    - Units
    - Table data
  - **collection of points**
    - Linear and exponential growth
    - Function notation

- ## <u>Arithmetic</u>
  - **basic arithmetic**
    - Linear equation word problems
    - Linear inequality word problems
    - Units
  - **ratios & units**
    - Ratios, rates, and proportions
    - Units
  - **percentages**
    - Percents
  - **statistics**
    - Data inferences
    - Center, spread, and shape of distributions
    - Data collection and conclusions

- ## <u>Algebra</u>
  - **common algebra mistakes**
    - Solving linear equations and linear inequalities
    - Solving quadratic equations
    - Operations with rational expressions
    - Operations with polynomials
    - Structure in expressions
  - **radicals**
    - Radicals and rational exponents
    - Radical and rational equations
  - **exponent rules**
    - Radicals and rational exponents
    - Structure in expressions

- **absolute value**
  - Solving linear equations and linear inequalities
  - Linear equation word problems
- **must be true**
  - Interpreting nonlinear expressions
  - Structure in expressions
- **point of intersection**
  - Solving systems of linear equations
  - Linear and quadratic systems
- **advanced algebra**
  - Radical and rational equations
  - Operations with rational expressions
  - Operations with polynomials
  - Polynomial factors and graphs
  - Function notation
- **dividing polynomials**
  - Operations with rational expressions
  - Polynomial factors and graphs
- **imaginary numbers**
  - Complex numbers

- ## <u>Properties</u>
  - **linear properties**
    - Graphing linear equations
    - Solving systems of linear equations
  - **quadratic properties**
    - Interpreting nonlinear expressions
    - Manipulating quadratic and exponential expressions
    - Polynomial factors and graphs
    - Nonlinear equation graphs
  - **function properties**
    - Polynomial factors and graphs
    - Nonlinear equation graphs
    - Function notation
  - **circle properties**
    - Circle equations

- <u>Models</u>
  - **linear models**
    - Interpreting linear functions
    - Linear equation word problems
    - Linear inequality word problems
    - Linear function word problems
    - Scatterplots
    - Linear and exponential growth
  - **quantity & value**
    - Systems of linear inequalities word problems
    - Systems of linear equations word problems
  - **geometry models**
    - Linear function word problems
    - Systems of linear equations word problems
    - Quadratic and exponential word problems
    - Volume word problems
  - **exponential models**
    - Linear and exponential growth
    - Interpreting nonlinear expressions
    - Quadratic and exponential word problems
    - Manipulating quadratic and exponential expressions
  - **rearrange formulas**
    - Interpreting nonlinear expressions
    - Manipulating quadratic and exponential expressions
    - Structure in expressions
    - Isolating quantities
  - **WTF models**
    - Systems of linear inequalities word problems
    - Systems of linear equations word problems
    - Scatterplots
    - Key features of graphs
    - Linear and exponential growth
    - Interpreting nonlinear expressions
    - Quadratic and exponential word problems
    - Manipulating quadratic and exponential expressions

- <u>Geometry</u>
  - **part over whole**
    - Angles, arc lengths, and trig functions
    - Circle theorems
  - **angle rules**
    - Congruence and similarity
  - **similar & congruent triangles**
    - Congruence and similarity
  - **cylinders & more**
    - Quadratic and exponential word problems
    - Volume word problems
  - **trigonometry**
    - Right triangle trigonometry
  - **advanced geometry**
    - Volume word problems
    - Right triangle word problems
    - Circle theorems

Frequently Asked Questions

how do you use this book?

Can I Use a Calculator?

Try not to. The real SAT will be divided into a No Calculator and a Calculator section, but this book does not make a distinction between these questions, mostly because it doesn't matter. **Most question types can appear in either section, so you need to know how to answer them without a calculator.** Also, you won't even need a calculator for the vast majority of questions in the Calculator section.

My advice is to have your calculator handy, but only reach for it if you absolutely need to. You should not be doing "8 times 7" in your calculator. You should not be doing "180 minus 43" either. You'll know when you're working on a true Calculator section question because the numbers will be huge or involve complicated decimals.

You're using this book to practice your SAT Math skills, so why not take the opportunity to also practice your arithmetic skills? Students who rely too much on their calculators tend to make a lot of careless mistakes. Challenge yourself as you practice. It will pay off on test day!

Is there a Guessing Penalty?

No. You do not lose points for wrong answers on the SAT. That's why **you should never leave an SAT question blank.**

On the Multiple Choice questions, guess B for questions where you have no idea. On the Free Response/Grid-in questions, guess 2 instead of leaving questions blank.

Are the Questions in Order of Difficulty?

For the most part, yes. Remember that **the Math sections on the real SAT will be roughly in order of difficulty** — easy questions at the beginning, hard questions at the end. Each packet in this book roughly goes in the same order.

But one very important thing to note is that the Free Response/Grid-in questions at the end of the sections are not necessarily harder than the Multiple Choice questions. In fact, the difficulty "resets" when you get to the Grid-ins. The No Calculator section is basically two sections in one:

- #1 to #15 — Multiple Choice
- #16 to #20 — Grid-in

Question #1 is usually very easy, and #15 is usually very difficult. However, #16 is usually an easy question! In these packets, this just means that you should not assume a Grid-in question is hard just because it doesn't have answer choices. On the SAT, it's important to know that the first few Grid-ins will be easy. **If you're running out of time, guess B on the hard Multiple Choice questions and go straight to the Grid-ins to pick up those easy points.**

What's the SAT's format?

The SAT Math has a 25-minute, 20-question No Calculator section and a 55-minute, 38-question Calculator section. If you have more questions about the exam, just go online and look them up. It's super easy to find information about the SAT! The Settele Tutoring website has an expanded FAQ section:

www.SetteleTutoring.com/faq

You didn't buy this book to learn SAT trivia. You bought it to practice the SAT Math. Get to work!

Math Packets

Start with the section on SAT-specific strategies. The rest of the packets will reference these strategies, so you need to know the vocabulary. For more direction, go back to the Introduction to find study plans and suggested lessons.

SAT-Specific Strategies

The Basics

Change your strategy, change your score! Improving your SAT scores requires that you adopt two big picture goals. Most obvious, you will need to **Memorize Formulas** and practice traditional algebra. Many SAT questions will not be very different from the kinds of problems that you see on your in-school Math tests. If you don't know the facts, formulas, or algebra skills, you won't be able to solve many of the questions.

But the more interesting goal is that you need to incorporate non-traditional strategies into your process as well. Avoid algebra when you can. It's messy, confusing, and prone to mistakes. Arithmetic is safer. With **Guess & Check, Arithmetize,** and **Plug Points Into Equations**, you're able to simplify the problems and reduce the chance of a careless mistake. Even if you're amazing at traditional Math, you need to be open-minded about these new strategies. The most common reason that Math scores don't improve is that people stubbornly refuse to incorporate the SAT-specific strategies into their process.

The Twists

At first, the hardest part will be figuring out which kinds of questions are better solved with the SAT-specific strategies. Years of Math classes in school have programmed you to see algebra everywhere. Your first instinct will almost always be the traditional approach, but you need to change that impulse.

Start by paying attention to your confusion. If a question feels hard, try a strategy. Don't think too far ahead about whether it will work. If the variables don't seem to matter, make up a number and **Arithmetize**. If a story has a lot of numbers, try working backwards from Choice B with **Guess & Check** instead. And most important, if a question has points and equations, then **Plug Points Into Equations**!

Packets

- Guess & Check
- Arithmetize
- Plug Points Into Equations
- Memorize Formulas
- Get Back to Basics

approximately 33 questions per test

worth approximately 330 points total

The SAT-specific strategies can work on <u>all topics</u>. They are extremely powerful tools that can help you earn a lot of points that you're currently losing. They can also help you add points from questions that do not use strategies. The strategies make you move faster, which frees up time to work on the truly difficult questions.

Some people might not consider **Memorize Formulas** or **Get Back to Basics** as SAT-specific strategies, since they're essentially what you need to do for school Math tests, as well. But the other three strategies are game-changers:

Guess & Check	4 questions
Arithmetize	7 questions
Plug Points Into Equations	5 questions

That's a total of 16 questions and approximately **160 points** for questions where you can avoid algebra!

★ HIGHLY RECOMMENDED ★

Watch the video lesson for the **Guess & Check, Arithmetize,** and **Plug Points Into Equations** packets — detailed walkthrough of all examples!

scan or visit:

SetteleTutoring.com/math

Important Ideas

Guess & Check

Work backwards when you can. Pick the answer choice that you think is right, or just start with B (because it's in the middle). Check it by using the information in the question or by plugging the choice into the equation. If it's wrong, try another choice.

Best for:
- long, multi-step stories
- complex algebra with integer answer choices
- "what is the value of x ?"
- "what is the solution?"

Not as good for:
- annoying answer choices, like fractions
- irregular final questions, like asking for $2x + 5$ instead of just x

Advanced tip — Guess & Check is associated with the multiple choice portion of the SAT, but it can still be used on some Grid-in questions. If you're totally stuck, why not guess something simple like 1 or 2 and see what happens?

Plug Points Into Equations

If a question includes points and equations, plug the points into the equations. It's really that simple!

Basic tip — It's usually obvious when a question includes equations, but you might need to do some work to find points to plug in. Most important, remember that graphs are really just collections of points, so pick something easy (like a y-intercept) and plug it into the equations.

Advanced tip — A story might also give you a point in the form of a sentence. For example, "On the tenth day, Roger had 26 coins," is really the point (10, 26). You can also use increases/decreases to come up with the point yourself. A simple example would be taking "the population started at 300 and doubled every 14 days," and turning it into the points (0, 300) and (14, 600). Be clever!

Arithmetize

Turn algebra into arithmetic. If they don't ask you to solve for the variables, then they probably don't matter — they're just a placeholder for a number. So replace the placeholder with a number!

1. Pick a simple number for the variable
2. Plug your number into the equation or story.
3. Solve for the "answer" value.
4. Plug your number into the answer choices.
5. Eliminate any choices that don't match your "answer" value. Check every choice!
6. If multiple choices remain, pick a new number and repeat the steps above. You only need to check choices that were not eliminated.

Best for:
- variables in question and in answer choices
- "equivalent expression"
- stories with equation answers

Not as good for:
- exponent questions

Basic tip — Don't be afraid of picking 0 and 1. Yes, they're likely to work in multiple answer choices, but they get you the right answer on the first try just as often. Also, if they fail, they fail quickly. It doesn't take much time or effort to Arithmetize with 0 and 1.

Advanced tip — Don't be afraid of picking weird or big numbers if the question calls for it. For example, 100 is a great number to Arithmetize with for percent questions. Similarly, 9 is good for square roots because it's a perfect square.

Memorize Formulas and Get Back to Basics

Use the rest of the packets in this book to learn and memorize the formulas, vocabulary, and skills that you'll need for the individual topics.

When questions are confusing, think about which packet seems most relevant and write down the basic ideas that you remember for that topic. In general, if you can do something, you probably should do it.

Guess & Check

The Basics

You've definitely used **Guess & Check** before. Use the answer choices to work backwards. It's much easier to test the numbers than to solve a complex equation. Plug the values from the choices in for x:

Example 1

$$\sqrt{10 - 3x} - 7 = x - 9$$

What is the solution set of the equation above?

A) $\{-2\}$

B) $\{3\}$

C) $\{-2, 3\}$

D) $\{-9, -2, 3\}$

The Twists

Sometimes **Guess & Check** is helpful because it lets you do slightly easier algebra. In this case, FOILing is easier than factoring, so plug an answer choice in for k and see if it gets you back to the original expression:

Example 2

The expression $\frac{1}{2}x^2 - 8$ can be rewritten as $\frac{1}{2}(x + k)(x - k)$, where k is a positive constant. What is the value of k ?

A) 2

B) 4

C) 8

D) 16

If there's a lot of information in the question, **Guess & Check** can still be confusing. But picking an answer choice at least gives you a starting point. Test Choice B first. If B is wrong, you can guess A or C next, depending on whether you need a bigger or smaller number.

Example 3

Veronica is organizing the carpool for her family reunion. Some of the cars seat 5 people each, and the rest seat 7 people each. If she organizes the carpool so that 55 people ride in 9 cars and each car is filled to capacity, how many of the cars seat 7 people each?

A) 3

B) 4

C) 5

D) 6

Exercise: Guess & Check

1

$$\frac{x+2}{5} = \frac{x-2}{3}$$

What is the solution to the equation above?

A) 8

B) 2

C) 0

D) −16

2

Which of the following is a solution to the equation $x = \sqrt{2x-3} + 3$?

I. 0

II. 2

III. 6

A) I only

B) II only

C) III only

D) II and III only

3

$$4x^2 - 8x - 5 = 0$$

Which of the following is a solution to the equation above?

A) 2.5

B) 0.5

C) 1

D) 5

4

A wildlife survey estimated that the population of Western fence lizards in an area was approximately 86% of the population of sagebrush lizards in the same area. If the survey found that the population of Western fence lizards in this area was about 1,200, which of the following represents the approximate population of sagebrush lizards in this area?

A) 1,400

B) 1,360

C) 1,290

D) 1,030

5

$$y = x^2$$
$$y = 10 - 3x$$

When the system of equations above is graphed in the xy-plane, the graphs of the equations intersect at point (a, b) where $a > 0$ and $b > 0$. What is the value of b ?

A) 2

B) 4

C) 14

D) 25

Arithmetize
SAT-specific strategies

The Basics

Arithmetize is a very valuable tool. However, it's not something that helps all that much for math class in school. It's very specific to the SAT. Even if you're amazing at algebra, there will be times when it's easier to work with actual numbers, just like with Guess & Check. But instead of using the numbers in the answer choices, **Arithmetize lets you pick your own numbers.**

If you NARROW YOUR FOCUS to just one value, you're more likely to understand how an equation changes that value. You're also less likely to make the most common algebra mistakes because you <u>only</u> have to worry about numbers instead of numbers <u>and letters</u>. The question below is basic algebra, but what happens if you **make all of the x's equal to 0** instead of solving with traditional math?

Example 1

Which expression is equivalent to
$(3x^2 - 7x + 9) - (4x^2 - 2x + 1)$?

A) $7x^2 - 9x + 10$

B) $x^2 - 5x - 8$

C) $-x^2 - 9x + 10$

D) $-x^2 - 5x + 8$

The Twists

Some tutors will tell you to never Arithmetize with 0 or 1, but that's nonsense. Even if those numbers don't work perfectly, they might eliminate some answer choices. At the least, the math is quick and less likely to cause mistakes. If you do end up with multiple choices that work, just choose a new number and try it in the choices you couldn't eliminate. This is why you should **always test all of the answer choices when you Arithmetize.** What happens when you make x equal to 0 in the example below?

Example 2

$$x^2 - 2x + 5$$

Which of the following is equivalent to the expression above?

A) $(x + 1)^2 + 4$

B) $(x + 1)^2 - 4$

C) $(x - 1)^2 + 4$

D) $(x - 1)^2 - 4$

Sometimes you can't **Arithmetize** for all the variables in a question. In this example, pick values for x and y, but not for a and b. Use your x and y to find a and b:

Example 3

If $x^2 + y^2 = a$ and $xy = b$, which of the following is equivalent to $2a + 4b$?

A) $(x + y)^2$

B) $2(x + y)^2$

C) $(x + 2y)^2$

D) $2(x + 2y)^2$

Exercise: Arithmetize

1

If $x \neq 0$, which of the following is equivalent to $\dfrac{1}{3x} - \dfrac{3}{x}$?

A) $-\dfrac{2}{3}$

B) $-\dfrac{1}{x}$

C) $-\dfrac{8}{3x}$

D) $\dfrac{2}{x}$

2

The volume of a right circular cylinder with radius r and height h is given by the equation $V = \pi r^2 h$. Which of the following expressions represents the volume of a second right circular cylinder with half the radius and half the height of the first cylinder?

A) $\dfrac{1}{2}V$

B) $\dfrac{1}{4}V$

C) $\dfrac{1}{8}V$

D) $\dfrac{1}{16}V$

3

Which of the following expressions is equivalent to $(3x - 2)^2 - 9x^2$?

A) $2(2 - 3x)$

B) $3(1 - 3x)$

C) $4(1 - 3x)$

D) $9(2 - x)$

4

$$y = \frac{2x^2(3x)^2}{6x^4}$$

In the equation above, $x \neq 0$. What is the value of y ?

A) 0

B) 1

C) 2

D) 3

5

$$B(t) = 20(2)^{2t}$$

The number of bacteria in a petri dish grows exponentially over time. The function B above models the number of bacteria after t hours in the petri dish. Based on the function, which of the following statements must be true?

A) The predicted number of bacteria in the petri dish doubles every half hour.

B) The predicted number of bacteria in the petri dish doubles every hour.

C) The predicted number of bacteria in the petri dish doubles every two hours.

D) The predicted number of bacteria in the petri dish doubles every four hours.

Plug Points Into Equations

SAT-specific strategies

The Basics

You might think of this strategy as a version of Guess & Check. But it deserves its own page because it's often overlooked. Questions that seem like they require a thorough knowledge of algebra and the properties of equations might actually be solved easily by just testing a point. A point that "works" in an equation will produce a valid result, like 2 = 2. A point that does not "work" will end with an equation that doesn't make sense, like 2 = 5. **When you Plug Points Into Equations, start with easy points:**

Example 1

x	$\dfrac{1}{2}$	1	$\dfrac{3}{2}$	2	$\dfrac{5}{2}$
$f(x)$	$\dfrac{13}{4}$	$\dfrac{7}{2}$	$\dfrac{15}{4}$	4	$\dfrac{17}{4}$

Some of the values of the function f are shown in the table above. Which of the following defines f?

A) $f(x) = \left(\dfrac{7}{2}\right)^x$

B) $f(x) = 4^x + \dfrac{5}{4}$

C) $f(x) = \dfrac{5}{2}x + 2$

D) $f(x) = \dfrac{1}{2}x + 3$

The Twists

It's easy to forget that lines and other graphs are just collections of points. Instead of trying to figure out the equation by looking at the whole line, take one point and plug it into the possible equations. This is especially helpful on the SAT because they design the graphs to trick you. Usually, the boxes don't mean what you think they mean:

Example 2

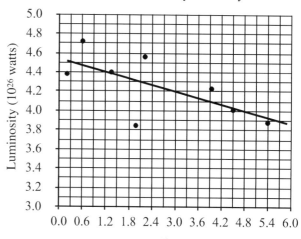

Mass and Luminosity of Nearby Stars

The scatterplot above shows the luminosity of 8 nearby stars, in 10^{26} watts, with respect to their solar masses in 10^{30} kilograms. The line of best fit is also shown. Based on the data in the scatterplot, which of the following equations best models the line of best fit, where m is the mass of the star, in 10^{30} kg, and $L(m)$ is the luminosity of the star, in 10^{26} watts?

A) $L(m) = \dfrac{9}{2} - \dfrac{9}{80}m$

B) $L(m) = \dfrac{9}{2} + \dfrac{9}{80}m$

C) $L(m) = \dfrac{9}{2} - \dfrac{1}{3}m$

D) $L(m) = \dfrac{9}{2} + \dfrac{1}{3}m$

Exercise: Plug Points Into Equations

1

Which of the following graphs represents the equation $y = 2(1.5)^x$?

A)

B)

C)

D)

2

A line in the xy-plane has a slope of $\dfrac{1}{3}$ and passes through the point $(-6, 5)$. Which of the following is an equation of the line?

A) $y = 3x - 1$

B) $y = 3x + 1$

C) $y = \dfrac{1}{3}x + 7$

D) $y = \dfrac{1}{3}x - 2$

3

A certain medicine is known to eliminate 50 percent of the bacteria remaining in a petri dish every 80 minutes after the medicine is first applied. Which of the following exponential functions best models the number of bacteria $P(t)$ that remains t minutes after the medicine is first applied to a petri dish containing 600 bacteria?

A) $P(t) = 80(0.5)^{\frac{t}{600}}$

B) $P(t) = 80(0.5)^{600t}$

C) $P(t) = 600(0.5)^{\frac{t}{80}}$

D) $P(t) = 600(0.5)^{80t}$

4

x	0	$3k$	$9k$
y	k	$3k$	$7k$

The graph of a line in the xy-plane includes the selected values of x and their corresponding values of y as shown in the table above, where k is a constant. Which of the following equations represents the line?

A) $2x - 3y = -3k$

B) $2x - 3y = -k$

C) $3x - 2y = k$

D) $3x - 2y = 3k$

Memorize Formulas
SAT-specific strategies

The Basics

The more interesting SAT-specific strategies — Guess & Check, Arithmetize, and Plug Points Into Equations — give you new ways to answer questions that you'd solve with traditional algebra if you were in school. But sometimes you'll have no choice but to use traditional formulas (or at least the traditional formulas will be much more efficient).

This example tests **the single most important formula for the SAT**. You <u>must</u> memorize the slope-intercept formula for linear equations. You will feel hopelessly lost without it. (The Linear Properties packet goes into much more detail about it.)

Example 1

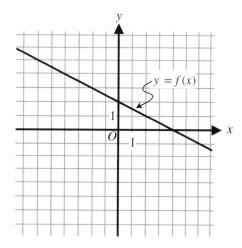

The linear function f is graphed in the xy-plane above. Which of the following equations represents the graph of f?

A) $f(x) = 2x + 4$

B) $f(x) = 2x - 2$

C) $f(x) = -\dfrac{1}{2}x + 2$

D) $f(x) = -\dfrac{1}{2}x + 4$

The Twists

The word "formula" should be interpreted loosely. Sometimes the SAT is testing how well we've **memorized mathematical vocabulary**. The distinction between a definition and a formula isn't very important. The key is that some questions are virtually impossible to answer if you don't know the relevant facts.

Example 2

$$y = -\frac{4}{5}x + 3$$
$$y = ax + b$$

In the system of linear equations above, a and b are constants. If the system has no solutions, what is the value of a ?

A) $-\dfrac{4}{5}$

B) $-\dfrac{1}{3}$

C) $\dfrac{5}{4}$

D) 3

Memorizing formulas can also include **knowing the steps** to solve certain types of problems. There is a formula to answer this next example, but it doesn't take much longer to perform the correct algebra operation to find the sum of the solutions. These algebra steps <u>must</u> be memorized for the SAT.

Example 3

What is the sum of the solutions to the equation $0 = x^2 - 14x - 32$?

Exercise: Memorize Formulas

1

$$|5 - x| = -4$$

The equation above has exactly how many solutions?

A) Zero

B) One

C) Two

D) Three

2

$$g(x) = \frac{x + 3}{x^2 - 9x + 8}$$

The function g above is undefined for which values of x?

A) $\{-3\}$

B) $\{-9, 8\}$

C) $\{1, 8\}$

D) $\{-8, -3, -1\}$

3

$$(3 - i)(2 + 4i)$$

Which of the following is equivalent to the expression above. (Note: $i = \sqrt{-1}$)

A) $2 + 10i$

B) $5 + 3i$

C) $6 - 4i$

D) $10 + 10i$

4

Data set X

Data set Y

Data sets X and Y are represented in the histograms above. Both data sets have the same mean. Which of the following is true about the two data sets?

A) Data set X and data set Y have the same standard deviation.

B) The standard deviation of data set X is greater than the standard deviation of data set Y.

C) The standard deviation of data set Y is greater than the standard deviation of data set X.

D) The standard deviations of data sets X and Y cannot be calculated.

Get Back to Basics

SAT-specific strategies

The Basics

In a sense, many of "The Basics" questions throughout this book and on the SAT are purely about **Memorizing Formulas** — if you know the relevant math fact, it's very unlikely that you'll get the question wrong. Many of "The Twists" questions still need you to memorize those same formulas, but you'll also need to sort through added layers of confusing stories, complex equations, and annoying steps. The **Get Back to Basics** strategy is all about "untwisting" whatever difficulties the SAT throws at you. There's always some underlying topic that's much more familiar to you.

Notice that the following example is almost identical to Example #2 from the **Memorize Formulas** packet. The only difference is that the equations and answers look much more confusing. We still need to memorize what "no solutions" means, but now we also need to "untwist" the equations so that we can better understand what we're given — we need to **Get Back to Basics**! What's the most basic equation of a line?

Example 1

$$3x - 2y = 7$$
$$a x + 5y = b$$

In the system of linear equations above, a and b are constants. If the system has no solutions, what is the value of a ?

A) $-\dfrac{15}{2}$

B) $-\dfrac{6}{5}$

C) $\dfrac{6}{5}$

D) $\dfrac{15}{2}$

The Twists

Sometimes it's hard to know what "The Basics" of a question are. The SAT can disguise things well. As you go through the packets, you'll get better at recognizing what the questions are testing. Stories make things even more confusing, but remember that the algebra is still the same algebra that you learned in school. **Get Back to Basics** by changing equations into the familiar ones that you're used to — lines, quadratics, and exponential functions. Which type is this?

Example 2

$$h = \frac{5t + 51}{2}$$

The equation above is used to estimate the height h, in inches, of an oak tree t years after it was planted. Based on the equation, which of the following must be true?

A) An oak tree's height increases by 51 inches every year.

B) An oak tree's height increases by 25.5 inches every year.

C) An oak tree's height increases by 5 inches every year.

D) An oak tree's height increases by 2.5 inches every year.

Exercise: Get Back to Basics

Note: This exercise consists of pairs of questions that are meant to show how the SAT twists up the basic ideas that you need to memorize. The first question in each pair will require little more than **Memorizing Formulas**. The second question will test these exact same formulas but with a twist that makes the question more difficult. **Get Back to Basics.** If you knew how to solve the "basic" version, then you should still be able to solve the "twisted" version. An extra step or two should "untwist" the question so that it gets back to the basic, familiar place that you're comfortable with.

1   Basics — LP

In the xy-plane, what is the y-intercept of the line with equation $y = 4x - 3$?

A) $(0, -4)$

B) $(0, -3)$

C) $(0, 3)$

D) $(0, 4)$

2   Twists — FP

$$f(x) = (x + 2)(x - 1)^2$$

Which of the following represents the y-intercept of the function f above?

A) $(0, 2)$

B) $(0, 1)$

C) $(0, -1)$

D) $(0, -2)$

3   Basics — stat

Town	Temperature
Bloomfield	98°
Chesterfield	88°
Georgetown	92°
Kentwood	84°
Portage	95°
Redford	79°
Roseville	95°

The table above shows the high temperature for seven towns in Michigan. What was the median temperature for the seven towns? (Disregard the degree symbol when gridding your answer.)

4   Twists — stat

Age	Frequency
17	3
18	4
19	11
20	7
21	8
22	9
23	4
25	1
27	1

The frequency chart above gives the distribution of ages for students in a college class. What is the median age of students in the class?

The slope of line ℓ is 3. When graphed in the xy-plane, line m is perpendicular to line ℓ. Which of the following could represent the slope of line m ?

A) -3

B) $-\dfrac{1}{3}$

C) $\dfrac{1}{3}$

D) 3

When graphed in the xy-plane, line ℓ passes through the points $(3, 7)$ and $(5, 4)$. Which of the following is an equation of a line that is perpendicular to line ℓ ?

A) $3x - 2y = 10$

B) $2x + 3y = 10$

C) $-2x + 3y = 10$

D) $-3x - 2y = 10$

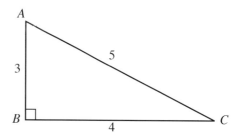

In right triangle ABC above, which of the following represents the value of $\tan C$?

A) $\dfrac{3}{5}$

B) $\dfrac{3}{4}$

C) $\dfrac{4}{5}$

D) $\dfrac{4}{3}$

In right triangle ABC, the length of $\overline{AB}$ is 3 and the length of hypotenuse $\overline{AC}$ is 5. Which of the following is equivalent to 0.8?

A) $\cos C$

B) $\sin C$

C) $\tan A$

D) $\tan C$

Basics — QP

The vertex of quadratic function f in the xy-plane is $(1, 4)$. Which of the following could be an equation of f?

A) $f(x) = (x + 1)^2 + 4$

B) $f(x) = (x - 1)^2 + 4$

C) $f(x) = (x + 4)^2 + 1$

D) $f(x) = (x - 4)^2 + 1$

Basics — CP

A circle with center $(8, -6)$ and radius 4 is graphed in the xy-plane. Which of the following represents the equation of the circle?

A) $(x + 8)^2 + (y - 6)^2 = 4$

B) $(x - 8)^2 + (y + 6)^2 = 4$

C) $(x + 8)^2 + (y - 6)^2 = 16$

D) $(x - 8)^2 + (y + 6)^2 = 16$

Twists — QP

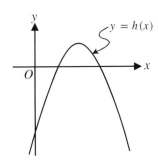

The graph of $h(x)$ is shown in the xy-plane above. If $a, b,$ and c are positive constants, which of the following equations could define h?

A) $h(x) = a(x + b)^2 - c$

B) $h(x) = a(x - b)^2 + c$

C) $h(x) = -a(x + b)^2 - c$

D) $h(x) = -a(x - b)^2 + c$

Twists — CP

$$x^2 + 8x + y^2 - 2y = 8$$

The equation above represents a circle in the xy-plane. What is the radius of this circle?

A) $\sqrt{8}$

B) 5

C) 8

D) 25

Free Points

The Basics

Well, they're not exactly free. But in general, Free Points questions tend to be relatively easy. Almost all of them will be in the Calculator section, but very few will actually require you to calculate anything. Most are just about correctly reading a graph or chart. In order to do that, you also need to read the question carefully, so underline key words to help you NARROW YOUR FOCUS to the right part of the figure.

The Twists

If a Free Points question appears near the beginning of a section, there probably won't be many twists. You might need to find a particular point or understand a trend (is it increasing or decreasing). More difficult Free Points questions will mess with the graph so that it's harder to read. **Pay attention to the units on the axes.** One box might not be one unit. For that matter, make sure that you're looking at the correct axis. Sometimes they'll ask for the *y*-value of a point, but the *x*-value will be an answer choice to trick you if you're not careful.

Some of the charts will be lists of points, usually using function notation instead of *y*. Even if you haven't worked with functions in math class in school, you should still be able to get these right. **Just think of *f(x)* as *y*.**

If the chart seems like the result of a survey, then things might be more complicated. Often, they ask about probability, but it's never the complex probability that you might have learned in school (combinations, permutations, and factorials). You're almost always looking for a fraction, where the numerator is the specific thing that they're asking for and the denominator is the group that they're asking you to pick from. Sometimes the group is the entire chart, but sometimes it's only a column or two. Once again, read carefully and you should be okay.

Packets

- read the graph
- charts & probability
- collection of points

approximately 7 questions per test

worth approximately 70 points total

Math	grph	grph	grph	chrt
ratio	ratio	arith	COP	COP	chrt
ratio	perc	perc	perc	stat	stat
CAM	CAM	CAM	CAM	stat	stat
CAM	rad/exp	abs/MBT	POI	POI	POI
LP	LP	LP	div/imag	alg+	alg+
LP	LP	LP	QP	QP	QP
LM	LM	LM	CP	FP	FP
QV	GM	XM	XM	RAF	WTF
geo+	trig	cyl/POW	ang/SCT	WTF	WTF

Important Ideas

Graphs

Pay attention to:
- axis labels
- units for each axis
- x-axis is horizontal (left and right)
- y-axis is vertical (up and down)

When they're talking about "greatest change" or "rate of change," they're probably talking about the slope of the line. **Steeper slopes mean greater rates of change**. Flat lines mean there is no change.

Most graphs will be linear or composed of lines. In other words, the rate of change will be constant over a certain interval. Here's a very basic example:

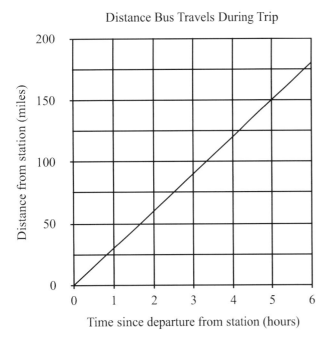

Distance Bus Travels During Trip

Since this graph is a line, we know that the bus traveled at a **constant speed**. In fact, the speed is given by the slope of the line.

Remember that graphs are one way of showing a **collection of points**. Use known points to calculate slope or to test equations. We know this bus travels 150 miles in 5 hours, which means it travels at a constant rate of 30 miles per hour. The **Plug Points Into Equations** strategy is extremely useful when you are given a graph.

Scatterplots

A scatterplot shows two things: the actual data collected (the dots) and the predicted trend (the line of best fit).

When a graph question asks you to compare the actual and estimated values, find the difference between the data point and the line of best fit at whatever value they ask for. Just make sure that you're looking at the correct axis.

Charts

Read the question carefully, and underline key words that tell you which columns and rows are important.

If they don't give you totals, you may need to calculate them yourself. But sometimes, the totals are misleading. If a chart question wants you to NARROW YOUR FOCUS to just a few rows or columns, you may need to adjust the totals to reflect the narrower range.

Usually, the "of" portion of the question tells you the denominator of the fraction.

Probability

Most probability starts as a fraction:

$$\frac{\text{desired outcomes}}{\text{total possible outcomes}}$$

Since fractions can be converted to decimals or percents, probability can be expressed that way too.

f(x) = y

In other words, most $f(x)$ charts are just lists of points that are in the format you're used to: (x, y).

Know how to translate from function notation to regular algebra. These questions ask the same thing:

"What is the value of $f(3)$?"
"What is the y-value when x is 3 ?"

Read the Graph

free points

The Basics

You can't get these wrong! Pay attention to slopes. Read all of the choices.

Example 1

The graph below shows the number of digital movie rentals, in millions, from 2002 to 2015.

Based on the graph, which of the following best describes the general trend in digital movie rentals from 2002 to 2015?

A) Sales generally increased each year since 2002.

B) Sales generally decreased each year since 2002.

C) Sales generally decreased until 2005 and then increased.

D) Sales generally decreased until 2007 and then increased.

Example 2

Based on the graph above, during which of the following periods was there the greatest change in the number of digital movie rentals?

A) 2006–2008

B) 2008–2010

C) 2011–2013

D) 2013–2015

The Twists

Don't let scatterplots or weird stories throw you off. It's still about slopes and points.

Example 3

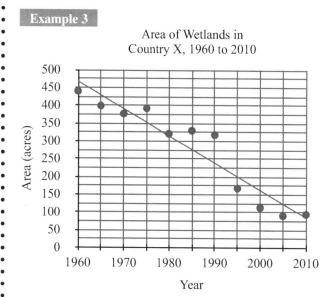

According to the line of best fit in the scatterplot above, which of the following best approximates the year in which the area of the wetlands in Country X was estimated to be 150 acres?

A) 1995

B) 2002

C) 2005

D) 2010

Example 4

For the year 1990, the actual area of the wetlands was approximately how much greater than the area predicted by the line of best fit?

A) 70

B) 140

C) 200

D) 250

Exercise: Read the Graph

Games Played versus Goals Scored

A statistician created the scatterplot above to analyze the relationship between games played and goals scored for 10 different soccer players.

1

How many goals were scored by the player who played in the most games?

A) 18

B) 24

C) 27

D) 37

2

Of the labeled points, which represents the player with the most goals scored per game played?

A) *A*

B) *B*

C) *C*

D) *D*

Rodrigo's Distance from Home

Rodrigo left home in his car and went to the dry cleaner to pick up his clothes. He then drove to a restaurant and ate dinner. Finally, he drove home on the same route after he finished dinner. The graph above shows Rodrigo's distance from home during the 5 hours he spent away from home.

3

According to the graph, which of the following statements is NOT true?

A) Rodrigo drove at a constant speed from his home to the dry cleaner.

B) Rodrigo was 2 miles away from home twice during the drive.

C) Rodrigo spent 3 hours at dinner.

D) Rodrigo spent 30 minutes at the dry cleaner.

4

According to the graph, how many total miles did Rodrigo drive during his trip?

A) 5

B) 6

C) 12

D) 30

Charts & Probability

free points

The Basics

Focus on the end of the question. Make sure that you select the right boxes for the numerator and denominator. **The "of" statement usually tells you the denominator.**

Example 1

	Trains	Buses	Total
Late	36	98	134
On-time	114	52	166
Total	150	150	300

The table shows the results of a study conducted by a transit agency that investigated whether trains or buses were more likely to arrive late to a certain mass transit stop. A random sample of 300 train and bus arrivals were selected for the study. What proportion of the arrivals were trains that were late?

A) $\dfrac{3}{25}$

B) $\dfrac{6}{25}$

C) $\dfrac{18}{67}$

D) $\dfrac{49}{150}$

Example 2

What fraction of the on-time arrivals were buses?

A) $\dfrac{52}{300}$

B) $\dfrac{52}{166}$

C) $\dfrac{52}{150}$

D) $\dfrac{52}{98}$

The Twists

Don't be confused by probability. They are still asking for the fraction. Use your calculator to find the decimal equivalent. Just be careful when they start asking for numbers from multiple boxes.

	Number of Stars			
	0	1	2	3
Comedy	3	8	6	8
Horror	4	5	9	7
Drama	1	10	7	7

A movie critic rates movies by giving them from 0 to 3 stars. The table above shows the critic's ratings for 75 movies in three genres.

Example 3

If one of the movies is selected at random, what is the probability that the selected movie is a drama that received 1 star?

A) 0.10

B) 0.13

C) 0.40

D) 0.43

Example 4

If a movie that received at least 2 stars is chosen at random, which of the following is closest to the probability that the movie was a comedy?

A) 0.19

B) 0.27

C) 0.32

D) 0.56

Exercise: Charts & Probability 1

1

	Bought product	Did not buy product
Saw advertisement	52	94
Did not see advertisement	32	122

The table above provides the results of an advertising survey of 300 people. The respondents were asked whether they bought a certain product and whether they had previously seen an advertisement for that product. If one of the people who bought the product is chosen at random for a follow-up survey, what is the probability that the person chosen saw the advertisement?

A) $\dfrac{32}{84}$

B) $\dfrac{52}{84}$

C) $\dfrac{52}{300}$

D) $\dfrac{84}{300}$

2

	Saw movie	Did not see movie	Total
Men	41	39	80
Women	22	58	80
Total	63	97	160

A marketing company gave 160 people a free ticket to see a certain movie. The table above shows the number of men and women who used the free ticket to see the movie. Which of the following is closest to the probability that a person who saw the movie is a woman?

A) 0.15

B) 0.35

C) 0.55

D) 0.65

Project	2005	2006	2007	2008
A	$1,200	$1,345	$1,512	$1,603
B	$3,378	$4,598	$4,622	$4,870
C	$916	$1,040	$1,155	$1,321
D	$2,040	$3,916	$5,008	$6,775
Total	$7,534	$10,899	$12,297	$14,569

The table above gives the annual budgets for four projects run by the Parks and Recreation Department of City X from 2005 to 2008.

3

Which of the following projects accounted for approximately one third of the money spent on all projects in the given year?

A) Project A in 2006

B) Project B in 2008

C) Project C in 2008

D) Project D in 2007

4

Which of the following best approximates the average rate of change in the annual budget for Project C from 2006 to 2008 ?

A) $140

B) $165

C) $240

D) $280

5

A certain game includes a deck of 24 cards with each of the whole numbers from 1 to 24 written on one of the cards. The deck is shuffled randomly. If a card is randomly selected from the deck, what is the probability that the number is a multiple of 5 ?

A) $\dfrac{1}{24}$

B) $\dfrac{1}{12}$

C) $\dfrac{4}{24}$

D) $\dfrac{5}{24}$

6

A student flips a coin that has an equal probability of landing heads side up and tails side up. The student flips the coin into the air 3 times. The coin landed heads side up 2 times and tails side up 1 time. If the student tosses the coin one more time, what is the probability that the coin will land tails side up?

A) 0.25

B) 0.5

C) 0.75

D) 1

7

Each of the integers from 1 to 10 is written on a piece of paper and placed into a bag. The odd numbers are written on blue paper, and the even numbers are written on red paper. If a student randomly selects a piece of paper from the bag, what is the probability that the number written on the paper is a multiple of 4, given that the selected piece of paper is red?

A) $\dfrac{1}{10}$

B) $\dfrac{1}{5}$

C) $\dfrac{2}{5}$

D) $\dfrac{1}{2}$

8

Number Correct	Music	No Music	Total
Less than 6	12	16	28
6 to 8	10	18	28
9 to 11	30	22	52
More than 11	28	14	42
Total	80	70	150

A study was conducted where the participants had to take a short test. Before the test began, the participants were allowed to choose whether or not to listen to music during the test. The results of the study are summarized in the table above. For the participants who chose not to listen to music, what proportion answered more than 8 questions correctly?

A) $\dfrac{1}{5}$

B) $\dfrac{6}{25}$

C) $\dfrac{18}{35}$

D) $\dfrac{47}{75}$

9

	Cover Style	
	Hard	Soft
Fiction	5	11
Nonfiction	9	7

The table shows the distribution of books on a shelf by cover style and genre. If a soft cover book is selected at random, what is the probability that the selected soft cover book is nonfiction?

Exercise: Charts & Probability 3

Questions 10-14 refer to the following information.

	Small	Medium	Large	Total
Red	10	18	4	32
Green	14	21	7	42
Blue	6	9	11	26
Total	30	48	22	100

The table above summarizes 100 shirts by size and color.

10

Approximately what percent of the shirts are small and blue?

A) 6%

B) 20%

C) 26%

D) 30%

11

What fraction of the red shirts are medium sized?

A) $\dfrac{9}{50}$

B) $\dfrac{3}{8}$

C) $\dfrac{9}{16}$

D) $\dfrac{2}{3}$

12

If one large shirt will be selected at random, what is the probability that the shirt will be green?

A) $\dfrac{7}{100}$

B) $\dfrac{7}{42}$

C) $\dfrac{7}{22}$

D) $\dfrac{42}{100}$

13

If one of the green shirts is selected at random, which of the following is closest to the probability that the shirt will be large?

A) 0.07

B) 0.17

C) 0.32

D) 0.42

14

If one of the shirts is selected at random, what is the probability that the shirt will not be large or blue?

A) 0.48

B) 0.52

C) 0.63

D) 0.78

Collection of Points

free points

The Basics

The correct strategy should be obvious — **Plug Points Into Equations** until you find the equation that fits. As you can see, $f(x)$ is just a fancy way of saying y.

Example 1

x	$f(x)$
1	-1
3	-7
5	-13

Some values of the linear function f are shown in the table above. Which of the following defines f?

A) $f(x) = 1 - 2x$

B) $f(x) = 2 - 3x$

C) $f(x) = 3 - 2x$

D) $f(x) = 7 - 4x$

$-1 = 1 - 2(1)$
$-1 = 1 - 2$ ✓
$-7 = 1 - 2(3)$
$-7 = -5$

Example 2

x	$g(x)$	$h(x)$
0	5	6
1	3	2
2	1	1
3	-1	2
4	-3	6

The table above shows some values of the functions g and h. For which value of x is $g(x) - h(x) = x$?

A) 0

B) 1

C) 2

D) 3

The Twists

Sometimes there's a story. You should still **Plug Points Into Equations**. It doesn't matter whether those points are listed in a chart or shown as a line on a graph.

Example 3

Temperature of a Solution

A chemist conducts an experiment by measuring the temperature T of a solution, in degrees Celsius, m minutes after a reactive agent has been added. Over the interval in the graph, the change in temperature is nearly linear. Which of the following equations best models the line of best fit?

A) $T(m) = 2m + 31$

B) $T(m) = 3.45m + 32$

C) $T(m) = 4.24m + 38$

D) $T(m) = 5m - 40$

Exercise: Collection of Points

x	1	2	3	4
$g(x)$	–4	1	6	11

The table above shows some values of the linear function g. Which of the following defines g ?

A) $g(x) = 2x - 6$

B) $g(x) = 3x - 7$

C) $g(x) = 5x - 9$

D) $g(x) = 7x - 11$

x	0	1	2	3	4
y	$\dfrac{12}{5}$	$\dfrac{19}{5}$	$\dfrac{26}{5}$	$\dfrac{33}{5}$	8

Which of the following equations relates y to x for the values in the table above?

A) $y = \left(\dfrac{7}{5}\right)^x + 1$

B) $y = \left(\dfrac{12}{5}\right)^x + \dfrac{7}{5}$

C) $y = \dfrac{19}{5}x + \dfrac{12}{5}$

D) $y = \dfrac{7}{5}x + \dfrac{12}{5}$

3

Weight of Different Finches

Finch	Ounces	Grams
grey-warbler finch	0.28	8.0
cocos finch	0.53	15.0
large cactus finch	0.95	27.0
mangrove finch	0.64	18.0

The table above gives the typical weights for four different Galapagos finches, expressed in both ounces and grams. If x ounces is equivalent to g grams, which of the following best represents the relationship between x and g ?

A) $x = 28.3g$

B) $g = 28.3x$

C) $g = 0.35x$

D) $g + x = 28.3$

Which of the following ordered pairs (x, y) satisfies the inequality $4y - 3x < 9$?

   I. $(1, -2)$

   II. $(3, 2)$

   III. $(-3, 1)$

A) II only

B) I and II only

C) II and III only

D) I, II, and III

Arithmetic

The Basics

Arithmetic questions are almost entirely in the Calculator section, which is good because the math can involve lots of numbers and lots of steps. This means that **staying organized is very important**. Showing your work can be the difference between right and wrong on Arithmetic questions. In fact, even if you're doing the work in your calculator, you should take the time to write down the steps on the page. The calculator isn't foolproof, and if you make a mistake, you're more likely to catch it if you write your steps down as you go.

The Twists

You know that warm, fuzzy feeling you get when you finish a math problem and your answer is also one of the choices? Unfortunately, the SAT loves to take advantage of your confidence. Don't rely on that feeling too much!

Many Arithmetic questions only involve three numbers. Subtract, then divide. Or is it divide, then subtract? Or is it multiply, then subtract? All three will be answer choices, so you won't notice if you've done the wrong thing. You'll be confident but wrong. Showing your work will help, as will taking the time to write out your units. But you should also make sure that you're always following PEMDAS — the order of operations.

For Statistics questions, you need to **Memorize** a lot of definitions. Again, the incorrect answer choices will be purposely misleading, so if you confuse median and mean, you will be lured into the wrong answer. Statistics questions also involve a lot of reading, so take the time to underline problem words. Sometimes, it only takes one word to make a long answer choice wrong.

Packets

- basic arithmetic
- ratios & units
- percentages
- statistics

approximately 11 questions per test

worth approximately 110 points total

Math	grph	grph	grph	chrt
ratio	ratio	arith	COP	COP	chrt
ratio	perc	perc	perc	stat	stat
CAM	CAM	CAM	CAM	stat	stat
CAM	rad/exp	abs/MBT	POI	POI	POI
LP	LP	LP	div/imag	alg+	alg+
LP	LP	LP	QP	QP	QP
LM	LM	LM	CP	FP	FP
QV	GM	XM	XM	RAF	WTF
geo+	trig	cyl/POW	ang/SCT	WTF	WTF

Important Ideas

PEMDAS

Remember to follow the order of operations:
- parentheses
- exponents
- multiplication/division
- addition/subtraction

But more importantly, follow the instructions in the question. Reading is half the battle on Arithmetic questions.

Statistics

The **mean** (or arithmetic mean) is the same as the average. Memorize the formula:

$$\text{average} = \frac{\text{sum of the numbers}}{\text{how many numbers}}$$

The **median** is the middle number in a set when the numbers are arranged from least to greatest.

The **mode** is the most common number in a set.

The **range** of a set is the biggest number minus the smallest number.

Standard deviation refers to how spread out the data is. If the numbers are all close to a clear middle, the set has a low standard deviation. If the numbers are spread out, the set has a high standard deviation.

Box plots have 5 components:

Sample size refers to the number of people involved in a survey.

Bias refers to factors that might make the results of a survey inaccurate.

Margin of error is a measure of the accuracy of a survey. The higher the margin of error, the less reliable the survey.

The most accurate surveys will have large sample sizes. More important, the survey will be given to a **random sample** of the population.

Ratios & Units

Rates usually mean that you need to multiply or divide. For example, "cookies cost $2 each" means you need to multiply the number of cookies by 2.

But they can also be written as fractions, or ratios. For example, "a bakery makes 36 cookies in 90 minutes" can be expressed as:

$$\frac{36 \text{ cookies}}{90 \text{ minutes}}$$

Mismatched units are the most common mistake on ratios questions, so **taking a second to write out the units could save you 10 points!** Start with a ratio and compare the units. If they don't match up, you can multiply by additional fractions to get the correct units. You'll know that you're done when the units cancel so that the top units on both sides are the same and the bottom units on both sides are the same.

If a car is traveling at 30 miles per hour, how many minutes does it take for the car to travel 2 miles?

$$\frac{30 \text{ miles}}{1 \text{ hour}} = \frac{2 \text{ miles}}{x \text{ minutes}} \cdot \frac{60 \text{ minutes}}{1 \text{ hour}}$$

$$\frac{30}{1} = \frac{120}{x} \rightarrow 30x = 120$$

$$x = 4 \text{ minutes}$$

Percentages

The SAT loves to twist percentages questions, so use the **OPEN** formula to make sure that everything is in the right place.

$$(\text{Original})(\text{Percent}) = \text{New}$$

When the question references percent change or uses phrases like "20% less than", modify the OPEN formula to represent a change from 100%.

$$(O)(1 \pm P) = N$$

Basic Arithmetic

arithmetic

The Basics

The SAT loves to mess with your head. One common trick involves the Free Response/Grid-in questions. You're probably aware that the Math questions are generally in order from easiest to hardest. Actually, each Math section is really two sections in one — multiple choice and grid-in — which means two sets of easy to hard. In other words, **the first Grid-in is generally pretty easy.** Unfortunately, they make you think it's hard by giving you a complicated story. Just follow instructions, and Guess & Check when you can.

Example 1

A cupcake store sold a total of 50 cupcakes on Tuesday. The store sells cupcakes in small packages of 4 and large packages of 6. If the store sold at least one large package of 6 cupcakes on Tuesday, what is one possible number of small packages of 4 cupcakes sold on Tuesday?

$$\underline{50-6} \qquad 1 \text{ package of } 6$$

$$44$$

The Twists

It may not be immediately obvious, but a lot of Basic Arithmetic questions involve **remainders**. Remember that a remainder is what's leftover when you can't divide a number evenly. Sometimes they ask for the remainder. Sometimes they want you to ignore it and focus on the division. Other times, you have to eliminate answers that don't divide evenly:

Example 2

Betsy is going to an amusement park. The park entrance fee is $15, and tickets for the rides cost $4 each. If Betsy wants to spend no more than $42 at the amusement park, what is the maximum number of ride tickets that she can buy after paying the entrance fee?

Exercise: Basic Arithmetic

1

An airplane has already flown 1,400 miles from its starting airport. If the airplane continues to fly at a constant speed of 550 miles per hour, how far will it be from its starting airport after another 5 hours of flying?

2

A car wash can clean at least 8 cars per hour and at most 14 cars per hour. Based on this information, what is one possible amount of time, in hours, that it could take the car wash to clean 112 cars?

3

A restaurant sells appetizers for $8 and entrees for $10. Mike orders 1 entree and a appetizers. If he spends at least $49 but no more than $59, what is one possible value of a ?

4

A group of workers in a factory must inspect a total of 150 widgets, and they decide that each of them will inspect the same number of widgets. When two of the workers called out sick, the remaining workers still had to inspect a total of 150 widgets, but each worker had to inspect an additional 20 widgets. How many workers were in the group originally?

5

Fletcher has m mice to feed to his pet snakes. If he feeds each snake 3 mice, he'll have 5 extra mice left over. In order to feed each snake 4 mice, he would need an additional 8 mice. How many pet snakes does Fletcher have?

Ratios & Units

arithmetic

The Basics

A ratio is a comparison of two values that takes the form of a fraction. Typically, you will set two ratios equal to each other by setting up a proportion. This lets you scale a rate up or down:

Example 1

A waiter makes $23 in tips during a 2-hour shift. At this rate, how much will the waiter make in tips during a 7-hour shift?

A) $6.57

B) $80.50

C) $115.00

D) $161.00

Sometimes they'll use more complicated words, like "directly proportional," but the idea is the same. The rate is consistent, so you can use fractions to compare two situations:

Example 2

The number of apples produced by a certain apple tree is directly proportional to the tree's age. If a 15-year-old tree produces 65 apples, how many apples will a 21-year-old tree produce?

The Twists

The most common twist by far is that the SAT will mess with the units. **Take 10 seconds to write out the units when you set up your ratios, and you could could easily save yourself 10 points.** This is a fully preventable careless mistake!

Example 3

A truck traveled 4 miles in 7 minutes. To the nearest tenth, what was the truck's average speed in miles per hour?

Most people solve the above example using two steps, but can you use ratios to do all of the work at once? Hint: you can convert units with more fractions!

$$\frac{4 \text{ miles}}{7 \text{ minutes}} = \frac{x \text{ miles}}{1 \text{ hour}} \bullet \underline{\hspace{2cm}}$$

As the questions get more complicated, keeping track of your units will become even more important. But the best part is that the units themselves allow you to check your work as you go:

Example 4

Angela spends $95 to buy 7 cakes for the office holiday party. She cuts each cake into quarters, then cuts each quarter into 3 pieces. If Kevin eats 5 pieces of cake during the party, how much did Angela spend on just Kevin's share of cake? (Round your answer to the nearest cent.)

Exercise: Ratios & Units 1

1

If a factory produces 550 shirts in 2 days, how many shirts does it produce in 7 days?

2

A fruit basket contains 2 apples for every 5 oranges. How many oranges are in the basket if it contains 10 apples?

A) 4

B) 13

C) 20

D) 25

3

A certain class contains 3 girls for every 2 boys. If there are 30 students in the class, how many girls are in the class?

A) 10

B) 18

C) 20

D) 45

4

The typical smartphone contains 34 milligrams of gold. What is the maximum number of smartphones that can be made with 5 grams of gold? (1 gram = 1,000 milligrams)

5

States Daphne plans to visit	15
Hours Daphne plans to drive each day	6
Average speed in miles per hour	45
Number of rest stops along the route	214
Number of highways along the route	36
Length of the route in miles	2,416

Daphne is going on a roadtrip. Based on the information in the table above, how many days will it take for Daphne to complete her roadtrip? (Round your answer to the nearest whole day.)

Exercise: Ratios & Units 2

Questions 6-8 refer to the following information.

2014 MLB Standings, AL West Division

Team	Home		Away	
	Wins	Losses	Wins	Losses
Dodgers	45	36	49	32
Giants	45	36	43	38
Padres	48	33	29	52
Rockies	45	36	21	60
D-backs	33	48	31	50

The table above shows the wins and losses for the 5 teams in the American League West Division of Major League Baseball during the 2014 season. Each team played a total of 162 games. Each team played 81 games at its home stadium and 81 games away (at another team's stadium).

6

To the nearest hundredth, what is the ratio of the first place team's total wins to the last place team's total wins?

7

If the Giants had only played 45 home games in 2014, how many home games would they have been expected to win, assuming they win home games at the same rate?

8

A team's Consistency Ratio compares the number of wins at home to the number of wins away. A team that is perfectly consistent will win 1 home game for every 1 away game and have a Consistency Ratio of 1. Based on the table, which team was the most consistent in 2014?

A) Dodgers

B) Giants

C) Padres

D) D-backs

9

Mike's bank account contained $1,000 in 2013. Exactly 4 years later, in 2017, the same account contained $2,056. If the amount of money in Mike's bank account increased by c dollars every 5 months, where c is a constant, what is the value of c ?

10

An ecologist calculates that a certain forest is growing at a rate of $2\frac{3}{5}$ of an acre every two years. Based on this ecologist's calculation, how many years will it take for this forest to grow 39 acres?

Exercise: Ratios & Units 3

11

Jim walks 18 feet in 13.9 seconds. At this rate, how many feet will Jim walk in 2 hours? (Round your answer to the nearest whole number of feet.)

12

In a different galaxy, aliens use a unit of weight called a *snark*, which is equivalent to 14.1 ounces. Those aliens also use a larger unit called a *blerg*, which is composed of 7 *snarks*. Based on these relationships, 30 *blergs* is equivalent to approximately how many pounds? (1 pound = 16 ounces)

A) 185

B) 238

C) 2,961

D) 3,360

13

A local concert venue can hold up to 1,200 people. The cost to put on a concert at the venue is $24,000, regardless of the number of people who attend. If the event organizers expect to sell only 85 percent of the tickets to a certain concert at the venue, what is the minimum amount they should charge per ticket so that they at least cover the cost of the concert?

A) $14.12

B) $17.00

C) $20.00

D) $23.53

14

A groundskeeper at a football stadium buys grass seed for the field. One bag of seed can plant $\frac{1}{5}$ of the field with grass. If a football field is approximately $1\frac{1}{3}$ acres, how many acres can be planted with 72 bags of seed? (Round your answer to the nearest tenth of an acre.)

15

A bus traveled 4 miles in 14 minutes. To the nearest tenth, what was the bus's average speed in meters per second? (Note: 1 mile is approximately 1,609 meters.)

Percentages

arithmetic

The Basics

Get used to thinking of percentages as decimals:

What is 12% of 275?

$X = (0.12)(275)$

What is 4% of 340?

$X = 0.04 (340)$

What is 200% of 68?

What is 1.9% of 320?

42 is what percent of 175?

$\dfrac{42}{175} = \dfrac{x \% (175)}{175}$ $x\% = 0.244$

24.4%

63.84 is 76% of what number?

Were the last two questions difficult? The problem is that your brain associates percentages with multiplication. The SAT takes advantage of this habit by creating situations where you actually need to divide. To combat this twist, you need to be "**OPEN**" to a new formula:

Original times Percentage Equals New

$$(O)(P) = N$$

Example 1

An ecologist discovered that 21.4% of the trees in a small grove were infected with a certain fungus. If 199 of the trees in the small grove were infected with the fungus, approximately how many total trees are in the grove? (Round your answer to the nearest whole number of trees.)

The Twists

Unfortunately, things still get complicated when the question asks about percent increase or decrease. What happens when you use the **OPEN** formula on this example?

Example 2

Last year, 916 babies were born in a certain hospital. This year, 958 babies were born in the same hospital. To the nearest tenth of a percent, what was the percent increase in the number of babies born in the hospital?

A) 1.0 %

B) 4.2 %

C) 4.4 %

D) 4.6 %

You need to start thinking of percent change as it relates to 100%. (This will be essential for Exponential Models questions.) When you're dealing with percent change, adjust the **OPEN** formula to reflect the increase (+) or decrease (–) from the original:

$$(O)(1 \pm P) = N$$

Example 3

Kim has 30% more french fries than Todd. If Kim has 65 french fries, how many french fries does Todd have?

A) 35

B) 45

C) 50

D) 85

Exercise: Percentages 1

1

A cable company charges $63.13 for television service after a 7% fee is added. What is the price of the television service before the fee was added?

A) $58.71

B) $59.00

C) $61.43

D) $62.06

2

A farmer sells watermelons and apples at a market. At the end of the day, approximately 6% of the watermelons and 3% of the apples remain unsold. If he started the day with 129 watermelons and 369 apples, which of the following is closest to the total number of fruits that remain unsold?

A) 15

B) 19

C) 26

D) 30

3

The weight of a person on Mars is approximately 60% less than his weight on Earth. If a person weighs 160 pounds on Earth, how much does he weigh on Mars, in pounds?

A) 60

B) 64

C) 96

D) 100

Questions 4 and 5 refer to the following information.

	Car Color		
	Red	Green	Total
2010	197	168	365
2015	217	128	345
Total	414	296	710

The table shows the number of red and green cars sold by a car dealership during 2010 and 2015.

4

Approximately what percentage of the cars sold in 2010 were red?

A) 28 %

B) 46 %

C) 48 %

D) 54 %

5

What was the approximate percent decrease in green cars sold from 2010 to 2015?

A) 24 %

B) 31 %

C) 40 %

D) 76 %

Exercise: Percentages 2

6

What is 200% of 8.4 ?

A) 1.68

B) 4.2

C) 16.8

D) 42

7

The total displacement of a ship is the amount of water, in tons, that would fill the space taken by the ship beneath the surface. The total displacement of the *Titanic* was approximately 68% of the displacement of the *Queen Mary*. If the total displacement of the *Titanic* was 52,310 tons, which of the following is the best approximation of the total displacement of the *Queen Mary*?

A) 163,469

B) 77,400

C) 35,571

D) 16,739

8

A farmer grew 60 pumpkins in 2009. He grew 40% more pumpkins in 2010. The number of pumpkins grown in 2010 was what fraction of the total number of pumpkins grown in 2009 and 2010?

9

Number of siblings	Percent of students
None	15%
One	30%
Two	45%
More than two	10%

The table above shows the distribution of the number of siblings for students in a debate club. If the number of students with exactly two siblings is 12 more than the number of students with exactly one sibling, what is the total number of students in the debate club?

10

A pool is filled with 16,000 gallons of water. The amount of water is decreased by p% to 12,160 gallons. What is the value of p ?

Exercise: Percentages 3

11

Which of the following represents x increased by 12%, where $x > 0$?

A) $0.12x$

B) $0.88x$

C) $1.12x$

D) $1.2x$

12

There are 9 juniors on the high school hockey team. If 30% of the students on the hockey team are juniors, how many students are on the hockey team?

A) 27

B) 28

C) 30

D) 36

13

The price of a television is $850. Zak has a coupon that gives him 20% off the price of the television. He must pay a 4% sales tax on the discounted price. To the nearest dollar, how much does Zak pay for the television. (Disregard the $ sign when gridding your answer.)

14

A movie theater gives senior citizens a 20% discount on movie tickets. If a senior citizen pays $11.20 for a movie ticket after the discount was applied, what was the original price of the movie ticket before the discount?

A) $8.96

B) $13.44

C) $14.00

D) $56.00

15

If 72 is 20% more than x, what is the value of x ?

A) 14

B) 58

C) 60

D) 86

16

An oil spill is estimated to cover an area measuring x square kilometers. After 2 days, the oil spill is estimated to cover an area 425% larger than the original area. Which of the following expressions represents the area of the oil spill, in square kilometers, after these 2 days?

A) $4.25x$

B) $5.25x$

C) $425x$

D) $525x$

Statistics

arithmetic

The Basics

Statistics questions vary widely, but there isn't usually much math involved. Mostly, you need to know these essential definitions:

mean

$$\text{average} = \frac{\text{sum of the numbers}}{\text{how many numbers}}$$

median

middle number when the set is arranged from least to greatest

mode

most common number in the set

range

maximum – minimum

standard deviation

measures deviation of the data; how much does it wander from the middle?

Example 1

Which dot plot shows the greater standard deviation?

Grades on History Test

Grades on Chemistry Test

The Twists

For whatever reason, the SAT loves presenting data not as a list of values but as a list of frequencies:

Example 2

Values of 12 Die Rolls

mode =

median =

mean =

Example 3

Ages of Softball Team Members

Age	Frequency
19	1
23	1
25	2
28	1
29	2
30	4
32	1
33	1
35	1
48	1

mode =

median =

mean =

Exercise: Basic Statistics

Number of States Visited by Seven Travel Bloggers

Blogger	States Visited
John	36
Rick	48
Marion	25
Tom	41
Susanne	37
Lillian	48
Amy	32

A survey was given to seven travel bloggers asking how many states each had visited. The results of the survey are given in the table above. What is the median number of states visited by these seven travel bloggers?

Sick Days Used by a Random Sample of Employees

Sick Days	Frequency
0	4
1	12
2	17
3	14
4	18
5	8
6	3
23	1

The table above gives the results of a survey of a random sample of employees at Company A who were asked to report the number of sick days that they used during a 12-month period. If the employee who took 23 sick days were removed from the data set, which of the following would change the most?

A) median

B) mean

C) mode

D) range

The tables below give the distribution of the average hours of sleep per night for 20 people in East Springfield and West Springfield.

East Springfield

Average Hours of Sleep	Frequency
5	3
6	4
7	4
8	5
9	4

West Springfield

Average Hours of Sleep	Frequency
5	1
6	2
7	4
8	10
9	3

Which of the following is true about the data shown above?

A) The standard deviation of hours of sleep in East Springfield is greater than the standard deviation of hours of sleep in West Springfield.

B) The standard deviation of hours of sleep in East Springfield is less than the standard deviation of hours of sleep in West Springfield.

C) The standard deviation of hours of sleep in East Springfield is the same as the standard deviation of hours of sleep in West Springfield.

D) The standard deviation of hours of sleep in East Springfield and West Springfield cannot be calculated with the data provided.

Questions 4-6 refer to the following information.

Number of Stars Awarded by Group

Team	4 stars	3 stars	2 stars	1 star	0 stars
Group A	12	23	19	3	3
Group B	47	8	2	0	3
Group C	11	16	28	4	1
Group D	17	19	4	8	12
Total	87	66	53	15	19

A new movie was shown to four different test groups of 60 people each. After the movie, each person was asked to rate the movie on a scale of 0 to 4 stars. The number of people in each group who awarded different numbers of stars is shown in the table above.

4

What was the mean number of stars awarded by Group B ?

5

The median number of stars awarded by Group A was how much greater than the median number of stars awarded by Group C?

6

Which of the following box plots could represent the number of stars awarded by Group D ?

A)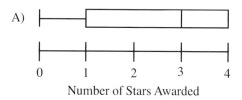

Number of Stars Awarded

B)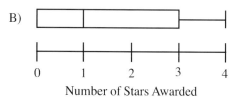

Number of Stars Awarded

C)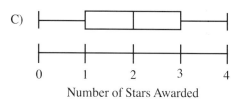

Number of Stars Awarded

D)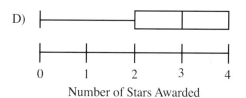

Number of Stars Awarded

▲

Average Wait Time for Appointments, 2010

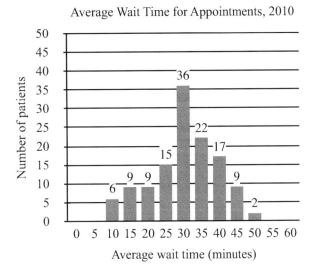

In 2010, a doctor's office with 2,000 total patients wanted to improve efficiency by lowering wait times. Roger surveyed 125 patients to determine how long they had spent in the waiting room before their appointment, rounded to the nearest 5 minutes. The results from Roger's survey are shown above.

In 2011, Roger conducted a similar survey at the same doctor's office. He asked 250 patients about their wait times and found that 6 patients had a wait time of 10 minutes. The office continued to serve 2,000 total patients.

7

Which of the following represents the range of the average wait times for Roger's 2010 survey?

A) 36

B) 40

C) 50

D) 60

8

Based on Roger's two surveys, which of the following most accurately compares the expected total number of patients with 10-minute wait times in each year?

A) The total number of patients with a 10-minute wait time in 2010 was expected to be equal to the total number of patients with a 10-minute wait time in 2011.

B) The total number of patients with a 10-minute wait time in 2010 was expected to be 2 times larger than the total number of patients with a 10-minute wait time in 2011.

C) The total number of patients with a 10-minute wait time in 2011 was expected to be 2 times larger than the total number of patients with a 10-minute wait time in 2010.

D) The total number of patients with a 10-minute wait time in 2011 was expected to be 125 times larger than the total number of patients with a 10-minute wait time in 2010.

9

Which of the following box plots could represent Roger's 2010 survey data?

A)

B)

C)

D)
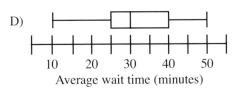

Mystery Averages

Occasionally, you'll need to calculate an average that's missing a value or that changes when a value is added or removed. Basically, you just need to **use the average formula twice**. It's very helpful to write the average formula on your page whenever you encounter a question that asks about it:

	Weight of Cats (pounds)			
Meg	9.8	10.4	10.1	9.5
AJ	x	8.7	9.3	9.0

Meg and AJ each have four cats, and the weights of their cats are given in the table above. The mean weight of Meg's cats is 0.9 pounds greater than the mean weight of AJ's cats. What is the value of x ?

Josephine has an average of 86% on five History exams. What is the minimum score she must earn on a sixth exam so that her overall average is at least 88%?

Exercise: Mystery Averages

10

A baseball pitcher averages 8 strikeouts per game over his first 4 games and 12 strikeouts per game over his next 2 games. To the nearest tenth, what is his average strikeouts per game for his first 6 games?

11

Hans is playing a game where players write a number from 1 to 50 on a blank card. He is playing with 5 other people, and the average of the first 3 players' cards is 9. If no two players write the same number, what is the maximum value that Hans can write on his card so that the average for all 6 players is still 9 ?

12

The average of x and 7 is a. The average of 4 and $3x$ is b. The average of $2x - 1$ and 8 is c. What is the average of a, b, and c in terms of x ?

A) $x + 3$

B) $2x + 6$

C) $3x + 9$

D) $6x + 18$

Surveys

Don't be intimidated by questions with a lot of text. You can Arithmetize or, like in Reading, avoid strong words and pick the weakest answer.

Example 6

A car dealership took a survey of the value of the cars on its lot. The survey showed that the mean car value was $10,000 and the median car value was $16,000. Which of the following situations could explain the difference between the mean and median car values?

A) The cars have values that are close together.

B) There are a few cars that are much more valuable than the rest.

C) There are a few cars that are much less valuable than the rest.

D) Many of the cars are valued between $10,000 and $16,000.

Example 7

An ice cream manufacturer surveys a small town of 10,000 people to determine whether the residents prefer chocolate or vanilla ice cream. The manufacturer surveyed 250 people over the age of 30 and found that 68% of them preferred chocolate ice cream. Which of the following must be true?

A) Exactly 68% of all the town's residents prefer chocolate ice cream.

B) Approximately 32% of all the town's residents prefer vanilla ice cream.

C) Approximately 68% of the town's residents over the age of 30 prefer chocolate ice cream.

D) Approximately 68% of the town's residents over the age of 30 like ice cream.

Exercise: Surveys

13

Sally conducts two surveys to determine the mean income in similarly-sized Floraltown and Parkville. She surveys 100 people in Floraltown and finds that the mean income is $55,000. She surveys 200 people in Parkville and finds that the mean income is $60,000. Which of the following must be true?

A) The majority of people in Parkville earn more than the majority of people in Floraltown.

B) Some people in Floraltown earn more than some people in Parkville.

C) The survey of Floraltown has a greater margin of error than the survey of Parkville.

D) The survey of Parkville has a greater margin of error than the survey of Floraltown.

14

A grocery store owner is debating whether to move his store to a new location 10 miles away. He conducts a survey at his current grocery store on a Tuesday morning, asking 150 of his customers whether they want the store to move to the new location. Which of the following factors makes it least likely that a reliable conclusion can be drawn from the survey?

A) Sample size

B) Population size

C) The time that the survey was given

D) The distance that the store would move

15

A small city wants to determine whether all city residents believe that a particular factory in the city should be taxed for emitting excess pollution. The city council conducts a survey of 300 people who work at the factory. The majority of those who were sampled were opposed to taxing the factory. Which of the following is true about the city council's survey?

A) It should have included more factory workers in its sample.

B) It shows that the majority of city residents oppose increasing taxes.

C) It shows that the majority of city residents oppose increasing taxes on this particular factory.

D) The survey is biased because its sample is not representative of all city residents.

Algebra

The Basics

Algebra makes up the vast majority of the SAT math section. The Properties and Models categories also test algebra, but they're separated out because they tend to test it in a different way. (More on that later.) This chapter is algebra stripped down to its most essential feature — solving for a variable.

The Twists

The **Common Algebra Mistakes** packet is basically 5 packets in one (Essential Algebra, Distribution, Fractions, Inequalities, and Factor & FOIL). They're meant to highlight the most basic algebra concepts. But also, the SAT knows the algebra mistakes that you're most likely to make, and the answer choices will reflect that. If you lose a negative, distribute incorrectly, or forget how to add fractions, you'll still get an answer that matches one of the choices. Be as careful as possible, and take note of the mistakes that you make most often. Self-awareness will help you prevent them. So will showing your work.

A few of the Algebra questions will involve some clever maneuvers, like manipulation of exponential bases, long division of polynomials, and multiplication by the conjugate. That might sound scary if you're not confident with algebra, but practice makes perfect. The rules of algebra don't change, so the more questions you see, the better you'll be at applying the rules in the correct situation. *Khan Academy* is a great resource to help you see a ton of Algebra questions.

If you haven't taken Algebra 2, factoring and functions will probably be difficult. But you shouldn't give up. The SAT-specific strategies can help. **Guess & Check** when the answer choices can be easily plugged back into an equation. **Arithmetize** when the value of x doesn't really matter. Use simple numbers like 0, 1, and 2 so that the math is easy. Arithmetizing can be strange at first, but it becomes more natural with practice.

Packets

- common algebra mistakes
- radicals
- exponent rules
- absolute value
- must be true
- point of intersection
- advanced algebra
- dividing polynomials
- imaginary numbers

approximately 13 questions per test

worth approximately 130 points total

Math	grph	grph	grph	chrt
ratio	ratio	arith	COP	COP	chrt
ratio	perc	perc	perc	stat	stat
CAM	CAM	CAM	CAM	stat	stat
CAM	rad/exp	abs/MBT	POI	POI	POI
LP	LP	LP	div/imag	alg+	alg+
LP	LP	LP	QP	QP	QP
LM	LM	LM	CP	FP	FP
QV	GM	XM	XM	RAF	WTF
geo+	trig	cyl/POW	ang/SCT	WTF	WTF

Important Ideas

Common Algebra Mistakes

Here's where most students tend to lose points:

negatives:

$$5 - (x - 2) = ?$$

$3 - x$ ✗

$7 - x$ ✓

distribution:

$$6 + x(2x - 3) = ?$$

$2x^2 + 3$ ✗

$2x^2 - 3x + 6$ ✓

greater/less than:

The cost, c, is at least $4

$c \leq 4$ ✗

$c \geq 4$ ✓

adding/subtracting fractions:

$$\frac{1}{2} + \frac{1}{4} = ?$$

$\frac{1}{2} + \frac{1}{4} = \frac{2}{6}$ ✗

$\frac{2}{4} + \frac{1}{4} = \frac{3}{4}$ ✓

denominators:

$$\frac{x}{2y} = 12$$

$\frac{x}{y} = 6$ ✗

$\frac{x}{y} = 24$ ✓

reducing:

$$\frac{2x + 6}{2x} = ?$$

6 ✗

$\frac{x + 3}{x}$ ✓

resolving exponents:

$$3(2)^2 = ?$$

$6^2 = 36$ ✗

$3(4) = 12$ ✓

FOILing:

$$(x + 3)^2 = ?$$

$x^2 + 9$ ✗

$x^2 + 6x + 9$ ✓

Use the Math Strategies

You might be able to **Guess & Check** if the choices are possible values of the variable. Look for questions like:

- which of the following could be the value of x?
- what value of x is a solution to the equation above?
- what is the least possible value of x?

You might be able to **Arithmetize** if you don't actually need to solve for the variables. Look for questions like:

- what is x in terms of y?
- which of the following is an equivalent form of the expression above?
- which of the following must be true?

Algebra Vocabulary

A **constant** is just a number. When they say that a letter is a constant, it means we don't know the number, so we're using a letter as a placeholder.

Sum means addition. **Difference** means subtraction. **Product** means multiplication.

"What is the value of $f(2)$?" means "What is the value of the equation when x equals 2?" so substitute 2 in for x.

Ways to Solve

If there's **one variable without an exponent**, try to get it by itself. Usually, x equals a number.

If there's **one variable with a squared exponent**, try to get everything equal to 0. Usually, you'll have to factor.

If there are **multiple variables and one equation**, move things around until you solve for what they want. Usually, "x in terms of y". Arithmetize.

If there are **multiple variables and two equations**, substitute or "stack" to eliminate one of the variables. Usually, a point of intersection.

Common Algebra Mistakes

algebra

The Basics

The SAT isn't simply testing algebra. The questions are designed to force errors. They're testing the most common mistakes! **Show Your Work** on every step.

Example 1

If $6x + 15 = 27$, what is the value of $2x + 5$?

Example 2

If $2a = 14$, what is the value of $4a + 8$?

Example 3

If $x > 0$ and $x^2 - 16 = 0$, what is the value of x ?

The Twists

The SAT also likes to phrase straightforward algebra in confusing ways. **Follow Instructions**. The odds are good that they're testing a simple algebra rule that you know well.

Example 4

When 2 times a number n is added to 8, the result is 6. What number results when 4 times n is added to 20?

A) -1

B) 4

C) 6

D) 16

Example 5

$$2x^2 - 6x + 1$$
$$4x^2 - 3x - 8$$

Which of the following is the sum of the two polynomials shown above?

A) $6x^2 - 9x - 7$

B) $6x^2 + 9x - 7$

C) $6x^4 - 9x^2 - 7$

D) $6x^4 + 9x^2 - 7$

Exercise: Essential Algebra

1

If $y = cx$, where c is a constant, and $y = 36$ when $x = 9$, what is the value of y when $x = 2$?

A) 4

B) 8

C) 18

D) 29

2

If $9 + 6t$ is 7 less than 28, what is the value of $3t$?

A) 2

B) 4

C) 6

D) 8

3

Which of the following is equivalent to the sum of the expressions $3 + y^2$ and $2y - 3$?

A) $y^2 + 2y$

B) $y^2 + 2y + 6$

C) $2y^3$

D) $3y^3$

4

If $5(a - b) = -8$, what is the value of $a - b$?

A) $-\dfrac{8}{5}$

B) $-\dfrac{5}{8}$

C) $\dfrac{5}{8}$

D) $\dfrac{8}{5}$

5

When 3 times n is added to 13, the result is 9. What is the value of $6n$?

A) -8

B) -4

C) $-\dfrac{4}{3}$

D) $\dfrac{3}{4}$

6

$$2x + x + 4 + x + 1 = x - 5 + x + 2$$

In the equation above, what is the value of x ?

A) –6

B) –4

C) –1

D) 6

7

The sum of $5x^2 - 4x + 7$ and $-x^2 - 2x + 8$ can be written in the form $ax^2 + bx + c$, where $a, b,$ and c are constants. What is the value of $a + b + c$?

8

If 2 times the number x is subtracted from 20, the result is 14. What number results when 8 times x is added to 5?

Distribution

The Basics

Don't let the SAT force the common mistake. Distribute to <u>all</u> parts.

Example 6

$$2(x + 5) + 6(x - 9) = 4x$$

What value of x is the solution of the equation above?

Example 7

Which of the following is equivalent to $4(x + 3) - 8$?

A) $12x - 8$

B) $4x + 4$

C) $4x - 5$

D) $4x - 20$

Example 8

$$(x^2 - 8) - (-5x^2 + 3)$$

Which of the following expressions is equivalent to the one above?

A) $6x^2 - 11$

B) $6x^2 - 5$

C) $-4x^2 - 11$

D) $-4x^2 - 5$

The Twists

Don't let weird instructions scare you. And don't lose negatives!

Example 9

$$(2ab^2 + 5a^2 - 4a^2b) - (-2ab^2 - a^2b + 5a^2)$$

Which of the following is equivalent to the expression above?

A) $4ab^2 - 3a^2b$

B) $4ab^2 - 3a^2b + 10a^2$

C) $4ab^2 - 5a^2b$

D) $4ab^2 - 5a^2b + 10a^2$

Example 10

$$3x(4x - 2) - 5(4x - 2) = ax^2 + bx + c$$

In the equation above, a, b, and c are constants. If the equation is true for all values of x, what is the value of $a + b$?

A) -14

B) -4

C) 12

D) 38

Exercise: Distribution

9

$$4(x^2y - 3xy^2) - (3x^2y + xy^2)$$

Which of the following is equivalent to the expression above?

A) $x^2y - 13xy^2$

B) $x^2y - 4xy^2$

C) $x^2y - 2xy^2$

D) $5x^2y$

10

$$x(x - 5) + 2(x + 5) - 5 = ax^2 + bx + c$$

In the equation above, a, b, and c are constants. If the equation is true for all values of x, what is the value of c?

A) –5

B) 0

C) 5

D) 10

11

$$5(t - 1) - 2(t + 2) = 2t$$

What value of t is the solution of the equation above?

A) –9

B) –1

C) 1

D) 9

12

$$(400x^2 + 1095) - 20(32 - 5x^2)$$

The equation above can be written in the form $ax^2 + c$, where a and c are constants. What is the value of $a + c$?

13

Which expression is equivalent to $(-x^2 - 9) - (6 + 3x - 3x^2)$?

A) $2x^2 - 3x - 15$

B) $2x^2 + 3x - 15$

C) $-4x^2 - 3x - 15$

D) $-4x^2 + 3x - 15$

14

$$2(x^2 - 4) - 3x(x + 1)$$

The expression above can be rewritten in the form $ax^2 + bx + c$, where a, b, and c are constants. What is the value of $a - b - c$?

Fractions

The Basics

Eliminate fractions by multiplying. Even if it's not necessary, eliminating fractions first makes algebra easier.

Example 11

If $\dfrac{x+3}{4} = y$ and $y = 5$, what is the value of x ?

A) 2

B) 8

C) 17

D) 23

Example 12

If $\dfrac{2}{7}t = \dfrac{3}{2}$, what is the value of t ?

A) $\dfrac{21}{4}$

B) $\dfrac{7}{3}$

C) $\dfrac{3}{7}$

D) $\dfrac{4}{21}$

The Twists

Fractions can get messy. Know what you can and cannot do with them.

Example 13

If $\dfrac{x}{y} = 3$, what is the value of $\dfrac{12y}{x}$?

A) 3

B) 4

C) 9

D) 36

Example 14

If $\dfrac{3}{7}x + \dfrac{2}{7}x = \dfrac{3}{8} + \dfrac{1}{2}$, what is the value of x ?

A) $\dfrac{49}{40}$

B) $\dfrac{28}{25}$

C) $\dfrac{5}{8}$

D) $\dfrac{14}{25}$

Exercise: Fractions

15

If $a = \dfrac{3}{4}b$ and $b = 28$, what is the value of $2a + 1$?

A) 7

B) 15

C) 21

D) 43

16

$$x - \dfrac{c}{5} = 0$$

If $x = 2$ in the equation above, what is the value of c ?

17

If $x - y + 15 = 0$ and $\dfrac{y}{2} = 6$, what is the value of xy ?

A) −36

B) −3

C) 3

D) 36

18

If $\dfrac{a+2}{a+4} = 6$, what is the value of a ?

A) $-\dfrac{22}{5}$

B) $-\dfrac{9}{4}$

C) $-\dfrac{4}{5}$

D) $-\dfrac{1}{2}$

19

If $\dfrac{x}{3} = \dfrac{x+12}{9}$, what is the value of $\dfrac{x}{3}$?

A) 1

B) 2

C) 3

D) 6

20

If $\dfrac{x}{y} = \dfrac{1}{2}$, what is the value of $\dfrac{16y}{x}$?

A) 4

B) 8

C) 16

D) 32

21

If $\dfrac{4}{9}h = \dfrac{3}{2}$, what is the value of h ?

Inequalities

The Basics

Most of these will be multiple choice. **Guess & Check** the answer choices.

Example 15

Which of the following numbers is NOT a solution of the inequality $2x + 1 \leq 5x - 2$?

A) -1

B) 1

C) 2

D) 4

Example 16

$$6 \leq 1 - x$$

Which of the following represents all of the solutions to the inequality above?

A) $x \leq 5$

B) $x \geq 5$

C) $x \leq -5$

D) $x \geq -5$

The Twists

Words like "least" and "greatest" sound scary, but you can usually pretend that the inequality is an equals sign.

Example 17

If $3a - 1 \leq 5$, what is the greatest possible value of $3a + 1$?

A) 1

B) 2

C) 7

D) 8

Example 18

If $x + y \leq 10$ and $y \geq 3$, what is the greatest possible value of x ?

A) 6

B) 7

C) 11

D) 13

Exercise: Inequalities

22

$$2x - 7 < 11$$

Which of the following represents the solutions to the inequality above?

A) $x < 18$

B) $x > 18$

C) $x < 9$

D) $x > 9$

25

If $5k - 2 \geq -12$, what is the least possible value of k ?

A) 2

B) 1

C) -2

D) -3

23

$$4x - 1 < 2x$$

Which of the following is a solution of the inequality shown above?

A) 0

B) 1

C) 2

D) 4

26

If $2x + 5 \leq -1$, what is the greatest possible value of $4x + 15$?

A) -11

B) -2

C) 1

D) 3

24

$$8x - 6y \leq 26$$

Which of the following inequalities is equivalent to the inequality above?

A) $2x - y \leq 6$

B) $3x - 4y \leq 13$

C) $4x - 3y \leq 13$

D) $4y - 3x \leq 6$

27

$$5 - 4x > 2x - 1$$

Which of the following represents the solutions to the inequality above?

A) $x < -1$

B) $x > -1$

C) $x < 1$

D) $x > 1$

Factor & FOIL

The Basics

FOILing is easy since the instructions are in the name. Show your work, and don't forget the middle term. If you don't feel confident, **Arithmetize** to make most Factor & FOIL questions much easier.

Example 19

$$2(x + 1)(3x + 4)$$

Which of the following is equivalent to the expression above?

A) $6x^2 + 8$

B) $6x^2 + 11x + 4$

C) $6x^2 + 14x + 8$

D) $12x^2 + 28x + 16$

Example 20

Which of the following is equivalent to $\left(\dfrac{x}{2} + y\right)^2$?

A) $\dfrac{x^2}{2} + y^2$

B) $\dfrac{x^2}{4} + y^2$

C) $\dfrac{x^2}{4} + \dfrac{xy}{2} + y^2$

D) $\dfrac{x^2}{4} + xy + y^2$

The Twists

If you understand FOILing, factoring shouldn't be much harder. And you can always check your answer by FOILing it out.

Example 21

$$4x^4 - 4x^2y^2 + y^4$$

Which of the following is equivalent to the expression shown above?

A) $(2x^2 - y^2)^2$

B) $(2x^2 - y^2)^4$

C) $(4x^2 - y^2)^2$

D) $(4x^2 - y^2)^4$

Even stuff that doesn't look like Factor & FOIL might include it somehow if there are squared terms involved.

Example 22

If $a^2 - b^2 = x$ and $a + b = y$, which of the following is equivalent to $a - b$?

A) $x - y$

B) xy

C) $\dfrac{x}{y}$

D) $\dfrac{y}{x}$

Exercise: Factor & FOIL

28

$$3(5x - 2)(2x - 5)$$

Which of the following is equivalent to the expression above?

A) $10x^2 - 29x + 10$

B) $10x^2 + 29x - 10$

C) $30x^2 - 87x + 30$

D) $30x^2 + 87x - 30$

29

$$f(x) = x^2 - 4k$$

In the function f above, k is a positive constant. Which of the following is an equivalent form of f?

A) $f(x) = \left(x - 2\sqrt{k}\right)\left(x + 2\sqrt{k}\right)$

B) $f(x) = \left(x - \sqrt{2k}\right)\left(x + \sqrt{2k}\right)$

C) $f(x) = \left(x - 2k\right)\left(x + 2k\right)$

D) $f(x) = \left(x - 2\sqrt{k}\right)^2$

30

$$(p + 2q)^2$$

Which of the following is equivalent to the expression above?

A) $p^2 + 4q^2$

B) $p^2 + 2pq + 2q^2$

C) $p^2 + 2pq + 4q^2$

D) $p^2 + 4pq + 4q^2$

31

$$(4x + 9)(4x - 9) = a\,x^2 - b$$

In the equation above, a and b are constants. Which of the following could be the value of a?

A) 2

B) 4

C) 8

D) 16

32

Which of the following is an equivalent form of $(2x - 5)^2 - (2x^2 - 5)$?

A) $2x^2 + 20$

B) $2x^2 + 30$

C) $2x^2 - 20x + 20$

D) $2x^2 - 20x + 30$

33

If $a^2 + b^2 = 12$ and $ab = 4$, which of the following is equivalent to $(a + b)^2$?

A) 12

B) 16

C) 20

D) 24

Radicals

algebra

The Basics

Just follow instructions. Remember that you "undo" a square root by squaring both sides.

Example 1

$$\sqrt{a-1} - x = 1$$

In the equation above, a is a constant. If $x = 3$, what is the value of a?

A) 3

B) 5

C) 17

D) 25

Example 2

If $x = 4\sqrt{3}$ and $3x = \sqrt{3y}$, what is the value of y?

A) 4

B) 12

C) 16

D) 144

The Twists

Occasionally you need to worry about solutions that don't actually work when plugged back into the equation (extraneous solutions). These are usually multiple choice questions, so you can **Guess & Check** from the start so that it's less of an issue:

Example 3

$$\sqrt{x+k} = x - 3$$

If $k = 3$, what is the solution set of the equation above?

A) $\{1, 6\}$

B) $\{1\}$

C) $\{3\}$

D) $\{6\}$

More important, don't get confused between squaring and square rooting. The SAT is counting on you to mess this up, so be careful!

Example 4

$$\sqrt{x} - \sqrt{16} = \sqrt{25}$$

In the equation above, what is the value of x?

A) 3

B) 9

C) 41

D) 81

Exercise: Radicals

1

$$\sqrt{4x^2 + 28} - k = 0$$

If $x > 0$ and $k = 8$ in the equation above, what is the value of x ?

A) 1

B) 3

C) 5

D) 7

2

$$\sqrt{3x + 22} + 4 = x + 2$$

What is the solution set of the equation above?

A) $\{-2\}$

B) $\{9\}$

C) $\{-2, 9\}$

D) $\{-2, 2, 9\}$

3

If $9\sqrt{2} = x\sqrt{18}$, what is the value of x ?

A) 1

B) 2

C) 3

D) 9

4

If $\sqrt{2a} = b$, what is a in terms of b ?

A) $\dfrac{b^2}{2}$

B) $\dfrac{b^2}{4}$

C) $\sqrt{\dfrac{b^2}{2}}$

D) $\sqrt{\dfrac{b^2}{4}}$

5

$$x = 2 + \sqrt{k - x}$$

If $k = 4$, what is the solution set of the equation above?

A) $\{0\}$

B) $\{3\}$

C) $\{0, 3\}$

D) $\{-3, 0, 3\}$

Exponent Rules

algebra

The Basics

Manipulating exponents is an essential part of algebra on the SAT. Some questions will incorporate the rules, but a few test them exclusively. You must memorize these!

Multiplication (add exponents)

$$x^6 \cdot x^2 = x^8$$

Division (subtract exponents)

$$\frac{x^6}{x^2} = x^4$$

Exponent to an Exponent (multiply exponents)

$$\left(x^6\right)^2 = x^{12}$$

Fractional Exponent (radical)

$$x^{\frac{1}{2}} = \sqrt{x} \qquad x^{\frac{2}{3}} = \sqrt[3]{x^2}$$

Negative Exponent (reciprocal)

$$x^{-1} = \frac{1}{x} \qquad \frac{1}{2x^{-3}} = \frac{x^3}{2}$$

The Twists

The hardest questions will incorporate multiple rules, so things can get tricky. In theory, you could Arithmetize, but in practice, there's just way too much going on. Knowing the rules is more efficient.

Example 1

Which of the following is equal to $\sqrt[4]{\dfrac{1}{b}}$, for $b > 0$?

A) b^{-4}

B) $b^{-\frac{1}{4}}$

C) $-b^4$

D) $-b^{\frac{1}{4}}$

Example 2

The expression $\dfrac{x^3 y^{-\frac{1}{2}}}{x^{-\frac{3}{2}} y^2}$, where $x > 1$ and $y > 1$ is equivalent to which of the following?

A) $\dfrac{1}{x^2 \sqrt[4]{y}}$

B) $\dfrac{x\sqrt{x}}{y^2\sqrt{y}}$

C) $\dfrac{x^4\sqrt{x}}{y\sqrt{y}}$

D) $\dfrac{x^4\sqrt{x}}{y^2\sqrt{y}}$

Exercise: Exponent Rules 1

1

If $2x^{-\frac{1}{3}} = k$, where $x > 0$, what is x in terms of k?

A) $\sqrt[3]{\dfrac{k}{2}}$

B) $-\sqrt[3]{\dfrac{k}{2}}$

C) $\dfrac{8}{k^3}$

D) $-\dfrac{8}{k^3}$

2

If $x^{\frac{y}{3}} = 81$ for positive integers x and y, and $x \leq 81$ what is one possible value of y?

3

Which of the following is equivalent to $4^{\frac{2}{3}}$?

A) $\sqrt[3]{4}$

B) $\sqrt{8}$

C) $2\sqrt{2}$

D) $2\sqrt[3]{2}$

4

Which of the following is equal to $a^{\frac{4}{3}}$, for all values of a?

A) $\sqrt[4]{a^{\frac{1}{3}}}$

B) $\sqrt[4]{a^3}$

C) $\sqrt[3]{a^{\frac{1}{4}}}$

D) $\sqrt[3]{a^4}$

5

If $\left(x^{a^2}\right)\left(x^{-b^2}\right) = x^{12}$, $x > 1$, and $a - b = 4$, what is the value of $a + b$?

A) 3

B) 4

C) 6

D) 8

6

If $a - 2b = 24$, what is the value of $\dfrac{3^a}{9^b}$?

A) 3^{24}

B) 3^{12}

C) 9^8

D) The value cannot be determined from the information given.

Exercise: Exponent Rules 2

7

$$\frac{\sqrt[3]{k^2}}{\sqrt[4]{k}}$$

If the expression above is equivalent to $k^{\frac{a}{b}}$ for all values of k, what is the value of $\frac{a}{b}$?

8

Which of the following is equivalent to $(x + y)^{-1}$, where $x > 0$ and $y > 0$?

A) $x - y$

B) $-x - y$

C) $\dfrac{1}{x + y}$

D) $\dfrac{1}{x} + \dfrac{1}{y}$

9

If $a = b^{16}$, where $a > 0$ and $b > 0$, which of the following expressions represents $\sqrt{a}$?

A) $b^{\frac{1}{2}}$

B) b^2

C) b^4

D) b^8

10

$$\left(4^{100} \cdot 8^{100}\right)^6 = 2^x$$

Based on the equation above, what is the value of x ?

A) 600

B) 1,200

C) 3,000

D) 6,000

11

Which of the following is equivalent to $\left(b^{\frac{2}{3}}\right)\left(\sqrt{b}\right)$, where $b > 0$?

A) $b^{\frac{1}{3}}$

B) $b^{\frac{1}{2}}$

C) $b^{\frac{3}{5}}$

D) $b^{\frac{7}{6}}$

12

$$\left(16\right)^{-\frac{1}{2}} = k$$

In the equation above, what is the value of k ?

A) -8

B) -4

C) $\dfrac{1}{8}$

D) $\dfrac{1}{4}$

13

$$\left(\sqrt{x^c}\right)^3 = x^{\frac{1}{4}}$$

In the equation above, c is a constant and $x > 0$. What is the value of c ?

14

Which of the following expressions is equivalent to $x^{\frac{3}{4}}y^{\frac{5}{4}}$, where x and y are positive?

A) $\sqrt[4]{x^3y^5}$

B) $\sqrt[15]{(xy)^4}$

C) $\dfrac{1}{\sqrt[4]{x^3y^5}}$

D) $\dfrac{1}{\sqrt[15]{(xy)^4}}$

15

$$3^{\frac{2}{a}} \cdot \sqrt[a]{2^2}$$

If a is a positive integer, which of the following is equivalent to the expression above?

A) $4^{\frac{1}{a}}$

B) $6^{\frac{1}{a}}$

C) $\sqrt[a]{13}$

D) $\sqrt[a]{36}$

16

$$\sqrt[4]{x^2 + 6x + 9}$$

Which of the following is equivalent to the expression above when $x > 0$?

A) $(x+3)^{\frac{1}{4}}$

B) $(x+3)^{\frac{1}{2}}$

C) $(x+3)^2$

D) $(x+3)^4$

17

$$x = \frac{8^5}{4^9}$$

What is the value of x in the equation above?

A) $\dfrac{1}{2}$

B) $\dfrac{1}{4}$

C) $\dfrac{1}{8}$

D) $\dfrac{1}{16}$

18

The expression $\left(x^{-2}y^{\frac{1}{2}}\right)\left(x^{\frac{2}{3}}y^2\right)$, where $x > 1$ and $y > 1$ is equivalent to which of the following?

A) $\dfrac{\sqrt[5]{y}}{\sqrt[3]{x}}$

B) $\dfrac{\sqrt[5]{y^2}}{\sqrt[4]{x^3}}$

C) $\dfrac{y\sqrt{y}}{x\sqrt[3]{x}}$

D) $\dfrac{y^2\sqrt{y}}{x\sqrt[3]{x}}$

Absolute Value

algebra

The Basics

Don't worry so much about the mathematical definition of absolute value. Just know that the <u>final</u> answer within the bars becomes positive.

Example 1

For what value of x is $|x - 2| - 2$ equal to 0?

A) −2

B) 0

C) 2

D) There is no such value of x.

Understanding how absolute value works can save you time. Calculations aren't always necessary.

Example 2

$$|21 - 4x| = -7$$

How many solutions does the equation above have?

A) Zero

B) Exactly one

C) Exactly two

D) More than two

The Twists

You should know what an absolute value graph looks like. It tends to show up on questions that ask about domain and range:

Example 3

Which of the following equations has a graph in the xy-plane for which y is always greater than or equal to 0 ?

A) $y = x - 3$

B) $y = x^2 - 3$

C) $y = x^3 - 3$

D) $y = |x - 3|$

If you ever need to actually solve an absolute value equation, you'll need to create two separate equations to capture both possibilities.

Example 4

$$|2x - 8| = 4$$

What is the least possible value of x that satisfies the equation above?

Exercise: Absolute Value

1

If $x > 0$, which of the following expressions is equal to 0 for some value of x?

A) $|x - 2| + x$

B) $|x - 2| - x$

C) $|2 - x| + x$

D) $|2 + x| + x$

2

$$|x - 5| = \frac{1}{2}$$

What is the least value of x that satisfies the equation above?

3

A point with coordinate n is plotted on a number line. Which of the following inequalities gives all of the values for x that are within 5 units of n?

A) $|x + n| \leq 5$

B) $|x - n| \leq 5$

C) $|x| + n \leq 5$

D) $|x| - n \leq 5$

4

$$|x - 7| = 0$$

The equation above has how many solutions?

A) Zero

B) Exactly one

C) Exactly two

D) Infinitely many

5

$$|3x - 6| = 12$$

Which of the following is a solution to the given equation?

A) 2

B) 4

C) 6

D) 10

6

$$|x - 2| = |10 - x|$$

What is the solution to the equation above?

A) –8

B) –6

C) 6

D) 8

Must Be True

algebra

The Basics

These can be tough. You either need to be really comfortable with algebra or really good at **Arithmetizing**.

Example 1

$$x = \frac{a}{b-a}$$

In the equation above, if a is positive and b is negative, which of the following must be true?

A) $x > 0$

B) $x = 0$

C) $x < 0$

D) x is undefined.

Example 2

$$y = \frac{\frac{1}{x}}{x + \frac{1}{x}}$$

In the equation above, $x \neq 0$. Which of the following must be true?

A) $y < 1$

B) $y = 1$

C) $y > 1$

D) y is an integer other than 1

The Twists

Remember that different types of numbers behave in different ways:

positive vs. negative

integer vs. fraction

Example 3

If $-1 < x < 0$, then which of the following must be true?

 I. $x < x^2$

 II. $x^2 < x^3$

 III. $x < x^3$

A) I only

B) II only

C) I and III only

D) I, II, and III

You may need to Arithmetize with different types of numbers to see the full picture:

Example 4

$$x = \frac{a}{b}$$

If $a < b$ and $b \neq 0$, which of the following must be true?

A) x is positive.

B) x is negative.

C) x is an integer.

D) None of the above.

Exercise: Must Be True

1

A parabola in the xy-plane has equation $y = ax^2 + bx + c$, where $a, b,$ and c are constants. If the parabola has vertex $(-1, 0)$, which of the following must be true?

A) $a = b + c$

B) $b = a + c$

C) $c = a + b$

D) $a + b + c = 0$

2

If $a^2 = b^2$, then which of the following must be true?

    I. $a = b$

    II. $a^3 = b^3$

    III. $a^{-2} = b^{-2}$

A) I only

B) III only

C) I and II only

D) I, II, and III

3

If $x + y > x$, which of the following must be true?

A) $x > 0$

B) $x < 0$

C) $y > 0$

D) $y < 0$

4

If a and b are constants such that $a \neq 0, b \neq 0$, and $a < b$, which of the following must be true?

    I. $\dfrac{a}{b} < 1$

    II. $ab > 0$

    III. $|a| < |b|$

A) None of these

B) I and II only

C) II and III only

D) I, II, and III

5

The linear function f is defined for all real numbers. If the graph of $y = f(x)$ in the xy-plane has a negative slope, which of the following must be true when $a \neq 0$?

    I. $f(a) > f(a + 1)$

    II. $f(0) > 0$

    III. $f(a) < f(2a)$

A) I only

B) III only

C) I and III only

D) II and III only

Point of Intersection

algebra

The Basics

Point of Intersection questions are some of the most repetitive SAT questions. Each test has at least two, and the method used to solve them doesn't change that much. You really need to get these right! If you're not comfortable with algebra, use **Guess & Check** when you can:

Example 1

$$4x - y = -12$$

$$2x + 3y = -34$$

What is the solution (x, y) to the system of equations above?

A) $(1, 16)$

B) $(-1, 8)$

C) $(-5, -8)$

D) $(-8, -6)$

Example 2

$$\frac{x}{3} = y$$

$$1 + 2(y + 2) = x$$

If (x, y) satisfies the system of equations above, what is the value of y?

A) 5

B) 10

C) 15

D) 20

The Twists

If there are no choices or if the question asks for a weird combination of the variables, you'll have to solve algebraically. Substitute when you can, and use the "stack" method when you can't. As always, try to make the algebra as easy as possible.

Example 3

$$\frac{1}{4}x + \frac{1}{2}y = 7$$

$$x - \frac{1}{4}y = 10$$

The system of equations above has solution (x, y).

What is the value of $\dfrac{x}{y}$?

Example 4

$$f(x) = x^2 - 8x + 16$$

$$g(x) = x - 2$$

The functions f and g are defined above. What is one possible value of a such that $f(a) = g(a)$?

Exercise: Point of Intersection

1

$$2x - y = 7$$
$$3x + 4y = 5$$

Which of the following ordered pairs (x, y) satisfies the system of equations above?

A) $(5, 3)$

B) $(5, -3)$

C) $(3, -1)$

D) $(-1, 2)$

2

$$x - y = -12$$
$$x + 2y = 24$$

According to the system of equations above, what is the value of x ?

3

$$y = x^2 + 1$$
$$2y - 5 = 9 - 2x$$

If (x, y) is a solution of the system of equations above and $x > 0$, what is the value of $x + y$?

4

$$y = \frac{3}{2}x + 1$$
$$y = (x - 6)(2x + 1)$$

How many ordered pairs (x, y) satisfy the system of equations shown above?

A) 0

B) 1

C) 2

D) Infinitely many

5

$$y > x - 6$$
$$4x > 12$$

Which of the following consists of the y-coordinates of all the points that satisfy the system of inequalities above?

A) $y > 6$

B) $y > 3$

C) $y > -3$

D) $y > -6$

6

$$y \leq 2x - 5$$
$$x - 2y > 4$$

Which of the following ordered pairs (x, y) satisfies the system of inequalities above?

A) $(3, 1)$

B) $(3, -2)$

C) $(2, 1)$

D) $(-1, -3)$

Advanced Algebra

algebra

The Basics

Most of these are just algebra with a lot of steps. There are more opportunities to accidentally make Common Algebra Mistakes, so be careful! Remember that **Arithmetizing** can make things easier.

Example 1

If $x \neq 4$ and $x \neq -1$, which of the following is equivalent to $\dfrac{1}{\dfrac{1}{x+1} + \dfrac{1}{x-4}}$?

A) $2x - 3$

B) $x^2 - 3x - 4$

C) $\dfrac{2x - 3}{x^2 - 3x - 4}$

D) $\dfrac{x^2 - 3x - 4}{2x - 3}$

Even when things look impossible, there's usually a convenient solution. Play around with the equation or **Guess & Check** a few numbers.

Example 2

$$x^3 - 4x^2 + 3x = 12$$

For what real value of x is the equation above true?

The Twists

You need to be comfortable working with functions. Try not to let the twists make you panic. **Plug Points Into Equations** when you can.

Example 3

$$h(x) = 2x^2 + c$$

For the function h defined above, c is a constant and $h(3) = 14$. What is the value of $h(-3)$?

A) 14

B) 4

C) –4

D) –14

Example 4

$$g(x) = x^2 - 4x + 3$$

The function g is defined above. If $g(k - 2) = 0$, what is one possible value of k ?

Exercise: Advanced Algebra

$$x - 2 = \frac{8}{x - 2}$$

In the equation above, which of the following is a possible value of $x - 2$?

A) 2

B) $2\sqrt{2}$

C) 4

D) 64

$$f(x) = 2 - x$$

$$g(x) = 5 - f(2x)$$

The functions f and g are defined above. What is the value of $g(4)$?

A) –3

B) –2

C) 7

D) 11

3

If $f(x) = \dfrac{x^2 - 4x + 9}{x + 2}$, what is $f(2)$?

$$f(x) = x^2 - x - 5$$

$$g(x) = 3x^3 - 3x^2 - 15x$$

The polynomials $f(x)$ and $g(x)$ are defined above. Which of the following polynomial functions is divisible by $2 - 3x$?

A) $p(x) = f(x) - g(x)$

B) $q(x) = f(x) - 2g(x)$

C) $r(x) = 2f(x) - g(x)$

D) $s(x) = 2f(x) - 3g(x)$

$$f(x) = ax - 3$$

In the function above, a is a constant. If $f(6) = -11$, what is the value of $f(-4)$?

Dividing Polynomials
algebra

The Basics

The SAT loves this type of question. This is difficult algebra, but if you know the process, the questions are fairly consistent. First, remember regular long division:

$$\frac{475}{3} = ?$$

You can also do long division with polynomials. If you're shooting for an 800, you need to know how to divide algebraically in case this comes up in the Grid-ins. But usually you can **Arithmetize**.

Example 1

$$\frac{x^3 - 4x^2 + 2x + 5}{x - 2}$$

Which of the following is equivalent to the expression above?

A) $x^2 - 2x - 2 + \dfrac{1}{x - 2}$

B) $x^2 - 2x + 6 - \dfrac{7}{x - 2}$

C) $x^2 - 6x - 10 + \dfrac{25}{x - 2}$

D) $x^2 - 6x + 14 - \dfrac{23}{x - 2}$

The Twists

Sometimes they ask for just a part of the whole process. Since the x carries through the whole equation, you can **Arithmetize**. Just stay organized.

Example 2

$$\frac{4x^2 - 3x + 7}{x + 2} = 4x - 11 + \frac{k}{x + 2}$$

If $x \neq -2$ above, what is the value of k ?

Exercise: Dividing Polynomials

$$\frac{2x^3 + 4x^2 - 5}{x + 3} = 2x^2 - 2x + 6 - \frac{A}{x + 3}$$

If $x \neq -3$ above, what is the value of A?

What is the remainder when $x^2 - 4x - 9$ is divided by $x - 7$?

A) -30

B) -2

C) 12

D) 68

The equation $\dfrac{20x^2 - 2x + 8}{k\,x + 2} = 5x - 3 + \dfrac{14}{k\,x + 2}$ is

true for all values of $x \neq -\dfrac{2}{k}$, where k is a constant.

What is the value of k?

The equation $\dfrac{18x^2 - 33x - 12}{6x + b} = 3x - 5 - \dfrac{17}{6x + b}$

is true for all values of $x \neq -\dfrac{b}{6}$, where b is a constant.

What is the value of b?

A) -5

B) -1

C) 1

D) 5

Imaginary Numbers

algebra

The Basics

Imaginary Numbers questions involve i, which is just a math constant, kind of like π.

$$i = \sqrt{-1}$$

Most of the time, this is an irrelevant fact meant only to confuse you. On easy questions, treat i like a variable and combine terms like you normally would.

Example 1

What is the sum of the complex numbers $7 + 4i$ and $3 + 8i$, where $i = \sqrt{-1}$?

A) 22

B) 22i

C) 10 + 12i

D) 21 + 32i

They always tell you that $i = \sqrt{-1}$, but the real formula to **Memorize** is $i^2 = -1$. If there's an i^2, replace it with -1.

Example 2

Which of the following complex numbers is equal to $(9 + 6i) - (4i^2 - 8i)$, for $i = \sqrt{-1}$?

A) $-13 - 14i$

B) $-5 + 2i$

C) $5 - 2i$

D) $13 + 14i$

The Twists

Harder questions will almost always involve the conjugate:

3 + 5i and 3 – 5i are conjugates

In math, it's bad to have radicals and imaginary numbers in the denominator of a fraction. Multiplying the numerator and denominator by the conjugate will solve the problem.

Example 3

Which of the following complex numbers is equivalent to $\dfrac{2}{3 + 5i}$? (Note: $i = \sqrt{-1}$)

A) $\dfrac{2}{3} + \dfrac{2i}{5}$

B) $\dfrac{2}{3} - \dfrac{2i}{5}$

C) $\dfrac{3}{17} + \dfrac{5i}{17}$

D) $\dfrac{3}{17} - \dfrac{5i}{17}$

Exercise: Imaginary Numbers

1

Which of the following complex numbers is equal to $(1 + 4i) - (5 - 2i)$, for $i = \sqrt{-1}$?

A) $-4 + 2i$

B) $-4 + 6i$

C) $4 + 2i$

D) $4 + 6i$

2

Which of the following complex numbers is equal to the product of $3 + 5i$ and $2 - i$, where $i = \sqrt{-1}$?

A) $1 + 7i$

B) $1 + 13i$

C) $5 + 4i$

D) $11 + 7i$

3

Which of the following complex numbers is equivalent to $\dfrac{5 - i}{4 + 6i}$? (Note: $i = \sqrt{-1}$)

A) $\dfrac{5}{4} - \dfrac{i}{6i}$

B) $\dfrac{5}{4} + \dfrac{i}{6i}$

C) $\dfrac{7}{26} - \dfrac{17i}{26}$

D) $\dfrac{7}{26} + \dfrac{17i}{26}$

4

$$\frac{10 - 3i}{2 - 5i}$$

If the expression above is rewritten in the form $a + bi$, where a and b are real numbers, what is the value of b ? (Note: $i = \sqrt{-1}$)

A) $\dfrac{3}{5}$

B) 1

C) $\dfrac{44}{29}$

D) $\dfrac{59}{29}$

5

Which of the following complex numbers is equivalent to $\dfrac{3 - 4i}{2i} + \dfrac{1 + 2i}{4}$? (Note: $i = \sqrt{-1}$)

A) $\dfrac{7}{4} + i$

B) $-\dfrac{7}{4} - i$

C) $\dfrac{3}{5} + \dfrac{4i}{5}$

D) $\dfrac{3}{5} - \dfrac{4i}{5}$

Properties

The Basics

While Algebra questions test your math skills, Properties questions test your **math knowledge**. Some of these questions are about equations, but many also include graphs. In fact, Properties questions are mostly about how algebra "looks" when graphed in the xy-plane.

Most of the questions will involve lines and quadratics (parabolas), so you'll need to be comfortable with the standard forms of both types of equations. Some of the harder questions test circle equations and polynomial functions. If you haven't taken Algebra 2, these questions might be tough! But they only test a handful of properties, so you can learn the most essential rules just for the SAT.

The Twists

Pretty much everything you need to know for Geometry is included in the Reference Chart at the beginning of each section, but for some reason, the SAT expects you to memorize all of the formulas and rules for lines, quadratics, functions, and circles. The next page and the individual packets will list the properties, but it's up to you to **Memorize the Formulas**!

The SAT also likes to twist the standard equations so that they're hard to recognize. A question might be worded in such a way that you have no idea that it's asking about a line. Use the packets to learn the patterns that line questions share, even when they're well-disguised.

If the variables don't have exponents, you're probably working with a line, so try to get back to $y = mx + b$. If there's an x^2, it's probably a quadratic, but also remember that you might need to FOIL some terms in order to find the hidden x^2. Circles have an x^2 and a y^2. Once you figure out what you're working with, try to get back to the standard form. Also, don't forget that you can **Plug Points Into Equations**, even when they're not in the standard form.

Packets

- linear properties
- quadratic properties
- function properties
- circle properties

approximately 12 questions per test

worth approximately 120 points total

Math	grph	grph	grph	chrt
ratio	ratio	arith	COP	COP	chrt
ratio	perc	perc	perc	stat	stat
CAM	CAM	CAM	CAM	stat	stat
CAM	rad/exp	abs/MBT	POI	POI	POI
LP	LP	LP	div/imag	alg+	alg+
LP	LP	LP	QP	QP	QP
LM	LM	LM	CP	FP	FP
QV	GM	XM	XM	RAF	WTF
geo+	trig	cyl/POW	ang/SCT	WTF	WTF

Important Ideas

Lines

Standard form: **y = mx + b**
- m = slope
- b = y-intercept
- (x, y) = points on the line

Memorize **slope formula**:

$$\text{slope} = \frac{\text{rise}}{\text{run}} = \frac{\Delta y}{\Delta x} = \frac{y_1 - y_2}{x_1 - x_2}$$

If you have **two points**, you can find the **slope** between them using slope formula.

Parallel lines have the same slope.

Perpendicular lines have negative reciprocal slopes.

Parallel lines will have **no solutions** because they never intersect.

Two lines have **infinitely many solutions** when they are the exact same line.

Often, you'll be explicitly told when you're working with a **line** or a **linear** function. Another clue is when the **x does not have an exponent.**

Functions

A **factor** is a term that divides evenly into a function. It also tells you where a function crosses the x-axis. Remember that if a function has an x-intercept at $x = 2$, then the term $(x - 2)$ will be a factor. Similarly, if $x = -2$ is an x-intercept, then $(x + 2)$ is a factor. Notice that the +/– sign changes!

When finding function values on a graph, do not confuse these two questions:

What is the value of f(3)? means "what is the y-value when x = 3?"

For what value of x does f(x) = 3? means "what is the x-value when y = 3?"

Quadratics

Standard form: **y = ax² + bx + c**
- a = smileyness/frownyness (opens up/down)
- b = not useful
- c = y-intercept
- (x, y) = points on the parabola

Root form: **y = (x – r)(x – s)**
- r = first root/solution/zero/x-intercept
- s = second root/solution/zero/x-intercept

Vertex form: **y = a(x – h)² + k**
- a = smileyness/frownyness (opens up/down)
- (h, k) = vertex

The **vertex** is also the **maximum or minimum** of the parabola. You can think of the vertex as the center, and parabolas are **symmetrical** over the vertex. In other words, the left side is the mirror image of the right side.

On very hard questions, you might not be able to factor, so you'll have to use quadratic formula:

$$x = \frac{-b \pm \sqrt{b^2 - 4ac}}{2a}$$

Circles

Standard form: **(x – h)² + (y – k)² = r²**
- (h, k) = center
- r = radius
- (x, y) = points on the outside of the circle

Complete the Square

To get a quadratic into vertex form or to get a circle into standard form, you might need to **complete the square:**

$y = x^2 + 10x + 4$ standard parabola

$y = (x^2 + 10x) + 4$ group a and b terms

$y = (x^2 + 10x + 5^2) + 4$ add $\left(\frac{b}{2}\right)^2$

$y = (x^2 + 10x + 25) + 4 - 25$ maintain balance

$y = (x + 5)^2 - 21$ simplify

Linear Properties

properties

The Basics

Know the equation of a line. Everything revolves around this equation:

$$y = mx + b$$

Example 1

Which of the following is the graph of the equation $y = 3x - 1$ in the xy-plane?

A)

B)

C)

D)

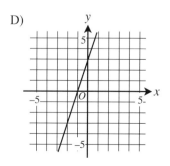

y-intercept

Given by b. Always has the coordinate $(0, b)$.

Example 2

If the line with equation $\dfrac{2}{3}x - \dfrac{3}{4}y = -2$ is graphed in the xy-plane, what is the y-coordinate of the y-intercept of the line?

slope

Given by m. Always constant — that's what makes it a line! You must **Memorize** slope formula:

$$\text{slope} = \frac{\text{rise}}{\text{run}} = \frac{\Delta y}{\Delta x} = \frac{y_1 - y_2}{x_1 - x_2}$$

Example 3

The graph of a line in the xy-plane passes through the points $(1, 11)$ and $(-1, 9)$. The graph of a second line has slope -2 and includes the point $(1, 2)$. If the two lines intersect at point (a, b), what is the value of $b - a$?

The Twists

In addition to the basic line formula, there are a few other terms and properties that you need to be comfortable with:

origin

the point (0, 0)

quadrant

one of the 4 sectors of the xy-plane

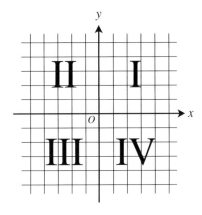

parallel

lines that are parallel have the same slope:

$$y = 2x - 1 \quad \text{and} \quad y = 2x + 6$$

perpendicular

lines that are perpendicular have negative reciprocal slopes:

$$y = 2x - 1 \quad \text{and} \quad y = -\frac{1}{2}x + 6$$

solution

the point of intersection

no solutions

Lines that do no intersect have no solutions. This only happens when lines are parallel.

infinitely many solutions

This just means that the two lines are the same, so they overlap/intersect at every point:

$$y = 2x - 1 \quad \text{and} \quad 2y = 4x - 2$$

Example 4

$$3x + 5y = 15$$
$$ax + by = 75$$

In the system of equations above, a and b are constants. If the system has infinitely many solutions, what is the value of $\dfrac{a}{b}$?

You don't need to use lines to solve Example 5, but thinking in terms of slopes and intercepts helps. Pretend that you have two separate equations:

Example 5

$$3kx - 4 = 3(x + 6) + 2(x - 5)$$

In the equation above, k is a constant. If the equation has no solutions, what is the value of k ?

Inequalities

Don't panic. Remember that the essence of a linear inequality is still a line with a slope and a y-intercept. After you graph the line, you need to "shade" up or down, depending on whether y is greater than or less than the line. The solution is where the two shaded regions overlap.

Example 6

$$y < -2x + 5$$
$$y \le -\frac{1}{3}x - 5$$

If the system of inequalities above is graphed in the xy-plane, which quadrant will contain no solutions to the system?

A) Quadrant I

B) Quadrant II

C) Quadrant III

D) There are solutions in all four quadrants.

Exercise: Linear Properties

1

A line in the xy-plane passes through the origin. If the slope of the line is $-\dfrac{2}{5}$, which of the following points lies on the line?

A) $(-5, -2)$

B) $(-2, 5)$

C) $(5, 2)$

D) $(10, -4)$

2

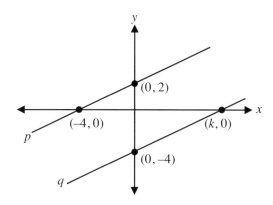

In the xy-plane above, line p is parallel to line q. What is the value of k ?

A) 2

B) 4

C) 6

D) 8

3

$$y \geq -6x + 360$$

$$y \geq 12x$$

In the xy-plane, if a point with coordinates (a, b) lies in the solution set of the system of inequalities above, what is the minimum possible value of b ?

4

The line $y = kx + c$, where k and c are constants, is graphed in the xy-plane. If the line contains the point (a, b), where $a \neq 0$ and $b \neq 0$, what is the slope of the line in terms of a, b, and c ?

A) $\dfrac{a - c}{b}$

B) $\dfrac{b + c}{a}$

C) $\dfrac{b - c}{a}$

D) $\dfrac{a}{c - b}$

5

$$5x + ay = 2$$

$$4x + 3y = 6$$

In the system of equations above, a is a constant. For what value of a will the system of equations have no solution?

A) $-\dfrac{15}{4}$

B) -1

C) 1

D) $\dfrac{15}{4}$

6

The graph of line ℓ in the xy-plane has intercepts at $(a, 0)$ and $(0, a)$. If $a \neq 0$, which of the following is true about the slope of the graph of line ℓ ?

A) It is positive.

B) It is negative.

C) It equals 0.

D) It is undefined.

7

$$4x - 5y = 20$$

Which of the following equations, when graphed in the xy-plane, is perpendicular to the graph of the equation above?

A) $4x + 5y = 20$

B) $5x - 4y = 20$

C) $5x + 4y = 20$

D) $5x + 8y = 10$

8

When graphed in the xy-plane, linear function f contains the points $(c, 4)$ and $(36, c)$, where c is a constant. If f passes through the origin, which of the following could be the value of c ?

A) 0

B) 3

C) 6

D) 12

9

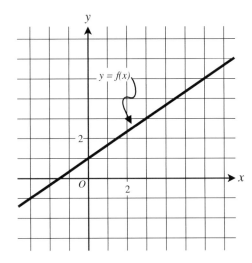

The linear function f is graphed in the xy-plane above. The slope of the graph of the linear function g is 3 times the slope of the graph of f. If the graph of g has an x-intercept at $(-1, 0)$, what is value of $g(6)$?

Quadratic Properties

properties

The Basics

Quadratic equations contain an x^2 term, and they form parabolas in the xy-plane. There are three main ways to express a quadratic equation, and each provides information about the graph. You need to **Memorize** all three formulas!

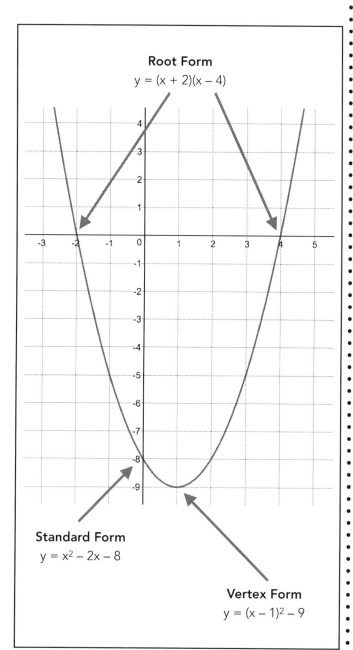

Root Form
y = (x + 2)(x – 4)

Standard Form
y = x² – 2x – 8

Vertex Form
y = (x – 1)² – 9

Root Form

Gives the points where the parabola crosses the x-axis, which are also known as:

- roots
- zeros
- solutions
- x-intercepts
- factors

$$y = (x - r)(x - s)$$

The roots are (r, 0) and (s, 0).

Standard Form

The most common way quadratics are expressed.

$$y = ax^2 + bx + c$$

The y-intercept is (0, c).
When **a > 0**, the parabola **opens upward** (smiles).
When **a < 0**, the parabola **opens downward** (frowns).

Vertex Form

Gives the vertex of the parabola, which is also known as the:

- turning point
- axis of symmetry
- maximum or minimum

$$y = a(x - h)^2 + k$$

The vertex is (h, k).
The **a-term** behaves the same as in standard form.

Example 1

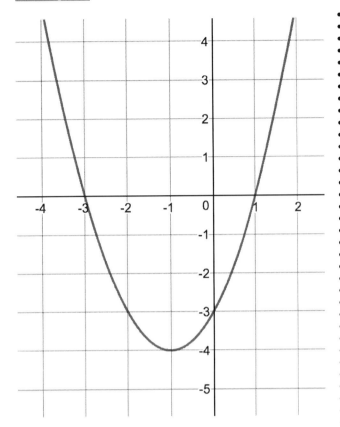

Root Form: _____

Standard Form: _____

Vertex Form: _____

Range: _____

Converting

Without a graph, you need to use algebra to move from one form to another. Use the Factor & FOIL packet for practice with those ideas. The one you might not remember is **completing the square**:

$y = x^2 + 10x + 4$ standard form

$y = (x^2 + 10x) + 4$ group a and b terms

$y = (x^2 + 10x + 5^2) + 4$ add $\left(\frac{b}{2}\right)^2$

$y = (x^2 + 10x + 25) + 4 - 25$ maintain balance

$y = (x + 5)^2 - 21$ simplify

Exercise: Convert Quadratics

Root → Standard

FOIL

1. $(x - 5)(x + 2)$

2. $(x - 3)(x + 3)$

3. $(2x - 1)(x + 4)$

Standard → Root

factor

4. $x^2 - 8x + 7$

5. $x^2 - 11x + 24$

6. $2x^2 - 16x - 18$

Standard → Vertex

complete the square

7. $x^2 - 8x + 21$

8. $x^2 + 2x + 5$

9. $x^2 - 6x - 20$

10. $x^2 + 2x - 9$

11. $x^2 - 10x + 24$

Exercise: Graphs of Quadratics

1

$$y = x^2 - 6x + 5$$

The equation above represents a parabola in the xy-plane. Which of the following equivalent forms of the equation displays the x-intercepts of the parabola as constants or coefficients?

A) $y = x(x - 6) + 5$

B) $y = (x - 3)^2 - 4$

C) $y = (x - 1)(x - 5)$

D) $y - 5 = x^2 - 6x$

2

$$y = (x + 1)(x - 3)$$

The equation above represents a parabola in the xy-plane. Which of the following equivalent forms of the equation displays the vertex of the parabola as constants or coefficients?

A) $y = x^2 - 2x - 3$

B) $y + 3 = x^2 - 2x$

C) $y = x(x - 2) - 3$

D) $y = (x - 1)^2 - 4$

3

The function f is defined by $f(x) = (x - 7)(x - 3)$. The graph of f in the xy-plane is a parabola. Which of the following intervals contains the x-coordinate of the minimum value of f?

A) $7 < x < 10$

B) $3 < x < 7$

C) $-7 < x < -3$

D) $-10 < x < -7$

4

The zeros of the polynomial function g are 2 and -4. If the range of g is the set of real numbers less than or equal to 9, which of the following could be the graph of $y = g(x)$ in the xy-plane?

A)

B)

C)

D)

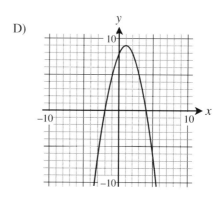

5

What is the sum of the solutions of
$(x + 4)(x - 9) = 0$?

A) 13

B) 5

C) -5

D) -13

6

$$x^2 - 5x - 6 = 0$$

If m is a solution of the equation above and $m > 0$,
what is the value of m ?

7

$$x^2 - 4x + 11$$

Which of the following is equivalent to the expression
above?

A) $(x + 2)^2 + 7$

B) $(x + 2)^2 - 7$

C) $(x - 2)^2 + 7$

D) $(x - 2)^2 - 7$

8

What are the solutions of the quadratic equation
$7x^2 - 21x - 70 = 0$?

A) $x = -2$ and $x = -5$

B) $x = -2$ and $x = 5$

C) $x = 2$ and $x = -5$

D) $x = 2$ and $x = 5$

9

The scatterplot below shows the number of bacteria in
a petri dish over a 12-hour period.

Number of Bacteria in Petri Dish

Which of the following equations best models the data
in the scatterplot?

A) $y = 2.31x^2 - 27.381x + 651.32$

B) $y = 2.31x^2 + 27.381x - 651.32$

C) $y = -2.31x^2 + 27.381x + 651.32$

D) $y = -2.31x^2 - 27.381x - 651.32$

10

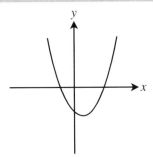

The parabola above has equation $y = ax^2 + bx + c$.
Which of the following is true about the parabola with
the equation $y = -ax^2 + bx - c$?

A) It has a positive y-intercept and opens upward.

B) It has a positive y-intercept and opens downward.

C) It has a negative y-intercept and opens upward.

D) It has a negative y-intercept and opens downward.

The Twists

Sometimes, the numbers won't work out in an easy way, and you'll need to rely on the **quadratic formula** to understand the parabola. Memorize it!

When $y = ax^2 + bx + c$, the roots are:

$$x = \frac{-b \pm \sqrt{b^2 - 4ac}}{2a}$$

Example 2

What are the solutions to $x^2 + 4x + 1 = 0$?

A) $x = -2 \pm \sqrt{3}$

B) $x = -2 \pm 2\sqrt{3}$

C) $x = -2 \pm \sqrt{6}$

D) $x = -2 \pm 2\sqrt{6}$

The SAT can also ask you for the **sum of the solutions**, which isn't hard when the equation is factorable. But you wouldn't want to work through the entire quadratic formula to find the sum when the equation is not factorable. What's the shortcut? (Note that this is the same equation as Example 2.)

Example 3

What is the sum of the solutions of $x^2 + 4x + 1 = 0$?

A) –4

B) –2

C) 2

D) 4

How to Memorize

Quadratic Formula can be intimidating, but it's something you need to know. If it helps, try to remember the two key pieces, both of which also reveal important information about the parabola.

axis of symmetry

$$x = \frac{-b}{2a}$$

gives the x-coordinate of the vertex

discriminant

$$b^2 - 4ac$$

gives the number and type of solutions:

- if discriminant > 0, then 2 real solutions
- if discriminant = 0, then 1 real solution
- if discriminant < 0, then 0 real solutions

Example 4

$$4x^2 = 8x + c$$

For what value of c does the quadratic equation above have no real solutions?

A) 5

B) 3

C) –3

D) –5

Exercise: Advanced Quadratics

11

$$y = 5x^2 + 1$$
$$y = k$$

In the system of equations above, k is a constant. For which value of k does the system of equations have exactly one real solution?

A) –2

B) –1

C) 1

D) 2

12

What is the sum of the solutions of $2x^2 + 6x - 10 = 0$?

A) –3

B) $-\dfrac{\sqrt{29}}{2}$

C) $\dfrac{\sqrt{29}}{2}$

D) 3

13

$$h(t) = -4.9t^2 + 30t + 5$$

The equation above expresses the approximate height h, in meters, of a projectile t seconds after it is launched vertically upward with an initial velocity of 30 meters per second from a platform that is 5 meters off the ground. After approximately how many seconds will the projectile hit the ground?

A) 5.8

B) 6.3

C) 6.8

D) 7.3

14

If $(3x + a)(2x + b) = 6x^2 + cx + 28$ for all values of x, and $a = 11 - b$, what are the two possible values for c ?

A) 4 and 7

B) 8 and 21

C) 12 and 14

D) 26 and 29

15

$$x^2 + \frac{m}{2} = \frac{n}{4}x$$

In the quadratic equation above, m and n are constants. Which of the following expressions represents the solutions of the equation?

A) $\dfrac{n \pm \sqrt{n^2 - 32m}}{2}$

B) $\dfrac{n \pm \sqrt{n^2 - 2m}}{2}$

C) $\dfrac{n \pm \sqrt{n^2 - 32m}}{8}$

D) $\dfrac{n \pm \sqrt{n^2 - 2m}}{8}$

Function Properties

properties

The Basics

Almost all of the SAT deals with functions and their properties. When you're working with lines and parabolas, the rules are fairly simple and easy to visualize, even without a graph. But when the SAT asks about "higher order" functions, things can get confusing. **Think back to parabolas and quadratics,** and you should be fine.

Example 1

$$y = a x^3 + b x^2 + c x + d$$

In the equation above, a, b, c, and d are constants. If the equation has x-intercepts at $-2, 1$, and 4, which of the following is a factor of $a x^3 + b x^2 + c x + d$?

A) $x - 2$

B) $x + 1$

C) $x + 2$

D) $x + 4$

Don't let the vocabulary confuse you. They tend to ask the same question in lots of different ways:

Example 2

In the xy-plane, the graph of function f has roots $0, -2$, and 2. Which of the following could define f ?

A) $f(x) = x(x - 2)(x + 2)$

B) $f(x) = x(x + 2)^2$

C) $f(x) = x(x - 2)^2$

D) $f(x) = x^2(x - 2)^2$

The Twists

When functions are graphed, you need to keep one more thing in mind. Sometimes the graph **"bounces"** on the x-axis.

Example 3

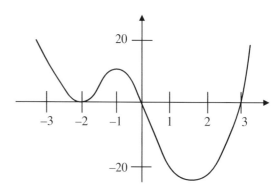

Which of the following could be the equation of the graph above?

A) $y = x(x - 2)(x + 3)$

B) $y = x(x + 2)(x - 3)$

C) $y = x(x - 2)^2(x + 3)$

D) $y = x(x + 2)^2(x - 3)$

There's also something called **remainder theorem**, which is a very confusing way of talking about factors and division:

> If f(a) = b, then b is the remainder when f(x) is divided by (x – a).

> If f(3) = 5, then 5 is the remainder when f(x) is divided by (x – 3).

Example 4

For polynomial function $g(x)$, the value of $g(-2)$ is 7. Which of the following must be true of $g(x)$?

A) $x + 2$ is a factor of $g(x)$.

B) $x - 2$ is a factor of $g(x)$.

C) The remainder when $g(x)$ is divided by $x + 2$ is 7.

D) The remainder when $g(x)$ is divided by $x - 2$ is 7.

Exercise: Functions and Factors

1

x	f(x)
2	5
0	2
−1	0
−3	−4

The function f is defined by a polynomial. Some values of x and $f(x)$ are shown in the table above. Which of the following must be a factor of $f(x)$?

A) $x - 2$

B) $x - 1$

C) $x + 1$

D) $x + 2$

2

In the xy-plane, the graph of function g has zeros at −5, 1, and 5. Which of the following could define g ?

A) $g(x) = (x + 5)(x - 1)(x - 5)$

B) $g(x) = (x + 5)(x + 1)(x - 5)$

C) $g(x) = (x + 5)^2(x - 1)$

D) $g(x) = (x - 5)^2(x + 1)$

3

If the function f has 4 distinct zeros, which of the following could represent the complete graph of f in the xy-plane?

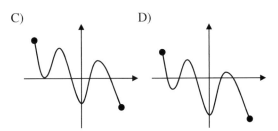

4

The polynomial $p^4 + 2p^3 - 3p^2 - 8p - 4$ can be written as $(p + 1)^2(p^2 - 4)$. What are all of the x-intercepts of the polynomial?

A) −1 and 4

B) −2, −1, and 2

C) −4, −1, and 4

D) −4, 1, and 4

Function Values

These get confusing because it's easy to mix up what they're asking for. Just remember that functions are collections of points, so you're either looking for the x or the y.

---▼---

Example 5

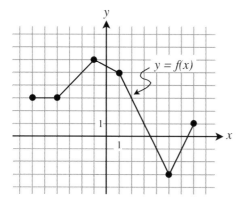

The complex function *f* is graphed on the *xy*-plane above. Which of the following are equal to 3 ?

I. $f\left(-\dfrac{9}{2}\right)$

II. $f(1)$

III. $f(2)$

A) II only

B) III only

C) I and III only

D) I, II, and III

Example 6

For what value of *x* is the value of *f(x)* above at its minimum?

A) 5

B) 3

C) −3

D) −6

---▲---

---▼---

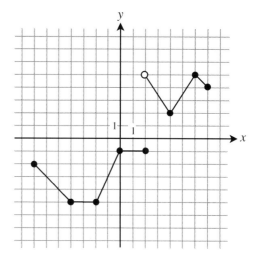

The complex function *f* is graphed on the *xy*-plane above for $-7 \le x \le 7$.

5

For what value of *x* does *f(x)* = 2 ?

A) −1

B) 2

C) 4

D) 5

6

If *k* is a constant such that the equation *f(x)* = *k* has exactly two real solutions, which of the following could be the value of *k* ?

A) −5

B) −3

C) 2

D) 4

7

$$g(x) = x + 4$$

The function *g* is defined by the equation above. For which of the following values of *x* does $f(x) + g(x) = 0$?

A) −6.5

B) −4

C) −3

D) −1

---▲---

Undefined

Remember that the rules of math state that you can't divide by 0. When a question asks for the value that makes a function undefined, they want you to **set the denominator of the fraction equal to 0**.

Example 7

Which of the following is a value of x for which the expression $\dfrac{5}{x^2 - 6x + 8}$ is undefined?

A) -2

B) 0

C) 4

D) 5

Translations

Functions can move and change, depending on what you do to them. Instead of thinking about the entire function, NARROW YOUR FOCUS to a point or two, and watch how that point changes. Or use your calculator!

Example 8

$$f(x) = (x - 2)^2 + 13$$

The function f is defined above and graphed in the xy-plane. The graph of f is translated k units to the left such that the image of f has equation $y = (x + 5)^2 + 13$. What is the value of k?

8

$$f(x) = \frac{x + 2}{(x + 2)^2 - 8(x + 2) + 16}$$

For what value of x is the function f above undefined?

A) -16

B) -2

C) 0

D) 2

9

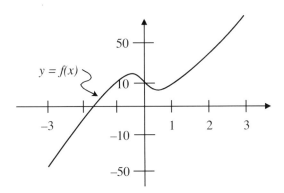

The function f is graphed in the xy-plane above. Which of the following could be the equation of $y = -f(x)$?

A) $y = -2x^3 + x - 10$

B) $y = 2x^3 - x + 10$

C) $y = -10x^3 + x - 2$

D) $y = 10x^3 - x + 2$

Circle Properties

properties

The Basics

Memorize the standard equation!

$$(x - h)^2 + (y - k)^2 = r^2$$

(h, k) is the center.

r is the radius.

Example 1

$$(x - 3)^2 + (y + 2)^2 = 4$$

center:

radius:

point on the circle:

graph it:

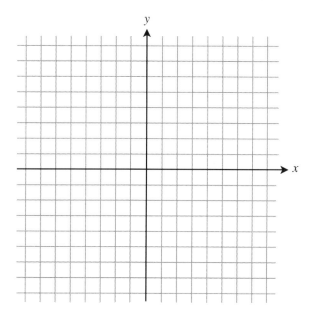

The Twists

Often, circle equations will not be in standard form, so you have to **complete the square** twice to get back to a usable equation:

$$x^2 + y^2 - 6x + 4y = -9$$

Group like terms:

$$(x^2 - 6x) + (y^2 + 4y) = -9$$

Complete the square:

add $\left(\dfrac{b}{2}\right)^2$

$$x^2 - 6x \underline{+9} = (x - 3)^2$$

$$y^2 + 4y \underline{+4} = (y + 2)^2$$

Maintain balance:

$$(x - 3)^2 + (y + 2)^2 = -9 \underline{+9 + 4}$$

$$(x - 3)^2 + (y + 2)^2 = 4$$

Example 2

What are the center and radius of the circle below?

$$x^2 + y^2 + 6x - 8y = 0$$

Exercise: Circle Properties

1

A circle in the xy-plane has center $(9, -4)$ and radius 5. Which of the following could be the equation of the circle?

A) $x^2 - 9x + y^2 + 4y + 25 = 0$

B) $x^2 + 9x + y^2 - 4y + 25 = 0$

C) $x^2 - 18x + y^2 + 8y + 72 = 0$

D) $x^2 + 18x + y^2 - 8y + 72 = 0$

2

Which of the following is an equation of a circle with center $(2, -4)$ and a circumference that includes the point $\left(1, -\dfrac{12}{5}\right)$?

A) $(x - 2)^2 + (y + 4)^2 = \dfrac{89}{25}$

B) $(x + 2)^2 + (y - 4)^2 = \dfrac{89}{25}$

C) $(x - 2)^2 + (y + 4)^2 = \dfrac{69}{5}$

D) $(x + 2)^2 + (y - 4)^2 = \dfrac{69}{5}$

3

A circle in the xy-plane has equation $(x - 4)^2 + (y - 5)^2 = 9$. Which of the following points lies in the interior of the circle?

A) $(-4, -5)$

B) $(1, 0)$

C) $(2, 3)$

D) $(3, 2)$

4

$$x^2 + y^2 - 2x - 12y = -12$$

The equation of a circle in the xy-plane is shown above. What is the radius of the circle?

A) 5

B) 6

C) 25

D) 36

Models

The Basics

If Properties questions test algebra theory, then Models questions test algebra in the real world. These are the story questions. Students absolutely hate them! I get it. Algebra is hard enough without weird situations that you need to decipher. The good news is that if you take the time to learn the rules, formulas, and properties for regular Algebra questions, you'll be able to apply that same knowledge to Models questions.

The Twists

The problem is that it's not always easy to figure out what type of Model you're dealing with. As you work through the packets, try to pay attention to the similarities between the questions in each exercise. **Get Back to Basics!**

Linear Models will obviously look like lines, so you can "untwist" them by returning to the safety of $y = mx + b$. Think in terms of slopes and y-intercepts. Quantity & Value models are essentially Point of Intersection questions, except that you'll be responsible for constructing the two equations. Luckily, they pretty much all follow the same format, so it should be relatively easy to learn the pattern and repeat it on the SAT. Rearrange Formulas questions will involve a complicated story, but it almost never matters. Just solve for the variable they ask for, and don't make the common algebra mistakes that they always try to trip you up on.

Some models won't have nice counterparts in the regular algebra world. Geometry Models are in this category because they don't actually involve much geometry. You can use area and perimeter equations to create an algebraic expression, and then it's all about solving for x. Exponential Models seem really complicated, but they also have a pattern that you can learn and repeat. WTF Models are the worst. They're just weird. There won't be much of a pattern, so you'll have to follow instructions and generate a model that works for the unique situation in the question. Just try your best!

Packets

- linear models
- quantity & value
- geometry models
- exponential models
- rearrange formulas
- WTF models

approximately 11 questions per test

worth approximately 110 points total

Math	grph	grph	grph	chrt
ratio	ratio	arith	COP	COP	chrt
ratio	perc	perc	perc	stat	stat
CAM	CAM	CAM	CAM	stat	stat
CAM	rad/exp	abs/MBT	POI	POI	POI
LP	LP	LP	div/imag	alg+	alg+
LP	LP	LP	QP	QP	QP
LM	LM	LM	CP	FP	FP
QV	GM	XM	XM	RAF	WTF
geo+	trig	cyl/POW	ang/SCT	WTF	WTF

Important Ideas

Linear Models

If it looks like a line, it probably is a line. Get back to the safety of $y = mx + b$. In the real world, the letters take on new meaning:

- m = slope = rate, cost per item, speed
- b = y-intercept = starting value, flat fee
- (x, y) = points on the line = same thing!

Don't forget that you can **Plug Points Into Equations** to test them out. The variable might be different, but you can still plug in given points or make up your own (**Arithmetize**) to better understand what a model means.

Quantity & Value

Sometimes, the answer choices will give you possible sets of equations. Other times, you'll need to come up with them yourself. Either way, the two equations tell you the same two things:

- quantity (or number) of items
- value (or cost) of those items

These questions often test the difference between greater than and less than signs, so remember:

- **at least 5** means that 5 is the minimum, so the sign should open away from the 5, so **x ≥ 5**
- **at most 5** means that 5 is the maximum, so the sign should open toward the 5, so **x ≤ 5**

Geometry Models

These do not usually involve complicated Geometry. The area and volume formulas are in the Reference Chart. Remember that the **perimeter is the sum of the lengths of all the sides**.

If it seems like you don't have to solve for the length or width, you can usually make them up. Arithmetizing will help you visualize what's going on. So will drawing pictures!

Exponential Models

It's important to know the difference between linear and exponential growth. Lines are straight, which means that they increase by the exact same amount every year/month/day/whatever. Exponential growth is not constant. It gets bigger faster. Think of what happens when you keep multiplying something by 2. First, 2 becomes 4, then 8, then 16, then 32, then 64, then 128, then 256, then 512... See how it's increasing by more and more each time? The rate of growth is not constant.

Exponential Models can be understood using a version of the OPEN formula:

$$(O)(1 \pm P)^t = N$$

The packet explains what this means, and seeing several examples will help you recognize the pattern. But percentages play a big role in Exponential Models, so you might want to refer to that packet as well. In fact, most mistakes on Exponential Models come from incorrectly converting percentages into decimals.

Rearrange Formulas

These are often included in multi-part questions, but they don't usually require an understanding of the story. Just rearrange the equation to solve for the variable they want. Arithmetizing helps a lot, especially if they ask you to compare two hypothetical situations.

WTF Models

The name says it all. Some are actually pretty straightforward and look a lot like the "value" part of Quantity & Value models. But most are unique. You might never see a similar question ever again. That makes it difficult to find a pattern, but comfort with algebra will help you navigate the weird stories. Arithmetizing also helps because it lets you visualize what's going on.

Linear Models

models

The Basics

Most models are just lines in disguise. Don't let the story distract you. Think in terms of slopes and intercepts:

$$y = mx + b$$

Example 1

$$L = 2.1m + 0.6$$

An entomologist uses the equation above to model the length L of a certain insect, in centimeters, in terms of the number of months m since it hatched. Based on the equation, what is the estimated increase, in centimeters, of the insect's length each month?

A) 0.6

B) 1.5

C) 2.1

D) 2.7

If things are a little jumbled, **Get Back to Basics.** Make the equation look like $y = mx + b$ and you'll understand what they're asking for:

Example 2

Mark is painting the outside of a house over the course of several days. Each day, he applies paint to a certain number of square feet of the house's exterior. The number of square feet he has left to paint at the end of each day can be estimated with the equation $n = 1{,}562 - 225d$, where n is the number of square feet left to paint and d is the number of days he has painted. What is the meaning of the number 1,562 in this equation?

A) Mark will paint the entire house in 1,562 days.

B) Mark has a total of 1,562 square feet to paint.

C) Mark paints at a rate of 1,562 square feet per hour.

D) Mark paints at a rate of 1,562 square feet per day.

The Twists

Don't get complacent. Linear models are designed to twist the normal stuff you know about lines. Stay on your toes, and you should be fine.

Example 3

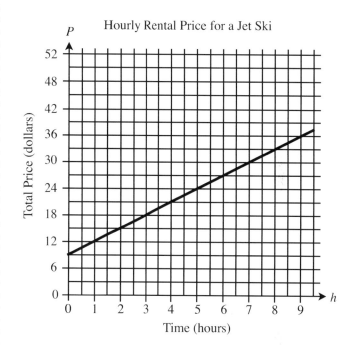

The graph above shows the price P, in dollars, to rent a jet ski for h hours. Which of the following expresses the relationship between h and P ?

A) $P = 9h$

B) $P = 3h + 9$

C) $P = h + 3$

D) $P = \dfrac{1}{2}h + 9$

Exercise: Linear Models 1

1

At a bakery, c cupcakes are made using f bags of flour. If $c = 3 + f$, how many additional bags of flour are needed to make each additional cupcake?

A) One

B) Two

C) Three

D) Four

▼

Questions 2-4 refer to the following information.

Fish species	Growth Constant
Blue snapper	3.4
Pike fin	4.1
Toothless guppy	2.4
Yellowback stickler	3.7
Striped grouper	3.4
Speckled guppy	4.4
Redfin velchfish	3.9
Spotted fluke	3.3

One method of estimating the length, in centimeters, of certain species of fish is to multiply the age of the fish, in years, by a growth constant that is unique to each species. The table above gives the growth constants for eight species of fish.

2

According to the information in the table, what is the approximate length of a 3-year-old speckled guppy?

A) 4.4 centimeters

B) 7.4 centimeters

C) 8.7 centimeters

D) 13.2 centimeters

3

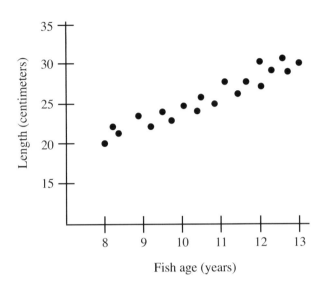

The scatterplot above gives the lengths of 20 fish of the same species based on their ages. Based on the graph and the table, the species on the scatterplot is most likely

A) Speckled guppy.

B) Yellowback stickler.

C) Toothless guppy.

D) Pike fin.

4

If a blue snapper and a yellowback stickler are each 8 centimeters long, which of the following is closest to the difference in their lengths 18 <u>months</u> from now?

A) 0.15

B) 0.30

C) 0.45

D) 0.60

▲

5

$$a = 9y + 13$$

The model above can be used to estimate the number of apples, a, produced by an apple tree, in terms of the tree's age y, in years, between 5 and 40 years after it is planted. Based on the model, what is the estimated increase in the number of apples produced by a tree each year?

A) 2.7

B) 3.9

C) 9

D) 13

6

A cargo ship weighing 255,000 tons can be loaded with crates that weigh 120 tons each. The total weight of the cargo ship and the crates cannot exceed 340,000 tons. If n represents the number of crates loaded onto the cargo ship, which of the following inequalities models the situation described above?

A) $120 \leq 340,000 - n$

B) $120n \geq 85,000$

C) $120n \leq 340,000$

D) $340,000 \geq 255,000 + 120n$

Questions 7 and 8 refer to the following information.

$$w = 80 + 8t$$

Devin uses the equation above to plan a workout routine, where w represents the total weight he wants to bench, in pounds, t weeks from now.

7

Devin's goal is to increase the total weight he can bench by at least 100 pounds. According to the equation, how many weeks will it take for Devin to achieve his goal?

A) 3

B) 13

C) 23

D) 33

8

Which of the following represents the number of weeks in terms of the total weight Devin wants to bench?

A) $t = w - 10$

B) $t = w + 10$

C) $t = \dfrac{w - 80}{8}$

D) $t = \dfrac{w + 80}{8}$

Exercise: Linear Models 2

Weather in Desert Springs in April

The scatterplot above shows data collected about the weather in Desert Springs during the month of April. A line of best fit for the data is also shown. According to the line of best fit, what is the predicted average temperature, in degrees Celsius, on a day with 3 cm of rainfall?

A) 35.73

B) 38.54

C) 47.27

D) 50.00

10

Height of a Tree

Year	Height (feet)
2010	46
2015	52

The height of a certain tree was measured in 2010 and 2015. If the tree grows at a constant rate, which of the following functions h models the height, in feet, of the tree t years after 2010 ?

A) $h(t) = 1.2t + 46$

B) $h(t) = 1.2(t - 2010) + 46$

C) $h(t) = 46t + 6$

D) $h(t) = 46(t - 2010) + 6$

A storage company calculates the price for a customer to rent a storage unit, in dollars, using the expression $35 + 2am$, where a is the area of the storage unit, in square feet, and m is the number of months the customer rents the storage unit. Which of the following is an accurate interpretation of the expression?

A) The company charges $2 per month for each square foot of storage space.

B) The company charges $35 per month for each square foot of storage space.

C) The minimum area of a storage unit is 2 square feet.

D) A customer must rent a storage unit for at least 2 months.

Quantity & Value
models

The Basics

The SAT consistently tests this type of model, so understanding its format is essential. It's best illustrated through an example:

Example 1

Mike has 15 coins worth a total of $2.70. If Mike only has dimes, worth $0.10 each, and quarters, worth $0.25 each, how many dimes does Mike have?

A) 6

B) 7

C) 8

D) 9

You could **Guess & Check**, but sometimes you won't have answer choices, so you also need to know how to construct Quantity & Value models:

Set your variables:

Quantity of coins:

Value of coins:

Find the point of intersection:

The Twists

Mathematically, there isn't one. Sometimes, the story disguises the fact that it's a QV model, but you'll start to recognize the pattern.

Example 2

Brad is organizing a wedding reception for 152 people. He has 18 tables where they can sit. Some of the tables can seat up to 6 people each, and the rest can seat up to 10 people each. Assuming that all of the tables are filled to capacity and every person has a seat, how many of the tables are 10-person tables?

Other times, you just need to choose the correct set of equations:

Example 3

Mona needs to order pizzas for a party. To make sure that everyone has enough food, she needs to order at least 12 pizzas. Regular pizzas cost $14 each, and pepperoni pizzas cost $16 each. Her budget for the party is no more than $180, and she has to order at least one pizza of each type. Which of the following systems of inequalities represents the conditions described if x is the number of regular pizzas and y is the number of pepperoni pizzas that Mona orders?

A) $14x + 16y \geq 180$
   $x + y \leq 12$
   $x \geq 1$
   $y \geq 1$

B) $14x + 16y \geq 180$
   $x + y \leq 12$
   $x \leq 1$
   $y \leq 1$

C) $14x + 16y \leq 180$
   $x + y \geq 12$
   $x \geq 1$
   $y \geq 1$

D) $14x + 16y \leq 180$
   $x + y \geq 12$
   $x \leq 1$
   $y \leq 1$

Exercise: Quantity & Value

1

A hardware store sells hammers and screwdrivers. Each hammer costs $5, and each screwdriver costs $3. If Dolores purchased a total of 11 hammers and screwdrivers for a combined price of $39, how many screwdrivers did she purchase?

2

A cargo plane is loaded with boxes weighing 50 pounds and crates weighing 125 pounds. The cargo plane can carry a maximum weight of 10,000 pounds. If there is a combined total of 90 boxes and crates to be loaded onto the cargo plane, which of the following systems of inequalities represents this situation in terms of x and y, where x is the number of boxes and y is the number of crates?

A) $125x + 50y \leq 10,000$
$x + y = 90$

B) $125x + 50y \geq 10,000$
$x + y = 90$

C) $50x + 125y \leq 10,000$
$x + y = 90$

D) $50x + 125y \geq 10,000$
$x + y = 90$

3

In a certain card game, red cards are worth 2 points and black cards are worth 5 points. If Kristen has 19 cards worth a total of 77 points, how many black cards does she have?

4

A golf club offers standard and premier memberships. The monthly cost of a standard membership is $3,500, and the monthly cost of a premier membership is $6,725. Last year, the golf club made $577,550 off of 130 total memberships. Which of the following systems of equations could be used to find the number of standard memberships, S, and the number of premier memberships, P, that the golf club had last year?

A) $\dfrac{S}{6,725} + \dfrac{P}{3,500} = \dfrac{1}{577,550}$
$S + P = 130$

B) $6,725S + 3,500P = 577,550$
$S + P = 130$

C) $3,500S + 6,725P = 130$
$S + P = 577,550$

D) $3,500S + 6,725P = 577,550$
$S + P = 130$

5

A certain type of flower can have either 12 petals or 14 petals. Layla frolics through a field containing this type of flower, and she picks 16 of them. Later, she counts the petals as she pulls them off of each flower. If Layla counts a total of 196 petals, how many of the flowers that she picked had 14 petals?

Geometry Models

models

The Basics

Geometry with a cute story is more about algebra than it is geometry. Most of these questions involve lengths and widths, so either make equations or **Arithmetize**.

Example 1

The length of a rectangular carpet is 5 feet shorter than twice its width. If the width of the carpet is w feet, which of the following expressions represents the perimeter, in feet, of the carpet in terms of w ?

A) $5 - 2w$

B) $4w - 10$

C) $6w - 10$

D) $2w^2 - 5w$

Example 2

An artist modified a rectangle by increasing its length by 20 percent and decreasing its width by n percent. These modifications decreased the area of the rectangle by 16 percent. Based on the artist's changes, what is the value of n ?

A) 16

B) 25

C) 30

D) 36

The Twists

A lot of Geometry Models are similar to other question types, so be flexible. What does this equation remind you of? Just make sure that it's set up the way the question wants. **Arithmetize** to play it safe.

Example 3

A gardener is planting a rectangular flowerbed with a 5-foot-wide path surrounding it. The equation $A = 5p + 100$ will relate the area A, in square feet, of the path to the perimeter p, in feet, of the flowerbed. Based on this design, how many feet will the perimeter of the flowerbed increase for each additional square foot of the path's area?

A) $\dfrac{1}{100}$

B) $\dfrac{1}{5}$

C) 5

D) 100

Exercise: Geometry Models

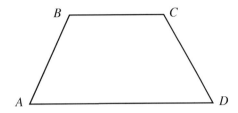

In quadrilateral *ABCD* above, *AD* is parallel to *BC*, and *AB* = *CD*. If *AD* and *BC* were each reduced by 25 percent, then by what percent would the area of *ABCD* decrease?

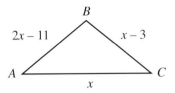

Note: Figure not drawn to scale.

In isosceles triangle *ABC* above, *AB* = *BC*. What is the perimeter of triangle *ABC* ?

A fish tank in the shape of a rectangular prism has a length of 30 centimeters, a width of 20 centimeters, and a height of 20 centimeters. The tank is filled halfway with water. If an additional 1,800 cubic centimeters of water are poured into the tank, what is the total height of water in the tank, in centimeters?

A) 10

B) 13

C) 16

D) 17

A room has an area of 153 square feet. If the width is 8 feet shorter than the length, what is the width of the room, in feet?

Exponential Models

models

The Basics

What makes exponential models different from everything else?

Linear growth
(the increase is constant)

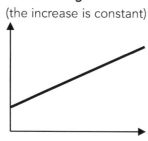

Exponential growth
(the increase increases)

Example 1

Grover has four job offers, each with different salary options. If he wants to accept the job that yields exponential salary growth, which of the four options should he choose?

A) At the end of each year that he works for the company, Grover's salary will increase by 1% of his initial salary.

B) At the end of each year that he works for the company, Grover's salary will increase by 2% of his initial salary and he'll receive a $500 annual bonus.

C) At the end of each year that he works for the company, Grover's salary will increase by 1.2% of his previous year's salary.

D) At the end of each year that he works for the company, Grover's salary will increase by $1000.

The Twists

Exponential equations make more sense in the context of a story, but the standard form of the equation can mirror the **OPEN** formula that you used for Percentages questions.

$$(O)(1 \pm P)^t = N$$

O = original amount

t = time (in days, months, years, etc.)

P = percent change per unit of time

    1 + P = rate of growth

    1 − P = rate of decay

N = new amount after t time has passed

Example 2

A population of bacteria in a petri dish grows at a rate of 2 percent per hour. If there were 120 bacteria in the petri dish to start, which equation best models the number of bacteria B in the petri dish after h hours?

A) $B = 120(0.02)^h$

B) $B = 120(1.02)^h$

C) $B = 120(1.2)^h$

D) $B = 120(2)^h$

Example 3

An antibiotic is introduced into a different petri dish when there are 800 bacteria present. The antibiotic kills the bacteria, and the population decreases by 12 percent every hour. To the nearest whole number, how many bacteria will remain in the petri dish after 3 hours?

Exercise: Exponential Models 1

Richard invests $100 in a stock that increases in value by 3% each year. How much money does Richard have after 5 years? (Round your answer to the nearest whole dollar.)

A cable company wants to increase the cost of a yearly contract by d dollars per year. This same yearly contract currently costs c dollars per year. Which of the following best models the cost y, in dollars, of a yearly contract for the cable company x years from now?

A) $y = c(d)^x$

B) $y = d(c)^x$

C) $y = cx + d$

D) $y = dx + c$

The population of wolves on a preserve has increased by approximately 80 percent every year since 2005. If there were 408 wolves on the preserve in 2011, how many wolves were there in 2005?

A pool of water evaporates by the same percentage every hour. If only 5% of the pool remains after 6 hours, by approximately what percent does the pool evaporate every hour?

A) 5%

B) 16%

C) 39%

D) 61%

$$C(x) = 150(1.04)^x$$

The equation above models the number of customers, $C(x)$, at a certain grocery store x years after it moves to a new location. Which of the following best models the number of customers at the grocery store m months after it moves to a new location?

A) $C(m) = 150(1.04)^{\frac{m}{12}}$

B) $C(m) = 150(1.04)^{12m}$

C) $C(m) = 150(1.003)^{12m}$

D) $C(m) = 150(1.60)^m$

A botanist calculates that a certain fungus has killed 4 percent of the trees in a forest every 10 years since 1940. If there were approximately 3,075 trees in the forest in 2010, approximately how many trees died between 1960 and 1980?

A) 206

B) 296

C) 2,337

D) 4,092

Exercise: Exponential Models 2

7

The initial value of an investment is $200, and the value of the investment increases by 3% each year. Which function gives the value of the investment V, in dollars, t years after the initial investment was made?

A) $V(t) = 200(0.03)^t$

B) $V(t) = 200(0.3)^t$

C) $V(t) = 200(1.03)^t$

D) $V(t) = 200(1.3)^t$

8

An investment firm claims that a certain stock will increase in value by 0.9% compared to each previous month. Which type of function best models the monthly value of the stock over time?

A) Increasing linear

B) Decreasing linear

C) Increasing exponential

D) Decreasing exponential

9

$$P(t) = 8(1.14)^t$$

The function P above models the population of gulls at a nesting site, where t represents the number of days after September 1. Which of the following is the best interpretation of the number 1.14 in this context?

A) The model estimates that there were 1.14 gulls at the nesting site on September 1.

B) The model estimates that the population at the nesting site increases by 1.14 gulls each day.

C) The model estimates that the population of the nesting site will grow by a factor of 1.14 each day.

D) The model estimates that the population at the nesting site will grow by a factor of 8 every 1.14 days.

10

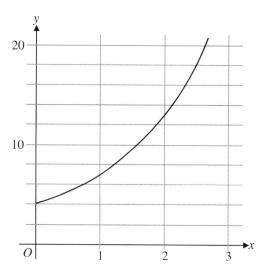

What is the equation of the graph shown?

A) $y = 2^x + 4$

B) $y = 3(2)^x + 1$

C) $y = 3(2)^x + 4$

D) $y = 4(2)^x$

11

A researcher found that for each hour that a class spent studying for a certain exam, the average number of points earned on the exam improved by 15%. Without studying, the class earned an average of 70 points on the exam. Which function best models the average number of points y that the class would get after studying for x hours?

A) $y = 15(0.7)^x$

B) $y = 15(1.7)^x$

C) $y = 70(0.15)^x$

D) $y = 70(1.15)^x$

12

A cylindrical tank is filled with water. A valve is opened to allow water to drain from the tank. In the first minute after the valve is opened, 5% of the water in the tank drains out. If the water continues to drain at this same rate, losing the same volume of water every minute until the tank is completely empty, which type of function best models the volume of water remaining in the tank as the number of minutes since the valve was opened increases?

A) Increasing exponential

B) Decreasing exponential

C) Increasing linear

D) Decreasing linear

13

$$V(w) = 720(0.9)^{\frac{w}{12}}$$

A pool of 720 gallons of water evaporates so that 10% of its volume is lost every 12 weeks. The function V above models the volume of water, in gallons, that remains in the pool w weeks after it begins to evaporate. Which of the following is the best interpretation of the number 0.9 in the function?

A) The number of gallons of water that evaporate from the pool every week

B) The number of gallons of water that evaporate from the pool every 12 weeks

C) The proportion of the volume of water that remains in the pool after one week

D) The proportion of the volume of water that remains in the pool after 12 weeks

14

An initial investment of 36 dollars grows by approximately 11.3% each year. Which of the following functions best models the value $V(t)$, in dollars, of the investment t years after the initial investment?

A) $V(t) = 1.113(36)^t$

B) $V(t) = 36(2)^{1.113t}$

C) $V(t) = 36(1.113)^t$

D) $V(t) = (36 \bullet 1.113)^t$

15

The height of a plant increased by 2% from the previous week for 10 consecutive weeks. If x is the number of weeks since the height began to increase and y is the height of the plant, which of the following equations could model the height of the plant over this time period?

A) $y = 0.2x + 4.35$

B) $y = 2x + 4.35$

C) $y = 4.35(1.02)^x$

D) $y = 4.35(2)^x$

16

The initial value of an investment is x dollars. Each year the value of the investment decreases by $p\%$. Which of the following expressions represents the value of the investment after 5 years?

A) $\dfrac{(xp)^5}{100}$

B) $\left(x - \dfrac{p}{100}\right)^5$

C) $x\left(1 - \dfrac{p}{100}\right)^5$

D) $\dfrac{p(1-x)^5}{100}$

Rearrange Formulas

models

The Basics

It's Algebra. And they add in a boring story. So it's Algebra, but worse.

Example 1

The speed s of an object is found by dividing the distance d the object travels by the time t that it takes the object to travel that distance. Which of the following equations give the distance d in terms of s and t ?

A) $d = st$

B) $d = \dfrac{s}{t}$

C) $d = \dfrac{t}{s}$

D) $d = t + s$

Example 2

$$E_k = \frac{1}{2}mv^2$$

An object's kinetic energy E_k is related to the mass of the object m and the velocity of the object v by the formula above. Which of the following expresses the square of the velocity of the object in terms of the kinetic energy of the object and the mass of the object?

A) $v^2 = 2mE_k$

B) $v^2 = \dfrac{E_k}{2m}$

C) $v^2 = \dfrac{2E_k}{m}$

D) $v^2 = \dfrac{2m}{E_k}$

The Twists

Sometimes they ask you to strip away the algebra and understand the relationship in terms of numbers. What's that called again? **Arithmetize!**

Example 3

A city planner lays out two rectangular plots of land with the same width. If the area of Plot A is three times the area of Plot B, the length of Plot B is what fraction of the length of Plot A?

A) $\dfrac{1}{2}$

B) $\dfrac{1}{3}$

C) $\dfrac{1}{6}$

D) $\dfrac{1}{9}$

Example 4

Containers A and B are in the shape of a right circular cylinder and have the same volume. If the radius of the base of Container A is 4 times the length of the radius of the base of Container B, what is the ratio of the height of Container A to the height of Container B?

A) $1 : 2$

B) $1 : 4$

C) $1 : 8$

D) $1 : 16$

Exercise: Rearrange Formulas

1

A dog walker uses the formula $p = 5dwm$ to estimate his weekly profit p, in dollars, based on the number of dogs he walks d for m minutes per walk for w walks per week. Which of the following correctly expresses w in terms of p, d, and m ?

A) $w = \dfrac{5p}{dm}$

B) $w = \dfrac{dm}{5p}$

C) $w = \dfrac{p}{5dm}$

D) $w = \dfrac{5dm}{p}$

2

If the height of a rectangular pyramid is multiplied by 6, its volume will be how many times greater?

(Note: The volume of a rectangular pyramid is found using the formula $V = \dfrac{1}{3}lwh$.)

A) 2

B) 6

C) 18

D) 216

Questions 3 and 4 refer to the following information.

Cadmium's formula: $\qquad L = \dfrac{(c + s)^2}{v}$

Cadmium's formula estimates the length of a wire L, in centimeters based on the current passing through the wire c, in amperes, the size of the wire s, in square centimeters, and the velocity v, in meters per second, of the wire in a vacuum.

3

Which of the following expressions is equivalent to $c + s$?

A) $\sqrt{\dfrac{L}{v}}$

B) $\sqrt{Lv}$

C) $(Lv)^2$

D) Lv^2

4

If the velocity of a wire is doubled, what happens to its length?

A) It is increased by 200 percent.

B) It is increased by 50 percent.

C) It is decreased by 50 percent.

D) It is decreased by 200 percent.

WTF Models

models

The Basics

These are models that don't fit one of the standard categories or formats. They don't necessarily have easily recognizable counterparts in the Algebra world. They can be difficult precisely because each one is unique. Or so it would seem…

1

During a typical week, Bill drinks w bottles of water and s bottles of soda. If each bottle of water is 16 ounces and each bottle of soda is 20 ounces, which of the following could represent the total number of ounces that Bill drinks in a week if he only drinks water and soda?

A) $20w + 16s$

B) $16w + 20s$

C) $36ws$

D) $320ws$

2

Stephanie bought a pair of pants and a blouse on sale. The pair of pants was 20% off the original price and the blouse was 15% off the original price. In total, Stephanie saved $36 because of the sale. Which equation models Stephanie's savings, where x is the original cost of the pair of pants and y is the original cost of the blouse?

A) $20x + 15y = 36$

B) $15x + 20y = 36$

C) $0.2x + 0.15y = 36$

D) $0.15x + 0.2y = 36$

The Twists

When they get weird, you can almost always solve easily, as long as you STAY CALM!

Arithmetize to visualize:

3

Luis rents a truck at a rate of $50 per day. Which of the following equations represents the total cost c, in dollars, to rent the truck for w weeks?

A) $c = \dfrac{50w}{7}$

B) $c = \dfrac{7w}{50}$

C) $c = 50w + 7$

D) $c = 50(7w)$

4

A population of Arctic hares increased by 10 percent from January to December of 2010. In 2011, the population decreased by 6 percent. If there were h Arctic hares at the end of 2011, which of the following represents the number of Arctic hares at the beginning of 2010?

A) $\dfrac{h}{(1.1)(0.94)}$

B) $\dfrac{h}{1.04}$

C) $(1.1)(0.94)h$

D) $1.04h$

5

Jody and Larry spent a combined $300 on furniture. If Larry spent $60 more than Jody, how much did Jody spend on furniture?

6

In a certain game, a *blerg* is worth 3 points less than a *snark*. If 5 *blergs* and 3 *snarks* are worth a total of 49 points, how many points is a *blerg* worth?

7

The sum of three numbers is 138. If one of the numbers, n, is half of the sum of the other two numbers, what is the value of n?

8

Ivy goes apple picking because she has nothing better to do. In the morning, she picks 19 red apples and 6 green apples. In the afternoon, she picks 5 more green apples. How many more red apples does Ivy need to pick so that 80% of all of her apples are red?

9

A baseball season consists of 162 games. A certain team wins 55 percent of its first 120 games. The coach of this team estimates that the team will make the playoffs if it wins at least 58 percent of its games over the entire season. In order to accomplish this, the team needs to win x games during the remainder of the season. Which of the following inequalities best describes the possible values of x such that the team makes the playoffs?

A) $(0.55)(120) - x \geq (0.58)(162)$, where $x \leq 42$

B) $(0.55)(120) + x \geq (0.58)(162)$, where $x \leq 42$

C) $(0.55)(120 + x) \geq (0.58)(162)$, where $x \leq 42$

D) $(0.55)(120 - x) \geq (0.58)(162)$, where $x \leq 42$

Multi-Part Models

Multi-part questions are still fairly independent of each other. In other words, if you don't know how to do the first question, it doesn't mean that you won't be able to answer any of them. Treat them as separate questions that just happen to refer back to the same information.

------- ▼ -------

Questions 10 through 15 refer to the following information.

Lauren is getting married and needs to decide on a venue for the reception. The table below shows the quoted prices for four different venues.

Venue	Hosting Fee, H (dollars)	Cost to hire a band, B (dollars)	Cost per plate of food, F (dollars per guest)
A	3,000	800	75
B	5,500	650	85
C	4,250	900	80
D	3,500	875	60

The total cost, c, for the reception is given by the formula $c = (H + B) + Fn$, where n is the number of guests.

10

Which of the following expresses the cost per plate of food in terms of $c, H, B,$ and n ?

A) $F = c - H + B - n$

B) $F = c - H - B - n$

C) $F = \dfrac{c - H + B}{n}$

D) $F = \dfrac{c - H - B}{n}$

11

For what number of guests, n, will the cost of having the wedding reception at Venue A exceed the cost of having the wedding reception at Venue D?

12

Lauren's friend Tabitha had her wedding reception at Venue B, but she received a 30 percent discount on the band because her uncle was the keyboard player. If Tabitha spent a total of $16,325, how many guests attended her wedding reception?

13

If Lauren wants to spend no more than $10,000 on her wedding reception, at which venue could she have the most guests without exceeding her budget?

A) Venue A

B) Venue B

C) Venue C

D) Venue D

14

If the cost of having a wedding reception at Venue C were plotted in the xy-plane with the number of guests, n, on the x-axis and the cost of the wedding reception, c, on the y-axis, which of the following best describes the y-intercept of the resulting graph?

A) The total cost of a wedding reception at Venue C

B) The minimum number of guests needed for a wedding reception at Venue C

C) The total cost of the hosting fee and the band at Venue C

D) The cost of one plate of food at Venue C

15

Lauren chooses Venue A and invites g guests to her wedding reception. However, Lauren knows that a guests will be invited but will not be able to attend her wedding reception. Which of the following inequalities could Lauren use to determine whether the number of guests who attend her wedding reception will keep the cost within her $10,000 budget limit?

A) $3,800 + 75(g - a) \geq 10,000$

B) $3,800 + 75(g - a) \leq 10,000$

C) $3,800 + 75g - a \geq 10,000$

D) $3,800 + 75g - a \leq 10,000$

Geometry

The Basics

Reference Chart! Reference Chart! Reference Chart! If you get a Geometry question wrong because you're too lazy to look back and double check a formula, you have no one to blame but yourself. REFERENCE CHART!!!

The Twists

Okay, so not everything you need is in the Reference Chart. There are a few constants and formulas that you need to memorize, but it's not nearly as many as you had to learn for Geometry class in school. If you hated Geometry (everybody seems to, for some reason) you can rest easy knowing that SAT Geometry is relatively simple.

There are a few question types that the SAT loves to repeat. Part Over Whole questions are all about circle sectors, and Similar Triangles questions are really just ratios. The process is so consistent that you should have no problem recognizing the pattern.

Cylinders also tend to come up a lot, but you usually just need the formula (reference chart!). Hexagons also appear from time to time, but that formula isn't given. (It's included on the next page, though.) They usually want you to solve hexagon questions by turning them into equilateral and/or 30-60-90 right triangles.

The Advanced Geometry packet has some of the most twisted questions. They usually take the familiar shapes and hide them by adding or subtracting pieces. As always, "untwist" the questions by **Getting Back to Basics** — rectangles, triangles, and circles. Even questions with three-dimensional shapes can often be solved by thinking in terms of the two-dimensional shapes that you're used to.

Packets

- angle rules
- similar & congruent triangles
- cylinders & more
- part over whole
- trigonometry
- advanced geometry

approximately 4 questions per test

worth approximately 40 points total

Math	grph	grph	grph	chrt
ratio	ratio	arith	COP	COP	chrt
ratio	perc	perc	perc	stat	stat
CAM	CAM	CAM	CAM	stat	stat
CAM	rad/exp	abs/MBT	POI	POI	POI
LP	LP	LP	div/imag	alg+	alg+
LP	LP	LP	QP	QP	QP
LM	LM	LM	CP	FP	FP
QV	GM	XM	XM	RAF	WTF
geo+	trig	cyl/POW	ang/SCT	WTF	WTF

Important Ideas

Reference Chart

$A = \pi r^2$
$C = 2\pi r$
$A = \ell w$
$A = \frac{1}{2}bh$
$c^2 = a^2 + b^2$
Special Right Triangles

$V = \ell wh$
$V = \pi r^2 h$
$V = \frac{4}{3}\pi r^3$
$V = \frac{1}{3}\pi r^2 h$
$V = \frac{1}{3}\ell wh$

The number of degrees of arc in a circle is 360.
The number of radians of arc in a circle is 2π.
The sum of the measures in degrees of the angles of a triangle is 180.

Angles

A right angle is 90°. Complementary angles add up to 90°.

A straight line is 180°. Supplementary angles add up to 180°.

The interior angles of a quadrilateral (4-sided figure) add up to 360°. Squares, rectangles, trapezoids, and parallelograms are all quadrilaterals.

The sum of the interior angles of any figure can be found using the formula below, where n is the number of sides the figure has:

$$\text{sum of interior angles} = 180(n - 2)$$

Vertical angles are congruent (equal). The angles b and c below are vertical angles.

Parallel lines create lots of congruent angles. If the lines below are parallel, then:

- $a = d = e = h$
- $b = c = f = g$

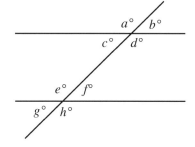

Circles

A fraction (or sector) of a circle contains the same fraction of the degrees, radians, circumference, and area. Whenever a question discusses a fraction of a circle, write down:

$$\frac{\text{part}}{\text{whole}}$$

A line that is tangent to a circle forms a right angle with the radius:

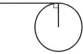

Triangles

Isosceles triangles have two congruent angles opposite two congruent sides.

Equilateral triangles have three equal sides, and all three angles are 60°.

The largest side of a triangle will be opposite the largest angle, and the smallest side will be opposite the smallest angle.

Triangles that have the same angle measures are similar. Their sides will be in proportion.

Area of a hexagon with sides of length x = $\frac{3\sqrt{3}}{2}x^2$

Trigonometry

The most important rule is soh-cah-toa, which helps you remember the meanings of the functions:

$$\sin = \frac{\text{opposite}}{\text{hypotenuse}} \qquad \cos = \frac{\text{adjacent}}{\text{hypotenuse}}$$

$$\tan = \frac{\text{opposite}}{\text{adjacent}}$$

Also:

$$\sin(x°) = \cos(90 - x°)$$

$$\cos(x°) = \sin(90 - x°)$$

Angle Rules

geometry

The Basics

Most Angle questions will involve filling in all or most of the angles based on a few that are given. The Reference Chart includes a few of the constants, but others need to be memorized.

REFERENCE

$A = \pi r^2$
$C = 2\pi r$

$A = \ell w$

$A = \frac{1}{2}bh$

$c^2 = a^2 + b^2$

Special Right Triangles

$V = \ell wh$

$V = \pi r^2 h$

$V = \frac{4}{3}\pi r^3$

$V = \frac{1}{3}\pi r^2 h$

$V = \frac{1}{3}\ell wh$

The number of degrees of arc in a circle is 360.
The number of radians of arc in a circle is 2π.
The sum of the measures in degrees of the angles of a triangle is 180.

Example 1

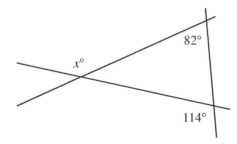

In the figure above, what is the value of x ?

The Twists

It's easy to get stuck on Angle questions if you don't know the rules, but knowing them might not be enough if you don't know when to apply them. These two rules, in particular, can be difficult to see:

Parallel Lines

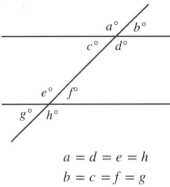

$$a = d = e = h$$
$$b = c = f = g$$

Isosceles Triangles

A pair of congruent sides opposite a pair of congruent angles.

Example 2

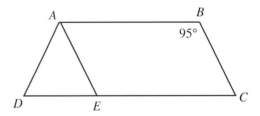

Note: Figure not drawn to scale.

In the figure above, $\overline{AB}$ and $\overline{CD}$ are parallel, $\overline{AE}$ and $\overline{BC}$ are parallel, and $AD = AE$. If the measure of $\angle ABC$ is 95°, what is the measure of $\angle ADE$?

Exercise: Angle Rules

1

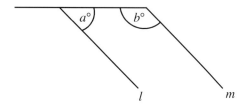

If line l is parallel to line m, which of the following describes the relationship between a and b?

A) $a = 360 - b$

B) $a = 360 + b$

C) $a = 180 - b$

D) $a = 180 + b$

2

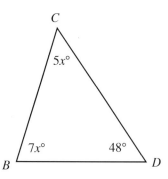

What is the measure of $\angle B$ in degrees?

A) 11

B) 33

C) 55

D) 77

3

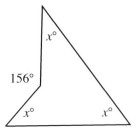

In the figure above, what is the value of x?

4

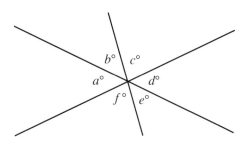

Note: Figure not drawn to scale.

In the figure above, if $b + c = d + e$, which of the following must be true?

A) $a = b$

B) $b = c$

C) $a = f$

D) $e = f$

Similar & Congruent Triangles
geometry

The Basics

Triangles are similar when they have the same angle measures. They'll be different sizes, but all of the sides will be in proportion. In school, there was only one requirement to know that two triangles were similar:

Similar Triangles — AA

If we know that two pairs of <u>A</u>ngles are the same, then we're good to go. Skip the proof and go straight to the proportions. It's usually obvious that all three pairs of angles look the same (AAA), but we only need two.

Example 1

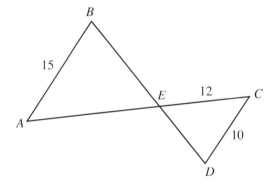

In the figure above, $\overline{AB} \parallel \overline{CD}$ and segment BD intersects segment AC at E. What is the length of AC ?

A) 18

B) 24

C) 29

D) 30

The Twists

If you hated Geometry class in school, Congruent Triangles are almost certainly the reason. Luckily, the SAT does not test congruence very much. You won't need to demonstrate all of the steps of your congruent triangle proof, but you will need to remember the possible last steps:

Congruent Triangles — SSS
              — SAS
              — ASA
              — AAS
              — HL (Hypotenuse-Leg)

This list includes almost every combination of sides and angles possible, so you might be better off **Memorizing** the exceptions. There are only two:

1) **AAA** — we know they're <u>similar</u>, not congruent
2) **ASS** — doesn't work! Remember it this way: *Proofs are easy if you're <u>not an ASS</u>!*

Example 2

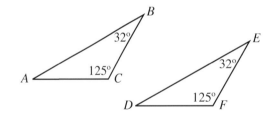

As shown above, $\triangle ABC$ and $\triangle DEF$ each have an angle measuring 32° and an angle measuring 125°. Which of the following statements, if true, would be sufficient to prove $\triangle ABC$ is congruent to $\triangle DEF$?

   I.   The measure of $\angle A$ is equal to the measure of $\angle D$.

   II. The length of $\overline{BC}$ is equal to the length of $\overline{EF}$.

   III. The length of $\overline{AC}$ is equal to the length of $\overline{DF}$.

A) I only

B) II only

C) II and III only

D) I, II, and III

Exercise: Similar & Congruent Triangles 1

1

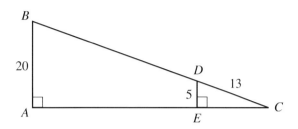

In the figure above, what is the length of *AC* ?

A) 12

B) 39

C) 48

D) 52

2

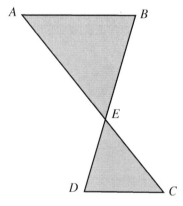

A gardener designed a flowerbed which is represented in the sketch above. The lengths represented by *AB*, *BE*, *AE*, and *CD* on the sketch represent lengths of 540 inches, 270 inches, 330 inches, and 180 inches, respectively. Segments *AC* and *BD* intersect at *E*, and ∠*BAE* and ∠*ECD* have the same measure. What is the value of *CE* ?

3

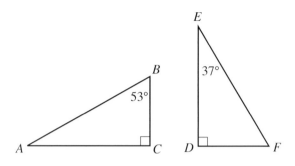

Triangles *ABC* and *DEF* are shown above. Which of the following is equal to the ratio $\dfrac{AC}{AB}$?

A) $\dfrac{DE}{DF}$

B) $\dfrac{DE}{EF}$

C) $\dfrac{DF}{EF}$

D) $\dfrac{EF}{DE}$

4

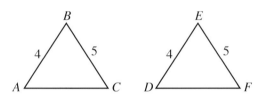

Note: Figure not drawn to scale.

Triangle *ABC* and triangle *DEF* have the side lengths shown above. Which of the following statements is sufficient to prove triangle *ABC* is congruent to triangle *DEF* ?

A) The measure of ∠*A* is equal to the measure of ∠*D*.

B) The measure of ∠*B* is equal to the measure of ∠*E*.

C) The measure of ∠*D* is equal to the measure of ∠*F*.

D) Triangle *ABC* is isosceles.

Exercise: Similar & Congruent Triangles 2

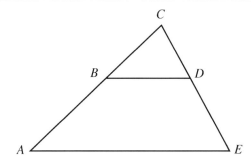

Note: Figure not drawn to scale.

In the figure above, $\overline{BD} \parallel \overline{AE}$ and $AC = 40$. The ratio of BD to AE is 2:5. What is the length of AB ?

A) 8

B) 16

C) 24

D) 30

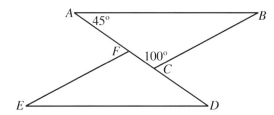

6

In the figure above, $\triangle ABC$ is congruent to $\triangle DEF$, where $\angle A$ corresponds to $\angle D$ and $\angle B$ corresponds to $\angle E$. What is the measure, in degrees, of $\angle AFE$? (Disregard the degree symbol when gridding your answer.)

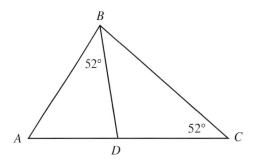

7

In the figure above, which of the following ratios has the same value as $\dfrac{AB}{BC}$?

A) $\dfrac{AB}{BD}$

B) $\dfrac{AC}{BC}$

C) $\dfrac{AD}{BD}$

D) $\dfrac{BD}{CD}$

8

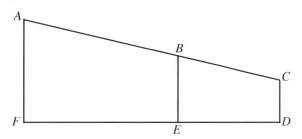

Note: Figure not drawn to scale.

In the figure above, $\overline{AF}$, $\overline{BE}$, and $\overline{CD}$ are parallel, $\overline{BC} = 5$, $\overline{DE} = 4$, and $\overline{EF} = 6$. What is the length of $\overline{AB}$?

A) 7

B) 7.5

C) 8

D) 8.5

9

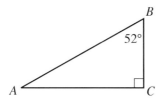

Triangle ABC above is similar to triangle DEF (not shown), where $\overline{AB}$ corresponds to $\overline{DE}$ and $\overline{BC}$ corresponds to $\overline{EF}$. If the perimeter of triangle DEF is half the perimeter of triangle ABC, what is the measure of $\angle D$?

A) 19°

B) 26°

C) 38°

D) 52°

10

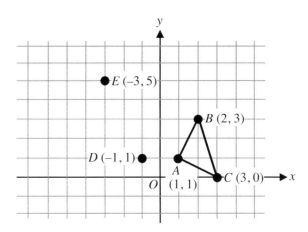

In the xy-plane above, point F (not shown) is placed so that $\triangle ABC$ is similar to $\triangle DEF$, where $\angle A$ corresponds to $\angle D$ and $\angle B$ corresponds to $\angle E$. Which of the following is a possible set of coordinates for point F?

A) $(-6, 0)$

B) $(-6, -1)$

C) $(-5, -1)$

D) $(-4, -1)$

Cylinders & More

geometry

The Basics

For some reason, the SAT really loves cylinders. They give you the formula. In the rare case that they ask about spheres, cones, or pyramids... well... they give you those formulas too.

REFERENCE

$A = \pi r^2$
$C = 2\pi r$

$A = \ell w$

$A = \frac{1}{2} bh$

$c^2 = a^2 + b^2$

Special Right Triangles

$V = \ell w h$

$V = \pi r^2 h$

$V = \frac{4}{3} \pi r^3$

$V = \frac{1}{3} \pi r^2 h$

$V = \frac{1}{3} \ell w h$

The number of degrees of arc in a circle is 360.
The number of radians of arc in a circle is 2π.
The sum of the measures in degrees of the angles of a triangle is 180.

Example 1

A company is designing packaging for a food product. The packaging is in the shape of a right circular cylinder, as shown above. The height of the packaging is 9 centimeters, and the volume must be exactly 144π cubic centimeters. What is the <u>diameter</u> of the packaging, in centimeters?

The Twists

Sometimes there are two cylinders. This one is similar to a Rearrange Formulas question.

Example 2

A grain silo in the shape of a right circular cylinder has a volume of 256 cubic yards. What is the volume, in cubic yards, of a second grain silo that is three times as tall and one half as wide?

Exercise: Cylinders & More

1

A packaging company is designing a jar in the shape of a right circular cylinder. The height of the jar will be 8 inches. If the internal radius will be between 2.45 and 2.50 inches, what is one possible integer value of the volume of the jar in cubic inches?

2

A container in the shape of a right circular cylinder is filled with water to a height of 20 inches. The base of the container has an area of 80 square inches. When a rock is dropped into the container, the height of the water rises to 22 inches total. What is the volume of the rock to the nearest cubic inch?

3

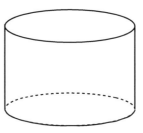

A container in the shape of a right circular cylinder is shown above. The radius of the base is equal to the height. If the volume of the container is 125π cubic centimeters, what is the <u>diameter</u> of the base of the container, in centimeters?

4

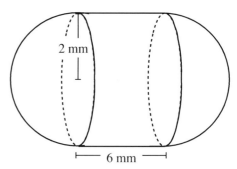

A pharmaceutical company designed a pill in the shape of a right circular cylinder with half of a sphere on both ends. What is the volume of the pill to the nearest cubic millimeter?

Part Over Whole

geometry

The Basics

A quarter of a circle contains a quarter of the degrees, a quarter of the area, and a quarter of the circumference. Use ratios to compare these attributes.

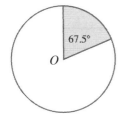

Point O is the center of the circle above. If the area of the entire circle is 64π, what is the area of the shaded region?

A) 11π

B) 12π

C) 13π

D) 14π

Reference Chart

Don't forget that the SAT gives you many of the formulas you need. Those relevant to Part Over Whole are highlighted:

REFERENCE

$A = \pi r^2$
$C = 2\pi r$

$A = \ell w$

$A = \frac{1}{2}bh$

$c^2 = a^2 + b^2$

Special Right Triangles

$V = \ell wh$

$V = \pi r^2 h$

$V = \frac{4}{3}\pi r^3$

$V = \frac{1}{3}\pi r^2 h$

$V = \frac{1}{3}\ell wh$

The number of degrees of arc in a circle is 360.
The number of radians of arc in a circle is 2π.
The sum of the measures in degrees of the angles of a triangle is 180.

The Twists

Like all Geometry questions, the SAT likes to disguise familiar questions so that they appear new and confusing. Chances are, if a question involves part of a circle, it's a Part Over Whole question.

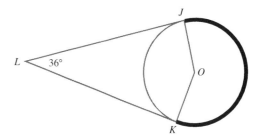

In the figure above, point O is the center of the circle and segments JL and KL are tangent to the circle at points J and K, respectively. If the radius of the circle is 10, what is the length of arc $\overset{\frown}{JK}$ (shown in bold)?

A) 8π

B) 12π

C) 20π

D) 60π

Exercise: Part Over Whole

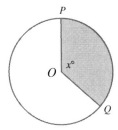

In the figure above, the circle has center O and radius 4. If the length of minor arc PQ is 3π, what is the value of x?

2

In a circle with center O, the central angle COD has a measure of $\dfrac{7\pi}{8}$ radians. The length of minor arc COD is what fraction of the circumference of the circle?

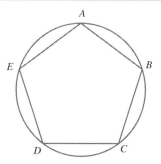

A regular pentagon is inscribed in the circle above. If the circumference of the circle is 100, what is the length of minor arc BD?

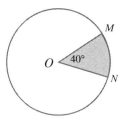

The area of the shaded region is π. What is the radius of circle O?

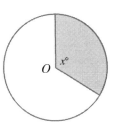

Note: Figure not drawn to scale.

In the figure above, the circle has center O and has radius 5. If the area of the shaded region is between 10 and 11, what is one possible <u>integer</u> value of x?

Trigonometry

geometry

The Basics

Trigonometry is complex, but the SAT mostly tests the simplest concepts. In fact, you will almost never need to use the SIN, COS, and TAN buttons on your calculator. If you think you need to, you probably did something wrong. Instead, start each Trigonometry problem by writing this on the page:

soh cah toa

This helps you remember that:

$$\sin = \frac{\text{opposite}}{\text{hypotenuse}}$$

$$\cos = \frac{\text{adjacent}}{\text{hypotenuse}}$$

$$\tan = \frac{\text{opposite}}{\text{adjacent}}$$

If there's no picture, draw a right triangle so that it's easier to visualize the trigonometric ratios.

Example 1

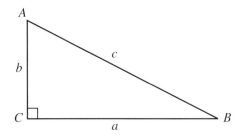

Given the right triangle ABC above, which of the following is equal to $\dfrac{a}{c}$?

A) $\sin B$

B) $\cos B$

C) $\tan B$

D) $\tan A$

The Twists

They'll complicate the triangles or give you side lengths that don't match with the trig fraction. Just remember that these are ratios!

Example 2

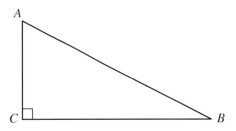

In the figure above, $\sin B = \dfrac{3}{5}$ and $AC = 12$. What is the length of BC ?

Formulas

The SAT doesn't give any Trigonometry formulas besides the fact that 2π radians equals 360 degrees. You need to know soh-cah-toa, and this:

Example 3

Why are the following two <u>essential</u> formulas true?

$$\sin (x°) = \cos (90 - x°)$$

$$\cos (x°) = \sin (90 - x°)$$

Exercise: Trigonometry

1

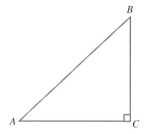

Note: Figure not drawn to scale.

Similar triangles *ABC* and *DEF* are shown above, where vertices *A*, *B*, and *C* correspond to vertices *D*, *E*, and *F*, respectively. If *EF* = 5 and *DE* = 13, what is the value of sin *A* ?

2

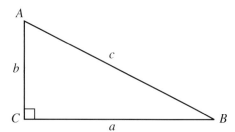

In right triangle *ABC* above, cos *B* = 0.8. What is the value of tan *A*?

3

One angle in a right triangle measures $a°$, where $\cos a° = \dfrac{3}{5}$. What is the value of $\sin(90° - a°)$?

4

Angle *x* has a measure of 900 degrees. What is the measure of angle *x* in radians?

A) 5π

B) 6π

C) 8π

D) 9π

5

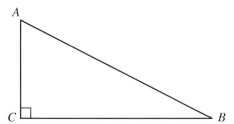

In triangle *ABC* above, $\overline{AC} = 3$ and $\overline{BC} = 4$. If point *D* (not shown) lies on $\overline{AB}$, what is the value of $\sin(\angle ACD) - \cos(\angle DCB)$?

Advanced Geometry

geometry

The Basics

Know the geometry rules. You'll need to solve a complicated puzzle, and it's not always clear which rules you're going to need. Be on the lookout for clues, and use the Reference Chart. Many Advanced Geometry questions involve the often-forgotten special right triangle ratios:

REFERENCE

$A = \pi r^2$
$C = 2\pi r$

$A = \ell w$

$A = \frac{1}{2}bh$

$c^2 = a^2 + b^2$

Special Right Triangles

$V = \ell wh$

$V = \pi r^2 h$

$V = \frac{4}{3}\pi r^3$

$V = \frac{1}{3}\pi r^2 h$

$V = \frac{1}{3}\ell wh$

The number of degrees of arc in a circle is 360.
The number of radians of arc in a circle is 2π.
The sum of the measures in degrees of the angles of a triangle is 180.

Example 1

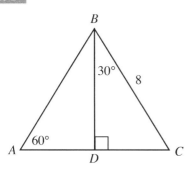

In $\triangle ABC$ above, what is the value of $\overline{BD}$?

A) 4

B) $4\sqrt{2}$

C) $4\sqrt{3}$

D) 6

The Twists

You have to be clever. Add and subtract shapes and pieces. Look for known angles and constants. Make triangles and draw radiuses. If the shape is three-dimensional, you can usually use two-dimensional shapes to solve.

Example 2

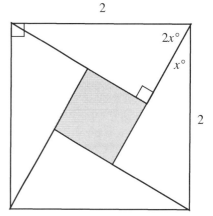

The large square above has sides of length 2. Which of the following represents the area of the small shaded square?

A) 2

B) 3

C) $\sqrt{3} - 1$

D) $4 - 2\sqrt{3}$

Exercise: Advanced Geometry 1

1

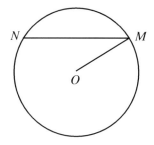

In the figure above, O is the center of the circle and OM is a radius. If the measure of angle OMN is $30°$, then the length of minor arc MN is what fraction of the circumference of circle O ?

2

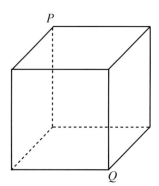

The cube above has edges of length 2. What is the length of line segment PQ (not shown)?

A) 2

B) $2\sqrt{2}$

C) $2\sqrt{3}$

D) $3\sqrt{2}$

3

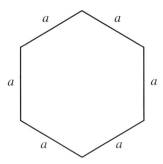

In the figure above, a regular hexagon has sides of length a. Which of the following represents the area of the hexagon in terms of a ?

A) $3a^2$

B) $6a^2$

C) $\dfrac{\sqrt{3}}{4}a^2$

D) $\dfrac{3\sqrt{3}}{2}a^2$

4

It is given that $\cos x = a$, where x is the radian measure of an angle and $0 < x < \dfrac{\pi}{2}$. Which of the following is equal to $-a$?

A) $\cos(-x)$

B) $\cos(\pi - x)$

C) $\cos(x + 2\pi)$

D) $\cos(2\pi - x)$

5

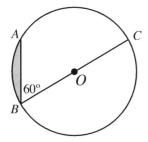

In the figure above, $\overline{AB} = 6$ and $\overline{BC}$ is a diameter of the circle with center O. What is the area of the shaded region?

A) $6\pi - 3\sqrt{3}$

B) $6\pi - 9\sqrt{3}$

C) $36\pi - 3\sqrt{3}$

D) $36\pi - 18\sqrt{3}$

6

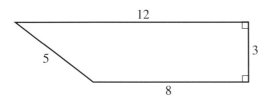

What is the area, in square units, of the figure above?

A) 27

B) 30

C) 36

D) 96

7

A square is inscribed in a circle with radius 4 meters. What is the area of the square in square meters?

A) $4\sqrt{2}$

B) 8

C) 16

D) 32

8

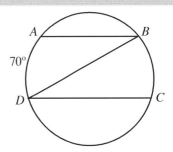

Note: Figure not drawn to scale.

In the circle above, $\overline{AB}$ is parallel to $\overline{CD}$. What is the measure of $\angle BDC$?

A) 35°

B) 45°

C) 55°

D) 65°

Exercise: Advanced Geometry 3

9

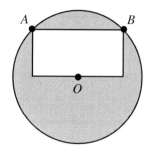

In the figure above, the radius of circle O is k. Vertex A and vertex B of the rectangle lie on the circle. Which of the following represents the area of the shaded region?

A) $\pi - k^2$

B) $k^2(\pi - \sqrt{2})$

C) $k^2(\pi - 1)$

D) $k^2(\pi - 2)$

10

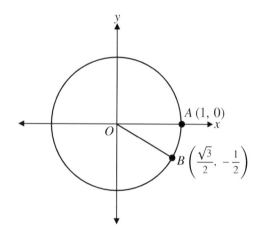

In the xy-plane above, a circle with radius 1 is centered on the origin. Which of the following is equivalent to the value of $\cos(\angle AOB)$?

A) $-\cos\left(\dfrac{\pi}{6}\right)$

B) $\sin\left(\dfrac{\pi}{6}\right)$

C) $\cos\left(\dfrac{\pi}{3}\right)$

D) $\cos\left(\dfrac{11\pi}{6}\right)$

11

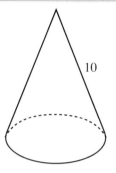

Note: Figure not drawn to scale.

The figure above is a right circular cone. The area of the base of the cone is 36π square inches. What is the volume of the cone in cubic inches?

A) 12π

B) 48π

C) 96π

D) 120π

12

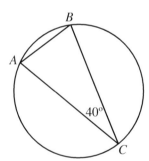

Note: Figure not drawn to scale.

Triangle ABC is inscribed in the circle above. Arc $\overset{\frown}{AB}$ is congruent to arc $\overset{\frown}{BC}$. What is the measure of $\angle B$?

A) $40°$

B) $70°$

C) $100°$

D) $140°$

Answers &
Explanations

Use the Table of Contents at the beginning of the book to find the answer pages for the packet that you're working on. Try not to jump to the answer immediately when you're stuck on a question. Learn to take risks and try the strategies before giving up.

Guess & Check

The Basics

Work backwards from the answer choices.

Example 1

Let's plug –2 in for x to test the value. We'll use parentheses to stay organized. It's easy to lose negatives:

$$\sqrt{10 - 3(-2)} - 7 = (-2) - 9$$

Show your work as you simplify the equation:

$$\sqrt{10 + 6} - 7 = -11$$

$$\sqrt{16} - 7 = -11$$

$$4 - 7 = -11$$

$$-3 = -11 \ \text{✗}$$

This result doesn't make sense, which means that –2 is not a valid solution. Eliminate Choices A, C, and D because they all contain –2. We could be done with the question if we want. One of the best things about Guess & Check is that once you've found the answer that works, you don't need to check the others. But since we only got to Choice B through elimination, it's a little safer to actually check 3 in the equation to make sure that we didn't make a careless mistake:

$$\sqrt{10 - 3(3)} - 7 = (3) - 9$$

$$\sqrt{10 - 9} - 7 = -6$$

$$\sqrt{1} - 7 = -6$$

$$1 - 7 = -6$$

$$-6 = -6 \ \text{✓}$$

Now we're confident that Choice B is the answer. There's another way to get this answer, but it uses algebra. In fact, it may have been your first instinct. But did you fall for the SAT's trap?

move the 7

$$\sqrt{10 - 3x} - 7 = x - 9$$

$$\frac{+7 \qquad +7}{\sqrt{10 - 3x} = x - 2}$$

square both sides

$$\left(\sqrt{10 - 3x}\right)^2 = (x - 2)^2$$

$$10 - 3x = (x - 2)(x - 2)$$

FOIL

$$10 - 3x = x^2 - 2x - 2x + 4$$

get = 0

$$10 - 3x = x^2 - 4x + 4$$

$$\frac{-10 + 3x \qquad + 3x - 10}{0 = x^2 - x - 6}$$

factor

$$0 = (x + 2)(x - 3)$$

$$x = -2 \qquad x = 3$$

This is a lot of algebra, and it suggests that Choice C is the answer. That's the trap! All of this algebra is correct, but it produces an "extraneous solution". Equations with radicals often produce an extra answer when we solve them, and we're supposed to <u>check</u> to see if all of our answers work in the original equation. We would need to plug –2 and 3 into the equation to find the extraneous solutions. But we were able to do that exact step originally — without all of the algebra — because the multiple choices limited us to just a few possible guesses.

If none of this makes much sense, that's actually a good thing. You're going to <u>love</u> the SAT strategies! On some questions, they let us avoid algebra altogether. On others, they at least make the algebra easier. And in many cases, they help us avoid trap answers. With Guess & Check, we didn't even notice that Choice C was a trap. The strategies reduce the risk of losing points needlessly.

Guess & Check

The Twists

Example 2

Lots of people look at a question like this and give up before they start. Or they get careless and ignore the twist — the fraction is going to cause problems if you try to factor. Instead, use the answer choices to Guess & Check different values for k in the second expression. Factoring is hard because you have to think about division and subtraction at the same time, which is more difficult with fractions. But FOILing is simple multiplication. Try Choice A:

$$\frac{1}{2}(x+2)(x-2)$$

FOIL the two binomials first:

$$\frac{1}{2}\left(x^2 - 2x + 2x - 4\right)$$

$$\frac{1}{2}\left(x^2 - 4\right)$$

Now distribute the fraction:

$$\frac{1}{2}x^2 - 2$$

This isn't what we want. The last number should be 8. Try Choice B:

$$\frac{1}{2}(x+4)(x-4)$$

Another great thing about Guess & Check is that the process is repetitive. Once you figure out what to do for the first choice, you can repeat the process until you find the right answer. So again, FOIL the binomials:

$$\frac{1}{2}\left(x^2 - 4x + 4x - 16\right)$$

$$\frac{1}{2}\left(x^2 - 16\right)$$

And distribute the fraction:

$$\frac{1}{2}x^2 - 8$$

That's it. We're done. No need to check the other choices. **The correct answer is Choice B.**

Example 3

This question has a lot of information. In fact, sorting through it all is what makes this question difficult. Guessing an answer choice gives you a place to start. You'll be surprised how often you can stumble your way to the right answer by using Guess & Check.

Start with Choice B. It's a middle number so you'll be able to move up or down if it doesn't work, depending on why it doesn't work. It helps to focus on the last part of the question. What does the answer choice represent?

4 cars that seat 7 people each

Turn that into math:

$$4 \times 7 = 28$$

What else do you know? Stay focused on the answer choice. If there are 4 cars that seat 7 people, then how many cars seat 5 people?

$$\begin{array}{r} 4 \times 7 = 28 \\ +5 \\ \hline 9 \end{array}$$

Guess & Check

The question tells us there are 9 cars total, so there must be 5 cars left. How many people are in those 5 cars?

$$4 \times 7 = 28$$
$$+5 \times 5 = 25$$
$$\overline{9}$$

Is that the right number of people?

$$4 \times 7 = 28$$
$$+5 \times 5 = \underline{25}$$
$$\overline{9} \qquad 53 \text{ ✗}$$

The question says we're supposed to have 55 people total. Our guess gave us only 53. We should try a larger number so that there are more 7-person cars. Guess Choice C, which means 5 cars that seat 7 people. The process is the same:

$$5 \times 7 = 35$$
$$+4 \times 5 = \underline{20}$$
$$\overline{9} \qquad 55 \text{ ✓}$$

Choice C is the correct answer. There's no need to check any of the other choices.

Guess & Check — The Twists

Guess & Check can also help you make algebra easier by reversing the process. Multiplication is usually easier than division, for example.

Use Guess & Check as a starting point when questions give you a lot of information.

Focus on what the answer choices mean.

Start with Choice B so that you can move up or down if B doesn't work.

If a question asks for the "least" or "greatest" possible value, then start with the least or greatest answer choice.

Stay organized and show your work!

Exercise: Guess & Check

#1 — Answer = A
You can Guess & Check in whatever order you like, and it's perfectly fine to check the easiest choices first. Choice C is 0, which is extremely easy to plug into the equation, producing $\frac{2}{5} \neq \frac{-2}{3}$. Next, Choice B is quickly shown to be wrong because the right side would be equal to 0: $\frac{4}{5} \neq \frac{0}{3}$. Rather than work with the risky negative in Choice D, check Choice A to find that it works: $\frac{10}{5} = \frac{6}{3}$. Both fractions reduce to 2.

#2 — Answer = C
This time, we need to check the Roman numerals, and we will need to test them all. Zero doesn't work because we can't take the square root of a negative: $0 \neq \sqrt{-3} + 3$. If we had solved algebraically, $x = 2$ would have appeared to be a valid solution, but it's extraneous. Guess & Check shows the problem much more quickly and easily than the algebra: $2 \neq \sqrt{1} + 3$. Only $x = 6$ creates a valid equation: $6 = \sqrt{9} + 3$.

#3 — Answer = A
Guess & Check the laziest choices first. Choice C is the easiest to check: $4 - 8 - 5 \neq 0$. Choice D would be next, but it fails too: $100 - 40 - 5 \neq 0$. If this were a No Calculator question, it might be best to convert the decimals into fractions because they're easier to multiply and square. We'd see that Choice B also fails: $4(\frac{1}{4}) - 8(\frac{1}{2}) - 5$ becomes $1 - 4 - 5 \neq 0$. At this point, Choice A might be too annoying to bother checking, so you'd pick it simply because of Process of Elimination. That's fine! But checking it confirms that it's correct: $4(\frac{5}{2})^2 - 8(\frac{5}{2}) - 5$ becomes $4(\frac{25}{4}) - \frac{40}{2} - 5$, which finally reduces to $25 - 20 - 5 = 0$.

#4 — Answer = A
Percentages are notoriously tricky on the SAT, and Guess & Check prevents the most common mistake. We prefer to multiply when we have percentages, so use a calculator to multiply the answer choices by 0.86. Choice A isn't exact, but it's definitely the closest to the 1,200 that the question requires. The trap is Choice B, which makes the mistake of taking 14% of 1,200 and adding it in. Percentages aren't

Guess & Check

reversible! Another common trap is Choice D, which is 86% of 1,200, but that is a misreading of what the question is asking for. The story tells us that there are more sagebrush lizards than Western fence lizards. Choice D reverses that relationship. You can sometimes Guess & Check the choices against the story without doing any math and just seeing that certain choices don't make sense with the instructions.

#5 — Answer = B

First, notice that the answer choices represent the y-coordinate of the point of intersection. Guess & Check by substituting the choice into y in the lazier equation, solving for x, then checking both values in the other equation. Checking Choice A in the first equation immediately produces a problem because $x = \sqrt{2}$, which is messy. It's fine to pause this check and try an easier choice instead. Choice B gives $x = 2$ because $4 = 2^2$. Plugging both x and y into the second equation produces a valid equation: $4 = 10 - 3(2)$. There's no need to check the other choices once you've proven the correct answer.

Arithmetize

The Basics

There are two main reasons that people struggle with Arithmetize. First, your instincts for algebra are so strong that you simply refuse to try other strategies. Without thinking, you start doing algebra whenever you see variables. But the second reason is that you don't know how to recognize when to Arithmetize. Example 1 is the most obvious Arithmetize situation because there are variables in both the question and the answer choices. Since we never need to do solve for x, we can make it whatever we want.

Example 1

If you follow the instruction and let $x = 0$, you'll very quickly have a much simpler equation:

$$(3(0)^2 - 7(0) + 9) - (4(0)^2 - 2(0) + 1)$$

$$(0 - 0 + 9) - (0 - 0 + 1)$$

$$(9) - (1)$$

The zeros cancel out most of this equation's messiness, and we can very quickly reduce the entire thing to the answer value 8. Do something to make this number stand out. You don't want to lose it.

$$9 - 1 = \underline{8}$$

Since the answer choices are supposed to represent equivalent expressions, they should also give us the answer value 8 when $x = 0$. Try each one:

Choice A
$$7(0)^2 - 9(0) + 10$$

$$0 - 0 + 10 = 10 \ \textbf{✗}$$

Choice B
$$(0)^2 - 5(0) - 8$$

$$0 - 0 - 8 = -8 \ \textbf{✗}$$

Choice C
$$-(0)^2 - 9(0) + 10$$

$$-0 - 0 + 10 = 10 \ \textbf{✗}$$

Choice D
$$-(0)^2 - 5(0) + 8$$

$$-0 - 0 + 8 = 8 \ \textbf{✓}$$

Only Choice D produces the same value that we got for the original expression. That's it! When typed out, this looks like more work than just solving algebraically. In fact, 0 is a great Arithmetize number because it can often make the right answer obvious with very little work. In this case, we know that all of the x-terms will disappear, so it's obvious that Choice D will be right based only on the value of the final term.

We could have picked any number as our value of x, and we still would have gotten Choice D. That's a big advantage of the Arithmetize strategy! Another advantage is that avoiding algebra helps us avoid traps. If you forget to distribute the negative, you'd likely pick the trap in Choice C:

algebra mistake
$$3x^2 - 7x + 9 - 4x^2 - 2x + 1$$

$$-x^2 - 9x + 10$$

Distributing correctly would get you the correct answer in Choice D:

$$3x^2 - 7x + 9 - 4x^2 + 2x - 1$$

$$-x^2 - 5x + 8$$

You may think that you're too good at math to make these kinds of mistakes, but that's exactly the kind of over-confidence that costs people points. The SAT is long, you will be tired, and mistakes will happen. It's inevitable. And when you make mistakes, your wrong answer will almost certainly be an answer choice, so you'll confidently pick the wrong answer without noticing a problem. Arithmetize and the other strategies help us skip the algebra steps that frequently lead to mistakes.

Arithmetize

The Twists

Example 2

If you remember how to complete the square, the algebra is easy. If you don't, you can still get the answer. Pick an easy number:

$$\text{Let } x = 0$$

What's the value of the original expression?

$$(0)^2 - 2(0) + 5$$

$$0 - 0 + 5 = \underline{5}$$

Underline or box the 5. That's the value that we want the answer choices to equal, so we don't want to forget it. In fact, that's the most confusing thing about Arithmetizing. You have a number that you picked that gets substituted and a number that you need the answer choices to equal after you substitute. Stay organized and you'll be fine.

Let's put 0 in for x in the answer choices. We need the choice to equal 5.

Choice A
$$(0 + 1)^2 + 4$$

$$(1)^2 + 4$$

$$1 + 4 = 5 \checkmark$$

Choice A works! But unlike Guess & Check, we <u>must</u> check every answer choice. Sometimes we pick a number that works for more than one choice. Checking everything is our way of being sure that we have the right answer:

Choice B
$$(0 + 1)^2 - 4$$

$$(1)^2 - 4$$

$$1 - 4 = -3 \text{ ✗}$$

Eliminate Choice B. Keep going:

Choice C
$$(0 - 1)^2 + 4$$

$$(-1)^2 + 4$$

$$1 + 4 = 5 \checkmark$$

Choice C also works. We'll have to try a different number, but let's finish checking with the numbers we have:

Choice D
$$(0 - 1)^2 - 4$$

$$(-1)^2 - 4$$

$$1 - 4 = -3 \text{ ✗}$$

Choice D can also be eliminated. We need to pick a new number for x and try again, but we don't need to check Choices B and D since we already know that they don't work. Stick with easy numbers:

$$\text{Let } x = 1$$

$$(1)^2 - 2(1) + 5$$

$$1 - 2 + 5 = \underline{4}$$

Arithmetize

Now we're substituting 1 in for x and looking for the choices to equal 4.

Choice A

$$(1+1)^2 + 4$$

$$(2)^2 + 4$$

$$4 + 4 = 8 \; \textbf{✗}$$

This time, Choice A didn't work. Choice C is probably the answer, but it's safer to check and know for sure:

Choice C

$$(1-1)^2 + 4$$

$$(0)^2 + 4$$

$$0 + 4 = 4 \; \textbf{✓}$$

Choice C is the correct answer. To be honest, solving this question is faster with algebra, so it's better to know how to complete the square. But Arithmetize is a great tool to help you pick up a few extra points. You won't always know how to solve using algebra, so Arithmetizing is a useful backup.

Example 3

When the algebra is really hard, Arithmetizing may be the only way to get an answer.

$$\text{Let } x = 1 \text{ and } y = 2$$

In this case, we won't Arithmetize for a and b because those variables are dependent on our values for x and y. Usually you can pick whatever numbers you want. However, if the question gives you rules to follow, make sure that you follow them.

Use x and y to find a and b:

$$(1)^2 + (2)^2 = a$$

$$1 + 4 = a$$

$$\underline{5 = a}$$

$$(1)(2) = b$$

$$\underline{2 = b}$$

Use the values of a and b to find the value of the expression in the question:

$$2a + 4b = 2(5) + 4(2)$$

$$2a + 4b = 10 + 8$$

$$2a + 4b = \underline{18}$$

There are a lot of numbers to keep track of. We should substitute the values we picked for x and y into each of the answer choices, and the right answer will equal 18.

Choice A

$$(1+2)^2$$

$$(3)^2 = 9 \; \textbf{✗}$$

Choice B

$$2(1+2)^2$$

$$2(3)^2$$

$$2(9) = 18 \; \textbf{✓}$$

Choice C

$$\left(1 + 2(2)\right)^2$$

$$(1+4)^2$$

$$(5)^2 = 25 \; \textbf{✗}$$

Choice D

$$2\left(1 + 2(2)\right)^2$$

$$2(1+4)^2$$

$$2(5)^2$$

$$2(25) = 50 \; \textbf{✗}$$

Arithmetize

Choice B was the only answer that equalled 18, so it must be the correct answer. If we had picked 0 for x or y, we might have ended up having to try new numbers. It really depends on the situation whether Arithmetizing with 0 is a good choice. Most of the time it works out, but you'll get better at knowing when to pick which numbers.

Arithmetize — The Twists

Always Arithmetize with all of the answer choices.

If two answer choices work, pick new numbers and try again with the choices you did not eliminate.

When there are a lot of variables, stay organized.

If the question gives you some rules to follow or equations that relate the variables, then pick random numbers for the independent variables and solve for the dependent variables.

Exercise: Arithmetize

#1 — Answer = C
We can't use zero, so choose the next best thing and Arithmetize $x = 1$. The expression becomes $\frac{1}{3} - \frac{3}{1}$. You can use common denominators to subtract: $\frac{1}{3} - \frac{9}{3} = -\frac{8}{3}$. Substituting 1 in for x in the answer choices gives Choice C as the only matching answer. Another easy Arithmetize is $x = 3$ because it makes the second term equal to 1.

#2 — Answer = C
Use the story to pick efficient numbers. If we make the radius and height both equal to 2, then they'll be easy to divide in half for the second part of the question. So if $r = 2$ and $h = 2$, then the volume of the first cylinder is $V = \pi(2)^2(2) = 8\pi$. Follow instructions and cut the radius and height in half for the second cylinder: $V = \pi(1)^2(1) = \pi$. We can see that the second cylinder is $\frac{1}{8}$ of the volume of the original cylinder. The trap answer is Choice B because people who use algebra often forget to square the half along with the radius:

$V = \pi(\frac{1}{2}r^2)(\frac{1}{2}h) = \frac{1}{4}\pi rh$. The square needs to be outside of the parentheses: $V = \pi(\frac{1}{2}r)^2(\frac{1}{2}h)$.

#3 — Answer = C
Start simple with $x = 0$ to Arithmetize. You should get that the original expression is 4, and Choices B and D can be eliminated. Both Choices A and C give a value of 4, so we need to try another number. When $x = 1$, the original expression becomes -8, and only Choice C gives that same value. There are a lot of places to make algebra mistakes or get confused in this question, but Arithmetizing makes them all disappear.

#4 — Answer = D
We can't pick zero, so Arithmetize with $x = 1$. It's important that you don't skip steps. The parentheses matter: $y = \frac{2(1)^2(3(1))^2}{6(1)^4}$. Because of PEMDAS, we need to solve parentheses and exponents before doing any multiplication: $y = \frac{2(1)(9)}{6(1)}$. This reduces to $\frac{18}{3} = 6$. Even with Arithmetize, there's still a chance that you make a mistake with all of the parentheses and exponents, but having numbers should make the error less likely if you show your work. If you do make the common mistake, you would likely get Choice B.

#5 — Answer = A
Since the question is asking about a change, we need to Arithmetize with two values to see the change. As always, keep it simple. If $t = 0$, then the exponent will simplify to 0, making $B(0) = 20$. You can Guess & Check the answers, but the laziest one to check is Choice B because then $t = 1$. Substituting into the equation: $B(1) = 20(2)^2 = 80$. Since 80 is more than double 20, Choice B is clearly wrong. Choices C and D are also illogical at this point: if the bacteria quadruple in an hour, then they would do much more than double in 2 or 4 hours. By Process of Elimination, we're left with Choice A. You can simply pick it and move on. If you want to prove it, make $t = \frac{1}{2}$. The exponent becomes 1, giving you $B(\frac{1}{2}) = 20(2) = 40$.

Plug Points Into Equations

The Basics

Equations are just collections of points.

Example 1

Both the points and the equations are annoying. Start with the easiest point to work with. Points with 0's and 1's are usually the easiest, so some people start here:

$$\left(1, \frac{7}{2}\right)$$

Test the point in <u>all</u> of the choices and eliminate any that don't work:

Choice A

$$\frac{7}{2} = \left(\frac{7}{2}\right)^1$$

$$\frac{7}{2} = \frac{7}{2} \checkmark$$

Choice B

$$\frac{7}{2} = 4^1 + \frac{5}{4}$$

$$\frac{7}{2} = \frac{16}{4} + \frac{5}{4}$$

$$\frac{7}{2} = \frac{21}{4} \; \boldsymbol{\times}$$

Choice C

$$\frac{7}{2} = \frac{5}{2}(1) + 2$$

$$\frac{7}{2} = \frac{5}{2} + \frac{4}{2}$$

$$\frac{7}{2} = \frac{9}{2} \; \boldsymbol{\times}$$

Choice D

$$\frac{7}{2} = \frac{1}{2}(1) + 3$$

$$\frac{7}{2} = \frac{1}{2} + \frac{6}{2}$$

$$\frac{7}{2} = \frac{7}{2} \checkmark$$

Choices A and D both work, so we'll have to check another point. Stick with the easy points. Another easy point is:

$$(2, 4)$$

Choice A

$$4 = \left(\frac{7}{2}\right)^2$$

$$4 = \frac{49}{4} \; \boldsymbol{\times}$$

Choice D

$$4 = \frac{1}{2}(2) + 3$$

$$4 = 1 + 3$$

$$4 = 4 \checkmark$$

Choice A gets eliminated, which means that **Choice D is the correct answer.** As it turns out, this second point was probably even easier than the first. Though, it doesn't really matter. Pick the point that you think is the easiest. Just make sure that you test all of the equations.

Plug Points Into Equations — The Basics

Plug points into equations. It's in the name!

This strategy lets you see what's happening at one point instead of trying to think about the entire equation. It makes things much easier to understand and visualize.

Usually the easiest points to plug in will include 0's and 1's, but pick the best point for the situation.

The Twists

Example 2

The SAT loves to twist graphs to mess with your expectations. As you can see, all of the choices have

Plug Points Into Equations

the exact same y-intercept, so this question really comes down to slopes.

You should be able to eliminate Choices B and D because they have positive slopes, but the graph is clearly negative.

You've probably been taught to look at the line and count the boxes. The line looks like it drops 1 box and runs 3 boxes, which would be a slope of $\frac{-1}{3}$.

To be sure, test an actual point in the equations. Even though there are lots of dots on the graph, we can ignore them. The question asks about the "line of best fit", so we need to use points from the line itself. The line looks like it includes the point $(3.0, 4.2)$. You can use your calculator to plug this point into the equations:

Choice A

$$4.2 = \frac{9}{2} - \frac{9}{80}(3.0)$$

$$4.2 = 4.5 - (0.1125)(3.0)$$

$$4.2 = 4.5 - 0.3375$$

$$4.2 = 4.1625$$

It's not exact, but that doesn't mean it's wrong. Remember that we got our point by looking at the graph. We were estimating, so it's possible that we were slightly off. Try Choice C and see if it's closer:

Choice C

$$4.2 = \frac{9}{2} - \frac{1}{3}(3.0)$$

$$4.2 = 4.5 - 1$$

$$4.2 = 3.5 \; \text{✗}$$

This is way off. The SAT twisted this graph by messing with the scale. You can't easily count the boxes to get the slope because the boxes don't mean the same thing. One box up and down is 0.1 units, but one box left and right is 0.3 units.

It's much safer to Plug Points Into Equations so that you can actually prove that the point lies on the equation. **Choice A is the correct answer because the point works in the equation, which is exactly what we'd expect from looking at the graph.**

Plug Points Into Equations — The Twists

The SAT changes the scales on graphs because they know you'll count the boxes to get the slopes. Don't let them trick you!

Lines and other graphs are just collections of points. Pick one and plug it into an equation to test it. This is essentially Guess & Check, but in this case you need to test all of the choices, or at least all of the choices that can't be easily eliminated.

Exercise: Plug Points Into Equations

#1 — Answer = D
Whenever we have graphs, the easiest points to plug in are almost always y-intercepts. Start there. Use the equation to find the y-value when $x = 0$. You need to remember that when 0 is an exponent, the base becomes 1, so we'd get a y-intercept of $(0, 2)$. This eliminates Choices B and C. The next easiest point would be where $x = 1$. Again, plug the value into the equation to find the correct y-value. The graph needs to include the point $(1, 3)$. This eliminates Choice A and leaves us with the correct answer, which is Choice D.

#2 — Answer = C
Hopefully, you can quickly eliminate Choices A and B because the slope for those lines is 3, not $\frac{1}{3}$. Don't bother building the equation. Checking the equations they give you is much easier. Plug the point into the equations. Choice C produces a valid result: $5 = \frac{1}{3}(-6) + 7$, which simplifies to $5 = -2 + 7$. Choice D simplifies to an invalid equation: $5 = -2 - 2$.

Plug Points Into Equations

#3 — Answer = C

The points aren't given directly, but the story can help you generate them. Since there are 600 bacteria to start, we can create the point $(0, 600)$. Plugging it into the equations, you'd see that Choices A and B are wrong because the 0 exponent becomes a base of 1: $600 = 80(1)$. The story describes the change, so we can easily turn a decrease of 50% every 80 minutes into the point $(80, 300)$. Choice C would reduce to an exponent of 1, which works: $300 = 600(0.5)$. Choice D would be a huge exponent of 80 times 80, so it's obviously wrong.

#4 — Answer = A

This question looks very hard, but it's incredibly easy if we robotically Plug Points Into Equations without worrying too much about why it works. The simplest point is $(0, k)$. Choice A would produce the valid equation $0 - 3k = -3k$. None of the other choices make sense when we plug in the same point. That's it! There's no need to build an equation from scratch or test the other points.

Memorize Formulas

The Basics

Traditional algebra can't be entirely avoided. There are some things that just need to be memorized.

Example 1

You <u>must</u> know how to recognize and build $y = mx + b$ equations. The fastest way to get this question is to focus on the y-intercept, which is 2. The b portion of the linear equation represents the y-intercept, and **only Choice C has a 2 in that spot**.

Big picture, you'll also need to memorize that m represents the slope of the line. Slope is calculated as the change in the y-values divided by the change in the x-values between two points. You can find this directly on the graph:

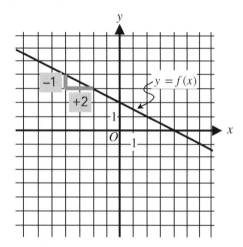

The slope would be $-\frac{1}{2}$, which also matches with Choice C. Everything about $y = mx + b$ can be found in the Linear Properties packet.

In this case, you could also have found the answer using Plug Points Into Equations, since all of our choices are equations and a graph is essentially a list of points. The easiest point is $(0, 2)$, and it would only work in Choice C. This is a reminder that the SAT strategies can help you when you're stuck, but there will be times when the <u>only</u> way to get the answer is by memorizing the right information.

The Twists

Example 2

It's obvious that this question involves lines in some way too. But we also need to memorize what "no solutions" means when we have linear equations. This phrase is code that the lines are parallel, which means that they have the <u>same slope</u>.

If you've memorized the structure of $y = mx + b$ equations, it's easy to see that a in the second line corresponds to the slope of $-\frac{4}{5}$ in the first line. **Choice A is a very quick answer if we've memorized these facts and formulas.** Without knowing what "no solutions" means, it would be very difficult to get this question right.

Example 3

More complex algebra has more formulas and facts to memorize. Quadratics involve a lot of vocabulary, but this question is also about skills. You need to know that the solutions for quadratic equations are most easily found through factoring. Hopefully, you've done a lot of factoring in school and know it well. It's much easier to learn through long-term repetition than short-term cramming for an SAT. But in case you need a refresher:

Quadratic equations in standard form look like this:

$$y = ax^2 + bx + c$$

Our equation matches this formula:

Memorize Formulas

$$y = \quad ax^2 \quad +bx \quad +c$$
$$y = \quad x^2 \quad -14x \quad -32$$

$$a = 1$$
$$b = -14$$
$$c = -32$$

When $a = 1$, we factor by finding two numbers that add to b and multiply to c. The negative complicates things, but you can always use trial and error. The value of c typically limits the possibilities:

multiply		add
$c = -32$		$b = -14$
8	–4	4
–8	4	–4
–32	1	–31
–16	2	–14

Once you've found the right factors, you can build the factored form of your quadratic equation. This is another formula that you need to memorize:

$$0 = (x - 16)(x + 2)$$

Find the solutions by setting each factor equal to 0. You basically have two equations to solve:

$$x - 16 = 0 \qquad x + 2 = 0$$

$$x = 16 \qquad x = -2$$

The question wants you to find the sum, which you need to memorize as addition:

$$16 + (-2) = 14$$

The sum is 14. This entire process should be quick and automatic by the time you take the SAT. Factoring is an essential piece of the algebra toolkit, as important as distributing or reducing fractions.

There's another formula that we can memorize as a shortcut. It wouldn't save much time on this question, but it would be very helpful if the quadratic were too complex to factor and we had to use quadratic formula (another thing to memorize). The sum of the solutions of any quadratic can be found with:

$$\text{sum of solutions} = \frac{-b}{a}$$

In our case, since $a = 1$ and $b = -14$:

$$\text{sum of solutions} = \frac{-(-14)}{1} = 14$$

Memorize Formulas — The Twists

Formulas are just the tip of the iceberg. The SAT also requires that you memorize math vocabulary, and there are plenty of skills that you need when questions can only be solved with traditional algebra.

The packets in this book cover everything you need to memorize for the SAT! The "Important Ideas" pages are excellent summaries.

Exercise: Memorize Formulas

#1 — Answer = A
The result of an absolute value equation can never be negative, so there's no possible way for the absolute value of $5 - x$ to equal -4. This is essentially the definition of absolute value. You will also need to memorize how to solve absolute value equations. (see the Absolute Value packet for more)

#2 — Answer = C
A function is undefined when the denominator (bottom) of any fraction is zero. Factor the denominator into $(x - 8)(x - 1)$, which gives the zeros $x = 8$ and $x = 1$. The SAT is hoping that you half-remember the definition of "undefined" and pick -3, which makes the numerator (top) equal to zero. A fraction is only undefined when the denominator is zero. (see the Function Properties packet for more)

Memorize Formulas

#3 — Answer = D

FOIL the two terms into $6 + 12i - 2i - 4i^2$. It's easy to combine like terms: $6 + 10i - 4i^2$. We're given a fact about imaginary numbers, but it's not particularly useful. The better fact to memorize is that $i^2 = -1$. Substitute: $6 + 10i - 4(-1)$. Simplify and combine like terms. There's a more complicated idea that you need to memorize about imaginary numbers in the denominators of fractions, but $i^2 = -1$ is enough for most cases. (see the Imaginary Numbers packet for more)

#4 — Answer = B

Standard deviation is a measure of the spread of a data set. Set X has greater spread, so it has a greater standard deviation. Set Y has lower deviation because the data points are closer to the middle value of 20. There's a lot that needs to be memorized for Statistics questions, and standard deviation is one of the more difficult concepts. SAT strategies will not be as effective, and you won't be able to solve if you don't even know what they're asking you for. (see the Statistics packet for more)

Get Back to Basics

The Basics

Many of the SAT's hard questions will really be easy questions with a few extra steps. They're annoying, but untwisting the question will involve getting it back to a more recognizable topic.

Example 1

Recall that in Example 2 from the Memorize Formulas packet we needed to know that "no solutions" is code that we have two lines with the same slope. In this case, the two lines don't look like lines. We need to "untwist" these equations and get back to the basic $y = mx + b$ formula that we're comfortable with. Start with the easier line:

$$3x - 2y = 7$$
$$\underline{-3x \qquad\qquad -3x}$$
$$-2y = -3x + 7$$

$$\frac{-2y}{-2} = \frac{-3x}{-2} + \frac{7}{-2}$$

$$y = \frac{3}{2}x - \frac{7}{2}$$

The equation looks messy, but it's very easy to extract the information we need: the slope is $\frac{3}{2}$. The second equation also needs to be untwisted, but the a makes it look harder. It's not! Just do the exact same steps that you used for the first line. A key idea built into the **Get Back to Basics** strategy is that math doesn't change, even when something looks a little weird. The same basic rules and steps will work.

$$ax + 5y = b$$
$$\underline{-ax \qquad\qquad -ax}$$
$$5y = -ax + b$$

$$\frac{5y}{5} = \frac{-ax}{5} + \frac{b}{5}$$

$$y = \frac{-a}{5}x + \frac{b}{5}$$

Again, it's now much easier to extract the slope, which is $\frac{-a}{5}$. Also, notice that I'm keeping the negative on the a, instead of moving it to the front of the fraction. Honestly, it's because I'm terrified of losing the negative! The answer choices make it clear that a lost negative will be hard to notice, since both the positive and negative version of each number are choices. Anticipate potential mistakes.

Now that we have the two slopes, we can follow the instructions given to us by the memorized vocabulary. If we need the same slope, then we can set the two slopes equal to each other:

$$\frac{3}{2} = \frac{-a}{5}$$

Multiply to solve for a:

$$-5 \cdot \frac{3}{2} = \frac{-a}{5} \cdot 5$$

$$-\frac{15}{2} = a$$

Choice A is correct. Looking back, is there any way you could have known the answer based on the equations we started with? I doubt it. At the least, you wouldn't have been confident.

In a way, the SAT is asking us for something very simple: when do lines have no solutions? But they added a lot of extra layers to the question to slow us down and shake our confidence. Don't be intimidated. If you've memorized the formulas and facts, you can work your way to the answer, one step at a time.

Get Back to Basics — The Basics

When questions and equations are confusing, bring them back to a form that is easier to work with.

The packets will help you understand what The Basics look like. Most of the really hard questions are just twisted versions of the basic math. Start by untwisting the question and you'll be on your way to solving it.

Get Back to Basics

The Twists

Example 2

Unlike Example 1, this question doesn't explicitly tell us that we're working with a line. Eventually, you need to be able to quickly recognize linear equations. The big clue is usually that we have two variables and zero exponents.

Once we know that we have a line, we should make it look like a line. Our basic linear equation is $y = mx + b$. Right now, the division is the twist that we need to deal with. We could multiply by 2 to get rid of the fraction, but it's actually better to divide both parts by 2:

$$h = \frac{5t}{2} + \frac{51}{2}$$

$$h = 2.5t + 25.5$$

$$y = mx + b$$

See how the values in this model match up with the parts of a line? That helps you NARROW YOUR FOCUS to just the part that the question is asking for.

All of the choices are asking for a rate — the increase in height every year. For lines, the rate of increase is the slope. Since m is the slope, we should pick the number that is in the m spot of our model.

Choice D is the correct answer. The story and the original equation make this seem like a really strange question that you've never encountered before. But Getting Back to Basics turns the weird equation into a standard line. Once you're at $y = mx + b$, this question is really easy.

Get Back to Basics — The Twist

Story questions make you think you're working with an equation you've never seen before. But it's usually the same stuff you've seen in math class.

Most story questions are lines, so try to make your equation look like the standard form of a line:

$$y = mx + b$$

Exercise: Get Back to Basics

#1 — Answer = B

You should memorize that the b term of a $y = mx + b$ equation represents the y-intercept. But you should also memorize that all y-intercepts have an x-coordinate of 0. We can Plug Points Into Equations: $y = 4(0) - 3$. This simplifies to $y = -3$, which is only true in Choice B. (see the Linear Properties packet for more)

#2 — Answer = A

Plug Points Into Equations. This isn't a line, but if we've memorized that all y-intercepts have an x-coordinate of 0, then we can plug the value into the equation: $f(0) = (0 + 2)(0 - 1)^2$. Simplify to find that $f(0) = 2$. Function notation is just another way of writing points, in this case $(0, 2)$. (see the Function Properties packet for more)

#3 — Answer = 92

Memorize Formulas. The median is the middle number when the data is arranged from least to greatest. 84 is a trap because it's the middle row, but the rows are not in any sort of order. (see the Statistics packet for more)

#4 — Answer = 20

The SAT loves to put data sets into frequency charts to confuse you. As you work your way to the middle, you need to account for the frequency of each age. For example, the chart tells us that 3 people are 17 years old. The middle numbers end up as two 20s, which just means that the median is 20. The trap is 21

Get Back to Basics

because it's the middle row if you don't untwist the frequency chart. (see the Statistics packet for more)

#5 — Answer = B

Memorize Formulas. Perpendicular slopes are negative reciprocals of each other. A slope of 3 is better thought of as the fraction $\frac{3}{1}$. The negative reciprocal is $-\frac{1}{3}$, which would be the slope of a perpendicular line. (see the Linear Properties packet for more)

#6 — Answer = C

There are a lot of twists to this question. First, we need to Get Back to Basics by turning the points into a slope. Plugging into the slope formula (which you need to memorize), we'd get $\frac{7-4}{3-5} = -\frac{3}{2}$. The perpendicular slope is the negative reciprocal, which is $\frac{2}{3}$. The answer choices are twisted versions of linear equations. Get back to the basic $y = mx + b$ that we're comfortable with. It can be tedious, but eventually you'll find that Choice C is the only one with a slope of $\frac{2}{3}$. (see the Linear Properties packet for more)

#7 — Answer = B

Memorize Formulas. By far, the most important trigonometry formula is soh-cah-toa, which reminds us of the ratios for each of the trig functions. In this case, "toa" reminds us that $\tan = \frac{\text{opposite}}{\text{adjacent}}$. As long as you focus on the correct angle, you will get $\frac{3}{4}$. (see the Trigonometry packet for more)

#8 — Answer = A

The most obvious twist in this question is that there's no picture. Draw one! The right angle <u>must</u> be B (because $\overline{AC}$ is the hypotenuse), but the rest is up to you. Basic trigonometry is much easier with a picture. You might need Pythagorean Theorem to find that the missing side $\overline{BC} = 4$. The rest is being comfortable converting fractions to decimals. You can try all of the answer choices, but only $\cos C = \frac{4}{5}$, which is 0.8 as a decimal. (see the Trigonometry packet for more)

#9 — Answer = B

Memorize Formulas. This entire question centers around the vertex form of a quadratic equation, which is $y = a(x - h)^2 + k$, where (h, k) is the vertex. Plugging that point into the formula gives Choice B. (see the Quadratic Properties packet for more)

#10 — Answer = D

We'll need the vertex for this question too, but first it's easier to think about the a-term. You need to memorize that parabolas open downward when the a-term is negative, so that eliminates Choices A and B. The picture tells us that the vertex is (b, c) because both coordinates are in the first quadrant, where the values would be positive. Plugging that point into the vertex formula, we'd see that the b-term would appear negative. This question looks very twisted because of all the letters, but it's still the same basic vertex formula that you need to memorize. (see the Quadratic Properties packet for more)

#11 — Answer = D

Memorize Formulas. The standard equation of a circle is $(x - h)^2 + (y - k)^2 = r^2$, where (h, k) is the center and r is the radius. Simply plugging the given information into the formula gives Choice D. (see the Circle Properties packet for more)

#12 — Answer = B

This question involves one of the SAT's most annoying twists. When we need to Get Back to Basics with circles, we need to complete the square twice. Almost everyone forgets how to "complete the square". The first step is to add in numbers that would create squared terms, but you need to add those same numbers to the other side, as well, for balance. This circle would be $(x + 4)^2 + (y - 1)^2 = 25$. Since the 25 represents the radius-squared, the radius would be 5. (see the Circle Properties packet for more)

Read the Graph

The Basics

Don't feel bad if these first two examples were hard. You'll get better at reading the graphs.

Example 1

Go through the choices, one at a time. It's really important that you read each one:

A) This is very tempting. It looks like the graph generally goes up. But the choice is trying to fool you. It says that the graph increases "each year since 2002," but that's not exactly true. For the first 5 years, the graph decreases, so it's not increasing "each year". If this choice said, "Sales generally increased between 2002 and 2015," then it would be right. But that one word — "each" — makes all the difference.

B) Clearly wrong. It's only decreasing a little at the beginning.

C) This is also tempting, but be careful. The SAT loves to mess with the units on the axes. The graph definitely decreases up until Year 5, but Year 5 does not represent 2005. Year 0 is supposed to be 2002, so Year 5 is actually 2007.

D) **And that's why Choice D is correct.** The graph decreases until 2007, and then increases afterward. Notice that we didn't really need to do any math. We just needed to be careful of the wording of the choices and the units on the axes.

Example 2

If you had difficulty with this question, it's probably because you were confused about what they were asking. The "greatest change" means the steepest slope. A lot of Read the Graph questions are about slope. The slope is steepest from Years 6 to 10, which correspond with 2008 to 2012. **Choice B is correct because it's the only one that falls within that range.** An important note — when they say "greatest change," it doesn't necessarily need to be a positive change. In this case, the graph is increasing. But on another question, the greatest change might actually be a decrease. Usually they're asking for the magnitude of the change, so the

direction doesn't matter. It can be steep up or steep down. But read carefully because they could ask specifically for the positive or negative change instead.

Also, be careful of Choice A. Once again, the SAT is trying to trick you by messing with the units on the graph. Years 6 through 8 are 2008 to 2010, not 2006 to 2008.

Read the Graph — The Basics

Read all of the choices carefully. Words that don't usually matter might make all the difference.

Check the units on both the x- and y-axes. They often mess with the units to trick you. Just training yourself to pause for a second before you circle an answer could save you 10 points.

If they're asking about the "change," they are probably asking about slopes. They're usually asking for the magnitude of the change, so the direction might not matter. The greatest change will have the steepest slope.

The Twists

Example 3

The main twist for this question is that scatterplots are confusing. But if you trust yourself, you'll do fine. The question wants to know the year when the area was estimated to be 150 acres. Find 150 on the y-axis. Draw a line across the graph until you intersect the line of best fit. What's the x-value of that point? **It's just after 2000, so Choice B is correct because 2002 is a good estimate.**

Be careful of Choice C. They're hoping that you think 2005 would be the middle of the box. It's not. Each box is a 5 year period, so 2005 would be the unlabeled line between 2000 and 2010. Once again, they're hoping you answer too quickly to pay attention to the units.

Read the Graph

The other trap answer is Choice A. The question specifically asks for the "estimated" value, which means that we need to look at the line of best fit, which is an estimate based on the data. The dots represent the actual data, so they're hoping that you're drawn to the dot at 1995 that's very close to the 150 line. But it's just not what they're asking for. Scatterplots include both actual data points and estimated best fit graphs, but the SAT questions will typically want some information from the best fit line, so you can usually ignore the dots.

Example 4

You can also trust your instincts on this question. They say 1990, so find that point on the x-axis. If you draw a line up, you'll see that there's a point on the line of best fit at approximately 240, and a data point at approximately 320 (halfway between the labeled lines of 300 and 350). The question sounds like they want a difference, so subtract those two values:

$$320 - 240 = 80$$

Choice A is close enough, so it's correct. Once again, we need to understand that scatterplots include both the actual data points (dots) and the estimated trend (line). In this case, though, they wanted you to consider both types of information.

Read the Graph — The Twists

Scatterplots look scary because there's a lot going on. Just know that the black **dots represent actual values** that were found with an experiment, survey, or something else scientific. The **line of best fit is an estimate** that lets us fill in the gaps. We can see a general trend, or even use the line of best fit to predict what would happen at places where we don't have actual data. So the twist is really just that they're throwing a lot of information at you and hoping you get too confused to answer. Untwist the question by focusing on the coordinates of the points and the units on the axes.

Exercise: Read the Graph

#1 — Answer = A
Start on the x-axis to find the player with the most games. It's the dot that is furthest to the right, specifically at around 37 games played. The y-coordinate of that point is 18.

#2 — Answer = C
This is similar to #1, but with a slight twist. Notice that the question is asking for "most goals scored per game played". That's a rate, so we'll need to compare two values as a ratio: goals scored divided by games played. Calculate the value for each point. Point A is approximately 14/27, which is 0.52. Point B is approximately 9/30, which is 0.3. Point C is 10/8, which is 1.25. Point D is 6/13, which is 0.46. The greatest number is at Point C. The most common mistake is flipping the fractions, putting the games played on the top, which would result in Choice B.

#3 — Answer = C
Choice A is true because the slope of the line from (0, 0) to (1, 4) is constant. The line represents Rodrigo's drive from home to the dry cleaner, and the slope represents his speed. Choice B is true because you can draw a line where y = 2, and you'll intersect the graph twice. Choice D is true because the flat line at y = 4 (when Rodrigo is at the dry cleaner) is 0.5 hours long. Choice C is <u>not</u> true because the flat line at the top of the graph (when he's at dinner) is 1.5 hours long, not 3 hours long. The twist is that the scale of the graph is not what you would expect. Always check the units!

#4 — Answer = C
The restaurant is 6 miles from Rodrigo's home, so he drove 6 miles to get there and 6 miles to get back home. That's a total of 12 miles. The twist is that you need to count the return trip home.

Charts & Probability

The Basics

The wording of the question is more important than the chart. In fact, you probably won't use most of the information in the chart. Instead, you'll need to use the question to pick out the right values from the right rows and columns.

Example 1

As you can tell by the answer choices, we're going to construct a fraction. We'll focus on the denominator (bottom number) first because it represents the group that we care about. In this case, we care about the entire chart. The "of" statement usually tells us where to look, and this question is asking about the "proportion of the arrivals". The entire chart is arrivals, so the denominator is 300.

Now we need to figure out which of the arrivals they're talking about. The question is pretty clear: "trains that were late". That's the top left box, which means our numerator (top number) is 36. The whole fraction is:

$$\frac{36}{300}$$

Since that's not a choice, we need to simplify. I'd start by dividing both parts by 3, and then reduce in little steps:

$$\frac{36}{300} = \frac{12}{100} = \frac{6}{50} = \frac{3}{25}$$

So Choice A is the answer.

Example 2

As we solve this one, notice that we're following the same process as Example 1. Charts & Probability questions follow a clear pattern.

This time, our "of" statement limits us to "the on-time arrivals". That means that our denominator will not be 300 because we don't actually care about the late arrivals. You might consider this a twist, but it happens often enough that it's just part of the basics. The total number of on-time arrivals is 166.

The numerator is the "buses" that were on-time. Again, the question does not care about late arrivals, so we're just looking at that middle row. The number of on-time buses is 52. So our full fraction is:

$$\frac{52}{166}$$

Sometimes we don't need to reduce, so Choice B is the answer. Notice that the wrong answers aren't random. The denominators match other numbers in the chart, including the 300 total arrivals that we used for the previous example. This lets us see what the SAT is up to. They are hoping that you look at the wrong parts of the chart, so you need to be especially careful that you're giving the SAT exactly what it's asking for. If you misread the question, your wrong answer will almost certainly be one of the choices.

Charts & Probability — The Basics

Start with the denominator, which is the group that the question cares about. Sometimes it's the entire chart. But sometimes it's just a few rows or columns. Often you can use the "of" statement to figure it out.

The numerator will always be a little more specific or narrow. You should always have a fraction with a smaller number on top of a bigger number. Reduce the fraction if needed.

The Twists

Example 3

The question is worded a little differently, but the pattern is the same. Start with the "of" statement, which says that we care about all "of the movies". The chart doesn't have a box for the total, but the description underneath tells us that there were 75 movies, so our denominator is 75.

Charts & Probability

Now just go to the specific place they tell you. We need "a drama that received 1 star," which is 10. Our fraction is:

$$\frac{10}{75}$$

The twist here is that they're asking about probability, but that doesn't really mean anything on the SAT. Essentially, our fraction means that, if we chose a movie randomly, 10 out of every 75 movies would be a 1-star drama. But both probability and fractions can also be expressed as decimals. Just divide 10 by 75 in your calculator, and you should get 0.13333… **This is approximately 0.13, so Choice B is the correct answer.**

Example 4

This question has a lot of twists. For one, there's no "of" statement. We need to figure out for ourselves which columns and rows they care about. Again, we're choosing a movie randomly, but it's "a movie that received at least 2 stars." They only care about the last two columns. We need to add up all of the values in those columns to get the total, but be careful of another twist — the 2 and 3 at the top are not going to be added in. Those are headers, meaning that they just tell us the number of stars. Add everything else to get our denominator:

$$6 + 9 + 7 + 8 + 7 + 7 = 44$$

As always, the numerator will be a smaller group chosen from the larger group. They want the comedies, which also need to be added together:

$$6 + 8 = 14$$

So our completed fraction is:

$$\frac{14}{44}$$

Put that in your calculator, and you'll get 0.318… which rounds to 0.32. **So Choice C is the answer.** It's harder to notice the traps when the answer choices are decimals, but these other numbers represent common mistakes. The most frustrating is Choice B,

which represents the probability of a comedy out of movies that received <u>exactly</u> two stars. Many people forget to include the 3-star column. These kinds of mistakes are easy to make if you're not paying attention, but they are unforgivable. Show your work and underline the key parts of the question so that you don't lose these points needlessly.

Charts & Probability — The Twists

Probability doesn't really matter on the SAT. You can think in terms of fractions. In fact, almost every chart question will involve fractions in some way, so that's a good place to start.

If the question is twisted because they don't give you a chart, try to get back to basics by building a fraction from the information in the question.

If there's no "of" statement, you'll need to figure out the denominator on your own. Read carefully. It's really just the group that you're choosing from. Which rows and columns do they care about? Which ones do they seem to be leaving out?

Exercise: Charts & Probability 1

#1 — Answer = B
The denominator is only the people who bought the product (left column). Add 52 and 32 to get that the denominator is 84. The numerator is only the people who bought the product <u>and</u> saw the advertisement, which is 52. The fraction is $\frac{52}{84}$.

#2 — Answer = B
The denominator is people who saw the movie, which is the left column only. The total is given as 63. The numerator is women who saw the movie, which is 22. The fraction is $\frac{22}{63}$, which is 0.35 as a decimal.

#3 — Answer = B
The twist is that the wording is different than what we're used to. Follow instructions. Each answer choice refers to one box in the chart. They want the box that represents "one third of the money spent on all projects in the given year", which means one third of the total for that year. To test Choice A, take the

Charts & Probability

total in 2006 ($10,899) and find one-third of it by dividing by 3, which should give you $3,633. That's way more than the box for Project A in 2006 ($1,345), so Choice A is incorrect. Repeat the process for Choice B. One third of the total for 2008 ($14,569) is $4,856, which is very very close to the box for Project B in 2008. Check the other choices to be sure, but none are closer than Choice B.

#4 — Answer = A

Find the total change for Project C from 2006 to 2008 by subtracting those boxes ($1,321 – $1,040 = $281). The twist is that they want the average rate of change, so Choice D is a trap. Divide $281 by 2 to find the change per year, which is approximately $140.

Exercise: Charts & Probability 2

#5 — Answer = C

Get Back to Basics. The twist is that there's no chart. It shouldn't matter. We can still build a fraction. The denominator is 24 because that's the total number of cards in the deck. The numerator is 4 because the only multiples of 5 in the deck are 5, 10, 15, and 20. There's no need to reduce.

#6 — Answer = B

This is a strange question that's more about the concept of probability than any sort of calculation. On any flip, this coin has an equal chance of landing on tails, which can be expressed as a probability of $\frac{1}{2}$ or 0.5. That's it. It doesn't matter that the student has flipped the coin previously. The coin doesn't remember the previous flips. Each flip is an independent event. They're hoping to trick you into thinking that the coin is "due" for another tails, which suggests that the probability has increased. That's just not how probability works in the real world.

#7 — Answer = C

Get Back to Basics. Like #5, this question does not have a chart, but we can still build a fraction. Start with the denominator, which is restricted to the red papers only. Even though there are 10 pieces of paper, our denominator will only include the 5 even numbers on the red papers. The numerator is easier, since only 2 numbers are multiples of 4 (4 and 8). The

fraction is $\frac{2}{5}$. The trap is Choice B, which is the reduced fraction when 10 is the denominator.

#8 — Answer = C

The first twist is that the denominator is limited to the "No Music" column, which is 70 total. The second twist is that "more than 8 questions" means that we need the boxes for "9 to 11" and "More than 11". Add 22 and 14 to get the numerator as 36. Reduce $\frac{36}{70}$ to $\frac{18}{35}$.

#9 — Answer = 7/18 or .388 or .389

The denominator is only the soft cover books, which is 18 total. The numerator is the 7 nonfiction books in that righthand column.

Exercise: Charts & Probability 3

#10 — Answer = A

The denominator is all 100 of the shirts. The numerator is the 6 shirts that are both small and blue. Divide: $\frac{6}{100} = 0.06$, which is 6%.

#11 — Answer = C

The denominator is the red shirts only, which is 32. The numerator is the medium red shirts, which is 18. Reduce $\frac{18}{32} = \frac{9}{16}$.

#12 — Answer = C

The denominator is the large shirts only, which is 22. The numerator is the green large shirts, which is 7.

#13 — Answer = B

Compare this question to #12. It's almost the exact same words, but the slight difference completely changes our answer. This time, the denominator is the green shirts only, which is 42. The numerator is still the 7 large green shirts.

#14 — Answer = C

The "of" statement tells us to include all of the shirts, so the denominator is 100. But the numerator is annoyingly limited. It's safest to exclude the "large" column and the "blue" row. That leaves four boxes in the top left, which we can add together: $10 + 18 + 14 + 21 = 63$. The fraction is $\frac{63}{100}$.

Collection of Points

The Basics

These questions take advantage of one of our most important Math strategies — Plug Points Into Equations. In fact, that's pretty much all it is!

Example 1

Start with the easiest point, which is (1, –1). Be organized, and start with Choice A:

$$-1 = 1 - 2(1)$$

$$-1 = 1 - 2$$

$$-1 = -1 \checkmark$$

But don't stop here! The SAT designs Collection of Points questions so that the first equation works for the first point. You should continue to test the same point in the other equations. Let's try Choice B:

$$-1 = 2 - 3(1)$$

$$-1 = 2 - 3$$

$$-1 = -1 \checkmark$$

Looks like we'll need to revisit both Choices A and B, but let's keep going with the point (1, –1). Sticking with the same point makes it less likely that you'll plug in the wrong value accidentally. Here's Choice C:

$$-1 = 3 - 2(1)$$

$$-1 = 3 - 2$$

$$-1 = 1 \; \boldsymbol{\times}$$

And Choice D:

$$-1 = 7 - 4(1)$$

$$-1 = 7 - 4$$

$$-1 = 3 \; \boldsymbol{\times}$$

Now let's retry Choices A and B using the next point, which is (3, –7). First, Choice A:

$$-7 = 1 - 2(3)$$

$$-7 = 1 - 6$$

$$-7 = -5 \; \boldsymbol{\times}$$

Since that doesn't work, we now know that Choice B has to be the correct answer. This is much easier and safer than trying to build the linear equation to match these points.

Example 2

Once again, we're just reading a chart, even if the chart is a little more complicated than the last one. You don't really need to know function notation in order to get this right. Just follow instructions. For Choice A, put the values from the 0 row into the right places:

$$g(x) - h(x) = x$$

$$5 - 6 = 0$$

$$-1 = 0 \; \boldsymbol{\times}$$

Cross out Choice A, and try Choice B:

$$3 - 2 = 1$$

$$1 = 1 \checkmark$$

Choice B is the correct answer. On this question, we don't need to check the other choices. It's almost the reverse of Example 1, where they gave us lots of points and we needed to choose the equation. Here, they're giving us the equation, and we need to choose the one point that fits. If you're feeling nervous, take another few seconds to check the other answers. Nothing wrong with being sure.

Collection of Points

The Twists

Example 3

The twist is that this is a graph, not a chart. But as the text says, a line is made up of points, so it's still a collection of points like the other two examples. Pick a spot where the line of best fit intersects the boxes. In the bottom left, it looks like the point (5, 50) lies on the line.

The story doesn't really matter. It's just a way to trick you, since the normal (x, y) points are now represented with m and $T(m)$. Get Back to Basics. The x-axis is still the x-axis, even when it has a different letter or name. The function notation still represents the y-values. So as always, Plug Points Into Equations. Let's start with Choice A:

$$50 = 2(5) + 31$$

$$50 = 10 + 31$$

$$50 = 41 \ \text{✗}$$

This isn't close enough, so we can eliminate Choice A. Let's try the same point in Choice B:

$$50 = 3.45(5) + 32$$

$$50 = 17.25 + 32$$

$$50 = 49.25 \ \text{✓}$$

It's not exact, but that's really close. If another choice works, we might need to try another point, but Choice B should definitely be kept. Let's try Choice C:

$$50 = 4.24(5) + 38$$

$$50 = 21.2 + 38$$

$$50 = 59.2 \ \text{✗}$$

This also isn't close enough. Let's try Choice D:

$$50 = 5(5) - 40$$

$$50 = 25 - 40$$

$$50 = -15 \ \text{✗}$$

Not even close. **Choice B is the correct answer because it's the only one that was close.**

Exercise: Collection of Points

#1 — Answer = C
Plug Points Into Equations. Start with the easiest point, which is (1, –4). Unfortunately, the point works in all four equations. Try the second point, which is (2, 1). This point only works in Choice C.

#2 — Answer = D
Plug Points Into Equations. Remember that anything raised to the 0 power is equal to 1. Testing the first point eliminates Choice A. Testing the second point

eliminates Choice C. Testing the third point eliminates Choice B, leaving Choice D as the answer. Fractions scare people, but they are relatively easy to work with for this question. Even when you get to $\left(\frac{12}{5}\right)^2$ for checking Choice B, you can take a shortcut. You can hopefully estimate that $\frac{144}{25} + \frac{7}{5}$ is much bigger than $\frac{26}{5}$. Remember that fractions are division, so $144 \div 25$ is approximately 6, which is already more than $26 \div 5$, which is approximately 5. Of course, if this were in the Calculator section, you could actually do all of the arithmetic in your calculator.

#3 — Answer = B

Plug Points Into Equations. According to the question, the Ounces column should be plugged in for x, and the Grams column should be plugged in for g. Test the point (0.28, 8.0) in each of the choices. It only fits in Choice B. It's not an exact match, but no other choice is close.

#4 — Answer = B

Plug Points Into Equations. Make sure that you plug in correctly, though. The twist is that y is the first variable in the equation, so it's easy to accidentally plug the point in backwards because you're used to x being first. Messing with your expectations is a common twist. Numerals I and II work, but III does not.

Basic Arithmetic

The Basics

As the packet says, these questions are usually much easier than they look. Try to turn the story into math by reading carefully and staying organized.

Example 1

It's best to look for a starting point or total. In this case, we know that the store sold "a total of 50 cupcakes". Write that number down. We're going to use it.

The question also says that the store sold "at least one large package of 6 cupcakes". Let's remove those 6 from our total by subtracting:

$$50 - 6 = 44$$

The end of the question tells us to find a possible number of "small packages of 4 cupcakes" that the store could have sold. We don't know how many 6-cupcake packages it sold, but it doesn't matter. There's more than one answer to this question. Since we've already taken care of the 6-cupcake package that we know of, we can just divide the remaining 44 cupcakes by 4:

$$\frac{44}{4} = 11$$

So 11 is one possible answer. On the test, there's no reason to find the other answers, but let's see how you might go about it. Since the store sold "at least one large package", we know that they could have sold more than one. Let's see what happens if we assume they sold two large packages.

Two large packages of 6 cupcakes each is 12 total cupcakes. Subtract that from our total of 50:

$$50 - 12 = 38$$

We can divide by 4 to see how many of the small packages they sold:

$$\frac{38}{4} = 9.5$$

This is a problem. We can't sell half of a package, so this answer does not work. We need a number that is evenly divisible by 4 (doesn't have a remainder). Let's see what happens if we assume the store sold three large packages, which would be 18 cupcakes:

$$50 - 18 = 32$$

$$\frac{32}{4} = 8$$

The math checks out, and 8 is another possible answer. We could keep going, and we'd find that the other possible answers are 5 and 2. There's a pattern to these answers, but it's not obvious. An equation would obscure the story, which is why we didn't bother to set one up.

This packet is filled with questions where your instinct for algebra can get you in trouble. Algebra doesn't account for questions that don't allow decimal answers. It's also easy to get stuck because we might end up with two variables. In this case, people often represent the number of 6-cupcake packages with a variable too:

$$4x + 6y = 50$$

This is impossible to solve with two unknown variables. By using arithmetic from the start, we're more likely to just pick a value for the 6-cupcake packages and move on to the next step. Algebra can create unnecessary hurdles.

Basic Arithmetic — The Basics

Find a starting point or total. Write it down.

Look for any rules or conditions that you need to take care of first. If they leave something open-ended or vague, it's okay to make assumptions so that you can continue to solve.

You don't need to waste time with an equation. The instructions are easy enough to follow one at a time. Arithmetic is better than algebra!

Basic Arithmetic

The Twists

Example 2

This question isn't all that different from the last example. There's a clear starting point: Betsy can't spend more than $42.

There's also a rule that we need to take care of. The question says that Betsy must pay the entrance fee of $15. Let's remove that amount from our total:

$$42 - 15 = 27$$

The question wants to know how many $4 rides Betsy can go on with the money that she has left. Let's divide to find out:

$$\frac{27}{4} = 6.75$$

Once again, we don't want a remainder because Betsy can't go on a fraction of a ride. We can ignore the decimal and focus on the fact that 4 goes into 27 6 times. **So the answer is 6.** Betsy can spend $24 on rides, but the remaining $3 are not enough to buy another ticket for another ride.

The main trap is rounding 6.75 up to 7 out of habit. Stories sometimes force us to break the normal rules of numbers and rounding. That's why algebra can get you in trouble if you make an equation for this story — it obscures the story, making it easier to forget that the normal rules might not apply.

Basic Arithmetic — The Twists

Be careful of remainders. Sometimes you need to ignore decimals and find a whole number.

Exercise: Basic Arithmetic

#1 — Answer = 4150
Multiply 550 miles per hour by the 5 hours to get 2,750 miles. Add in the 1,400 miles already traveled to get a total of 4,150 miles.

#2 — Answer = anything from 8 to 14
Divide 112 cars by 14 cars per hour to get 8 hours. Or divide 112 cars by 8 cars per hour to get 14 hours. Either answer works, and so would any number in between. In this case, decimals are okay because you can have fractions of an hour.

#3 — Answer = 5 or 6
If you start with $59, you'll first subtract out the $10 for the one entree, leaving you with $49. Divide that by $8 per appetizer to find the value of a. You'll get 6.125, but you can't have a fraction of an appetizer, so the answer would be 6. If you start with $49, subtracting out the one entree leaves you with $39. Divide that by $8 per appetizer to get 4.875. This time, you have to round up because you started with a minimum, and you don't want to end up below the minimum, so the other answer is 5.

#4 — Answer = 5
Guess & Check. Pick a number of workers that divides evenly into 150. If there were 10 workers originally, each would inspect 15 widgets ($150 \div 10 = 15$). When 2 workers are out sick, there are 8 workers left to inspect the same number of widgets, but that does not divide evenly ($150 \div 8 = 18.75$). You can't have a worker inspect a fraction of a widget, so you need to try a different number. If there were 5 workers originally, each one would inspect 30 widgets ($150 \div 5 = 30$). If 2 workers were out sick, each of the remaining 3 workers would inspect 50 widgets ($150 \div 3 = 50$), which is 20 additional widgets, exactly what the question wants.

#5 — Answer = 13
The twist is that the number of mice does not matter. Focus on the number of snakes. Let $x =$ the number of snakes. Create an equation using the given information. One side will be $3x + 5$ (three mice per snake plus five extra mice). Set that equal to $4x - 8$ (four mice per snake, but eight mice short). Solve for x to find that Fletcher has a ridiculous 13 snakes. You could also Guess & Check, but it might be confusing with so many conditions.

Ratios & Units

The Basics

It's very easy to stick to a pattern with Ratios questions. Notice that, in all of the examples, the process is pretty much the same, even when the wording is different.

Example 1

Start by creating a fraction that captures the rate, or the two values that we want to compare:

$$\frac{\$23}{2 \text{ hours}}$$

Set this fraction equal to another ratio that compares the same types of values. We don't know the $ amount, but we do know the number of hours. Make sure that your units are consistent:

$$\frac{\$23}{2 \text{ hours}} = \frac{\$x}{7 \text{ hours}}$$

Cross multiply:

$$2x = 161$$

Divide to get x by itself:

$$x = \$80.50$$

So Choice B is the answer. You can probably do all of this in your calculator, but you should get in the habit of showing work. It'll pay off when the questions get twisted.

Example 2

This question uses some advanced math vocabulary, "directly proportional", to ask the same thing. We're clearly dealing with rates and comparisons, so we'll use ratios again. Start by creating a fraction that captures the rate:

$$\frac{15 \text{ years}}{65 \text{ apples}}$$

Set this fraction equal to another ratio that compares the same types of values:

$$\frac{15 \text{ years}}{65 \text{ apples}} = \frac{21 \text{ years}}{x \text{ apples}}$$

Cross multiply, and divide:

$$15x = 1,365$$

$$x = 91 \text{ apples}$$

That's it! **The answer is 91.**

Ratios & Units — The Basics

Use fractions to compare rates. Make sure that your units are consistent across the tops and bottoms of the fractions.

Cross multiply and divide to solve for x.

The Twists

Example 3

Let's use the same pattern that we did for the basic examples. Start by identifying an easy rate:

$$\frac{4 \text{ miles}}{7 \text{ minutes}}$$

Now look for a similar rate that we can compare it to by setting them equal. In this case, speed is a rate that we could write as a fraction:

$$\frac{4 \text{ miles}}{7 \text{ minutes}} = \frac{x \text{ miles}}{1 \text{ hour}}$$

As you can see, the units are not correct. Most people will convert hours to minutes with a simple substitution:

$$\frac{4 \text{ miles}}{7 \text{ minutes}} = \frac{x \text{ miles}}{60 \text{ minutes}}$$

Ratios & Units

Cross-multiply and divide:

$$7x = 240$$

$$x = 34.28571429 \text{ miles}$$

Rounding to the nearest tenth means that the answer is 34.3.

In this case, it was easy to change the units so that they matched, but it's going to get harder. We can anticipate the twist by using multiple fractions to get the units the same. Remember that you can reduce fractions when you have the same number on the top and bottom:

$$\frac{5x}{5y} = \frac{\cancel{5}x}{\cancel{5}y} = \frac{x}{y}$$

The same is true for units. When the same unit is on the top and the bottom, we can cancel them out. We can use this property to get rid of the units that don't match and get new units that do match:

$$\frac{4 \text{ miles}}{7 \text{ minutes}} = \frac{x \text{ miles}}{1 \, \cancel{\text{hour}}} \cdot \frac{1 \, \cancel{\text{hour}}}{60 \text{ minutes}}$$

For more complex Ratios & Units questions, we'll keep multiplying by rates until the units match up with the other side of the equation. In fact, this strategy will help you keep track of all the information because it checks itself — you'll know you're done when all the "bad" units are gone.

Example 4

Start with whatever rate you find first in the problem. Some people start at the end because the question usually gives you some sort of rate. But you can also start at the beginning:

$$\frac{\$95}{7 \text{ cakes}}$$

The question wants to know how much was spent on Kevin's share of cake, so that already matches up one of the units — dollars to dollars.

$$\frac{\$95}{7 \text{ cakes}} = \frac{\$x}{5 \text{ pieces}}$$

But the bottom units don't match. Find a rate that contains one of the bottom units. It doesn't matter what you choose, as long as you put the new ratio on the same side of the equals sign as the fraction that has the unit you're trying to cancel. In this case, we'll work from the start of the question again and use the left side of the equation:

$$\frac{1 \text{ cake}}{4 \text{ quarters}} \cdot \frac{\$95}{7 \text{ cakes}} = \frac{\$x}{5 \text{ pieces}}$$

We can cancel the "cakes", but we don't want "quarters" either. Luckily, there's one more ratio:

$$\frac{1 \, \cancel{\text{quarter}}}{3 \text{ pieces}} \cdot \frac{1 \, \cancel{\text{cake}}}{4 \, \cancel{\text{quarters}}} \cdot \frac{\$95}{7 \, \cancel{\text{cakes}}} = \frac{\$x}{5 \text{ pieces}}$$

We know we're done because we have "dollars" in both numerators and "pieces" in both denominators. Now we multiply all the numbers to get back to the simple proportion that we had with the basic examples. Remember that when fractions are on the <u>same side</u> of an equals, we multiply along the tops and along the bottoms.

$$\frac{1 \times 1 \times 95}{3 \times 4 \times 7} = \frac{x}{5}$$

$$\frac{95}{84} = \frac{x}{5}$$

When fractions are on <u>opposite sides</u> of an equals, we cross multiply top to bottom and bottom to top:

$$84x = 475$$

Divide:

$$x = \$5.654761905$$

We need to round to the nearest cent, so $5.65 is the correct answer.

Was this complicated? Absolutely! But if you write out the units, you can go step by step in an

Ratios & Units

organized way. And you could have just as easily put the ratios on the other side:

$$\frac{\$95}{7 \text{ cakes}} = \frac{\$x}{5 \text{ pieces}} \cdot \frac{3 \text{ pieces}}{1 \text{ quarter}} \cdot \frac{4 \text{ quarters}}{1 \text{ cake}}$$

$$\frac{95}{7} = \frac{12x}{5}$$

$$84x = 475$$

$$x = \$5.65$$

Same answer!

Ratios & Units — The Twists

Always write your units. You won't necessarily know if they matter when you read the question, but it'll be obvious when the ratios don't match.

When a unit appears in the numerator and denominator on the <u>same</u> side of an equals, you can cancel it out. Find ratios in the question that eliminate "bad" units so that you're left with what you want.

Once your units match on <u>opposite</u> sides of an equals, multiply along the tops and bottoms to condense your ratios into a simple proportion. Cross-multiply and divide, as usual.

Exercise: Ratios & Units 1

#1 — Answer = 1925

Set up a ratio: $\frac{550 \text{ shirts}}{2 \text{ days}} = \frac{x \text{ shirts}}{7 \text{ days}}$. Cross-multiply and divide to find that x equals 1,925 shirts.

#2 — Answer = D

Set up a ratio: $\frac{2 \text{ apples}}{5 \text{ oranges}} = \frac{10 \text{ apples}}{x \text{ oranges}}$. Cross-multiply and divide to find that x equals 25 oranges.

#3 — Answer = B

Set up a ratio: $\frac{3 \text{ girls}}{2 \text{ boys}} = \frac{x \text{ girls}}{30 \text{ students}}$. The twist is that the units don't match. You need to adjust the ratio so

that the units are consistent. Add the 2 boys and 3 girls to find that there are 3 girls for every 5 students. This is a common fix when the units don't match up — add the two parts to get a whole. The new ratio should be: $\frac{3 \text{ girls}}{5 \text{ students}} = \frac{x \text{ girls}}{30 \text{ students}}$. Cross-multiply and divide to find that x equals 18.

#4 — Answer = 147

Here's one way to set up the ratios:
$$\frac{1 \text{ phone}}{34 \text{ mg}} = \frac{x \text{ phones}}{5 \text{ grams}} \cdot \frac{1 \text{ gram}}{1,000 \text{ mg}}$$
Multiply along the tops to get: $\frac{1}{34} = \frac{x}{5,000}$
Cross-multiply and divide to get x equals 147.06, so the maximum number of phones is 147.

#5 — Answer = 9

The twist is that there is information in the chart that you won't need to use, which is very rare on the SAT. Focusing on the units will help you figure out what matters: $\frac{x \text{ days}}{1 \text{ trip}} = \frac{1 \text{ day}}{6 \text{ hours}} \cdot \frac{1 \text{ hour}}{45 \text{ miles}} \cdot \frac{2,416 \text{ miles}}{1 \text{ trip}}$.
Multiply along the fractions to find the proportion: $\frac{x}{1} = \frac{2,416}{270}$. Divide to get 8.95 days, which rounds up to 9.

Exercise: Ratios & Units 2

#6 — Answer = 1.47

The Dodgers are the first place team because they have the most wins (45 home + 49 away = 94 total). The D-backs are the last place team because they have the fewest wins (33 home + 31 away = 64 total). The question wants the ratio of the first place team to the last place team, so the fraction is $\frac{94}{64}$, which is 1.47 as a decimal.

#7 — Answer = 25

"Same rate" means you need a ratio. Since you're only asked about home games, focus only on the first two columns. The total number of home games is 81 (45 wins + 36 losses). The ratio should compare the win rate for those 81 games to the win rate for the 45 games described in the question:
$\frac{45 \text{ wins}}{81 \text{ games}} = \frac{x \text{ wins}}{45 \text{ games}}$. Cross-multiply and divide to find that x is equal to 25 wins.

Ratios & Units

#8 — Answer = B

This is a made up stat, so just follow instructions. Create a ratio for each team: $\frac{\text{wins at home}}{\text{wins away}}$. The question wants the team with a ratio that is closest to 1. The Dodgers' ratio is 0.92. The Giants' is 1.05. The Padres' is 1.66. The D-backs' is 1.06. The Giants' ratio is closest to 1.

#9 — Answer = 110

They've twisted the standard Ratios question so that it's hard to know what's going on. There are two key ideas that pop off the page that help us know that we need to use ratios. One is that they're clearly asking us to compare two types of values — dollars and months. The other is that the increase is <u>constant</u>, which tells us that we can set our two fractions equal to each other. Just be careful that you capture the <u>change</u> in the dollar amount by subtracting: $2{,}056 - 1{,}000 = 1{,}056$. Your ratios should be:

$\frac{\$c}{5 \text{ months}} = \frac{\$1{,}056}{4 \text{ years}} \cdot \frac{1 \text{ year}}{12 \text{ months}}$. Simplify the ratios to: $\frac{c}{5} = \frac{1{,}056}{48}$. Cross-multiply and divide to find c is 110.

#10 — Answer = 30

It doesn't matter that one of the ratios includes a fraction within a fraction. Just turn it into a decimal: $\frac{2.6 \text{ acres}}{2 \text{ years}} = \frac{39 \text{ acres}}{x \text{ years}}$. Cross-multiply and divide to get that x is equal to 30 years.

Exercise: Ratios & Units 3

#11 — Answer = 9324

Set up the ratios:
$\frac{18 \text{ feet}}{13.9 \text{ sec}} = \frac{x \text{ feet}}{2 \text{ hours}} \cdot \frac{1 \text{ hour}}{60 \text{ min}} \cdot \frac{1 \text{ min}}{60 \text{ sec}}$
Simplify to $\frac{18}{13.9} = \frac{x}{7{,}200}$. Cross-multiply and divide to get 9,323.7, which rounds to 9,324.

#12 — Answer = A

Set up the ratios:
$\frac{1 \text{ snark}}{14.1 \text{ ounces}} = \frac{7 \text{ snarks}}{1 \text{ blerg}} \cdot \frac{30 \text{ blergs}}{x \text{ pounds}} \cdot \frac{1 \text{ pound}}{16 \text{ ounces}}$
Simplify to $\frac{1}{14.1} = \frac{210}{16x}$. Cross-multiply and divide to get that x is equal to 185.0625.

#13 — Answer = D

The twist here is that only 85 percent of the tickets are sold. You're probably better off not using ratios. Take 85% of 1,200 to find the number of tickets sold, which is 1,020. Divide $24,000 by 1,020 to find the cost per ticket, which is approximately $23.53. If you want to use ratios, you can incorporate the 85%, but you'll have to be clever:

$\frac{\$x}{\text{ticket sold}} = \frac{\$24{,}000}{1{,}200 \text{ tickets available}} \cdot \frac{100 \text{ tickets available}}{85 \text{ tickets sold}}$

#14 — Answer = 19.2

Set up the ratios:

$\frac{x \text{ acres}}{72 \text{ bags}} = \frac{1\frac{1}{3} \text{ acres}}{1 \text{ field}} \cdot \frac{\frac{1}{5} \text{ field}}{1 \text{ bag}}$

The twist is that you have fractions in fractions. Luckily, both fractions are over 1, so you can just drop the denominators. Convert the mixed number to $\frac{4}{3}$ to make things easier. Multiply and divide to get 19.2 acres. One possible trap is rounding too early. If you make $1\frac{1}{3}$ into 1.3, you'll get the wrong final answer. This is a good example of why fractions are generally better than decimals.

#15 — Answer = 7.7

Set up the ratios:
$\frac{4 \text{ miles}}{14 \text{ min}} = \frac{x \text{ meters}}{1 \text{ sec}} \cdot \frac{1 \text{ mile}}{1{,}609 \text{ meters}} \cdot \frac{60 \text{ sec}}{1 \text{ min}}$
Simplify to $\frac{4}{14} = \frac{60x}{1{,}609}$. Cross-multiply and divide to get x equal to 7.6619, which rounds to 7.7.

Percentages

The Basics

Remember that decimals and percentages are really the same thing. To convert a percentage to a decimal, you move the decimal point two spaces to the left:

$$12\% = 0.12$$
$$112\% = 1.12$$
$$1.2\% = 0.012$$

The first four of these short questions are probably pretty easy, but you might have been stumped by the last two. We'll use the **OPEN** formula at the bottom of the page to solve all of these questions too:

What is 12% of 275?

$$(O)(P) = N$$

$$(275)(0.12) = N$$

$$33 = N$$

What is 4% of 340?

$$(O)(P) = N$$

$$(340)(0.04) = N$$

$$13.6 = N$$

What is 200% of 68?

$$(O)(P) = N$$

$$(68)(2.00) = N$$

$$136 = N$$

What is 1.9% of 320?

$$(O)(P) = N$$

$$(320)(0.019) = N$$

$$6.08 = N$$

42 is what percent of 175?

$$(O)(P) = N$$

$$(175)(P) = 42$$

$$P = \frac{42}{175}$$

$$P = 0.24 = 24\%$$

63.84 is 76% of what number?

$$(O)(P) = N$$

$$(O)(0.76) = 63.84$$

$$O = \frac{63.84}{0.76}$$

$$O = 84$$

It's important to be able to convert quickly between percentages and decimals. Be careful that you don't confuse 40% and 4%. They should be written as 0.4 and 0.04, respectively. For the second to last question, remembering that decimals and percentages blend together was important. Otherwise, we might have thought that the answer was 0.24%. Just think about it — could 42 be 0.24% of 175? No way! 0.24% is a very, very small part of a number, so 42 is too big. We need to convert our decimal back to a percentage, and 24% makes much more sense.

The SAT really likes to twist Percentages questions so that you're dividing instead of multiplying, just like in the last two examples above. The **OPEN** formula is just one way to prevent the common mistake of multiplying when you're supposed to divide. Another way to prevent it is to reread the question once you have your answer. If you had multiplied 63.84 and 0.76, you'd have gotten 48.5. Does it make sense for 63.84 to be 76% of 48.5? No! The question suggests that we should get a number bigger than 63.84, not

Percentages

smaller. This method of checking your answer is even easier when you have a story.

Example 1

In this case, it's easy to see how the story fits into the OPEN formula. We're looking for the original number of trees in the grove. And don't forget to write 21.4% as a decimal.

$$(O)(P) = N$$

$$(O)(0.214) = 199$$

$$O = \frac{199}{0.214}$$

$$O = 929.9 \approx 930$$

Rounding will get you an answer of 930. Notice that our answer makes sense with the story. Only 21.4% of the trees are infected, so we'd expect 199 to be considerably smaller than our answer, which is supposed to be all of the trees in the grove. If we had multiplied instead, we would have gotten an answer of approximately 43, which wouldn't make sense — if 199 trees in the grove are infected, how could there be only 43 total trees in the grove? Most people are too lazy to check whether their Percentages answers make sense with the question, especially because the wrong answer choices will almost always include the common mistakes. Don't be lazy and you could save yourself 10 points!

Percentages — The Basics

You can think of percentages as decimals. Move the decimal point two places to the left to turn a percentage into a decimal. Be careful:
- 80% would be 0.8
- 8% would be 0.08
- 1.8% would be 0.018
- 800% would be 8.0

When you convert percentage questions into equations, be careful with variables that represent the percentage. Divide the variable by 100, or double check if you've solved for the variable in its percentage form or decimal form.

Use the OPEN formula so that you don't get tricked by the SAT's percentage questions:

<u>O</u>riginal times <u>P</u>ercentage <u>E</u>quals <u>N</u>ew

(O)(P) = N

The Twists

Example 2

Some people might use the percent/increase formula here, and that's totally fine:

$$\% \text{ inc/dec} = \frac{\text{new} - \text{old}}{\text{old}} \times 100$$

But we're going to try the **OPEN** formula instead:

$$(O)(P) = N$$

$$(916)(P) = 958$$

$$P = \frac{958}{916}$$

$$P = 1.046 = 104.6\,\%$$

That's weird. How could we have 104.6%? That seems like a lot. Actually, this is a much better way to think about percentages than you're used to from

Percentages

school. You're used to taking a percentage and then adding or subtracting it from your original amount. Think about how you calculate the tip at a restaurant — you probably take 20% and then add it to the bill.

$$\$18 \text{ bill} \times 20\% \text{ tip}$$

$$18 \times 0.20 = 3.60$$

$$\text{total} = \$18 + \$3.60 = \$21.60$$

A more efficient way to do this is to just multiply the bill by 1.2, which is 120%. In other words, you're paying 100% of the bill, plus an additional 20%.

$$\$18 \times 1.20 = \$21.60 \text{ bill and tip}$$

Something similar is happening with these babies. This year, there were 104.6% of the babies as last year. In other words, there were 100% of the babies as last year, plus an additional 4.6% of last year's babies. **Since the question is asking about the increase, the answer is D.**

If you can get comfortable with this way of thinking, Percentages will be easy on the SAT and in life in general. Whenever you're dealing with percent change, you can think of the percentage as a change from 100%. You can adjust the **OPEN** formula to reflect that:

$$(O)(1 \pm P) = N$$

The 1 represents 100% of the original, and you'd choose plus or minus depending on whether you were calculating a percent increase or decrease.

$$(916)(1 + P) = 958$$

$$1 + P = \frac{958}{916} = 1.04585$$

$$P = 0.04585 \approx 4.6\%$$

Example 3

The hardest part about percent increase/decrease is figuring out which thing is the "original" and which

is the "new". If you switch them, you'll get the wrong answer. But in this case, I think it's pretty clear — Todd is the original because Kim has 30% more than he does. In other words, Kim's fries are based on Todd's. So we could plug all of this information into the modified **OPEN** formula:

$$(O)(1 \pm P) = N$$

$$(T)(1 + 0.30) = K$$

$$T(1.3) = 65$$

$$T = \frac{65}{1.3}$$

$$T = 50$$

And that makes sense. We know that Kim is supposed to have more fries than Todd. **So Choice C is the correct answer.**

But if we had accidentally switched the original and new values, we should have been able to catch our mistake. Here's what would have happened:

$$(65)(1.3) = T$$

$$84.5 = T$$

That's close enough to Choice D that you might pick it. But if you take a second to pause and think about the story, you should catch your mistake. The question says Kim should have 30% more fries than Todd, but that wouldn't make sense if Todd had 85 fries and Kim only had 65. Taking 10 seconds to check your answer against the story could save you 10 points!

Another common mistake occurs when you take 30% of Kim's fries and then subtract:

$$65 \times 0.30 = 19.5$$

$$65 - 19.5 = 45.5$$

This is very similar to the example above about paying a bill in a restaurant. Your instinct is to do

Percentages

percentages in two steps, so this mistake feels very natural. The problem is that you're treating Kim's fries like they're the original amount. You might be thinking, "why does it matter? Isn't Todd plus 30% the same as Kim minus 30%?" Unfortunately, no. And until you realize this, you'll continue to struggle on Percentages questions. Let's look at it this way:

You go to a store to buy a new phone. The phone costs $100. You have a coupon for a 10% discount. How much do you pay after the discount? You can probably do the math in your head — $90 for the phone. But let's say that there's a 10% tax on the discounted price. How much do you pay in total after the tax is added to the $90?

Some people think it's back to $100. After all, you took 10% off with the coupon and added 10% back on with the tax. Seems like it all evens out.

Wrong! You would actually pay $99 for the phone. How is that possible? Where did the extra dollar go?

$100	original cost of phone
−$10	10% discount $(100 \times 0.10 = 10)$
$90	new price/original
+$9	10% tax $(90 \times 0.10 = 9)$
$99	final cost

As you can see, the value of 10% changes because the base amount that we're taking 10% of also changes. Percentages are dependent on the original amount. So to bring it back to the Example, 30% of Todd's fries is not the same as 30% of Kim's fries. You need to accept this or you'll keep making mistakes on Percentages questions!

Luckily, the OPEN formula is our best defense against all of these potential mistakes. **This formula was specifically designed by me, Mike Settele, to prevent SAT mistakes after years of watching students struggle with the various percentage formulas that they had learned in school.** I'm very proud of the OPEN formula!

Its big advantage is that the plus/minus (±) makes percent change much more intuitive. In Example 3, we're told that "Kim has 30% <u>more</u> fries <u>than</u> Todd."

The "than" tells us that we'll need the percent change version of the formula, and the "more" tells us that we'll need a plus. Once we have the plus, it's fairly easy to see that Kim is the "new" value because the addition tells us that the "new" should be bigger than the "original". When you use the OPEN formulas, the text of the question should intuitively match the structure of the equation. Don't overthink it and you should be fine!

Percentages — The Twists

Use the modified OPEN formula when questions ask about percent change:

$$(O)(1 \pm P) = N$$

The twist is usually that it's easy to accidentally confuse the "original" and "new" values. Untwist these questions by double checking that your answer makes sense with the story.

Some clue words can help you build the right version of the OPEN formula:

% of = standard formula: $OP = N$
than = % change formula: $O(1 \pm P) = N$
more/greater/increase = $1 + P$
fewer/less/decrease = $1 - P$

Exercise: Percentages 1

#1 — Answer = B
It's easy to use the OPEN formula here because they're directly asking you for the original amount. And since it's a tax, you can test out your new understanding of percentages. You're paying 107% of the cost. $(O)(1 + 0.07) = 63.13$. Solve and you'll get 59 exactly. You could also Guess & Check. The answer choices represent the original cost of the service before the fee. Multiply each answer choice by 1.07 to find the cost after the 7% fee is added. (1.07 x 59.00 = 63.13)

#2 — Answer = B
The "% of" language tells us to use the standard OPEN formula (without the 1±). Match the fruit to the

Percentages

correct percentage. 6% of the 129 watermelons (129 x 0.06) is 7.74, or 8 watermelons left. 3% of the 369 apples (369 x 0.03) is 11.07, or 11 apples. Add them together to get 19 pieces of fruit.

#3 — Answer = B

This is a great example of how the modified OPEN formula can save you points. Since Mars is based on Earth, Earth is the original and Mars is the new. And since it's "less than", you'll use subtraction: $(E)(1 - P) = M$. Putting in the numbers, you'll see that the percentage actually changes into something you might not expect: $(160)(0.40) = M$. That's a very common twist because the SAT knows that percent decrease is a little counterintuitive. Multiply 160 by 0.40 to get that a person's weight on Mars is 64 pounds. Watch out for this twist. It helps to think about it in terms that you're more familiar with. If a store offers a "10% off" sale, you don't pay 10% of what an item costs. You pay 90% of what it costs.

#4 — Answer = D

This is more like a Charts & Probability question. Focus on the denominator first. They're only asking about cars sold in 2010, so the denominator is 365. The numerator is red cars sold in 2010, which is 197. Divide 197 by 365 to get 0.54, which is 54%. You can also use the OPEN formula, where the original number of cars is 365 and the new is just the 197 red ones.

#5 — Answer = A

A perfect opportunity to use the modified OPEN formula: $(168)(1 - P) = 128$. Solving for P gets you 24%. But be careful. If you use the OPEN formula without the 1, you'll get that P is 76%, which is an answer. That's because, like with #3, the number of green cars in 2015 is 76% of the number in 2010, but that's a decrease of 24%. Just remember that when they talk about percent decrease, you're going to want to get that negative into the formula so that you don't fall for the trap.

Exercise: Percentages 2

#6 — Answer = C

Occasionally, the SAT asks a straightforward, story-free percentage question. Good for us! The "% of"

tells us to use the standard OPEN formula and that 8.4 is the original: $(8.4)(2.00) = N$. Multiply for the answer.

#7 — Answer = B

Again, the "% of" tells us to use the standard OPEN formula. Before you put values in, you should show your work with the names of the ships to make sure that you're plugging things into the right places: $Q(0.68) = T$. The displacement of the *Titanic* will be the New value. Substituting and dividing will get you a value for the *Queen Mary* that is a little different from Choice B, but it's not close to any other choice.

#8 — Answer = 7/12 or .583

Get Back to Basics. There is a twist at the end, but the beginning is very basic. The "% more" is a clue that we'll need the OPEN formula with a "1+" to represent the increase: $(60)(1 + 0.40) = N$. Solving for the New gets us 84 pumpkins in 2010. But that's not the answer! The question wants us to build a fraction with the numerator as the pumpkins in 2010 and the denominator as the total for both 2009 and 2010. Once you have it, simplify it to an answer that you can bubble: $\frac{84}{60 + 84} = \frac{84}{144} = \frac{7}{12}$.

#9 — Answer = 80

Get Back to Basics. Write the OPEN formula down so that you have something to anchor the way you think about this question. They're clearly asking us for the Original number of students. And we're given 12 as a New value of some sort. The Percentage requires a little thought, but you can hopefully see that 12 is the difference between one and two siblings, which is 15% (45% – 30%). The formula should be: $O(0.15) = 12$. Divide to solve for the original.

#10 — Answer = 24

This question has a few twists, and it maybe highlights the one drawback of the OPEN formula. It should be easy to build the correct formula by following the story: $(16,000)(1 - P) = 12,160$. Solving for P gets 0.24, but that's not the answer. The way the question is phrased, we need to provide the percentage as an actual percentage, not as a decimal. It's tempting to bubble 0.24 because it's the value of P that we found, but the SAT will typically want the percentage number in the same way that

Percentages

we would say it. In an equation, it's easier to think of "24 percent" as 0.24, but the SAT will almost always want the answer as 24.

Exercise: Percentages 3

#11 — Answer = C
The OPEN formula is an excellent guide. The clue word "increased" tells us to use: $(x)(1 + 0.12) = N$. Clean it up to get Choice C. You really can't be falling for traps like Choice A, which shows 12% of x. The difference between a "percent of" and a percent change is very important on the SAT.

#12 — Answer = C
The "% of" tells us to use the standard OPEN formula: $(x)(0.30) = 9$. We're definitely being asked for the original number of players on the team, which comes out to 30.

#13 — Answer = 707
You can absolutely do this in two steps with two OPEN formulas. The New after the discount would become the Original for the tax calculation. But one benefit of Percentages is that they can be calculated simultaneously: $(850)(1 - 0.20)(1 + 0.04) = N$. The discount is a $1-$ term, and the tax is a $1+$ term, but the multiplication lets us do both changes at once because the order doesn't matter. Simplify and solve: $(850)(0.8)(1.04) = 707.2$. Don't forget to round!

#14 — Answer = C
Follow the story and build the correct OPEN equation: $(x)(1 - 0.20) = 11.20$. Solve for $x = 14$. The trap is Choice B, which is what you get if you take 20% of $11.20 and add it to the $11.20. Percentages are not reversible like that! If you're still making those kinds of mistakes, you need to find more practice because this is a very preventable error, and they will absolutely include questions on every single SAT that try to get you to make this mistake. Choice A is an even worse error because that price makes absolutely no sense with the story. How could a discounted price be more than the original price?

#15 — Answer = C
The question makes it clear that we need the percent change OPEN formula: $(x)(1 + 0.20) = 72$. Solve for $x = 60$.

#16 — Answer = B
This is an evil question! Use the answer choices to help you Sense the Difficulty. The wording of the question sounds like we'll need the percent change version of the OPEN formula because it says "larger than". If we take the time to follow the normal rules, we'd get: $(x)(1 + 4.25) = N$. This would simplify to Choice B. Obviously, Choice A is a trap. They really want you to turn 425% into a decimal and move on. If this were a real test, the question number would warn you about the potential trap because later questions are supposed to be harder — if it feels too easy, it's probably a trap. But big picture, Percentages questions are notoriously tricky and trap-heavy. Whenever you have a Percentages question, you should be on high alert. Show Your Work to avoid traps as much as possible.

Statistics

The Basics

You <u>must</u> memorize these words. Here are some helpful tricks to remember them:

The **mean** is the average, but it's also sometimes called the "arithmetic mean". It's <u>mean</u> that so many words <u>mean</u> average.

The **median** is the middle number, but the set has to be arranged in order. If you're just learning to drive, you probably know that the <u>median</u> is the barrier in the <u>middle</u> of the road.

The **mode** is the most common number. Both mode and most start with <u>mo</u>-.

The **range** is the biggest number minus the smallest number. A singer's range is the highest note she can sing to the lowest note she can sing.

You will never need to calculate **standard deviation** on the SAT, but you still need to know what it is. Focus on the word "deviation". If you deviate from a path, you wander off of it. Essentially, standard deviation is a measurement of how far the data points wander from the path. The more they wander, the greater the standard deviation. Let's look at the dot plots in Example 1 to see standard deviation in action.

Example 1

Compare the two test results. The grades on the History test are all over the place. They wander a lot. But the grades on the Chemistry test bunch together. It looks like they're following the same path.

Since the History test grades deviate more from the middle, this dot plot shows a greater standard deviation. The grades on the Chemistry test have a low standard deviation. The SAT will only ever ask you to compare two sets of values. One will clearly deviate more than the other.

You can usually visualize the difference by looking at the shape of the dots, bars, or frequencies:

Grades on History Test

Grades on Chemistry Test

The Chemistry test has a clear peak that towers above the axis because most of the data is bunched around 82. It's harder to tell what the central value is for the History test. The data looks more like rolling hills, with none of the hills standing out too much from the others. In general, the taller the peak, the lower the standard deviation.

> ### Statistics — The Basics
>
> Know the definitions of mean, median, mode, range, and standard deviation. You will be asked to compare values and understand the difference between these terms.
>
> Memorize the average formula:
>
> $$\text{average} = \frac{\text{sum of the numbers}}{\text{how many numbers}}$$

The Twists

Example 2

The twist is almost always that they list the data values by frequency. For some reason, a lot of students struggle to make sense of this. This Example presents the data as a **histogram**. Another twist is that the values of the rolls are very similar to the

Statistics

frequencies, so it's hard to even know what you're looking at. Let's break it down.

The first bar says that the number 1 was rolled 4 times total. The second bar says that the number 2 was rolled 3 times total. The number 3 wasn't rolled at all. The number 4 was rolled once. Both 5 and 6 were rolled twice each.

So the x-axis is just listing all of the possible rolls on a 6-sided die. The y-axis is telling us how many times each value came up. The mode will be the most common number, which means we need to find the tallest bar. **In this case, the mode is 1.**

The median is the middle number, but we need to take into account that there are multiples of each roll. We could just create a list with four 1s, three 2s, etc:

$$\{1, 1, 1, 1, 2, 2, 2, 4, 5, 5, 6, 6\}$$

Cross off one number from each end until you get to the middle number:

$$\{\cancel{1}, \cancel{1}, \cancel{1}, \cancel{1}, \cancel{2}, 2, 2, \cancel{4}, \cancel{5}, \cancel{5}, \cancel{6}, \cancel{6}\}$$

When we eliminate five numbers from each side, we're left with two 2s. Normally, we'd need to take the average when there are two middle numbers, but **since they're the same, we know that the median is 2.** If we're careful, we could have found the median by crossing off on the graph directly. Just remember that you need to cross off 1 four times, and so on:

Values of 12 Die Rolls

The mean is the most annoying of the three to find. Again, we can't forget that there are four 1s. You should fill out the average formula like this:

$$\text{average} = \frac{\text{sum of the numbers}}{\text{how many numbers}}$$

$$\text{average} = \frac{4(1) + 3(2) + 1(4) + 2(5) + 2(6)}{12}$$

We're still adding the numbers, but we're multiplying as well. You can read the numerator like this: there are four 1s, three 2s, (we left out the 3s because there are none), one 4, two 5s, and two 6s. We divide by 12 because there were 12 rolls. Simplify:

$$\text{average} = \frac{4 + 6 + 4 + 10 + 12}{12}$$

$$\text{average} = \frac{36}{12} = 3$$

The mean is 3. This may seem strange since 3 wasn't ever rolled, but it doesn't matter. The mean is the average, which is a calculation, not an actual data point.

Example 3

Histograms come up on the SAT once in a while, but **frequency charts** are very common. They give the same information. In this case, the left column corresponds to the x-axis on our histogram — it lists our values. The right column corresponds to the y-axis on the histogram — it gives the frequency, or how many times each age should be counted.

The mode is still easy to find. It's the value with the highest frequency, so **the mode is 30** because there are 4 people who are 30 years old. A common mistake is to think that the mode is 1 because there are a lot more 1s in this chart than any other number. But just think about what that would mean in the context of the story: the most common age of softball team members is 1? What's a 1-year-old doing playing softball?! You need to incorporate the frequencies into all of your calculations, but you also need to remember that the frequencies are not

Statistics

actually part of your data. The frequency is a way to count the values, but it's the actual values that determine all of our statistical calculations.

The median requires careful attention. We can "cross off" values like we did on the histogram, but it's a little harder since we don't have a graph. If we add up all of the frequencies, we'll see that there are 15 players on the team. That means the median will be the 8th number in the set, no matter which way you count. Count from both ends just to be safe:

Ages of Softball Team Members

Age	Frequency	
19	1	1
23	1	2
25	2	3, 4
28	1	5
29	2	6, 7
30	4	5, 6, 7, **8**
32	1	4
33	1	3
35	1	2
48	1	1

Notice that we're counting Age 25 twice. We need to make sure that we don't forget about the frequency of the values. **So the eighth number and the median are 30.** Another way to get there is to use tally marks, adding one on each end until you reach the middle. But again, you'll need to be careful that the number of tally marks for each row is equal to the frequency for that row.

We should calculate the average/mean the same way that we did before, multiplying the value by the frequency:

$$\text{avg} = \frac{1(19) + 1(23) + 2(25) + 1(28) + 2(29) + 4(30) + 1(32) + 1(33) + 1(35) + 1(48)}{15}$$

Simplify:

$$\text{avg} = \frac{19 + 23 + 50 + 28 + 58 + 120 + 32 + 33 + 35 + 48}{15}$$

$$\text{avg} = \frac{446}{15}$$

$$\text{avg} = 29.7\overline{33}$$

So the average is approximately 29.73. I strongly advise you not to enter all of this information into your calculator at once. Students enter numbers (or the entire equation) incorrectly all the time, and they don't think to check their work because they trust the calculator too much. The safest approach would be to use the calculator for just one step at a time, writing the results down as you go. Whenever I calculate an average with lots of data, I write the multiplication step down next to each row before adding and then dividing:

	Age	Frequency
19	19	1
23	23	1
50	25	2
28	28	1
58	29	2
120	30	4
32	32	1
33	33	1
35	35	1
48	48	1
446	**÷**	**15**

Statistics — The Twists

The most common twist is that you'll be given the list of data in a frequency chart or histogram. Don't forget that the frequency of each value needs to be taken into account when you find the median and mean. Stay organized, and don't do all the steps in your calculator. Writing them down will help you catch mistakes.

Statistics

Exercise: Basic Statistics

#1 — Answer = 37
This is just a simple list of values, but they're not in order. It's easier to find the median if they're organized from least to greatest: {25, 32, 36, 37, 41, 48, 48}. The middle number is 37.

#2 — Answer = D
The SAT is trying to slow you down. You don't actually need to calculate all of these values if you know your Statistics terms. The number 23 is so far away from the rest of the numbers that removing it won't affect the median, mean, or mode significantly. The range, however, changes a lot. It goes from 23 days to 6 days. In different ways, mean, median, and mode are all measurements of the middle of a data set. Range is a measurement of the <u>ends</u> of a data set. Since we're changing the end, we're going to have a bigger effect on the term that involves the ends.

#3 — Answer = A
Standard deviation measures how spread out the data values are. East Springfield has an even spread, but West Springfield bunches around 8 hours of sleep. In other words, East Springfield has greater deviation from the "path" than West Springfield. You can try drawing hills and mountains (like Example 1) to visualize the difference between the frequencies. East Springfield has a very slight hill at 8 hours, but it doesn't stick out much compared to the "heights" of the other rows around it. West Springfield has a very high peak at 8 hours, and the surrounding rows are significantly lower. The taller the peak, the lower the deviation.

#4 — Answer = 3.6
Don't forget to take the frequencies into account. Your average formula should be:
$\text{avg} = \frac{47(4) + 8(3) + 2(2) + 0(1) + 3(0)}{60}$. That simplifies to $\frac{216}{60}$, which is 3.6.

#5 — Answer = 1
Since each group has 60 members, the median will be the average of the 30th and 31st numbers. You can count from either direction. The median of Group

A is 3, and the median of Group C is 2. The difference is 1.

#6 — Answer = A
Box plots are annoying. They tell you 5 things. The easiest is that the lines outside the box mark the (1) minimum and (2) maximum of the set. In this case, that doesn't really help us. The line inside the box is the (3) median of the set, which would eliminate choices B and C, since the median of Group D is 3. The ends of the box tell us (4) the first quartile and (5) the third quartile.

Basically, the quartiles are like the medians of the median. The regular median divides a set into two halves. The quartiles are the medians of each of the two halves. In this case, the first quartile would be the average of the 15th and 16th numbers, and the third quartile would be the average of the 45th and 46th numbers. (We take the average because the halves contain an even number of numbers.) Both the 15th and 16th numbers (starting from 0) would be in the 1 star column for Group D, so the first quartile is 1, which matches with Choice A.

#7 — Answer = B
Be careful! Even though the x-axis of the chart includes values from 0 to 60, the range is only the values in the set. So the maximum is at 50, and the minimum is at 10. The range is the difference between these: 50 – 10 = 40.

#8 — Answer = B
If you picked Choice A, you fell for the oldest trick in the SAT book — hard questions shouldn't be easy! Is it really going to be the case that solving this question comes down to seeing that 6 = 6 ? No way! There's clearly something more complicated going on here. In fact, the story tells us that Roger surveyed 125 patients in 2010, but he surveyed 250 patients in 2011. So even though 6 people responded with a 10-minute wait time in each year, those 6 people represent different proportions of the survey. In 2010, you could represent the 10-minute wait times as $\frac{6}{125}$. In 2011, it would be $\frac{6}{250}$. You could get the fractions to have the same denominator to compare them more easily. You'd see that twice as many people

Statistics

responded with a 10-minute wait time in 2010: $\frac{6}{125} = \frac{12}{250}$. That means that Choice B is the answer. We'd expect that a larger portion of the 2,000 patients had 10-minute wait times in 2010 because those 6 people represent a larger portion of the 125 person sample. Always pay attention to where you are in the test — at the least, you could probably eliminate Choice A and take a better guess if you are aware that it's too easy to be correct on a hard question. Sense the difficulty!

#9 — Answer = B

Unfortunately, all of the choices show a median of 30, so that doesn't help. Choice A is wrong because the maximum and minimum are incorrect. Choice B is correct because the first quartile occurs at 25 (average of the 31st and 32nd numbers) and the third quartile occurs at 35 (average of the 94th and 95th numbers). This question shows why you need to be comfortable finding medians without writing out all of the values. It's just not possible with 125 data points! (See #6 for more details on box plots.)

Mystery Averages

Example 4

Mystery averages aren't particularly hard, but students have trouble because there's a lot of information. You'll almost always have to do the average formula twice. Start with the set where you have all the values:

$$\text{Meg's avg} = \frac{9.8 + 10.4 + 10.1 + 9.5}{4}$$

$$\text{Meg's avg} = \frac{39.8}{4} = 9.95$$

The question says that Meg's average is 0.9 pounds greater than AJ's:

$$9.95 - 0.9 = 9.05$$

Now build another average equation for AJ's cats with the data we have:

$$9.05 = \frac{x + 8.7 + 9.3 + 9.0}{4}$$

Multiply both sides by 4 to eliminate the fraction:

$$36.2 = x + 8.7 + 9.3 + 9.0$$

Add everything up, then subtract to get x by itself:

$$36.2 = x + 27$$

$$36.2 - 27 = x$$

$$9.2 = x$$

AJ's mystery cat weighs 9.2 pounds.

Example 5

This one is twisted because we don't have the specific values for Josephine's test scores. But here's a little trick: they don't matter. Let's see why by using our average formula:

$$\text{average} = \frac{\text{sum of the numbers}}{\text{how many numbers}}$$

We know two of these pieces:

$$86 = \frac{\text{sum of the numbers}}{5}$$

The question tells us that Josephine's average on 5 tests is 86. Multiply by 5 to find the sum:

$$430 = \text{sum of the numbers}$$

You can think of this as the total points that Josephine earned on all the tests combined. But honestly, it doesn't really matter how you think of it. The point is that we calculated the sum <u>because we could</u>. We're essentially using the Get Back to Basics strategy. We may not know where the question is headed, but we trust that the basic average formula is somehow part of the solution. Trust the process.

Statistics

As we said earlier, Mystery Averages usually involve two average formulas, so let's set it up again, but this time we need to factor in a 6th exam:

$$88 = \frac{\text{sum of the numbers}}{6}$$

Again, let's calculate the sum simply because we can. Multiply both sides by 6 to get:

$$528 = \text{sum of the numbers}$$

Now we have two sums (430 and 528). What should we do with them? Well, what <u>can</u> we do with them? The 430 represents five exams, and 528 represents what happens when we add in a sixth exam. Why not subtract to see the difference?

$$528 - 430 = 98$$

So Josephine needs a 98 on her sixth exam to bring up her average. Notice how we didn't know at the beginning that this would be our last step. That's exactly how Get Back to Basics is supposed to work: we do what we <u>can</u> do, and it's almost always what we <u>should</u> do. Formulas are very helpful because they keep us organized, even when we're not sure how to combine all of the information in the question. If a question asks for the average/mean, always start by writing the formula on your page. Plug in what you can and see what happens!

Mystery Averages — Summary

If you need to find a missing value, you'll probably need to use the average formula twice. It's okay if you feel like you're stumbling through this process. Just set up the formula and plug in the numbers that you know. You only need 2 of the 3 values to keep moving through the question.

There might also be circumstances where you need to make up some values. Sometimes there are rules to follow, but other times you can make up whatever numbers you want by Arithmetizing. (HINT: this will help on the Exercise!)

Exercise: Mystery Averages

#10 — Answer = 9.3
Start by finding the total number of strikeouts for the first 4 games. Use the average formula to stay organized. You'll multiply the average by the number of games (8 x 4) to find the sum of the strikeouts (32). Do the same thing for the next 2 games. Multiply the average by the number of games (12 x 2) to find the sum of the strikeouts in those 2 games (24). Now find the average for the 6 games by adding the two sums (32 + 24) and dividing them by 6 games ($\frac{56}{6}$) to get an average of 9.3 strikeouts per game.

#11 — Answer = 24
This is a very twisted question. Start with the basics. You can find the sum of the first 3 cards using the average formula: $9 = \frac{\text{sum}}{3}$. The sum of the first 3 cards is 27. Use a new average formula to account for all 6 players: $9 = \frac{27 + x + y + z}{6}$. In order for Hans's number to be as high as possible, the other players should have numbers as low as possible. And remember that no two players can write the same number. The formula should be: $9 = \frac{27 + 1 + 2 + z}{6}$. Solve to find that Hans's card is 24.

#12 — Answer = A
Arithmetize. Let $x = 1$. The average of 1 and 7 would make $a = 4$. The average of 4 and 3 would make $b = 3.5$. The average of 1 and 8 would make $c = 4.5$. Find the average of a, b, and c: $\frac{4 + 3.5 + 4.5}{3} = 4$. Plug 1 in for x in all the choices. Only Choice A gives you 4. If you do this algebraically, there's a high chance that you get it wrong and pick Choice C, so use the strategies. It should be obvious that Arithmetize is worth trying — there are an insane <u>four variables</u> in this question!

Surveys

Example 6

Survey questions are barely math. They involve a lot of reading, and one word can make all the difference, so pay attention.

Statistics

This question requires deep understanding of the difference between mean and median. Both are measures of the "center" of the data, but they are different definitions of the center. Why would the mean value ($10,000) be less than the median value ($16,000)? Let's look at another hypothetical situation to better understand the difference between mean and median.

Imagine a seesaw:

The seesaw has a midpoint. The triangle represents the hinge, or fulcrum, that lets the seesaw tilt. The triangle is the <u>median</u>. It's a fixed midpoint because both sides have the same length of seesaw. Remember that the median is the middle number, so if there are 5 numbers on one side of the median, there have to be 5 numbers on the other side. In seesaw-terms, if there are 5 feet of seesaw on the left side, there have to be 5 feet of seesaw on the right side.

But let's visualize the midpoint a different way. The <u>mean</u> is represented by a ball that we place in the middle when we start. If we have two people on the seesaw who are about the same weight, then the seesaw will be balanced. It won't want to tilt in either direction.

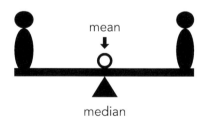

When this happens, the mean/average will be pretty close to the middle. The ball won't roll toward either side. But what if a fat person sat on one side?

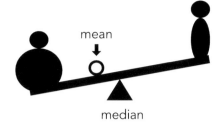

The median is still fixed in the middle of the seesaw because we haven't changed the length of either side. But we <u>have</u> changed the weight, and the ball rolls toward the fat person. In other words, the median doesn't care about the values of the data — it's the middle number no matter what the numbers are. But the mean <u>does</u> care about the values — it gets pulled toward the side that has the more extreme values.

Let's replace our people with the values from the Example. We'll also say that the dealership has 100 cars on the lot, just so we can visualize it better.

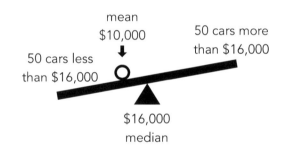

There's still the same length of seesaw on both sides of the hinge. The median is the middle, so the "length" of the set is the same on each side, which is why there are 50 cars on each side.

But the mean is $10,000, which is closer to the "less than $16,000" side. The principle is the same as when we were using fat and skinny people — the ball is rolling toward the side that has more extreme values. In other words, the 50 cars on the left cost a lot less than $16,000, but the 50 cars on the right cost only a little more than $16,000.

To sum up, the median tells us that the dealership has 50 cars that cost less than $16,000 and 50 cars that cost more than $16,000. But the mean tells us that the 50 cars that are less than $16,000 are <u>way less</u> than $16,000. The side with smaller values

Statistics

actually has a greater "weight", which pulls the mean down.

This matches with Choice C, which is the correct answer. If you're still a little confused, that's okay. This is a really hard question and concept.

Example 7

This question is a little easier because it's less about numbers and more about words. We need to be careful of strong words that take the survey's conclusion too far. Let's go choice-by-choice:

A) The word "exactly" is a problem. The survey found that 68% prefer chocolate, but it wasn't a survey of the entire town. Only 250 people got asked. It <u>might</u> be the case that 68% of the 10,000 residents also prefer chocolate, but is it really that hard to imagine 67% or 70% of them preferring chocolate? A survey gives us an estimate, but it's not exact. <u>In general, the more people you ask (the greater the sample size), the more accurate the result (the lower the margin of error).</u>

B) This choice is tempting, but "all" is a strong word. Go back to the survey. They didn't ask every type of person. They only asked "people over the age of 30". That means that the results of the survey only apply to people over the age of 30. Maybe kids really like vanilla. We just don't know, so we can't jump to conclusions about what everybody in the town would think. <u>In general, a survey should ask a group of people that represents the overall makeup of the town (a random sample of the residents).</u> When a survey is limited, we also have to limit our conclusions.

C) This choice seems okay. "Approximately" is a good word because it leaves some room on either side in case our survey is slightly off. And the conclusion is limited to residents over the age of 30, just like the survey. **Let's keep this choice.**

D) This is identical to Choice C, except that it says that 68% like ice cream. That's not what our survey asked. Maybe some of the people who said they prefer chocolate don't actually like ice cream. They might just pick chocolate if they

were forced to eat ice cream. If given the choice, they might not eat either flavor. Just like with Choice B, we can't jump to conclusions that go beyond the scope of the survey. We need to stick to what was asked.

Choice C is the correct answer because it basically just restates the survey. We don't jump to any conclusions, and the word "approximately" leaves some wiggle room in case the survey is a little off. Once you know how survey questions work, they become much less intimidating.

Surveys — Summary

Read carefully. Eliminate answer choices that are too strong. Don't jump to conclusions that aren't supported by the survey.

The **sample size** is the number of people who were surveyed. The larger the sample size, the more accurate the survey.

Ideally, a survey should ask a **random sample** of the population that represents the overall population.

Bias is bad. It means that the survey might be inaccurate because it did not ask a random sample. For example, if you asked a group of old people if they have a smartphone, you'd probably get a very different result than if you asked a random sample of the population. For various reasons, old people are probably less likely to have a smartphone than the average person, so the results of the survey would be biased.

Biased results have a high **margin of error**, which is a measurement of the accuracy of a survey or poll. A larger sample size means a lower margin of error.

Exercise: Surveys

#13 — Answer = C

Go through the choices. Choice A is not necessarily true. It's possible that Parkville has a higher income because only a few residents have much higher incomes than everyone else, which would pull up the mean (think back to the seesaw analogy from Example 6). Choice B is not necessarily true because everyone in Floraltown could earn $55,000 and everyone in Parkville could earn $60,000. It's unlikely, but it's still possible. Choice C must be true because the sample size for Floraltown (100 people) was less than the sample size for Parkville (200 people). In general, the greater the sample size, the smaller the margin of error.

#14 — Answer = C

Look for wrong answers. Choice B is definitely wrong because the population size would not affect the accuracy of the survey. Choice D is tempting. The distance probably affects the <u>result</u> of the survey, but it does not affect its accuracy. Choice A is second best because sample size does usually affect the accuracy of a survey. But 150 people seems like a good number. More important, the time that the survey was given is a big problem. A Tuesday morning is a very odd time if you're looking to get a sense of what a random sample of your customers think. Most people would be at work during that time. The Tuesday morning shoppers might have strange schedules that would allow them to travel to a different location more easily. In general, you want a survey to sample a group of people who represent the overall population. If the SAT ever makes you choose whether a survey is inaccurate because of sample size or because of bias, you should lean toward bias.

#15 — Answer = D

This survey is biased because it is only asking people who work at the factory. It's understandable that they would oppose taxing the factory. It might cost them their jobs. And since the survey only asked factory workers, we can't draw conclusions about what the entire city might think. People who don't work at the factory might support the tax.

Common Algebra Mistakes

The Basics

In general, when solving for x, work your way toward the variable — from the outside in.

Example 1

Subtract 15 from both sides:

$$
\begin{array}{rr}
6x + 15 = & 27 \\
- 15 & - 15 \\
\hline
6x = & 12
\end{array}
$$

Divide both sides by 6:

$$\frac{6x}{6} = \frac{12}{6}$$

$$x = 2$$

That's not the answer! The SAT almost always wants something else, so go back to the question. In this case, they want the value of $2x + 5$, so plug our value for x back in:

$$
\begin{aligned}
2x + 5 &= 2(2) + 5 \\
&= 4 + 5 \\
&= 9
\end{aligned}
$$

The correct answer is 9. If you're clever with algebra, you might notice that there's a shortcut. A lot of SAT algebra questions have one. If we divide our original equation by 3, we get straight to the answer:

$$\frac{6x + 15 = 27}{3}$$

$$2x + 5 = 9$$

It's not necessary to use these shortcuts, but try to look for them. You'll get better at finding them, and they might help a lot on twisted questions.

Example 2

Divide both sides by 2:

$$\frac{2a}{2} = \frac{14}{2}$$

$$a = 7$$

Plug back into the expression they want:

$$
\begin{aligned}
4a + 8 &= 4(7) + 8 \\
&= 28 + 8 \\
&= 36
\end{aligned}
$$

The answer is 36. But once again, there's a shortcut:

$$2\,(2a = 14)$$

$$4a = 28$$

$$
\begin{aligned}
4a + 8 &= (28) + 8 \\
&= 36
\end{aligned}
$$

Example 3

We could add 16 to both sides, then take the square root:

$$
\begin{array}{rr}
x^2 - 16 = & 0 \\
+ 16 & + 16 \\
\hline
x^2 = & 16
\end{array}
$$

$$\sqrt{x^2} = \sqrt{16}$$

$$x = 4$$

But you might also want to get in the habit of factoring when you have x^2 terms:

$$x^2 - 16 = 0$$

$$(x + 4)(x - 4) = 0$$

So technically x could be 4 or –4, but the question says $x > 0$, so **only +4 works.**

Common Algebra Mistakes

$$4n + 20 = 4(-1) + 20$$
$$= -4 + 20$$
$$= 16$$

So Choice D is the correct answer.

Example 5

Combine like terms. The twist is that they're counting on you to forget how to combine variables with exponents. But don't let them make you second guess yourself! Just think about it for a second. What's $x + x$?

$$x + x = 2x$$

$$(x)(x) = x^2$$

The same rules apply here. We add the coefficients, not the exponents:

$$\begin{array}{r} 2x^2 - 6x + 1 \\ +4x^2 - 3x - 8 \\ \hline 6x^2 - 9x - 7 \end{array}$$

Choice A is the answer.

Common Algebra Mistakes — The Basics

Show your work.

Work toward the variable, usually by adding/subtracting first, then multiplying/dividing. But each situation is different.

Pay attention to what they're asking for. The SAT knows that you're used to being done once you've solved for x. They will try to trick you by asking for something else. This final step will be easy, but it will also be easy to miss if you're not in the habit of rechecking the question.

Look for shortcuts. You might be able to manipulate the equation to get to your answer faster.

The Twists

Example 4

The twist is that this is not an equation. Untwist it by turning the words into equations. The first one is straightforward:

$$2n + 8 = 6$$

Read it back to be sure: two times n plus 8 equals 6. That matches our original question pretty well. Now solve for n:

$$\begin{array}{rcr} 2n + 8 = & & 6 \\ -8 & & -8 \\ \hline 2n & = & -2 \end{array}$$

$$\frac{2n}{2} = \frac{-2}{2}$$

$$n = -1$$

Now go back to the question. What do they want? If you skip this step, you'll pick Choice A, which is wrong. They want you to do one more thing:

Common Algebra Mistakes — The Twists

This is the math section, so when they twist questions by describing math with words, you need to untwist them by creating equations. Always double check that your equation matches the text.

Know how to combine like terms. The wrong answer choices will make you second guess yourself:

$$2x^2 + 3x^2 = 5x^2$$

The exponents don't change when you're adding and subtracting.

Common Algebra Mistakes

Exercise: Essential Algebra

#1 — Answer = B
Use the first values of x and y to find the value of c: $36 = c(9)$. So $c = 4$. Use the value of c to find the other value of y: $y = (4)(2)$. So $y = 8$.

#2 — Answer = C
Turn the words into an equation: $9 + 6t = 28 - 7$. The twist is that "7 less than" is hard to place. Subtraction is almost always at the end of the equation. Solve the equation to find that $t = 2$. But the question wants the value of $3t$, which is 6.

#3 — Answer = A
When you add the two expressions together, the 3 and –3 cancel out, leaving just $y^2 + 2y$. If you were even a little unsure, you could Arithmetize with a simple value, like $y = 2$.

#4 — Answer = A
You do not need to solve for a or b. Divide both sides by 5 to find that $a - b = -\frac{8}{5}$. People struggle with this question because they are robotically programmed to do algebra and solve for variables. The SAT is deliberately trying to short-circuit your robotic brain. Always look to the actual question to see what they want before you start mindlessly solving an equation.

#5 — Answer = A
Turn the words into an equation: $3n + 13 = 9$. Solve for n, which is $-\frac{4}{3}$. But the question wants the value of $6n$, which is –8. You could also see that if $3n$ is –4, then $6n$ would be double that.

#6 — Answer = B
Combine like terms and the equation should simplify to: $4x + 5 = 2x - 3$. Solve for $x = -4$.

#7 — Answer = 13
Get Back to Basics. Ignore the weird wording at the end. They're telling you to sum two expressions. Do it. When you add the equations together, you should get: $4x^2 - 6x + 15$. Line this up with the $ax^2 + bx + c$ that they want, and you'll see that each letter corresponds to a number (coefficient). Add the coefficients to get 13.

#8 — Answer = 29
Turn the words into an equation: $20 - 2x = 14$. Solve and you'll get that $x = 3$. The question wants the value of $8x + 5$, which is $24 + 5 = 29$.

Distribution

The Basics
One of the most common mistakes on the SAT is distributing incorrectly. These mistakes are unacceptable. They're incredibly easy to prevent, especially now that you know the SAT is looking to catch you making them.

Example 6

Distribute to both parts:

$$2(x + 5) + 6(x - 9) = 4x$$

$$2x + 10 + 6x - 54 = 4x$$

Combine like terms:

$$8x - 44 = 4x$$

Solve for x:

$$\begin{array}{r} 8x - 44 = \quad 4x \\ -8x \quad\quad\quad -8x \\ \hline -44 = -4x \end{array}$$

$$\frac{-44}{-4} = \frac{-4x}{-4}$$

$$11 = x$$

The correct answer is 11.

Example 7

Distribute to both parts:

$$4(x + 3) - 8$$

231

Common Algebra Mistakes

$$4x + 12 - 8$$

Combine like terms:

$$4x + 4$$

The correct answer is Choice B. You could also Arithmetize if you want. It's very quick and requires absolutely no distribution:

Let $x = 0$

$$
\begin{aligned}
4(x + 3) - 8 &= 4((0) + 3) - 8 \\
&= 4(3) - 8 \\
&= 12 - 8 \\
&= \underline{4}
\end{aligned}
$$

- A) $12(0) - 8 = -8$ ✗
- B) $4(0) + 4 = 4$ ✓
- C) $4(0) - 5 = -5$ ✗
- D) $4(0) - 20 = -20$ ✗

Example 8

You might be tempted to factor these expressions, but notice that the answer choices are all written without parentheses. That probably means we should get rid of the parentheses, not add more. Distribute the negative to both parts of the second term:

$$(x^2 - 8) - (-5x^2 + 3)$$

$$x^2 - 8 + 5x^2 - 3$$

Combine like terms:

$$6x^2 - 11$$

The correct answer is Choice A. But once again, Arithmetize works because we're never asked to solve for x. It's just a placeholder. If you make a lot of algebra mistakes, you need to switch your default position from algebra to strategies. You cannot afford

to lose points on something like this, so starting with the strategy is worthwhile if it prevents the error:

Let $x = 0$

$$(0^2 - 8) - (-5(0)^2 + 3)$$

$$(-8) - (3) = \underline{-11}$$

- A) $6(0)^2 - 11 = -11$ ✓
- B) $6(0)^2 - 5 = -5$ ✗
- C) $-4(0)^2 - 11 = -11$ ✓
- D) $-4(0)^2 - 5 = -5$ ✗

Let $x = 1$

$$(1^2 - 8) - (-5(1)^2 + 3)$$

$$(-7) - (-2) = \underline{-5}$$

- A) $6(1)^2 - 11 = -5$ ✓
- C) $-4(1)^2 - 11 = -15$ ✗

Arithmetizing here definitely takes longer than the algebra, but it's worth the time if it guarantees that you earn the points.

Distribution — The Basics

Make sure that you distribute coefficients and negatives to all parts within parentheses. The SAT is trying to catch you making a mistake, so you have to be careful.

The Twists

Example 9

The twist here is that they sometimes throw a lot of similar-looking variables at you. They're just trying to confuse you. If you're organized, it shouldn't matter. Don't try to do too much at once. Distribute first, then write the result, then combine like terms.

Common Algebra Mistakes

You're more likely to notice a mistake when you see the result of each step.

Distribute the negative to all parts:

$$(2ab^2 + 5a^2 - 4a^2b) - (-2ab^2 - a^2b + 5a^2)$$

$$2ab^2 + 5a^2 - 4a^2b + 2ab^2 + a^2b - 5a^2$$

Combine like terms:

$$2ab^2 + 2ab^2 \;\; \cancel{+5a^2}\; \cancel{-5a^2}\;\; - 4a^2b + a^2b$$

$$4ab^2 - 3a^2b$$

Choice A is the correct answer. But yet again, Arithmetizing could have saved you if you were overwhelmed by all of this. The number 1 makes a lot of the complexity instantaneously disappear because any number multiplied by 1 is still the number. You're left with just the coefficients:

Let $a = 1$
Let $b = 1$

$$(2ab^2 + 5a^2 - 4a^2b) - (-2ab^2 - a^2b + 5a^2)$$

$$(2 + 5 - 4) - (-2 - 1 + 5)$$

$$(3) - (2) = \underline{1}$$

A) $4 - 3 = 1$ ✓

B) $4 - 3 + 10 = 11$ ✗

C) $4 - 5 = -1$ ✗

D) $4 - 5 + 10 = 9$ ✗

I wouldn't Arithmetize with bigger numbers here because the exponents quickly make the strategy inefficient. But I don't know… making both variables equal to 1 seems easy enough and fast enough to try. Have some faith in the strategies, and I think you'll find that they work better than algebra in a lot of unexpected places.

Example 10

If you're confused by the wording of this question, that's okay. It's just a twist to scare you. Get Back to Basics. You should at least know how to clean up the left side of the equation. Distribute to all parts:

$$3x(4x - 2) - 5(4x - 2)$$

$$12x^2 - 6x - 20x + 10$$

Combine like terms, and you'll get:

$$12x^2 - 26x + 10 = ax^2 + bx + c$$

The equation and the question are both saying that the numbers in front of the variables line up with a, b, and c. Put them on top of each other to see:

$$12x^2 - 26x + 10$$
$$ax^2 + \;\; bx + \;\; c$$

All this talk about "constants" just means that:

$$a = 12$$
$$b = -26$$
$$c = 10$$

Finish the question by following the remaining instructions. What is the value of $a + b$?

$$a + b = 12 + (-26)$$
$$= 12 - 26$$
$$= -14$$

The correct answer is Choice A. You might have actually had an impulse to Arithmetize here because there are so many variables. Unfortunately, it doesn't work. The main reason is that we need the x's to match the coefficient to the other letters. This type of question is the rare case where a question looks like Arithmetize but the strategy fails. Don't let that deter you from Arithmetizing <u>whenever</u> you're confused. It helps way more often than not. And if it fails, it usually fails quickly, so you won't waste much time.

Common Algebra Mistakes

> ### Distribution — The Twists
>
> Don't be intimidated by lots of variables or weird instructions. If it looks like you'll have to distribute, then just do it. Stay organized!

Exercise: Distribution

#9 — Answer = A

Distribute to all parts and you should get: $4x^2y - 12xy^2 - 3x^2y - xy^2$. Combine like terms. The x^2y terms cannot be combined with the xy^2 terms. They have different exponents, so they're not actually "like" terms. Arithmetizing $x = 1$ and $y = 1$ also works very quickly.

#10 — Answer = C

Ignore the right side for now. Distribute to all parts on the left side to get: $x^2 - 5x + 2x + 10 - 5$. Combine like terms to get: $x^2 - 3x + 5$. The coefficients of the terms on the left match up with the terms on the right, so $c = 5$. For some reason, a lot of people forget the –5 that's immediately to the left of the equals. My guess is that they start combining like terms <u>while</u> they're distributing, so they aren't thinking about the stuff that isn't near the parentheses. Show your work for every step!

#11 — Answer = D

Distribute to all parts to get: $5t - 5 - 2t - 4 = 2t$. Combine like terms: $3t - 9 = 2t$. Solve for t to get that $t = 9$. Since all of the answer choices represent t, you could easily Guess & Check instead of distributing and solving.

#12 — Answer = 955

Distribute to all parts: $400x^2 + 1095 - 640 + 100x^2$. Combine like terms: $500x^2 + 455$. The twist is that you need to add the coefficients: 500 + 455 = 955.

#13 — Answer = A

Distribute the negative to all parts: $-x^2 - 9 - 6 - 3x + 3x^2$. Combine like terms: $2x^2 - 3x - 15$. Arithmetizing is a bit more annoying for this question. Looking ahead to the answer

choices, $x = 0$ wouldn't help because every answer would give us –15. The next logical value is $x = 1$, but it only eliminates Choices B and C. You could continue with $x = 2$, but you might also be at a point where you can see the algebra more clearly and notice that the correct answer needs a $-3x$ because of the distribution.

#14 — Answer = 10

Distribute to all parts: $2x^2 - 8 - 3x^2 - 3x$. Combine like terms: $-x^2 - 3x - 8$. Subtract the coefficients as instructed: $-1 - (-3) - (-8) = 10$. Remember that you can't have negative answers in the Grid-ins, so if you get one, you know you've made a mistake. The most common mistake is, in fact, losing the negatives in the instructions and just using the negatives from the coefficients: $-1 - 3 - 8 = -12$.

Fractions

The Basics

If you're confused by fractions, it's probably because you vaguely know that there are rules that you're supposed to follow, but you don't remember what the rules are. The SAT mostly focuses on multiplication:

Example 11

The second equation tells us the value of y, so plug it into the first equation so that you're only dealing with one variable:

$$\frac{x + 3}{4} = 5$$

To eliminate a fraction, multiply both sides by the denominator (bottom number).

$$\left(\frac{\cancel{4}}{1}\right)\frac{x + 3}{\cancel{4}} = 5\left(\frac{4}{1}\right)$$

$$x + 3 = 20$$

Solve for x:

Common Algebra Mistakes

$$x = 17$$

Choice C is the correct answer. You could also Guess & Check pretty easily, since all of the answer choices represent x by itself.

Example 12

Notice that in the first example, we eliminated the 4 on the bottom by multiplying by 4, but I wrote the $\frac{4}{1}$ as a fraction. That's because we are essentially eliminating fractions by multiplying by their reciprocals (reversing the top and bottom). We'll do the same thing here:

$$\frac{2}{7}t = \frac{3}{2}$$

$$\left(\frac{7}{2}\right)\frac{2}{7}t = \frac{3}{2}\left(\frac{7}{2}\right)$$

Multiplying the top by 7 eliminates the 7 on the bottom, and multiplying the bottom by 2 eliminates the 2 on the top. Now simplify the right side by multiplying across the tops and bottom of the fractions:

$$t = \frac{3 \times 7}{2 \times 2}$$

$$t = \frac{21}{4}$$

The answer is Choice A. It would be a lot harder to Guess & Check on a question like this. Even though the answers still represent t by itself, we'd have to plug in fractions, which are a little harder for our brains to comprehend. Use your judgment.

Fractions — The Basics

Eliminate fractions by multiplying by the reciprocal (the fraction flipped upside-down).

When you multiply fractions together, multiply across the numerators and denominators.

The Twists

Example 13

The SAT loves this type of question for some reason. The easiest way to solve it is by Arithmetizing. Pick numbers for x and y that would make the first equation true.

Let $x = 3$ and $y = 1$

$$\frac{x}{y} = 3 \qquad \frac{3}{1} = 3$$

Now put those numbers into the other expression:

$$\frac{12y}{x} = \frac{12(1)}{(3)}$$

$$= \frac{12}{3}$$

$$= 4$$

Choice B is the correct answer. You could also solve this algebraically if you know how to manipulate fractions. You can essentially flip the first equation upside down:

$$\text{If } \frac{x}{y} = 3, \text{ then } \frac{y}{x} = \frac{1}{3}.$$

The second expression can be rewritten to emphasize the variables so that you can substitute:

$$\frac{12y}{x} = \left(\frac{12}{1}\right)\left(\frac{y}{x}\right)$$

$$= \left(\frac{12}{1}\right)\left(\frac{1}{3}\right)$$

$$= \frac{12}{3}$$

$$= 4$$

Common Algebra Mistakes

Knowing how to flip fractions upside-down will help you on some harder questions, but Arithmetize when you can.

Example 14

Surprisingly, adding fractions is harder than multiplying them. We can add the left side no problem:

$$\frac{3}{7}x + \frac{2}{7}x$$

$$\frac{5}{7}x$$

But the right side can't be added easily because we don't have a <u>common denominator</u>. We can get a common denominator by multiplying, but notice that the process is different this time. Both the numerator and denominator are multiplied by the same number. This lets us change how the number looks without changing its value. Since $\frac{4}{4} = 1$, we're not actually changing the value of the term.

$$\frac{3}{8} + \frac{1}{2}$$

$$\frac{3}{8} + \frac{1}{2}\left(\frac{4}{4}\right)$$

$$\frac{3}{8} + \frac{4}{8}$$

$$\frac{7}{8}$$

Solve for x by eliminating the fraction on the left with the reciprocal, just like we did in Example 12:

$$\frac{5}{7}x = \frac{7}{8}$$

$$\left(\frac{7}{5}\right)\frac{5}{7}x = \frac{7}{8}\left(\frac{7}{5}\right)$$

$$x = \frac{49}{40}$$

Choice A is the correct answer.

Fractions — The Twists

You can Arithmetize on many Fractions questions (especially when you don't actually have to solve for x). Just make sure that the numbers you pick follow the rules/equations in the question.

When you add or subtract fractions, you <u>must</u> have a common denominator. Add or subtract the tops, but keep the bottom the same.

Multiplying the top and bottom of the fraction by the same number lets you change how a fraction looks without changing its value because you're really only multiplying by 1.

Exercise: Fractions

#15 — Answer = D
Substitute 28 in for b in the first equation. Multiply to get that $a = 21$. But that's not the answer. Plug 21 into the expression they ask for: $2(21) + 1 = 43$.

#16 — Answer = 10
Substitute 2 in for x. Solve for c by subtracting 2 from both sides, then multiplying both sides by –5.

#17 — Answer = A
Multiply the second equation by 2 to solve for $y = 12$. Substitute 12 in for y in the first equation. Solve for $x = -3$. Multiply x and y as instructed to get –36.

#18 — Answer = A
Get Back to Basics. Even though this fraction has variables, you can still multiply both sides by the denominator to eliminate it. If you multiply both sides by $a + 4$, you'll get $a + 2 = 6(a + 4)$. Distribute, then get all the variables on the same side. You should solve for $a = -\frac{22}{5}$.

#19 — Answer = B
You could cross-multiply to get: $9x = 3x + 36$. Or you could just multiply both sides by 9 to cancel the fraction on the right side and reduce with the 3 on the left side: $3x = x + 12$. Either way, solve to find

Common Algebra Mistakes

that $x = 6$. But the question wants the value of $\frac{x}{3}$, so the answer is 2.

#20 — Answer = D
Arithmetize. Let $x = 1$ and $y = 2$. Substitute those values into the second expression to get $\frac{32}{1}$.

#21 — Answer = 27/8
Eliminate the fraction by multiplying both sides by $\frac{9}{4}$, the reciprocal of $\frac{4}{9}$. You'll get that h is equal to $\frac{27}{8}$.

Inequalities

The Basics

Inequalities tend to make people forget everything they know about algebra. But they shouldn't! All of the same rules apply, except that the equals sign is replaced with a less than or greater than sign.

Example 15

Whenever possible, Guess & Check. It's absolutely the easiest way if you have the option:

$$2(-1) + 1 \le 5(-1) - 2$$
$$\text{A)} \quad -2 + 1 \le -5 - 2$$
$$-1 \le -7 \; ✗$$

That's it! **Choice A is the correct answer.** This inequality doesn't make sense because −1 is <u>not</u> less than −7, but the question wants us to find a value that does <u>not</u> work: "which of the following numbers is NOT a solution". Even though the NOT is in capital letters, it's easy to miss once you start doing the math. It's a good idea to underline it so that you don't forget about it.

If you want to solve this algebraically, you would do the exact same steps as if it were an equals sign. Start by getting all the x's on one side:

$$
\begin{array}{rcl}
2x + 1 & \le & 5x - 2 \\
-2x & & -2x \\
\hline
1 & \le & 3x - 2 \\
+2 & & +2 \\
\hline
3 & \le & 3x
\end{array}
$$

$$\frac{3}{3} \le \frac{3x}{3}$$

$$1 \le x$$

Since x has to be greater than or equal to 1, Choice A would be the only answer that does <u>not</u> fall in that range.

Example 16

You could also solve this one with Guess & Check. You'd need to try different numbers to eliminate the wrong answers. But if you solve algebraically, you need to take into account the <u>only</u> thing that's strange about Inequalities. It starts out the same as Example 15:

$$
\begin{array}{rcl}
6 & \le & 1 - x \\
-1 & & -1 \\
\hline
5 & \le & -x
\end{array}
$$

From here, we have to be careful. We should divide by −1 to get x by itself. But when we do, we have to reverse the inequality sign:

$$5 \le -x$$

$$\frac{5}{-1} \le \frac{-x}{-1}$$

$$-5 \ge x$$

Notice that the inequality sign used to open to the right, but now it opens to the left. To make our answer match the choices, we can flip it once more, but this time we're reversing the entire inequality:

$$x \le -5$$

Choice C is the correct answer. If you're unsure, use Guess & Check to confirm. Pick a number within your answer range:

Common Algebra Mistakes

Let $x = -6$

$$6 \leq 1 - (-6)$$

$$6 \leq 1 + 6$$

$$6 \leq 7 \checkmark$$

–6 works, which we'd expect based on our answer. But let's try –4 also. This guess should <u>not</u> work because it's outside the inequality's range:

Let $x = -4$

$$6 \leq 1 - (-4)$$

$$6 \leq 1 + 4$$

$$6 \leq 5 \text{ ✗}$$

As expected, x is less than –5, but not greater than –5.

Inequalities — The Basics

Don't confuse the inequality signs. Remember that the larger side faces the side with the greater value:

- $4 < 5$
- $5 > 4$

Guess & Check is usually the most efficient way to solve Inequalities questions. Just be careful if they ask for a number that does <u>not</u> satisfy the inequality.

The rules of Algebra still apply to Inequalities. Solve for x the same way you normally would.

The only exception is when you multiply or divide by a negative number. You <u>must</u> switch the direction of the inequality sign.

The Twists

Example 17

You know that Inequalities give you a range of values. This question is twisted to make you think that you need to find one specific value within a very wide range, but it's actually really easy. The greatest possible value will occur at the "equals" part of this "less than or equal to" inequality.

Let's start by looking at what we have and what we want:

$$3a - 1 \leq 5 \qquad 3a + 1 \text{ ?}$$

You could solve for a, but you're much better off using a shortcut to go directly from question to answer. Add 2 to both sides of the inequality:

$$\begin{array}{r} 3a - 1 \leq 5 \\ +2 +2 \\ \hline 3a + 1 \leq 7 \end{array}$$

So the greatest possible value of 3a + 1 is 7 because the expression has to be less than or equal to 7. **The correct answer is Choice C.** If you had solved for $a \leq 2$, you'd still plug 2 into the a in $3a + 1$.

Example 18

This question is even more confusing because you have two inequalities, but we can trust that the signs will behave as if they were equals signs. Both inequalities have wide ranges, but the "greatest possible value" part tells us that those ranges overlap at one point that is greater than all the others. That point is where the lines intersect. Honestly, if you're ever confused by inequalities, you can usually just rewrite the equations with equals signs and solve. If the inequality matters, it's usually pretty easy to add it back in at the end.

$$y = 3$$
$$x + y = 10$$

Common Algebra Mistakes

Substitute 3 in for y:

$$x + 3 = 10$$

Now solve for x:

$$\begin{array}{rcl} x + 3 & = & 10 \\ -3 & & -3 \\ \hline x & = & 7 \end{array}$$

So the greatest possible value of x is 7. **And the correct answer is Choice B.**

Inequalities — The Twists

When the SAT asks for greatest or least possible values on Inequalities questions, they're almost always asking for a point of intersection. You can pretend the inequality signs are just equals signs.

However, there might be hard questions where this is a bad assumption that gets you in trouble, so pay attention to where you are in the Math section. If it's supposed to be a hard question, double check your math by graphing the inequalities.

Exercise: Inequalities

#22 — Answer = C
Add 7 to both sides, then divide by 2 to get that $x < 9$.

#23 — Answer = A
Guess & Check. Plugging in 0 for x gives the inequality: $-1 < 0$. This is true, so Choice A is the answer.

#24 — Answer = C
Divide the inequality by 2, and you'll get: $4x - 3y \leq 13$.

#25 — Answer = C
Guess & Check. Start with the smallest number since the question is asking for the least possible value. Plugging in Choice D gives $-17 \geq -12$, which is not true. Choice C gives $-12 \geq -12$, which is true.

#26 — Answer = D
It's difficult to Guess & Check because the answer choices do not represent the value of x. We'll have to solve algebraically. Subtract 5, then divide by 2 to simplify the first inequality to $x \leq -3$. The greatest possible value of x is –3, so plug –3 in for x in the second expression. You'll get that x is equal to 3.

#27 — Answer = C
Solve for x by adding $4x$ and 1 to both sides to get: $6 > 6x$. Divide by 6 to get $1 > x$. The twist is that this inequality is backwards, and it's easy to jump to the wrong conclusion and pick Choice D. When you flip the inequality, you have to flip the sign: $x < 1$. If you had turned the inequality into an equals sign, you'd be stuck with both Choice C and Choice D at the end. But it's easy to Guess & Check from there. Pick an easy number that would be right for one inequality and wrong for the other. The easiest is $x = 0$. In the original equation, 0 works because $5 > -1$ is true. That means that 0 is a valid solution, and so it should also work in our answer. Since $0 < 1$ is true, Choice C is our answer. Choice D produces a bad inequality: $0 > 1$.

Factor & FOIL

The Basics

Hopefully you've taken Algebra 2 and have become a pro at both of these operations. But if not, we'll see that you can also Arithmetize on many Factor & FOIL questions.

Example 19

First, distribute the 2. It only gets distributed to one of the parenthetical terms (one of the binomials). When we FOIL, we'll technically be distributing it to the other term as well:

$$2(x + 1)(3x + 4)$$

$$(2x + 2)(3x + 4)$$

Now you can FOIL. Remember what it stands for: First, Outer, Inner, Last. You should get:

Common Algebra Mistakes

$$6x^2 + 8x + 6x + 8$$

If you want, you can use the Box Method to FOIL instead:

	$3x$	$+4$
$2x$	$6x^2$	$8x$
$+2$	$6x$	8

Add the terms:

$$6x^2 + 8x + 6x + 8$$

$$6x^2 + 14x + 8$$

So Choice C is the answer. As I said, you can also Arithmetize:

Let $x = 0$

$$2(x+1)(3x+4) = 2\left((0)+1\right)\left(3(0)+4\right)$$
$$= 2(1)(4)$$
$$= 8$$

Which choices also equal 8 when $x = 0$?

    A) $6(0)^2 + 8 = 8$ ✓

    B) $6(0)^2 + 11(0) + 4 = 4$ ✗

    C) $6(0)^2 + 14(0) + 8 = 8$ ✓

    D) $12(0)^2 + 28(0) + 16 = 16$ ✗

That eliminates Choices B and D, but we need to Arithmetize with a new number to choose between A and C:

Let $x = 1$

$$2(x+1)(3x+4) = 2\left((1)+1\right)\left(3(1)+4\right)$$
$$= 2(2)(7)$$
$$= 28$$

Which choice (of A and C only) equals 28 when $x = 1$?

A) $6(1)^2 + 8 = 6 + 8 = 14$ ✗

C) $6(1)^2 + 14(1) + 8 = 6 + 14 + 8 = 28$ ✓

Once again, Choice C is the correct answer. Knowing how to FOIL is definitely the better way to solve, but Arithmetizing gives you another tool that should guarantee you this question. It's better to take a little more time on questions like these to make sure that you don't make any careless errors.

And notice that Arithmetizing completely gets rid of the FOILing. That's because we only FOIL when we can't combine the terms in the parentheses. Once we Arithmetize, the terms can be combined, so we just add or subtract and move on. One of Arithmetize's great strengths is that it completely eliminates some of the most error-prone algebra steps, such as distributing, FOILing, and factoring.

Example 20

In this case, Arithmetizing is probably the better way to solve. Pick smart numbers that get rid of the fraction:

Let $x = 2$ and $y = 1$

$$\left(\frac{x}{2} + y\right)^2 = \left(\frac{2}{2} + 1\right)^2$$
$$= (1+1)^2$$
$$= (2)^2$$
$$= 4$$

Which choice also equals 4?

A) $\dfrac{(2)^2}{2} + (1)^2 = \dfrac{4}{2} + 1 = 3$ ✗

B) $\dfrac{(2)^2}{4} + (1)^2 = \dfrac{4}{4} + 1 = 2$ ✗

C) $\dfrac{(2)^2}{4} + \dfrac{(2)(1)}{2} + (1)^2 = \dfrac{4}{4} + \dfrac{2}{2} + 1 = 3$ ✗

D) $\dfrac{(2)^2}{4} + (2)(1) + (1)^2 = \dfrac{4}{4} + 2 + 1 = 4$ ✓

Common Algebra Mistakes

Choice D is the correct answer. Is the algebra faster? Maybe. But it's easy to make a mistake, so make sure that you FOIL correctly:

$$\left(\frac{x}{2} + y\right)^2$$

$$\left(\frac{x}{2} + y\right)\left(\frac{x}{2} + y\right)$$

$$\frac{x^2}{4} + \frac{xy}{2} + \frac{xy}{2} + y^2$$

$$\frac{x^2}{4} + \frac{2xy}{2} + y^2$$

$$\frac{x^2}{4} + xy + y^2$$

Same answer, but you've got to know how to multiply and add fractions. Also, make sure that you don't forget to FOIL. Many students mistakenly pick Choices A or B because they just square each term. That's a common algebra mistake! Write out both terms so that you can actually FOIL them correctly, without losing the middle term.

Factor & FOIL — The Basics

FOIL when you have two binomials.
- multiply the First terms
- multiply the Outer terms
- multiply the Inner terms
- multiply the Last terms
- combine like terms (usually in the middle)

Remember that squaring a binomial means you have to FOIL, so write out both of the terms so that you don't forget. This is a very common mistake:

$$(x + y)^2 = x^2 + y^2 \; \boldsymbol{\times}$$

There's going to be a middle term:

$$(x + y)^2 = x^2 + 2xy + y^2 \; \checkmark$$

If you don't trust yourself to FOIL correctly, Arithmetize so you can still get these questions right.

The Twists

Example 21

The twist is the factoring because it takes a little more effort than FOILing. In this question, they're also twisting the exponents to make you second-guess yourself. Basically, we can eliminate Choices B and D right from the start. If those binomials were to the 4th power, we'd have a very complicated answer with a <u>lot</u> of terms. In Choices A and C, it makes sense that squaring a square gets you a 4th power. Here's a simpler version:

$$\left(x^2\right)^2 = \left(x^2\right)\left(x^2\right)$$
$$= (x)(x)(x)(x)$$
$$= x^4$$

The coefficient 2 in front of the x would also be squared, so **the correct answer is Choice A.** We can FOIL it out to be sure:

$$\left(2x^2 - y^2\right)^2 = \left(2x^2 - y^2\right)\left(2x^2 - y^2\right)$$
$$= 4x^4 - 2x^2y^2 - 2x^2y^2 + y^4$$
$$= 4x^4 - 4x^2y^2 + y^4 \; \checkmark$$

If you were at all confused, you <u>must</u> take a chance and Arithmetize. Seeing that the x-terms change in the answer choices, I'd make sure that I don't get rid of x, but I'd let y disappear and see what happens:

Let $x = 1$
Let $y = 0$

$$4(1)^4 - 4(1)^2(0)^2 + (0)^4$$

$$4 - 0 + 0 = \underline{4}$$

A) $(2 - 0)^2 = 4 \; \checkmark$
B) $(2 - 0)^4 = 16 \; \boldsymbol{\times}$
C) $(4 - 0)^2 = 16 \; \boldsymbol{\times}$
D) $(4 - 0)^4 = $ something too big! $\boldsymbol{\times}$

Common Algebra Mistakes

Example 22

Only a fool wouldn't Arithmetize here. There are too many variables! Make up random numbers for a and b, and then use them to solve for x and y:

Let $a = 2$
Let $b = 1$

$$a^2 - b^2 = x \qquad a + b = y$$
$$2^2 - 1^2 = 3 \qquad 2 + 1 = 3$$

$$x = 3 \qquad\qquad y = 3$$

And don't forget what they're asking for:

$$a - b = ?$$
$$2 - 1 = \underline{1}$$

It's a little weird that the numbers we picked originally aren't getting plugged into the answer choices, but we're just following instructions. Stay organized so that you don't lose track of your variables and the answer value we want, which is 1.

A) $x - y = 3 - 3 = 0$ ✗

B) $xy = (3)(3) = 9$ ✗

C) $\dfrac{x}{y} = \dfrac{3}{3} = 1$ ✓

D) $\dfrac{y}{x} = \dfrac{3}{3} = 1$ ✓

It's annoying that two answers worked, but it doesn't take much effort to pick new numbers. Once you're good at Arithmetizing, you'll be able to use the remaining answer choices to help you pick smart values to plug in. In this case, I see that the problem was that x and y were the same, so the two fractions ended up looking the same. This time, I want to pick numbers that give me different values for x and y:

Let $a = 3$
Let $b = 1$

$$a^2 - b^2 = x \qquad a + b = y$$
$$3^2 - 1^2 = 8 \qquad 3 + 1 = 4$$

$$x = 8 \qquad\qquad y = 4$$

$$a - b = ?$$
$$3 - 1 = \underline{2}$$

C) $\dfrac{x}{y} = \dfrac{8}{4} = 2$ ✓

D) $\dfrac{y}{x} = \dfrac{4}{8} = \dfrac{1}{2}$ ✗

Now it's obvious that Choice C is the answer. The algebraic method might be faster, but if I didn't tell you that it involves factoring and FOILing, how would you know? In other words, what would you do if you saw a question like this in the midst of the real SAT?

Hopefully, you can Get Back to Basics by noticing the squared variables. You would see them, and instantly be reminded of factoring & FOILing because they almost always involve a squared term. It's really a matter of learning the pattern and turning it into a reflex. Once Factor & FOIL are on your mind, you should do what you can:

$$a^2 - b^2 = (a + b)(a - b)$$

This is the DOTS rule (Difference of Two Squares). It's a special kind of factoring that you need to memorize. When you have a squared term minus a squared term, they can be factored just like we did above. Now, we have:

$$x = (a + b)(a - b)$$

Next, substitute what we know. They gave us that $a + b = y$, and $(a + b)$ is one of our factors. We can substitute:

$$x = (a + b)(a - b)$$
$$x = y(a - b)$$

242

Common Algebra Mistakes

Pay attention to the question. They're asking for the value of $a - b$, so we're almost done. Just divide both sides by y to get $a - b$ alone:

$$\frac{x}{y} = \frac{y(a - b)}{y}$$

$$\frac{x}{y} = a - b$$

Again, Choice C is the correct answer. If that was confusing, that's okay. There's absolutely no reason to worry about the algebra solution.

Arithmetize shows its power on this question. Most people who see this question on a test would stare at it for a minute or two, hoping to notice the algebra shortcut but never finding it. They'd be forced to give up. Arithmetize gives you a way to save the points. It's like a parachute that you can release when you notice that you're free falling. Your real decision is not <u>whether</u> to pull the ripcord, but <u>when</u> to pull it. Why waste a full minute staring at a question and praying that the shortcut reveals itself? Pull the ripcord as soon as you notice that you're falling! Release the parachute and start Arithmetizing within just a few seconds. At the least, now you're not staring — you're solving.

Factor & FOIL — The Twists

Raising a binomial to the 3rd or 4th power is a mess, so it's usually not the answer. Don't let the higher exponents scare you. Use logic to find an answer, but FOIL it out if you can as a check.

If a question involves a squared term, it probably involves factoring or FOILing. Maybe it's a pure algebra question, or maybe it involves graphing quadratics. Either way, get in the habit of immediately jumping to Factor & FOIL in your mind when you see a squared term, especially if the question seems really hard.

When in doubt, Arithmetize.

Exercise: Factor & FOIL

#28 — Answer = C
Arithmetize. Let $x = 0$. Plugging in gives you $3(-2)(-5)$, which is 30. Only Choice C also equals 30 when you substitute 0 in for x.

#29 — Answer = A
Arithmetize. Since there are radicals in several answers, let $k = 4$. You can make $x = 0$, since the x-term doesn't seem to change in the answer choices. The original expression would be: $0^2 - 4(4) = \underline{-16}$. Plugging into the choices gives: A) $(-4)(4) = -16$, B) $(-\sqrt{8})(\sqrt{8}) = -8$, C) $(-8)(8) = -64$, D) $(-4)^2 = 16$. Only Choice A gives –16. The algebraic solution involves applying the DOTS factoring rule, but it's obviously risky because of the radicals.

#30 — Answer = D
Arithmetize. Let $p = 1$ and $q = 2$. That makes the original expression equal to 25. Only Choice D also equals 25 when you substitute. You could also FOIL, which is probably easier… if you don't make the common algebra mistake and pick Choice A!

#31 — Answer = D
FOIL the left side to get that $a = 16$.

#32 — Answer = D
Arithmetize. Letting $x = 0$ won't eliminate everything, but it's very fast at getting rid of two choices. The original expression is $(-5)^2 - (-5) = \underline{30}$, which eliminates Choice A and Choice C (the trap answer). You can finish it by starting over with $x = 1$. The main expression would be $(2 - 5)^2 - (2 - 5) = \underline{12}$, which will only match with Choice D: $2 - 20 + 30 = \underline{12}$.

#33 — Answer = C
You might try to Arithmetize. It's a great idea, but this is the rare case where the numbers don't work out. Instead, Get Back to Basics and FOIL the last expression: $(a + b)^2 = a^2 + 2ab + b^2$. Rearrange the expression, and you'll see that you have everything you need: $(a^2 + b^2) + 2(ab)$. Substitute: $12 + 2(4)$. Simplify to get 20.

Radicals

The Basics

The rules of algebra still apply. Show your work, and stay organized.

Example 1

Do what the question says and substitute for x:

$$\sqrt{a-1} - 3 = 1$$

Add 3 to both sides. Remember that you want to solve toward the variable, from the outside in. Don't start squaring things just yet. The 3 is further away from the variable, so we should deal with that first:

$$
\begin{array}{rcl}
\sqrt{a-1} - 3 & = & 1 \\
+3 & & +3 \\
\hline
\sqrt{a-1} & = & 4
\end{array}
$$

Now you can square both sides to get rid of the square root:

$$\left(\sqrt{a-1}\right)^2 = 4^2$$

$$a - 1 = 16$$

Solve for a:

$$a = 17$$

Choice C is the correct answer. You also could have Guess & Checked. It's definitely safer if you're not confident with advanced algebra.

Example 2

Start by going from two equations to one. Substitute the first equation in for x in the second equation:

$$3\left(4\sqrt{3}\right) = \sqrt{3y}$$

$$12\sqrt{3} = \sqrt{3y}$$

You could square both sides here, but you have to make sure you square everything correctly. Instead, let's break apart what we have into separate terms:

$$12 \cdot \sqrt{3} = \sqrt{3} \cdot \sqrt{y}$$

As you can see, both sides have a root 3. Eliminate them:

$$12 = \sqrt{y}$$

Now it's easier to solve by squaring:

$$12^2 = \left(\sqrt{y}\right)^2$$

$$144 = y$$

Choice D is the correct answer. Guess & Check would be difficult here because the numbers get big and radicals are weird. Of course, if this were the Calculator section, you could convert all of these radicals into decimals and let the calculator do the Guessing & Checking for you.

Radicals — The Basics

Obey the normal rules of algebra.

Don't start squaring things until you have to.

Sometimes it's better to break apart radicals so that you can understand what's really going on. Most of the breaking apart will involve multiplication.

The Twists

Example 3

There is absolutely no reason to solve this algebraically. In fact, doing so would make it very likely that you get this question wrong. You only have a handful of possible values of x, so just Guess & Check them!

First, let's get rid of k by substituting as instructed:

Radicals

$$\sqrt{x + 3} = x - 3$$

Guess $x = 1$ (from Choices A and B)

$$\sqrt{1 + 3} = 1 - 3$$

$$\sqrt{4} = -2$$

$$2 = -2 \ \boldsymbol{\times}$$

This doesn't work, so we can cross off Choices A and B. Sometimes you need to include the negative root, but this is not one of those times. I'm honestly not really sure why, except that the SAT doesn't want you to include it here. I guess because then the original equation wouldn't be a function? If you have no idea what I'm talking about, then don't worry about it! It doesn't matter. Let's keep checking:

Guess $x = 3$ (from Choice C)

$$\sqrt{3 + 3} = 3 - 3$$

$$\sqrt{6} = 0 \ \boldsymbol{\times}$$

Looks like Choice D will be the answer, but let's make sure:

Guess $x = 6$ (from Choice D)

$$\sqrt{6 + 3} = 6 - 3$$

$$\sqrt{9} = 3$$

$$3 = 3 \ \checkmark$$

Choice D is the correct answer. If you solved algebraically and fell for the trap answer Choice A, then shame on you! You were warned about extraneous solutions and you didn't bother to check for them. Will you be any more likely to remember on the real test? I don't think so. You don't get extra points for solving the "textbook" way. Guess & Check when you can!

Example 4

This question is very easy, but it's also very easy to make a careless mistake. The SAT is really trying hard to trick you here. Start by simplifying the radicals:

$$\sqrt{x} - \sqrt{16} = \sqrt{25}$$

$$\sqrt{x} - 4 = 5$$

Add 4 to both sides to get the x-term alone:

$$\sqrt{x} = 9$$

Now be careful! A lot of students pick Choice A here because they're moving too quickly. They see a square root and a 9, and their brains just really want the answer to be 3. It's not!

$$\left(\sqrt{x}\right)^2 = 9^2$$

$$x = 81$$

The correct answer is Choice D. What a mean little twist that question was!

Radicals — The Twists

If the answers are solution sets, don't bother solving algebraically. Just Guess & Check the choices.

Be very careful when working with square roots. It's very easy to skip steps because you're moving too quickly. Be thorough. Show your work. Stay organized.

Exercise: Radicals

#1 — Answer = B
Guess & Check. Substitute 8 in for k. Choice B gives $\sqrt{36 + 28} - 8 = 0$, which simplifies to $\sqrt{64} - 8 = 0$. If you choose to solve algebraically, add 8 to both sides before you square both sides.

Radicals

#2 — Answer = B

Guess & Check. If $x = -2$, then $\sqrt{16} + 4 = 0$, which is <u>not</u> true (the SAT does not include the negative root). This eliminates every choice except Choice B. Check it anyway to be sure: $\sqrt{49} + 4 = 11$.

#3 — Answer = C

Simplify the radical on the right by breaking apart the 18 into two radicals: $9\sqrt{2} = x\sqrt{9} \bullet \sqrt{2}$. Simplify further: $9\sqrt{2} = 3x\sqrt{2}$. The value of x is 3.

#4 — Answer = A

Square both sides: $2a = b^2$. Divide by 2: $a = \dfrac{b^2}{2}$. You can also Arithmetize by picking a value for a that produces a nice square root, like $a = 2$ or $a = 8$.

#5 — Answer = B

Guess & Check. Substitute 4 in for k. Check 0 first: $0 = 2 + \sqrt{4}$. This does <u>not</u> work (the SAT does not include the negative root), so Choice B is the answer. Check it to be sure: $3 = 2 + \sqrt{1}$.

Exponent ·Rules

The Basics

Unfortunately, you have to memorize these. It's guaranteed that they'll test at least one of these rules at least once per test. Since you'll be working with high exponents or weird combinations of exponents, Arithmetizing probably won't work. If you want a top score, spend some time on *Khan Academy* drilling these rules over and over and over again until you're comfortable with them.

Exponent Rules — The Basics

Learn the rules.

The Twists

Example 1

Almost every question will at least <u>feel</u> twisted. And the answer choices will be so similar that you won't have a good sense whether you're right or wrong. Try to go one step at a time so that you don't miss anything:

$$\sqrt[4]{\frac{1}{b}}$$

Start by turning the radical into a fractional exponent:

$$\left(\frac{1}{b}\right)^{\frac{1}{4}}$$

When a fraction is raised to an exponent, both the numerator and denominator are raised to that exponent:

$$\frac{1^{\frac{1}{4}}}{b^{\frac{1}{4}}}$$

But since 1 to any exponent is still 1, we're really looking at an expression like this:

$$\frac{1}{b^{\frac{1}{4}}}$$

We can move the *b*-term from the denominator to the numerator by negating the exponent.

$$b^{-\frac{1}{4}}$$

Choice B is the correct answer.

Example 2

This is a twisted mess. In general, I prefer to get rid of negative exponents first. They're confusing to look at, but getting rid of them is just about moving the term within the fraction. Plus, since the answer choices don't have any negative exponents, it's probably a good idea to get rid of them:

$$\frac{x^3 \bullet x^{\frac{3}{2}}}{y^2 \bullet y^{\frac{1}{2}}}$$

You have a few options for what to do next, but look ahead to your answers for ideas. Since it looks like there are both regular exponents and radicals in the choices, I'm going to convert the fractional exponents into radicals. There's no point in combining the two *x*-terms using the multiplication rule, since the answer choices tell me that I'd have to split them apart again anyway:

$$\frac{x^3\sqrt{x^3}}{y^2\sqrt{y}}$$

If you've come this far, you really can't get this question wrong, even if you don't actually know how to make our expression look exactly like the correct answer. Just use Process of Elimination:

A) Our *x*-term is on the top, and there's no reason why it would go back to the bottom. This is clearly wrong.

B) The bottom matches, but the top is different. Still, our version of the numerator has a lot of *x*'s, but this choice has somehow gotten rid of most of them. That's suspicious.

C) You probably recognize that our numerator needs to change in some way, but our

Exponent Rules

denominator seems fully simplified. Why would we suddenly lose the squared y-term? The bottom of this answer choice doesn't match our expectations.

D) This choice has the same denominator that we do. Plus, the numerator seems to have a lot of x's, just like ours. The distribution of the exponents on the x's is slightly different, but this is definitely the choice that is closest to our version of the expression. **Choice D is the best guess, and it's also the correct one.**

The final step, which you might be unsure about, is simplifying a radical. Essentially, we can split the $\sqrt{x^3}$ into two multiplied pieces:

$$\frac{x^3 \cdot \sqrt{x^2} \cdot \sqrt{x}}{y^2\sqrt{y}}$$

And since $\sqrt{x^2} = x$, we can pull an x out of the radical, leaving us with:

$$\frac{x^3 \cdot x \cdot \sqrt{x}}{y^2\sqrt{y}}$$

$$\frac{x^4\sqrt{x}}{y^2\sqrt{y}}$$

Confused? Yes! It's confusing! The exponent rules are annoying, especially when one question makes you apply multiple rules. But remember that most of these questions will be multiple choice, so you can let the choices suggest steps that you should take. You can also "meet in the middle", like we did. We knew enough to change the original expression a little bit, and then we compared the choices to what we had and found the closest match. Never forget that the choices limit the possibilities. We don't need to "solve" every question completely, like we need to for school. Our job is to "find" the right answer, and we don't get extra points for a perfect process. Just get to the end however you can.

> **Exponent Rules — The Twists**
>
> Go one step at a time. Write down everything you do so that you can easily check your work.
>
> Good luck!

Exercise: Exponent Rules 1

#1 — Answer = C

Divide both sides by 2. Raise each side to the -3 to cancel out the $-\frac{1}{3}$ (since you multiply the exponents, and this would make the exponent on the x equal to 1). You should have: $x = \left(\frac{k}{2}\right)^{-3}$. The exponent gets "distributed" to both the numerator and denominator: $x = \frac{k^{-3}}{2^{-3}}$. You can make the negative exponents positive by flipping the fraction: $x = \frac{2^3}{k^3}$. Simplify by raising 2 to the third power, which is 8. At the least, you should be able to eliminate Choices B and D because negatives don't ever jump from the exponent to the bases.

#2 — Answer = 3, 4, 6, or 12

You have no choice but to Arithmetize. Pick values for x that would get you to 81 when raised to an exponent. The easiest is probably $x = 81$. That means that the exponent needs to simplify to 1, which happens when $y = 3$ because $81^{\frac{3}{3}} = 81$. As another example, if $x = 9$, the exponent must be 2, which means that y must equal 6 because $9^{\frac{6}{3}} = 81$. You can get $y = 12$ when $x = 3$, and $y = 4$ when $x = 27$.

#3 — Answer = D

Rewrite the fractional exponent as a radical: $\sqrt[3]{4^2}$. Simplify to 16, then break it apart into factors: $\sqrt[3]{8} \cdot \sqrt[3]{2}$. The first term is a perfect cube that can be simplified to 2, so $2\sqrt[3]{2}$ is the answer. Even if you only know how to get $\sqrt[3]{16}$, you should still be able to eliminate Choices B and C because they're square roots and not cube roots, as well as Choice A because the 16 wouldn't become a 4 without changing something else.

Exponent Rules

#4 — Answer = D

Memorize Formulas. Rewrite the fractional exponent as a radical: $\sqrt[3]{a^4}$. There's no need to simplify further.

#5 — Answer = A

Start by using the rules of exponents. When you multiply exponential numbers with the same base, you add the exponents, so $x^{a^2-b^2} = x^{12}$. Since the bases are the same, you can focus on the exponents: $a^2 - b^2 = 12$. This should make you instantly think of factoring. Use the Difference of Two Squares rule to get: $(a-b)(a+b) = 12$. Since we're told that $a - b = 4$, we can substitute and solve: $4(a+b) = 12$. So $a + b = 3$.

#6 — Answer = A

Arithmetize. They never ask us to solve for a or b, so assume that they don't matter. As usual, it's best if we can work a zero into our Arithmetizing. Just make sure that you follow the rule established by the first equation. If we Arithmetize $a = 24$ and $b = 0$, then we've followed the rule ($24 - 2(0) = 24$) and created an excellent situation for the second expression: $\frac{3^{24}}{9^0}$. Since anything raised to the zero power is 1, this simplifies to 3^{24}. That's it! If you want to solve with traditional algebra, focus on the second part first. You can reduce the fraction using exponent rules, but first you need to get both the numerator and denominator to have the same base. Since $9 = 3^2$, you can substitute so that everything has 3 as a base: $\frac{3^a}{3^{2b}}$. When you are dividing exponential numbers, you subtract the exponents: 3^{a-2b}. It's no coincidence that the exponent is the exact same expression that they gave you at the beginning of the question. Just substitute to find the answer: 3^{24}. This is a hard question, but at the least, absolutely nobody should have picked Choice D. Sense the difficulty. This question is too hard for the easy "I give up" answer choice to be correct. Don't ever pick the "cannot be determined" choice on hard questions. It might be correct on an easy question, but you'd be able to prove that it's right.

Exercise: Exponent Rules 2

#7 — Answer = 5/12 or .416 or .417

Convert the radicals into fractional exponents: $\frac{k^{\frac{2}{3}}}{k^{\frac{1}{4}}}$. When the bases are the same and we're dividing, we subtract the exponents: $k^{\left(\frac{2}{3}-\frac{1}{4}\right)}$. At this point, it's really just about knowing how to subtract fractions by getting common denominators: $\frac{8}{12} - \frac{3}{12} = \frac{5}{12}$.

#8 — Answer = C

Memorize Formulas. If you know what a negative exponent means, this is incredibly easy. We can get rid of the negative by moving the base to the other part of the fraction: $\frac{(x+y)^{-1}}{1} = \frac{1}{(x+y)^1}$. Choice D is wrong because we can't split the grouping apart into two fractions. That's never allowed with fractions.

#9 — Answer = D

Take the square root of both sides to get the $\sqrt{a}$ that they're looking for. The rest is easier if you convert the radical on the b into a fractional exponent: $\sqrt{b^{16}} = (b^{16})^{\frac{1}{2}}$. When an exponent is raised to an exponent, we multiply the exponents, so $16 \cdot \frac{1}{2} = 8$.

#10 — Answer = C

Memorize Formulas. The calculator won't save you because the numbers are way too big! The right side of the equation gives a big clue — we should think in terms of base 2. Convert the 4 and 8 into 2s: $\left((2^2)^{100} \cdot (2^3)^{100}\right)^6$. Working from the inside out, when we have an exponent raised to an exponent, we multiply the exponents, so you'll multiply each exponent by 100: $\left(2^{200} \cdot 2^{300}\right)^6$. Still inside the parentheses, when two terms with the same base are multiplied, we add the exponents: $\left(2^{500}\right)^6$. The last step is to once again raise an exponent to an exponent by multiplying the exponents: $2^{3,000}$.

#11 — Answer = D

Make both exponents into fractions by converting the radical: $\sqrt{b} = b^{\frac{1}{2}}$. When multiplying terms with the same base, we add the exponents, which essentially

Exponent Rules

turns this into a common denominators question: $\frac{2}{3} + \frac{1}{2} = \frac{4}{6} + \frac{3}{6}$.

#12 — Answer = D

Get rid of the negative by moving the term and exponent into the bottom of a fraction: $(16)^{-\frac{1}{2}} = \frac{1}{(16)^{\frac{1}{2}}}$. Turn the fractional exponent into a radical and simplify: $\frac{1}{\sqrt{16}} = \frac{1}{4}$.

Exercise: Exponent Rules 3

#13 — Answer = 1/6 or .166 or .167

Convert the radical into a fractional exponent, which would include the c as the numerator: $\sqrt{x^c} = x^{\frac{c}{2}}$. When we raise an exponent to an exponent, we multiply the exponents: $(x^{\frac{c}{2}})^3 = x^{\frac{3c}{2}}$. Set the two fractional exponents equal to each other and solve: $\frac{3c}{2} = \frac{1}{4}$.

#14 — Answer = A

Memorize Formulas. Since the denominators of both fractional exponents are the same, we can put both terms under the same radical when we convert. That gets Choice A in just one step. At the least, you should be able to eliminate the other answers. Why would we get a 15? The two exponents won't mix like that. And there's no negative exponent, so we shouldn't introduce actual fractions.

#15 — Answer = D

Normally, we'd want to convert the radical into a fractional exponent, but this time it's better to convert the fractional exponent into a radical: $3^{\frac{2}{a}} = \sqrt[a]{3^2}$. Since both terms are an a-root, we can put them under a single radical. Simplify the exponents and multiply the resulting terms: $\sqrt[a]{9 \cdot 4}$.

#16 — Answer = B

Arithmetize actually works well here. The easiest number that we're allowed to pick is $x = 1$, which would simplify the original equation to $\sqrt[4]{16}$, which is 2. Only Choice B would give the same value: $(4)^{\frac{1}{2}} = \sqrt{4} = 2$. If you want to solve algebraically, you should start by factoring the quadratic into $(x + 3)^2$. Convert the radical into a fractional

exponent: $\left((x + 3)^2\right)^{\frac{1}{4}}$. When an exponent is raised to an exponent, multiply the exponents. Reduce the resulting fraction to get Choice B.

#17 — Answer = C

Without a calculator, you need to convert both bases into 2s: $\frac{(2^3)^5}{(2^2)^9}$. Simplify the exponents by multiplying: $\frac{2^{15}}{2^{18}}$. When we divide, we subtract the exponents: 2^{-3}. Convert this into a fraction and simplify: $\frac{1}{2^3} = \frac{1}{8}$.

#18 — Answer = D

This is extremely difficult to manipulate. Your best bet is to focus on the easiest part. The y-terms wouldn't change all that much when we multiply these two parenthetical groups. If you turned the fractional exponent into a radical, you'd end up with $y^2\sqrt{y}$ pretty quickly. Only Choice D has that term, and so you could pretty confidently guess that answer without working with the x-terms at all. The actual way to simplify the x's is to use the first exponent rule to start. When we multiply terms with the same base, we add the exponents. We'd need to get common denominators, but we would get $x^{-\frac{4}{3}}$. Move it to the bottom of the fraction to get rid of the negative, then convert the fractional exponent into a radical: $\frac{1}{\sqrt[3]{x^4}}$.

Simplifying the radical would confirm Choice D.

Absolute Value

The Basics

The mathematical definition of Absolute Value is a little confusing. Technically, the absolute value of a number is its distance from 0. Basically, it's the positive version of a number:

$$|4| = 4$$

$$|-4| = 4$$

It's helpful to think of absolute value bars as "special" parentheses that magically turn a number positive. But there's one thing that you <u>cannot</u> do:

$$|x - 7| = x + 7 \text{ ✗}$$

No! They don't work like that. They turn the <u>result</u> positive. So we'd need to put a number in for x to see what's really going on:

$$|3 - 7| = |-4| = 4$$

Luckily, most Absolute Value questions can be solved by using Guess & Check or Arithmetize, which means that you're usually putting in numbers anyway.

Example 1

You're given three possible values of x. Try them!

Let $x = -2$

$$|(-2) - 2| - 2 = 0$$

$$|-4| - 2 = 0$$

$$4 - 2 = 0 \text{ ✗}$$

Cross out Choice A. Let's try B:

Let $x = 0$

$$|(0) - 2| - 2 = 0$$

$$|-2| - 2 = 0$$

$$2 - 2 = 0 \text{ ✓}$$

That's it! No need to check anything else. **Choice B is the correct answer.**

Example 2

This is a good example of the Memorize Formulas strategy at its most pure. This question involves absolutely no actual math. You just need to know the definition of absolute value. Since the result of the absolute value expression will <u>never</u> be negative, there are no solutions. **Choice A is correct, simply based on the definition of absolute value.**

Absolute Value — The Basics

Absolute Value bars are like "special" parentheses that turn the <u>result</u> positive. As always, solve for whatever is in those parentheses first, then do the absolute value.

But if they're asking for the number of solutions, pay attention to the resulting value. Absolute value expressions will never produce a negative result.

The Twists

Example 3

The question is worded in a confusing way, but essentially it's asking which graph will have only positive values of y (because $y \geq 0$).

You should be able to use your knowledge of graphs to see that Choices A, B, and C will all dip below the x-axis because they all have a y-intercept of (0, –3). Essentially, we're Plugging Points Into Equations and choosing the easiest possible point of $x = 0$.

But if we put 0 in for x in Choice D, we see that it does not have a negative value:

$$y = |0 - 3|$$

Absolute Rules

$$y = \left| -3 \right|$$

$$y = 3$$

In fact, Choice D is correct because an absolute value function cannot be negative. Remember, it turns whatever result we get positive, so even negative values of x will become positive. The graph of Choice D looks like this:

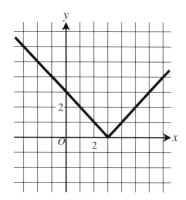

Example 4

While most absolute value questions don't involve math and only test the definition, we occasionally have to deal with the twist and actually solve an absolute value equation. The key is that there are two possible equations, and we need to solve them both. The first is obvious. Just drop the absolute value bars:

$$2x - 8 = 4$$

$$2x = 12$$

$$x = 6$$

This is going to give you the trap answer in most cases. The actual twist is that we need to account for the possibility that the absolute value bars turned a negative into a positive. In other words, the result of the absolute value could have been –4, which the bars would have made into a positive, disguising another solution. Create an expression with the negative value:

$$2x - 8 = -4$$

$$2x = 4$$

$$x = 2$$

We can now see that the least possible value is 2. Absolute value reminds me a lot of Inequalities. For the most part, the normal rules of algebra still apply, but there's one weird thing that we need to watch for. With absolute value, it's the fact that we sometimes need two equations to find all of the solutions. With inequalities, it's that multiplying or dividing by a negative flips the direction of the inequality. The SAT loves to test whether you've memorized these kinds of algebra quirks.

Absolute Value — The Twists

Absolute value graphs "bounce" off the x-axis because they cannot be negative.

If you need to solve an absolute value equation, you'll need to make two equations to account for the positive and negative results.

Exercise: Absolute Value

#1 — Answer = B
You can Arithmetize with a few numbers to test out the choices. But if you understand absolute value, Choice B is the only possible answer. The absolute value bars make the value inside them positive. The only way to get the entire expression equal to 0 is with subtraction.

#2 — Answer = 9/2 or 4.5
To solve absolute value equations, you need to create two equations that represent the positive and negative values. If you solve $x - 5 = \frac{1}{2}$, you'll get that $x = \frac{11}{2}$. But you also need to solve $x - 5 = -\frac{1}{2}$ to find x when the absolute value is negative. You will get the answer, which is $x = \frac{9}{2}$.

#3 — Answer = B
Arithmetize. But you'll need to be clever. If $n = 10$, then both $x = 6$ and $x = 14$ should satisfy the

Absolute Value

inequality. Since 6 doesn't work in Choices A and C, you can eliminate them. Try negative values next. If $n = -10$, then both $x = -6$ and $x = -14$ should satisfy the inequality. Choice D doesn't work when x is –6: $|-6| - (-10) \leq 5$ can be simplified to $6 + 10 \leq 5$. It works in Choice B, though.

#4 — Answer = B

If we try to make two equations for this absolute value, we will have some trouble. Zero is the same, whether it's negative or positive. You can just solve the one equation: $x - 7 = 0$. The only solution is $x = 7$.

#5 — Answer = C

Guess & Check. Plugging Choice C into the equation creates a valid result: $|18 - 6| = 12$. The properties of absolute value equations don't really matter for this question.

#6 — Answer = C

Guess & Check. There is no sane reason to try algebra here. You know that absolute value equations make negatives hard, and the answer choices make it clear that negatives matter. The smart first guess is Choice C because it's the smallest positive number. It produces a valid equation: $|6 - 2| = |10 - 6|$. Again, the properties of absolute value expressions don't really matter here because both numbers are already positive: $|4| = |4|$.

Must Be True

The Basics

The SAT used to have a lot of these questions. The ACT still does, but they mostly test Geometry. Essentially, these are perfect Arithmetize questions. Having real numbers is much better than trying to think about the situation using only logic. Remember, the SAT is trying to trick you, so you shouldn't really trust your logic. At least support your theory with numerical proof.

Example 1

Pick some easy-to-use numbers. Just make sure that you obey any rules that they give you. In this case, a must be positive, and b must be negative.

Let $a = 1$
Let $b = -2$

$$x = \frac{a}{b - a}$$

$$= \frac{1}{-2 - 1}$$

$$= \frac{1}{-3}$$

$$x = -\frac{1}{3}$$

So x is negative. **That matches with Choice C, which is the correct answer.** See how easy these are if you use numbers?

Example 2

This question looks like it's going to be a huge mess, but it's extremely easy if you Arithmetize. Again, pick a number that makes your life easy:

Let $x = 1$

$$y = \frac{\frac{1}{1}}{1 + \frac{1}{1}}$$

And just like that, the fractions-within-fractions that make this question look hard disappear:

$$y = \frac{1}{1 + 1}$$

$$y = \frac{1}{2}$$

Will y always equal $\frac{1}{2}$? No. If we had picked a different value for x, we would have gotten a different value for y. But this one point is enough for us to eliminate all of the wrong answers. **Only Choice A is true based on our result.** Whenever you see algebra that looks hard, you should at least try to Arithmetize. The odds are good that it will work.

Must Be True — The Basics

Arithmetize. Obey the rules in the question.

The Twists

Example 3

Different kinds of numbers will behave differently when you put them into equations. Exponents, in particular, make things tricky. Compare:

positive number greater than 1

$$x = 2$$
$$x^2 = 4 \qquad \text{Numbers get bigger.}$$
$$x^3 = 8$$

positive number less than 1

$$x = \frac{1}{2}$$
$$x^2 = \frac{1}{4} \qquad \text{Numbers get smaller!}$$
$$x^3 = \frac{1}{8}$$

negative number less than –1

$$x = -2$$
$$x^2 = 4 \qquad \text{Numbers all over the place!}$$
$$x^3 = -8$$

Must Be True

And this question is telling us to work with a negative number that's greater than −1:

Let $x = -\dfrac{1}{2}$

    I. $-\dfrac{1}{2} < \dfrac{1}{4}$ ✓

    II. $\dfrac{1}{4} < -\dfrac{1}{8}$ ✗

    III. $-\dfrac{1}{2} < -\dfrac{1}{8}$ ✓

So the correct answer is Choice C. Notice how unexpected the result was. This is why picking numbers is so helpful! Though, some people still get this wrong because they have trouble seeing Roman numeral III. They want $-\dfrac{1}{8}$ to be the smaller number, but we have to think in terms of a number line. Which number would be further to the left, $-\dfrac{1}{8}$ or $-\dfrac{1}{2}$?

Example 4

The worst twist is when the SAT expects you to try these different kinds of numbers without telling you to. That's why the key to these questions is that the choice <u>must</u> be true. It's not enough for it to be true sometimes. For this example, most people will Arithmetize with some obvious numbers that match the inequality rule at the beginning:

Let $a = 1$
Let $b = 2$

$$x = \dfrac{1}{2}$$

We quickly see that both Choices B and C are wrong. But we can't just assume that Choice A is right. We need to prove it. That will require some cleverness. We would be wise to try some negative numbers:

Let $a = -2$
Let $b = -1$

$$x = \dfrac{-2}{-1} = 2$$

But that doesn't change our answer at all. We need to really challenge ourselves to specifically prove Choice A wrong, which means somehow getting a negative number. We just saw that two negatives make a positive, but what about one negative?

Let $a = -2$
Let $b = 2$

$$x = \dfrac{-2}{2} = -1$$

There we go! We've now proven Choice A wrong, which **leaves us with Choice D**. When you encounter these situations, just remember to try different combinations of positive and negative integers and fractions. Use the choices to NARROW YOUR FOCUS to numbers that are likely to have an effect.

Must Be True — The Twists

Different types of numbers behave in different ways, so it's best to try a variety and eliminate choices as you go. Try positive and negative integers and fractions.

Exercise: Must Be True

#1 — Answer = B
Plug Points Into Equations. You have the values for x and y, so substitute into the parabola:
$0 = a(-1)^2 + b(-1) + c$. This simplifies to:
$0 = a - b + c$. Add b to both sides to get Choice B.

#2 — Answer = B
Arithmetize. Try different kinds of numbers to prove each of the numerals wrong. If $a = 1$ and $b = -1$, then the original equation is true, but numerals I and II are not. Since numeral III can be rewritten as $\dfrac{1}{a^2} = \dfrac{1}{b^2}$, it must be true because we already know that $a^2 = b^2$.

Must Be True

#3 — Answer = C

If you subtract x from both sides, you'll eliminate the x's and simplify the inequality to $y > 0$, which is Choice C. You could also Arithmetize.

#4 — Answer = A

Arithmetize. Your first instinct will be simple positive numbers, like $a = 1$ and $b = 2$. That's fine, but it won't eliminate any of the numerals. You can't just pick choice D, though. Sense the difficulty. They wouldn't ask a question like this if it were that easy. There must be a twist. Try to twist up your Arithmetize by trying negatives. If $a = -1$ and $b = 1$, you'd eliminate numerals II and III. Since there's no choice that lets us pick numeral I all by itself, we now have enough proof to pick Choice A. We can prove numeral I wrong by picking two negatives, like $a = -2$ and $b = -1$.

#5 — Answer = A

This is very hard! You definitely need to be comfortable with function notation, but it's hard to visualize no matter how good you are at math. You could Arithmetize by making up a line with a negative slope: $f(x) = -2x + 5$. Testing numeral I means picking two consecutive integers for x. In our example, we could see that $f(1) = 3$ and $f(2) = 1$, which makes numeral I true. We could try some other values of a, including negatives, but we'll continue to see that numeral I is true. The logical reason is that $a + 1$ will always be one unit to the right of a on the x-axis, and since the slope is going down, moving to the right on the x-axis will always give lower values. If we tried numeral II in our equation, we'd find it true. To see that it's not always true, we'd need another equation, like $g(x) = -2x - 5$. Now, $g(0) = -5$, which is less than 0. Essentially, numeral II is asking about the y-intercept. There's no reason the y-intercept <u>must</u> be greater than 0, so numeral II is false. Numeral III is the hardest to prove false. Most people will try positive numbers. Using our original equation $f(x) = -2x + 5$, we could use $a = 2$ and see that $f(2) = 1$ and $f(4) = -3$. In this case, numeral III is false because 1 is not less than –3. But if we had made $a = -2$, we would have gotten a different result: $f(-2) = 9$ and $f(-4) = 13$. This time, numeral III is true. This goes to show that we can't necessarily trust the first numbers that we Arithmetize, and that we need to try a few combinations for each condition. Regardless, numeral I is the only statement that must be true. You might also try quickly sketching some lines to visualize what's happening. The key is that you can't do all of this in your head, thinking only in abstract mathematical concepts. Give your brain something to hold onto. Numbers, equations, and graphs all turn your logic into something real that you can see and manipulate.

Point of Intersection

The Basics

Usually we think of a Point of Intersection on a graph, but most of the SAT questions that test this idea will not use a graph at all. That's why the Point of Intersection questions are considered Algebra and not Linear Properties.

Example 1

If you Plug Points Into Equations, make sure that you test the point in <u>both</u> equations:

Choice A

$$4(1) - (16) = -12$$

$$4 - 16 = -12$$

$$-12 = -12 ✓$$

$$2(1) + 3(16) = -34$$

$$2 + 48 = -34 ✗$$

This is why you check both points! The SAT loves to trick you by making the point work in one equation, but not the other. If you know that they're trying to trap you like this, it's easy to avoid the mistake.

Choice B

$$4(-1) - (8) = -12$$

$$-4 - 8 = -12$$

$$-12 = -12 ✓$$

$$2(-1) + 3(8) = -34$$

$$-2 + 24 = -34$$

$$22 = -34 ✗$$

Once again, the point works in the first equation, but not in the second equation.

Choice C

$$4(-5) - (-8) = -12$$

$$-20 + 8 = -12$$

$$-12 = -12 ✓$$

$$2(-5) + 3(-8) = -34$$

$$-10 - 24 = -34$$

$$-34 = -34 ✓$$

Now we're done. **Choice C is the correct answer because the point satisfies both equations.** There's no need to check Choice D since we've already proven that Choice C works.

If you want a faster way to solve, use the "stack" method (Elimination) to get rid of one of the variables. You need to have a positive and negative version of the same variable so that you can add the equations and cross them out. Start by multiplying the first equation by 3 so that we can get a $-3y$ to match the $+3y$ in the second equation:

$$3 \left[4x - y = -12 \right]$$

I know it's weird to see an equals sign in parentheses, but I think it helps you remember to distribute the 3 to all parts:

$$12x - 3y = -36$$

Now we can "stack" the equations and add them together. We conveniently eliminate the y's:

$$\begin{aligned} 12x - 3y &= -36 \\ + \ 2x + 3y &= -34 \\ \hline 14x \quad\ &= -70 \end{aligned}$$

Divide by 14:

$$\frac{14x}{14} = \frac{-70}{14}$$

$$x = -5$$

Since Choice C is the only answer where $x = -5$, you don't need to plug back in to solve for y.

Point of Intersection

Sometimes you will, though. In general, the "stack" method is the fastest way to solve most Point of Intersection questions. Unless...

Example 2

...there's an easy way to substitute. This example gives us equations that have an x or y all by itself. We should substitute one equation in for the variable in the other equation. But first, it's a good idea to eliminate things that make our lives complicated. Solve the fraction problem now and it won't cause headaches later on:

$$\frac{x}{3} = y$$

$$x = 3y$$

This is much easier to work with. You can substitute $3y$ in for x in the second equation:

$$1 + 2(y + 2) = 3y$$

Distribute and combine like terms:

$$1 + 2y + 4 = 3y$$

$$2y + 5 = 3y$$

Subtract:

$$\begin{array}{r} 2y + 5 = 3y \\ -2y \quad\quad -2y \\ \hline 5 = \ y \end{array}$$

No need to solve for x. **Choice A is the correct answer.** It's worth pointing out, however, that Choice C is the value of x. The SAT does this a lot. They want you to solve for the wrong variable, and then be so excited that you forget to check back with the question. Get in the habit of rereading the question so that you are sure that you've solved for the correct variable and aren't falling for a trap.

Point of Intersection — The Basics

You will almost never need to graph a Point of Intersection question.

If the choices give you points, then Plug Points Into Equations, like we always do. Just make sure that you check both equations.

If one of the equations is equal to a variable that's all by itself, you can probably substitute.

The most common way to solve Point of Intersection questions is by using the "stack" method (Elimination). Choose a number that will allow you to eliminate one of the variables. Make sure that you multiply all parts of the equation by that number.

The Twists

Example 3

The fractions do a good job of twisting this Point of Intersection question so that it looks hard to solve. Untwist it by getting rid of the fractions:

First equation:

$$4 \left[\frac{1}{4}x + \frac{1}{2}y = 7 \right]$$

$$x + 2y = 28$$

Second equation:

$$4 \left[x - \frac{1}{4}y = 10 \right]$$

$$4x - y = 40$$

Let's re-stack them so we can get a better look:

$$x + 2y = 28$$
$$4x - y = 40$$

We should try to eliminate a variable. We can easily eliminate the y's if we multiply the bottom

Point of Intersection

equation by 2, but I'm going to do it the hard way to show you something else. If we want to eliminate the x's instead, we'll need to multiply the top equation by <u>negative</u> 4. That means we need to also distribute the negative to the entire equation:

$$-4\left[x + 2y = 28\right]$$

$$-4x - 8y = -112$$

Re-stack the equations, and add them together:

$$\begin{array}{r} \cancel{-4x} - 8y = -112 \\ + \;\; \cancel{4x} - \;\;y = \quad 40 \\ \hline -9y = \;\; -72 \end{array}$$

Divide by –9:

$$\frac{\cancel{-9}y}{\cancel{-9}} = \frac{-72}{-9}$$

$$y = 8$$

Another twist here is that they don't want the value of x or y. We need both to find the value of $\frac{x}{y}$. Plug 8 in for y so that we can find x. It's easier to use the second equation:

$$x - \frac{1}{4}(8) = 10$$

$$x - 2 = 10$$

$$x = 12$$

Now find the value of the expression:

$$\frac{x}{y} = \frac{12}{8}$$

$$\frac{x}{y} = \frac{3}{2}$$

So $\frac{3}{2}$ or 1.5 are both correct answers. This definitely seems like a hard question, but it's not significantly different from the basic Point of Intersection questions. In fact, the process for solving these is almost always the same. With practice, you should be able to get these questions right every time without much effort.

Example 4

This one looks different. Or does it? Get Back to Basics. There are two equations, and the question seems to be asking when they're equal to each other. That's exactly what a point of intersection is! Follow instructions by setting f equal to g. We'll also replace the x's with a's, since that's what we're supposed to do with functions:

$$a^2 - 8a + 16 = a - 2$$

The squared term tells us that we're probably going to need to factor. We usually factor when everything is on one side of the equation and the other side is equal to 0. Let's move everything over to the left side:

$$\begin{array}{r} a^2 - 8a + 16 = \quad a - 2 \\ -a + 2 \quad -a + 2 \\ \hline a^2 - 9a + 18 = 0 \end{array}$$

Factor:

$$a^2 - 9a + 18 = 0$$

$$(a - 6)(a - 3) = 0$$

So our solutions are:

$$a = 6 \text{ and } a = 3$$

Both 6 and 3 are correct answers.

Point of Intersection — The Twists

Make equations easier to work with. Eliminate fractions by multiplying to Get Back to Basics.

Whenever they give you two equations, it's probably a Point of Intersection question. Sometimes they use functions or weird phrasing to confuse you. Basically, if you're looking for where two equations equal each other, it's a Point of Intersection question.

Point of Intersection

Exercise: Point of Intersection

#1 — Answer = C

Guess & Check. The only point that works in both equations is (3, –1). You can also use the "stack" method by multiplying the first equation by 4 and eliminating the y-terms.

#2 — Answer = 0

Use the "stack" method. Multiply the first equation by 2 so that you can eliminate the y-terms: $2x - 2y = -24$. The addition of the two equations gets you $3x = 0$.

#3 — Answer = 7

Substitute the first equation in for the y-term in the second equation. After you distribute the 2, you should get: $2x^2 + 2 - 5 = 9 - 2x$. Since this is a quadratic, move the terms so that everything is on one side and equal to 0. You should get: $2x^2 + 2x - 12 = 0$. You can divide by 2 to make it easier to factor: $x^2 + x - 6 = 0$. The factors are –3 and 2, but the question wants only positive values of x, so $x = 2$. Substitute 2 in for x into the first equation to find that $y = 5$. Add 2 and 5 as instructed to get that $x + y = 7$.

#4 — Answer = C

The easiest way to solve this is by graphing a rough sketch, which is rare for Point of Intersection questions. Even without a calculator, you should be able to see that the line has a y-intercept of 1, and the parabola has a y-intercept of –6. Since the parabola opens upward (because $a > 0$), the line must intersect it twice. Solving algebraically is very long, and the numbers don't work out nicely. You could set the equations equal to each other, and then manipulate so that one side is equal to 0. Use the discriminant to find the number of solutions (see Quadratic Properties packet for more information on all of these rules about intercepts and discriminants).

#5 — Answer = C

You could easily graph a rough sketch, but you'd still need to find the point of intersection. Simplify the second inequality: $x > 3$. Substitute 3 in for x in the first inequality. Since 3 is basically the minimum value of x, you'd be finding all of the y-values where x is greater than 3. You should get $y > -3$.

#6 — Answer = B

Guess & Check. Choice A works in the first inequality, but not in the second. Choice B works in both. Just be careful that you plug the values into the right variables. The SAT is hoping that you get confused, since x is first in the bottom equation but y is first in the top.

Advanced Algebra

The Basics

Use the SAT math strategies to solve if you're not comfortable with algebra. Mostly, you just need to be clever.

Example 1

There's absolutely no reason to do this algebraically. Watch how easy it is to Arithmetize:

Let $x = 0$

$$\cfrac{1}{\cfrac{1}{(0)+1} + \cfrac{1}{(0)-4}}$$

$$\cfrac{1}{\cfrac{1}{1} - \cfrac{1}{4}}$$

$$\cfrac{1}{\cfrac{3}{4}}$$

Remember that dividing by a fraction is the same as multiplying by its reciprocal:

$$1 \cdot \frac{4}{3} = \frac{4}{3}$$

So our answer choice should also be $\frac{4}{3}$ when we put 0 in for x. This part should be quick:

A) $2(0) - 3 = -3$ ✗

B) $(0)^2 - 3(0) - 4 = -4$ ✗

C) $\dfrac{2(0) - 3}{(0)^2 - 3(0) - 4} = \dfrac{3}{4}$ ✗

D) $\dfrac{(0)^2 - 3(0) - 4}{2(0) - 3} = \dfrac{4}{3}$ ✓

You could probably see that Choice D would be the correct answer just by looking at the expressions. This is by far the best way to answer this question. Using 0 makes it very simple, and there's no rule that says we can't.

But here's the algebra in case you're curious:

$$\cfrac{1}{\cfrac{1}{x+1} + \cfrac{1}{x-4}}$$

Start by getting a common denominator for the bottom fractions:

$$\cfrac{1}{\left(\dfrac{x-4}{x-4}\right)\dfrac{1}{x+1} + \dfrac{1}{x-4}\left(\dfrac{x+1}{x+1}\right)}$$

$$\cfrac{1}{\dfrac{x-4}{(x+1)(x-4)} + \dfrac{x+1}{(x+1)(x-4)}}$$

We can now add the two fractions, and while we're at it, we should FOIL the two binomials:

$$\cfrac{1}{\dfrac{2x-3}{x^2 - 3x - 4}}$$

Once again, dividing by a fraction is the same as multiplying by the reciprocal, so we'll end up flipping the bottom fraction upside-down:

$$\frac{x^2 - 3x - 4}{2x - 3}$$

We still got that Choice D is the correct answer. But there's a lot to keep track of. Arithmetizing is better.

Example 2

This is a very hard question. Your instinct is probably to subtract 12 and get the whole equation equal to 0. Not a bad idea, but it's basically impossible to factor cubic functions (x^3).

There's not much else you can do except try different things and see what happens. Maybe if we moved the negative term to the other side:

$$x^3 + 3x = 4x^2 + 12$$

Hmm… We can factor out some stuff:

$$x(x^2 + 3) = 4(x^2 + 3)$$

261

Advanced Algebra

Whoa. That worked out well. Divide out the common term to make the answer obvious:

$$x \, \cancel{(x^2 + 3)} = 4 \, \cancel{(x^2 + 3)}$$

$$x = 4$$

The correct answer is 4. This is why you shouldn't give up on a question just because you don't see a clear path to the solution. It might be a question that you skip at first so that you don't run out of time on the section, but you could return to it and just keep trying different things. What we did here is a version of "factoring by grouping", which you probably learned at some point in Algebra 2 and forgot. Honestly, it's not particularly useful on the SAT.

Guess & Check actually works well here. The SAT usually picks small numbers for these Advanced Algebra questions. It's unlikely that you'll end up with a fractional answer on such a hard question. But who knows? Try a few simple things:

Let $x = 0$

$$0^3 - 4(0)^2 + 3(0) = 12$$
$$0 - 0 + 0 = 12 \; ✗$$

Let $x = 1$

$$1^3 - 4(1)^2 + 3(1) = 12$$
$$1 - 4 + 3 = 12 \; ✗$$

Let $x = 2$

$$2^3 - 4(2)^2 + 3(2) = 12$$
$$8 - 16 + 6 = 12 \; ✗$$

At this point, it's starting to get tedious, but it feels like we're getting closer. Plus, I see lots of 3s and 4s in the equation, especially since 12 is a multiple of both. I'd keep going:

Let $x = 3$

$$3^3 - 4(3)^2 + 3(3) = 12$$
$$27 - 36 + 9 = 12 \; ✗$$

Let $x = 4$

$$4^3 - 4(4)^2 + 3(4) = 12$$

Yes, 4^3 is hard, but you hopefully notice that $4(4)^2$ is also three 4s multiplied together. They cancel:

$$\cancel{4^3} \; \cancel{-4(4)^2} + 3(4) = 12 \; ✓$$

The point is, don't be afraid to try things. Sometimes you'll have no idea what you're doing until the answer just falls into your lap. Even after taking countless SATs and seeing thousands and thousands of math questions, I still find myself stumped occasionally. I just play with the equation a bit, trusting that something will happen that gets me closer to the answer. The SAT likes to trick you, but there's only so much they can do. Persistence will eventually beat them.

Advanced Algebra — The Basics

Arithmetize! It can make a lot of the tough algebra much much easier.

Don't give up so easily. Try some simple manipulations so that you can see the equation in a slightly different way. Eventually something will click and you'll know what to do.

The Twists

Example 3

If you haven't learned function notation yet, these questions can seem impossible. But we can follow our Plug Points Into Equations strategy. The only difference is that the point is written a little differently than we're used to. The first sentence of this question actually gives us a point:

$$h(3) = 14$$

Advanced Algebra

This is really the point (3, 14). The 3 goes in place of x because that's just how function notation works. We often say that $f(x) = y$, and so we can see how that would give us an (x, y) coordinate:

$$f(x) = y$$
$$f(1) = 2$$

$$(1, 2)$$

The f is not a variable. It's kind of like a definition, just like the question says. In this Example, they're telling us that they've made up an equation, and they're calling it h:

$$h(x) = 2x^2 + c$$

The problem is that we don't know part of the equation because they used c instead of a number. But we can figure out what c is because they also gave us a point that works in the equation. Let's take the point (3, 14) and plug it into the function:

$$14 = 2(3)^2 + c$$

$$14 = 2(9) + c$$

$$14 = 18 + c$$

$$-4 = c$$

Once again, Plugging Points Into Equations makes our lives much easier. The rest of the question tells us to find the y-value when $x = -3$. Here's how it would look with function notation, but remember that the –3 on the left is really only instructions that tell us to put –3 in for x. We can also replace c with –4 now that we know its value:

$$h(-3) = 2(-3)^2 - 4$$

$$h(-3) = 2(9) - 4$$

$$h(-3) = 18 - 4$$

$$h(-3) = 14$$

So Choice A is the correct answer.

Example 4

This is a very twisted functions problem, but we should trust our strategies. We're still being given a point, but it's weird because it has a variable in it:

$$g(k - 2) = 0$$

$$(k - 2, 0)$$

As always, Plug Points Into Equations, even if they're really weird. In this case, $x = k - 2$:

$$0 = (k - 2)^2 - 4(k - 2) + 3$$

FOIL and distribute:

$$0 = k^2 - 4k + 4 - 4k + 8 + 3$$

Combine like terms:

$$0 = k^2 - 8k + 15$$

Factor:

$$0 = (k - 5)(k - 3)$$

The possible values of k are 5 and 3. Either would be a correct answer. Once you recognize that they're giving you a point and an equation, this very difficult question becomes pretty easy to untwist.

Advanced Algebra — The Twists

Don't be intimidated by function notation. Remember that if $f(x) = y$, then you probably have points (x, y) that you can plug into the function/equation f.

Even if points seem weird, trust the strategies. Plug Points Into Equations.

Advanced Algebra

Exercise: Advanced Algebra

#1 — Answer = B

You could Guess & Check by trying the three easy answers. When they don't work, you're left with Choice B. To solve algebraically, put the left side over 1, and cross-multiply to get $(x-2)^2 = 8$. Take the square root of both sides, then simplify the resulting radical.

#2 — Answer = D

To get $g(4)$, plug 4 in for x, which makes the second equation $g(4) = 5 - f(8)$. Find $f(8)$ using the first equation. You should get –6. Use that value in the second equation: $g(4) = 5 - (-6)$. Don't lose the negative, and you'll get 11.

#3 — Answer = 5/4 or 1.25

Plug Points Into Equations. You're given half a point ($x = 2$) and need to find the other half. Just plug 2 in for x. There's no need to try to factor or anything. This is Advanced Algebra because it's about functions, not because the math is particularly difficult.

#4 — Answer = C

You can Arithmetize, but you'll have to be very organized. To solve algebraically, factor the second equation: $g(x) = 3x(x^2 - x - 5)$. It's no coincidence that one of the factors is exactly the same as $f(x)$. This tells us that the correct answer will be a function that is divisible by both $x^2 - x - 5$ and $2 - 3x$. If you're clever with algebra, you can multiply these two factors together to better understand what the correct answer will be composed of:
$(2 - 3x)(x^2 - x - 5) =$
$2(x^2 - x - 5) - 3x(x^2 - x - 5)$. The second term is the exact same as $g(x)$. The first term is simply 2 times $f(x)$. You can rewrite this as $2f(x) - g(x)$, which is Choice C. Don't worry if this confuses you. It's basically the upper limit of the SAT's difficulty, so you're unlikely to see something exactly like this again.

#5 — Answer = 7/3 or 2.33

Plug Points Into Equations. The first part tells us that the point (6, –11) is included in the function. Plug it in: $-11 = a(6) - 3$. Solve to find that $a = -\frac{4}{3}$. Now that you know the full function, you can find $f(-4)$. Plug the values into the function: $-\frac{4}{3}(-4) - 3$. You should get $\frac{7}{3}$.

Dividing Polynomials

The Basics

First, you should remember how to do regular long division:

$$3\overline{)475}$$

3 goes into 4 once:

$$\begin{array}{r} 1 \\ 3\overline{)475} \end{array}$$

Multiply 3 by 1:

$$\begin{array}{r} 1 \\ 3\overline{)475} \\ 3 \end{array}$$

Subtract:

$$\begin{array}{r} 1 \\ 3\overline{)475} \\ -3 \\ \hline 1 \end{array}$$

Drop down the 7:

$$\begin{array}{r} 1 \\ 3\overline{)475} \\ -3 \downarrow \\ \hline 17 \end{array}$$

Divide 17 by 3:

$$\begin{array}{r} 15 \\ 3\overline{)475} \\ -3 \downarrow \\ \hline 17 \end{array}$$

Multiply by 5:

$$\begin{array}{r} 15 \\ 3\overline{)475} \\ -3 \downarrow \\ \hline 17 \\ -15 \end{array}$$

Subtract and drop the 5:

$$\begin{array}{r} 15 \\ 3\overline{)475} \\ -3 \downarrow \\ \hline 17 \\ -15 \\ \hline 25 \end{array}$$

Divide 3 into 25, and finish the long division:

$$\begin{array}{r} 158 \\ 3\overline{)475} \\ -3 \downarrow \\ \hline 17 \\ -15 \\ \hline 25 \\ -24 \\ \hline 1 \end{array}$$

There's still a 1 left, but here's where we'll stop. Your calculator would keep dividing and give you a decimal, but we want the 1 as a remainder. When we use long division on polynomials, we'll always have a remainder. The process is similar to long division of numbers, but there are a few quirks that make it even harder. To be honest, 99% of SAT testers do <u>not</u> need to know this. You can almost always Arithmetize, and if you can't, you can probably skip the question and spend your time on other questions. If that sounds like you, skip the next page until you see the word **Arithmetize** again.

Example 1

Set it up like this:

$$x - 2\overline{)x^3 - 4x^2 + 2x + 5}$$

Even though we have two numbers on the outside, we only use the first one in the division process. How many times does x go into x^3?

$$\begin{array}{r} x^2 \\ x - 2\overline{)x^3 - 4x^2 + 2x + 5} \end{array}$$

Just like before, we multiply, but now we'll use the entire $x - 2$ term:

Dividing Polynomials

$$\begin{array}{r} x^2 \\ x-2\overline{\smash{\big)}\,x^3-4x^2+2x+5} \\ \underline{x^3-2x^2} \end{array}$$

This part is where everybody messes up. Just like before, we need to subtract, but we need to make sure that we subtract the <u>entire</u> term. That means we'll need to distribute a negative:

$$\begin{array}{r} x^2 \\ x-2\overline{\smash{\big)}\,x^3-4x^2+2x+5} \\ \underline{-(x^3-2x^2)} \end{array}$$

That $-2x^2$ is going to become positive after we distribute, so our subtraction will end with:

$$\begin{array}{r} x^2 \\ x-2\overline{\smash{\big)}\,x^3-4x^2+2x+5} \\ \underline{-x^3+2x^2} \\ -2x^2 \end{array}$$

Just like before, we'll drop down the next term:

$$\begin{array}{r} x^2 \\ x-2\overline{\smash{\big)}\,x^3-4x^2+2x+5} \\ \underline{-x^3+2x^2}\downarrow \\ -2x^2+2x \end{array}$$

How many times does x go into $-2x^2$?

$$\begin{array}{r} x^2-2x \\ x-2\overline{\smash{\big)}\,x^3-4x^2+2x+5} \\ \underline{-x^3+2x^2}\downarrow \\ -2x^2+2x \end{array}$$

Multiply $x-2$ by $-2x$, and subtract. Make sure that you don't forget to distribute the negative:

$$\begin{array}{r} x^2-2x \\ x-2\overline{\smash{\big)}\,x^3-4x^2+2x+5} \\ \underline{-x^3+2x^2}\downarrow \\ -2x^2+2x \\ \underline{-(-2x^2+4x)} \\ -2x \end{array}$$

Bring down the 5:

$$\begin{array}{r} x^2-2x \\ x-2\overline{\smash{\big)}\,x^3-4x^2+2x+5} \\ \underline{-x^3+2x^2}\downarrow\downarrow \\ -2x^2+2x \downarrow \\ \underline{-(-2x^2+4x)}\downarrow \\ -2x+5 \end{array}$$

Divide $-2x$ by x:

$$\begin{array}{r} x^2-2x-2 \\ x-2\overline{\smash{\big)}\,x^3-4x^2+2x+5} \\ \underline{-x^3+2x^2}\downarrow\downarrow \\ -2x^2+2x \downarrow \\ \underline{-(-2x^2+4x)}\downarrow \\ -2x+5 \end{array}$$

Multiply and subtract:

$$\begin{array}{r} x^2-2x-2 \\ x-2\overline{\smash{\big)}\,x^3-4x^2+2x+5} \\ \underline{-x^3+2x^2}\downarrow\downarrow \\ -2x^2+2x \downarrow \\ \underline{-(-2x^2+4x)}\downarrow \\ -2x+5 \\ \underline{-(-2x+4)} \\ 1 \end{array}$$

We're out of terms to drop, and x does not divide into 1. So just like before, we have a remainder. Here's how we'd write this result as an expression:

$$x^2-2x-2+\frac{1}{x-2}$$

So the main answer is just a polynomial, but the remainder is a fraction, where the denominator is the same denominator as our original expression. **The correct answer is Choice A.**

As you can see, Dividing Polynomials questions are a nightmare. You won't always be able to **<u>Arithmetize</u>**, but it can make things much much easier:

Dividing Polynomials

Arithmetize

Let $x = 0$

$$\frac{(0)^3 - 4(0)^2 + 2(0) + 5}{(0) - 2}$$

$$\frac{0 - 0 + 0 + 5}{0 - 2} = -\frac{5}{2}$$

Now we have a value that our answer choices should equal when x is 0:

Choice A

$$(0)^2 - 2(0) - 2 + \frac{1}{(0) - 2}$$

$$-2 - \frac{1}{2}$$

$$-\frac{5}{2} \checkmark$$

Remember, we have to check all of the choices. We wouldn't know that the answer is A if we hadn't done it the long way first. So let's keep going:

Choice B

$$(0)^2 - 2(0) + 6 - \frac{7}{(0) - 2}$$

$$6 + \frac{7}{2} \text{ ✗}$$

Choice B is clearly wrong. Notice that Arithmetizing is still hard. It's very easy to lose a negative near the fraction.

Choice C

$$(0)^2 - 6(0) - 10 + \frac{25}{(0) - 2}$$

$$-10 - \frac{25}{2} \text{ ✗}$$

That's going to be way less than $-\frac{5}{2}$. Keep going.

Choice D

$$(0)^2 - 6(0) + 14 - \frac{23}{(0) - 2}$$

$$14 + \frac{23}{2} \text{ ✗}$$

Doesn't work. **So only Choice A gave us a valid answer, and now we can confidently choose it.** Arithmetizing is still a pain, but that's because Dividing Polynomials questions are among the most difficult on the SAT. Anything we can do to make them a little easier is worthwhile, and Arithmetizing is probably safer than long division because there are fewer negatives to lose.

There's one other way to solve these. You may have learned about synthetic division in school. Personally, I find the process confusing and error prone, but if you're already comfortable with it, you can use it to solve instead of long division. If you've never heard of it before, don't worry about it. Learning it isn't worth it for this one question. Just Arithmetize!

Dividing Polynomials — The Basics

First of all, don't do this unless you have to. If you can factor, that's definitely the best solution. But you'll know when you hit a true Dividing Polynomials question because it will look almost exactly like the Example.

Try to Arithmetize, but remember to check all of the choices, and be careful with negatives, especially around the fraction at the end.

If you can, learn how to do the long division. You might not be able to Arithmetize on certain twisted versions of these.

The Twists

Example 2

This one looks like we won't be able to Arithmetize because there are no answer choices, but actually we can! The x carries through the whole equation, so we can pick a number.

Dividing Polynomials

Let $x = 0$

$$\frac{4(0)^2 - 3(0) + 7}{(0) + 2} = 4(0) - 11 + \frac{k}{(0) + 2}$$

$$\frac{7}{2} = -11 + \frac{k}{2}$$

$$11 + \frac{7}{2} = \frac{k}{2}$$

$$\frac{22}{2} + \frac{7}{2} = \frac{k}{2}$$

$$\frac{29}{2} = \frac{k}{2}$$

$$29 = k$$

Wow! That wasn't bad at all. **The correct answer is 29.** This is another great question to stress the idea that sometimes things on the SAT just work out if you let them. Try something! Don't let a confusing question paralyze you. Even if you Arithmetize and it doesn't work, you probably won't waste much time, especially if you're using 0.

In case you're curious, here's how the work for the long division would look:

$$\begin{array}{r} 4x - 11 \\ x + 2 \overline{)4x^2 - 3x + 7} \\ -(4x^2 + 8x) \\ \hline -11x + 7 \\ -(-11x - 22) \\ \hline 29 \end{array}$$

Since 29 is the remainder, we'd write our answer like this:

$$4x - 11 + \frac{29}{x + 2}$$

And the 29 is exactly where our k was in the original equation.

Dividing Polynomials — The Twists

Even when they twist the question by removing the choices or introducing another variable, there's still a chance you can Arithmetize. If you've got the time, try something!

Exercise: Dividing Polynomials

#1 — Answer = 23
Arithmetize. If $x = 0$, then the equation simplifies to $-\frac{5}{3} = 6 - \frac{A}{3}$. Solve for A, and you'll get 23. You can also do long division, and the remainder will be –23, but the negative is included in the equation already, in front of the fraction.

#2 — Answer = C
You have to do this the long way. When you divide, you should get $x + 3 + \frac{12}{x - 7}$. The remainder would be 12.

#3 — Answer = 4
This is much easier than it looks. Focus on the division. What would you need to divide $20x^2$ by in order to get $5x$? The value of k would have to be 4. You could do the long division to test it. You could also Arithmetize from the start. You can't pick 0 for x because that would eliminate the k term. But if you make $x = 1$, the equation becomes $\frac{26}{k + 2} = 2 + \frac{14}{k + 2}$. Subtract the fraction to get: $\frac{12}{k + 2} = 2$. Cross-multiply: $12 = 2k + 4$. Solve, and you'll find that $k = 4$.

#4 — Answer = B
Arithmetize. If $x = 0$, the equation becomes: $-\frac{12}{b} = -5 - \frac{17}{b}$. Get the b's on the same side: $\frac{5}{b} = -5$. Solving will get you $b = -1$. You can solve algebraically using a similar process as question #3, but it's harder because you have to be very comfortable with long division.

268

Imaginary Numbers

The Basics

There are two very distinct types of Imaginary Numbers questions. One is much easier than the other, so the Basics/Twists difference is very obvious. If you see imaginary numbers in a question, take note of where you are in the section. If you're near the beginning, it's probably the easy kind. If you're near the end, it's probably a little twisted. Luckily, both types follow a fairly repetitive pattern to solve.

Example 1

Follow instructions by writing these two expressions as a sum:

$$7 + 4i + 3 + 8i$$

Combine like terms:

$$10 + 12i$$

That's it. **Choice C is the correct answer.** Easy Imaginary Numbers questions will really be about combining like terms. You can pretend the i is a variable. Yet another example of how the SAT throws weird things at you just to make you doubt yourself.

Example 2

This is also mostly standard Algebra. Distribute that negative to both parts:

$$(9 + 6i) - (4i^2 - 8i)$$

$$9 + 6i - 4i^2 + 8i$$

Here's the rare case where we need to actually use i to solve. This is why:

$$i = \sqrt{-1}$$
$$i^2 = \left(\sqrt{-1}\right)^2$$
$$i^2 = -1$$

We need to make this substitution:

$$9 + 6i - 4(-1) + 8i$$

There are a lot of negatives, so we need to be careful:

$$9 + 6i + 4 + 8i$$

Combine like terms:

$$13 + 14i$$

Choice D is the correct answer.

Imaginary Numbers — The Basics

i doesn't usually matter on easy questions. Just combine like terms.

If you have an i^2, replace it with -1. But make sure that you don't lose any negatives.

The Twists

Example 3

Hard Imaginary Numbers questions will be easy to recognize. They almost always have i in the denominator of a fraction. We need to get it out of there. In math, we want to avoid having i in the denominator for a reason that isn't really important. Just learn this process.

We need to multiply the top and bottom by the <u>conjugate</u>, which is kind of like an opposite version of a binomial. As the directions say, $3 + 5i$ and $3 - 5i$ are conjugates. Here's how we multiply:

$$\frac{2}{3 + 5i} \left(\frac{3 - 5i}{3 - 5i} \right)$$

Notice that we're really just multiplying by 1. This is how we change the way the fraction looks without actually changing its value. Let's rewrite it so that it's easier to see the next few steps:

$$\frac{2(3 - 5i)}{(3 + 5i)(3 - 5i)}$$

Imaginary Numbers

The numerator is easy. Just distribute:

$$\frac{6 - 10i}{(3 + 5i)(3 - 5i)}$$

The denominator isn't as tricky as it seems. You might recognize that it's the factored form of a Difference of Two Squares (DOTS) situation. FOIL it out to be sure:

$$\frac{6 - 10i}{9 - 15i + 15i - 25i^2}$$

As we'd expect with DOTS, there's no middle term because the $15i$'s cancel:

$$\frac{6 - 10i}{9 - \cancel{15i} + \cancel{15i} - 25i^2}$$

$$\frac{6 - 10i}{9 - 25i^2}$$

Remember that we can replace i^2 with –1. That will completely remove the i from the denominator:

$$\frac{6 - 10i}{9 - 25(-1)}$$

As always, watch those negatives when we combine the terms:

$$\frac{6 - 10i}{9 + 25}$$

$$\frac{6 - 10i}{34}$$

The answer choices split apart the numerator, which we can do by dividing each piece by 34:

$$\frac{6}{34} - \frac{10i}{34}$$

Reduce:

$$\frac{3}{17} - \frac{5i}{17}$$

Choice D is the correct answer. Even though this is definitely more twisted than the basic questions, it's actually not that different from regular algebra. So even if this is the first time you've ever worked with imaginary numbers, you should be able to apply your other algebra skills to these questions and get them right. Just watch those negatives!

Even if this beyond your algebra skill, you can still increase your odds of guessing correctly. Notice that Choices A and B look a <u>lot</u> like the original expression. These are traps answers. The SAT is hoping that you're so confused that you do something simple and move on, but we can't just chop up a fraction like that. The bottom is a group, so we need to take it apart very carefully with lots of weird steps (as we just saw with the conjugate). If you recognize that this is supposed to be a hard question, you can confidently cross out the choices that are way too easy. That would leave you with a 50/50 guess between Choices C and D. That's not bad for doing literally zero work! Look for opportunities like this when you're totally stumped by a hard question. You should at least know that hard questions won't have easy answers.

Imaginary Numbers — The Twists

When there's an imaginary number in the denominator of a fraction, multiply both the top and bottom by the conjugate to eliminate it.

Exercise: Imaginary Numbers

#1 — Answer = B
Distribute the negative to both parts to get: $1 + 4i - 5 + 2i$. Combine like terms. The i doesn't really matter.

#2 — Answer = D
Product means multiply: $(3 + 5i)(2 - i)$. FOIL to get: $6 - 3i + 10i - 5i^2$. Replace the i^2 with –1, then combine like terms. Don't lose the negative!

#3 — Answer = C
Multiply the numerator and denominator by the conjugate, which is $4 - 6i$. You'll have to FOIL. You should get: $\dfrac{20 - 30i - 4i + 6i^2}{16 - 36i^2}$. Replace the i^2 with

Imaginary Numbers

-1, then combine like terms to get: $\dfrac{14 - 34i}{52}$.
Reduce and break apart the fraction. At the least, you should be able to tell that Choices A and B are way too easy for a hard question. Cross them out and guess between C and D.

#4 — Answer = C

Get Back to Basics. We can tell by the setup that this will involve the conjugate, even if the actual wording of the question is strange. Multiply the numerator and denominator by the conjugate, which is $2 + 5i$.
After you FOIL, you'll get: $\dfrac{20 + 50i - 6i - 15i^2}{4 - 25i^2}$.
Replace the i^2 with -1, which makes both terms positive. Combine like terms to get: $\dfrac{35 + 44i}{29}$. As the question says, the b term is the one in front of the i.
You can break apart the fraction to get it: $\dfrac{35}{29} + \dfrac{44i}{29}$.

#5 — Answer = B

In order to add fractions, you need a common denominator, which is $4i$ in this case. Multiply the first fraction by $\dfrac{2}{2}$ and the second fraction by $\dfrac{i}{i}$. You should get: $\dfrac{6 - 8i + i + 2i^2}{4i}$. Replace the i^2 with -1, then combine like terms: $\dfrac{4 - 7i}{4i}$. You can't have i in the denominator, so you have to multiply both the numerator and denominator by i for the same reason that you usually multiply by the conjugate. You'll get: $\dfrac{4i - 7i^2}{4i^2}$. Replace the i^2's with -1 to get: $\dfrac{4i + 7}{-4}$.
Divide each term by -4 to separate the two terms: $-i - \dfrac{7}{4}$, which can be rearranged into Choice B.

Linear Properties

The Basics

There's such a wide variety of SAT questions that involve lines that students often feel like there's too much that they need to memorize. In fact, almost everything boils down to $y = mx + b$. When they give you lines in other formats, Get Back To Basics.

Example 1

This is very transparently about $y = mx + b$. I prefer to start with the b because it's a little easier to find on a graph. Let's compare:

$$y = mx + b$$
$$y = 3x - 1$$

The y-intercept is –1. That means we can eliminate Choices B and D.

The slope is 3, which means we'll rise 3 boxes and run (to the right) 1 box. **Choice C is the correct answer.** Choice A has a slope of $\frac{1}{3}$, which is a common way the SAT tries to trick you. It's very important that you remember that slope is rise over run. Remember it this way: first you need to rise in the morning, then you can go for your run. If you run first, you're just sleepwalking!

Example 2

If you want, you can manipulate this equation until it's back into $y = mx + b$ form. But the easier way to solve this is to use the Plug Points Into Equations strategy. Whenever we're talking about intercepts, we already know one half of the point. In this case, the y-intercept will have an x-coordinate of 0 (because it intercepts the y-axis). Plug 0 in for x:

$$\frac{2}{3}(0) - \frac{3}{4}y = -2$$

$$-\frac{3}{4}y = -2$$

Multiply by the reciprocal to eliminate the fraction:

$$\left(-\frac{4}{3}\right) \cdot -\frac{3}{4}y = -2\left(-\frac{4}{3}\right)$$

$$y = \frac{8}{3}$$

There's nothing else you need to do. **The correct answer is $\frac{8}{3}$.**

Example 3

Get Back to Basics. This question has a lot of steps, but you can find your way through this mess by continuously bringing yourself back to $y = mx + b$.

We start with 2 points that lie on a line. When you have 2 points, find the slope between them. Don't worry about why. Just know that it'll probably be important because lines are all about slopes and intercepts:

$$\text{points} = (1, 11) \text{ and } (-1, 9)$$

$$\text{slope} = \frac{y_1 - y_2}{x_1 - x_2}$$

$$= \frac{11 - 9}{1 - (-1)}$$

$$= \frac{2}{2}$$

$$\text{slope} = 1$$

Let's start filling in our $y = mx + b$:

$$y = (1)x + b$$

It's not much, but it's a start. Now what? Well, what else can we plug into this linear equation? We have 2 points, and we have an equation. Use our favorite strategy — Plug Points Into Equations:

$$11 = (1)(1) + b$$

$$11 = 1 + b$$

$$10 = b$$

Linear Properties

And just like that, we now have the equation for our first line:

$$y = x + 10$$

Move on to the second line, again focusing on $y = mx + b$. We are given the slope and a point on the line. Plug in what you know:

$$y = mx + b$$

$$2 = (-2)(1) + b$$

$$2 = -2 + b$$

$$4 = b$$

So our second line has the equation:

$$y = -2x + 4$$

The question wants the point of intersection, so we can set the two lines equal to each other (because they'll have the same y-value at the intersection point).

$$x + 10 = -2x + 4$$

Solve for x:

$$
\begin{array}{rcl}
x + 10 & = & -2x + 4 \\
+2x - 10 & & +2x - 10 \\
\hline
3x & = & -6
\end{array}
$$

$$\frac{3x}{3} = \frac{-6}{3}$$

$$x = -2$$

We're so close. We have the x-coordinate of the point of intersection (which the question tells us is a), but we need the y-coordinate. Pick an equation and Plug Points Into Equations:

$$y = x + 10$$
$$y = (-2) + 10$$
$$y = 8$$

The point of intersection is (–2, 8), but the question wants the value of $b - a$, so we have one last step:

$$b - a = 8 - (-2)$$

$$b - a = 10$$

The correct answer, after a very long process, is 10. This is a long question, but it's not particularly hard if you stay focused on lines and $y = mx + b$.

Linear Properties — The Basics

Everything revolves around $y = mx + b$. When in doubt, return to this standard.

m is the slope. You must memorize the various slope formulas. First you have to rise in the morning, then you can go for your run. If you run, then rise, you're sleepwalking!

$$\text{slope} = \frac{\text{rise}}{\text{run}} = \frac{\Delta y}{\Delta x} = \frac{y_1 - y_2}{x_1 - x_2}$$

b is the y-intercept, which always has an x-coordinate of 0.

(x, y) are points on the line. Don't forget one of our most essential strategies: Plug Points Into Equations.

The Twists

Example 4

It's important that you become familiar with all of the terms and ideas described in The Twists. The rules about parallel lines tend to be the most important. Yes, they have the same slope, but a lot of questions ask about parallel lines without explicitly saying so. When they talk about "infinitely many" or "no solutions", they're really talking about parallel lines.

Linear Properties

When lines have no solution, they must have the same slope but different intercepts. When they have infinitely many solutions, they must have the same slope and the same intercepts.

In Example 4 we should try to get the equations to look exactly the same because they're supposed to be the same line. The first problem is that 15 does not equal 75. Let's fix that:

$$5 \left[3x + 5y = 15 \right]$$

$$15x + 25y = 75$$

If these equations have infinitely many solutions, then the coefficients also need to be equal:

$$15x + 25y = 75$$
$$ax + by = 75$$

$$a = 15$$
$$b = 25$$

It's really that simple. Now just finish up by finding the value of the expression:

$$\frac{a}{b} = \frac{15}{25}$$

$$\frac{a}{b} = \frac{3}{5}$$

So $\frac{3}{5}$ or 0.6 are both valid answers. This is a good example of a question where the math is relatively easy. The difficulty comes from understanding what they're asking.

Example 5

The SAT often asks about lines without really asking about lines. This question can be solved without thinking about lines at all, but incorporating $y = mx + b$ into our thinking makes it easier to visualize what's happening and keep track of our work. I strongly encourage you to think about lines whenever they ask about "no solutions" and there's no quadratic equation involved (more on parabolas in the Quadratic Properties packet).

In this case, you can pretend that each side of the equation is its own linear equation:

$$y = 3kx - 4$$
$$y = 3(x + 6) + 2(x - 5)$$

If you were given this, you'd probably Get Back to Basics and simplify the second equation by distributing and combining like terms:

$$y = 3x + 18 + 2x - 10$$

$$y = 5x + 8$$

We know that "no solutions" is code for "same slope", so compare the slopes of the two equations. They should be the same, so we can create a separate equation to show that:

$$y = 3kx - 4$$
$$y = 5x + 8$$

$$3k = 5$$

Solve for k:

$$k = \frac{5}{3}$$

That's it! The answer is just $\frac{5}{3}$. Maybe you could have pulled that number out of the original equation, but breaking it apart helps us NARROW OUR FOCUS to what really matters — the slopes.

Example 6

This is the rare case where you actually need to graph the inequalities. Some of my students are very methodical when they graph lines. They draw out the axes and make little boxes or tick marks. If you have to graph something on the SAT without a calculator, chances are good that the little details won't matter much, so don't waste time making a pretty graph when a rough sketch will do.

To start, ignore the inequality signs. Just graph these as lines, focusing on slopes and intercepts. It should look something like this:

Linear Properties

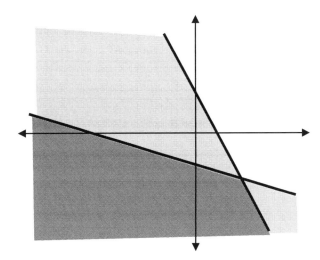

The top equation has a positive y-intercept and a steep negative slope. The bottom equation has a negative y-intercept and a flatter negative slope. They should clearly intersect in the 4th Quadrant.

Now we have to shade the solution sets. Both equations have a "$y <$ " shading so we need to shade where the y's are less than the line. In other words, shade down:

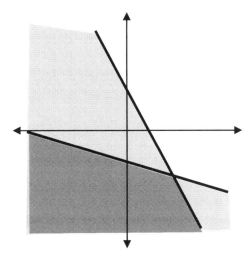

The two shaded regions overlap in the bottom left, and that's what we want. Solutions to the system will be shaded by <u>both</u> inequalities. So there are definitely solutions in Quadrants III and IV.

The benefit of a rough sketch is that you can adjust it as needed. It's unclear at first, but if we extend our lines, we'll see that there are also solutions in Quadrant II:

So the correct answer is Choice A. There are no solutions in Quadrant I, mostly because our second line never passes through that quadrant.

One other thing to note: technically our first line should be dashed because it uses the < symbol, and not the ≤ symbol. In other words, the solution set does not include the line itself, and we normally use a dashed line to show that. But it doesn't matter for this question. Again, rough sketches are usually all you need.

Linear Properties — The Twists

We normally think of solutions as points of intersection, but some Linear Properties questions involve twists that require a deeper understanding of how lines work.

Parallel lines have no solutions.

…unless they are exactly the same line. In that case, the lines have infinitely many solutions.

Inequalities intersect, but they also have shaded solution sets that overlap. Graph the lines normally, but shade either up or down depending on whether y is > or < the rest of the equation.

Linear Properties

Exercise: Linear Properties

#1 — Answer = D
Plug Points Into Equations. First, you have to make the equation. The $y = mx + b$ equation of this line is $y = -\frac{2}{5}x$. There's no b because the line passes through the origin. The only point that works is Choice D. If you picked anything else, shame on you! You got tricked by the SAT. They purposely designed those wrong answers to lure you in, and you didn't do enough to check that your instincts were right.

#2 — Answer = D
Parallel lines have the same slope. Find the slope of the line p by using the slope formula. The slope is $\frac{1}{2}$. Use the slope formula a second time for line q: $\frac{1}{2} = \frac{0-(-4)}{k-0}$. Simplify and solve for k. Alternatively, once you have the slope of line q, you could Get Back to Basics and build a $y = mx + b$ equation: $y = \frac{1}{2}x - 4$. Plug Points Into Equations to finish the job: $0 = \frac{1}{2}(k) - 4$.

#3 — Answer = 240
Treat the inequalities like equals signs, and set them equal to each other: $12x = -6x + 360$. Solve for $x = 20$. The question wants b, which corresponds to y, so substitute x into the easier equation: $y = 12(20)$. (see the Common Algebra Mistakes packet for more on Inequalities)

#4 — Answer = C
Plug Points Into Equations. The line becomes: $b = ka + c$. Since k represents the slope, you can just rearrange the equation to solve for k. Subtract c and divide by a to get Choice C.

#5 — Answer = D
Lines have no solutions when they are parallel. You can rearrange the two equations so that they're in $y = mx + b$ form. The first equation would be: $y = -\frac{5}{a}x + \frac{2}{a}$. Don't let the messiness bother you. The second equation would be: $y = -\frac{4}{3}x + 2$. Only the slopes matter. Parallel lines have the same slope, so set the two slopes equal to each other: $\frac{-5}{a} = \frac{-4}{3}$. Cross-multiply and divide to solve for a.

#6 — Answer = B
Arithmetize. If $a = 1$, then the points are (1, 0) and (0, 1). Sketch them on a rough graph, and you'll see that the slope is clearly negative.

#7 — Answer = C
Get Back to Basics. Perpendicular lines have negative reciprocal slopes. The safest way to answer this question is to get each of the equations back into basic $y = mx + b$ form. The original equation should be $y = \frac{4}{5}x - 4$. The perpendicular slope would be $-\frac{5}{4}$. Only Choice C has the that slope.

#8 — Answer = D
Plug Points Into Equations. First, create the equation of this line. You don't know the slope, so the best you can do is say that the equation won't have a b because the line passes through the origin: $y = mx$. You can plug one of the points into the equation: $4 = mc$. Doesn't help much. Try the other point: $c = 36m$. We're kind of stuck when we have two variables in one equation, but luckily we don't have just one equation — we have two! We can solve this like a system. Substitute the second equation in for c in the first: $4 = m(36m)$. Simplify to get $\frac{1}{9} = m^2$ and $\frac{1}{3} = m$. Substitute into the second equation to find $c = 36(\frac{1}{3})$. If the end was confusing, you could still Guess & Check at various points in this process. Remember to try different things, working both backwards and forwards, whenever you're stuck.

#9 — Answer = 14
First, find the slope of the graph of $f(x)$. You can count the boxes, and you'll see that the slope is $\frac{2}{3}$. The question says that $g(x)$ has a slope that is 3 times larger, which would be 2. Using the slope and the given x-intercept, you can use $y = mx + b$ to find the equation of $g(x)$: $0 = (2)(-1) + b$. Solving for b, you'd get that $g(x) = 2x + 2$. Now find that $g(6) = 2(6) + 2$, which is 14.

Quadratic Properties

The Basics

Hopefully, the first page of this packet gives you a good summary of the most essential quadratic ideas. It's really important to know all of the different vocabulary since they'll constantly switch the words they use, just to confuse you. The Vertex Form tends to be the one that people have the most trouble with. For some reason, it's more important on the SAT than it was in school.

Example 1

The root form is usually the easiest place to start. This graph has x-intercepts at –3 and 1, so:

Root Form
$$y = (x + 3)(x - 1)$$

You can't really get the entire standard form from the graph. You can only find that the y-intercept (c-term) is –3. You'll have to FOIL the root form for the rest:

$$y = (x + 3)(x - 1)$$

$$y = x^2 - x + 3x - 3$$

Standard Form
$$y = x^2 + 2x - 3$$

You can get the vertex form just by looking at the vertex of the graph. The vertex is at (–1, –4). Plug those points into the right places, remembering that the x-value will be negated (in this case the two negatives make a positive):

Vertex Form
$$y = (x + 1)^2 - 4$$

You can also find the vertex form by completing the square with the standard form. Just to show you how it's done:

$$y = x^2 + 2x - 3$$

$$y = (x^2 + 2x) - 3$$

$$y = (x^2 + 2x + 1) - 3 - 1$$

$$y = (x + 1)^2 - 4$$

Completing the square is an important skill on the SAT. It's a quick way to switch between different versions of a quadratic equation, and it'll be essential for Circle Properties questions. Completing the square is described in more detail right before the Exercise.

The **range** of any function is the set of possible y-values. For a parabola, the limit will be the vertex, which is also the maximum or minimum. In this case, the range can be expressed as:

$$y \geq - 4$$

The parabola turns when y is –4, but it continues on toward infinity on either side. It does so symmetrically, meaning that the two sides of the parabola are mirror images of each other across the vertex, or axis of symmetry. Notice that (–2, –3) and (0, –3) are both the same "distance" from the turning point. You go one unit up and one unit over on each side of the vertex. The next easily recognizable points are (–3, 0) and (1, 0), which are both 4 units above and 2 units over from the vertex. That's symmetry!

Quadratic Properties — The Basics

Know the three versions of a quadratic equation.
- Root Form gives the x-intercepts, but remember that the values on the graph are negated in the equation.
- Standard Form gives the y-intercept (the c-term), and tells you whether the graph opens up ($+a$) or down ($-a$). Standard form is the $y = mx + b$ of quadratics. When in doubt, get back to standard form.
- Vertex Form gives the vertex, or turning point, of the parabola. Remember that the x-value is negated in the equation. Parabolas are symmetrical across the vertex.

Factor, FOIL, and complete the square to move between forms.

Quadratic Properties

Exercise: Convert Quadratics

#1 — Answer = $x^2 - 3x - 10$

#2 — Answer = $x^2 - 9$

#3 — Answer = $2x^2 + 7x - 4$

#4 — Answer = $(x - 7)(x - 1)$

#5 — Answer = $(x - 8)(x - 3)$

#6 — Answer = $2(x - 9)(x + 1)$

#7 — Answer = $(x - 4)^2 + 5$

#8 — Answer = $(x + 1)^2 + 4$

#9 — Answer = $(x - 3)^2 - 29$

#10 — Answer = $(x + 1)^2 - 10$

#11 — Answer = $(x - 5)^2 - 1$

Exercise: Graphs of Quadratics

#1 — Answer = C
Factor this equation into $y = (x - 1)(x - 5)$. The x-intercepts are the roots. Even without factoring, you should notice that only Choice C is in the root form.

#2 — Answer = D
FOIL to get this equation into $y = x^2 - 2x - 3$. Complete the square to get the equation into vertex form: $y = (x - 1)^2 - 4$. Even without FOILing or completing the square, you should notice that only Choice D is in the vertex form. Sometimes, it really is entirely about Memorizing Formulas and vocab.

#3 — Answer = B
The minimum value is the vertex, which is halfway between the two roots. Since the equation is given in root form, you just need to know that the roots are 7 and 3. The vertex will be between 7 and 3, specifically at 5. Choice B includes that value.

#4 — Answer = A
The question gives you two pieces of information. Focus on the zeros first. Only Choices A and B have zeros at 2 and –4. The range of the function must be less than or equal to 9. Choice A is the answer because the maximum occurs at $y = 9$.

#5 — Answer = B
Since the quadratic is already in root form, the solutions are easy to find. The solutions are –4 and 9. Add them together to get 5.

#6 — Answer = 6
Factor into $(x - 6)(x + 1) = 0$. The solutions are 6 and –1. Since the question wants a positive solution, the answer is 6. A common mistake on this question is to factor too quickly, getting some combination of ±2 and ±3 as the solutions. Show your work and check it!

#7 — Answer = C
Complete the square: $(x - 2)^2 + 7$. You can also Arithmetize, but you should really learn how to complete the square if you are shooting for a top score.

#8 — Answer = B
Get Back to Basics. The twist is that the squared term has a 7. Divide the whole equation by 7 in order to get back to the standard form: $x^2 - 3x - 10 = 0$. Factor into $(x - 5)(x + 2) = 0$. The solutions are –2 and 5. If you were at all unsure, it's easy to Guess & Check. Just test the different possible values of x in the original equation.

#9 — Answer = C
Sketch a parabola that roughly lines up with the dots. You'll see that the y-intercept is around 650. Since it's positive, you can eliminate the choices with negative c-terms, which are Choices B and D. Since the parabola opens downward, the a-term must be negative, so Choice C is the answer. This is entirely about Memorizing Formulas for the standard form of a quadratic. The story is irrelevant.

#10 — Answer = B
This question has a huge twist! Most people pick Choice D because they see that the new equation

Quadratic Properties

has a negative a-term and a negative c-term. If you did, you didn't use the graph at all. That's a big problem! Remember that the SAT rarely gives you information that you don't use. The graph is a parabola with the equation $y = a x^2 + bx + c$. It opens upward, so the a-term is clearly positive. When it becomes negative in the new equation, the new parabola will open downward, which lets you eliminate Choices A and C. That part is exactly as we expected. But the y-intercept of the original graph is negative, which means that the original value of the c-term is also negative. Arithmetize to make this easier to understand. The y-intercept in the graph could be –2, which would make $c = -2$. When that is plugged into the new equation, the c-term becomes negative, but it's a double negative! Arithmetize: $y = -a x^2 + bx - (-2)$. Two negatives make a positive, which means that the y-intercept of our new graph will also be positive.

The Twists

Example 2

If you want a top score, you need to memorize quadratic formula. Questions that use it are rare, but it's basically impossible to get them right without it.

First, be clear about what your values are. This equation is in standard form, so it's easy:

$$x^2 + 4x + 1 = 0$$

$$a = 1$$
$$b = 4$$
$$c = 1$$

Plug those values into the quadratic formula:

$$x = \frac{-b \pm \sqrt{b^2 - 4ac}}{2a}$$

$$x = \frac{-(4) \pm \sqrt{(4)^2 - 4(1)(1)}}{2(1)}$$

$$x = \frac{-4 \pm \sqrt{16 - 4}}{2}$$

$$x = \frac{-4 \pm \sqrt{12}}{2}$$

$$x = \frac{-4 \pm \sqrt{4} \cdot \sqrt{3}}{2}$$

$$x = \frac{-4 \pm 2\sqrt{3}}{2}$$

$$x = -2 \pm \sqrt{3}$$

The correct answer is Choice A. A common mistake is dividing by 2 before you've simplified the radical. Remember that the plus/minus means that the two terms on the top are "connected". We have to divide into both, kind of like distribution.

Example 3

If a quadratic can be factored, it's very easy to find the solutions. Getting the sum would then be as simple as adding them together. We did that for #5 in the Graphs of Quadratics exercise.

We could also find the sum with solutions that we get from quadratic formula. Since we already did that for this equation in the previous example, we could sum them like this:

$$-2 + \sqrt{3} \quad + \quad -2 - \sqrt{3}$$

$$-2 + \cancel{\sqrt{3}} \quad + \quad -2 - \cancel{\sqrt{3}} = -4$$

But if we had to go through the entire process of plugging into quadratic formula, this would take a long time. And with all the steps, the chance of a mistake is high, so we could waste a lot of time getting the wrong answer. Luckily, there's a shortcut that is much more efficient. Memorize this formula:

$$\text{sum of solutions} = \frac{-b}{a}$$

Using a quadratic equation in standard form, we can get to the sum very quickly:

$$x^2 + 4x + 1 = 0$$

279

Quadratic Properties

$$\text{sum of solutions} = \frac{-4}{1} = -4$$

Within seconds, we know that the answer is Choice A. It can be overwhelming to memorize all of these formulas for quadratics (and we still have a few more to go!), so use your judgment. If you're struggling with regular factoring, then the quadratic formula and sum of the solutions formula aren't big priorities.

Example 4

Most students have seen the axis of symmetry formula at some point, and it's another way of finding the vertex if you can't complete the square. But the discriminant confuses people and isn't taught as thoroughly in school. Here's the simplest explanation so that you can understand why it tells us the number of solutions.

Let's look at the quadratic formula, but I'm going to ignore the denominator just to make things easier:

$$x = \frac{-b \pm \sqrt{b^2 - 4ac}}{2a}$$

$$x = -b \pm \sqrt{b^2 - 4ac}$$

Notice that the discriminant ($b^2 - 4ac$) is the entire piece under the radical. It's also important to remember that the plus/minus is the real reason that we can get <u>two</u> solutions out of one equation. Essentially, we can split this into two equations:

$$x = -b + \sqrt{b^2 - 4ac}$$

$$x = -b - \sqrt{b^2 - 4ac}$$

If the discriminant is a positive number (> 0), then we'll have two real solutions because we'll be adding and subtracting a number. So for example, you could have solutions that look like this:

$$x = 5 + \sqrt{4}$$

$$x = 5 - \sqrt{4}$$

In this case, the discriminant is 4, and the solutions would be 7 and 3. <u>A positive discriminant means two solutions.</u>

But if the discriminant is 0, then we'll only have one solution because our two equations will end up being the same:

$$x = 5 + \sqrt{0}$$

$$x = 5 - \sqrt{0}$$

In this case, $5 + 0$ and $5 - 0$ are both 5. So even though the plus/minus gives us two equations, the two equations give us the same answer. <u>When the discriminant is 0, we'll only have one solution.</u>

If the discriminant is less than 0, things will get weird:

$$x = 5 + \sqrt{-4}$$

$$x = 5 - \sqrt{-4}$$

You can't take the square root of a negative number. Technically, this quadratic would still have two solutions, but they would be imaginary solutions:

$$x = 5 + 2i$$

$$x = 5 - 2i$$

This parabola would not cross the x-axis. <u>So when the discriminant is less than 0, we have no real solutions</u> because we can't take the square root of a negative number.

Now let's get to the actual question for Example 4. We have a quadratic, but it's not in standard form, so we should move these variables to the left side:

$$4x^2 = 8x + c$$

Quadratic Properties

$$4x^2 - 8x - c = 0$$

And so our values for the coefficients:

$$a = 4$$
$$b = -8$$
$$c = -c$$

This is still confusing! $c = -c$? What? This is one of the SAT's favorite twists on quadratics. They know that negatives are already a problem, so they use them to confuse you about what the actual values are. Just know that c is a constant here. It could be a positive or a negative number. We don't yet. But we do know that moving it to the left side is changing how it looks, and we need to reflect that change throughout the question.

Let's put our values into the discriminant expression. And since we want "no real solutions", we should create an inequality where the discriminant is less than 0:

$$b^2 - 4ac < 0$$

$$(-8)^2 - 4(4)(-c) < 0$$

Start simplifying:

$$64 + 16c < 0$$

Let's solve for c:

$$16c < -64$$

$$c < -4$$

This means that we'll have 0 solutions when c is less than –4. **The only choice that satisfies our inequality is Choice D, so it must be the correct answer.** As we said before, the $-c$ is still weird. Our actual quadratic equation with Choice D would be:

$$4x^2 - 8x - (-5) = 0$$

$$4x^2 - 8x + 5 = 0$$

So technically our c was negative all along, but the c-term in the standard form is actually positive because the two negatives make a positive. Watch out for twists like this. If you want to prevent the confusion, you could have kept the c where it was and moved the $4x^2$ to get:

$$0 = -4x^2 + 8x + c$$

The discriminant would be the same:

$$8^2 - 4(-4)(c) < 0$$

$$64 + 16c < 0$$

$$16c < -64$$

$$c < -4$$

Quadratic Properties — The Twists

Memorize quadratic formula:

$$x = \frac{-b \pm \sqrt{b^2 - 4ac}}{2a}$$

Be comfortable with the discriminant:
- If $b^2 - 4ac > 0$, then 2 real solutions
- If $b^2 - 4ac = 0$, then 1 real solution
- If $b^2 - 4ac < 0$, then 0 real solutions

Pay attention to negatives when working with the a, b, and c constants in the quadratic's standard form. The SAT likes to twist these around so that the negatives are hidden within the constants.

You might also find use for:

$$\text{sum of solutions} = \frac{-b}{a}$$

$$\text{axis of symmetry} = \frac{-b}{2a}$$

Quadratic Properties

Exercise: Advanced Quadratics

#11 — Answer = C

By far the easiest way to do this is by creating a quick sketch. Since $y = k$ will be a horizontal line, the vertex of the parabola will be where the system has one solution. You can find the x-coordinate of the vertex with $\frac{-b}{2a}$. The twist is that there is no b-term because there's no term with just one x. You should eventually find that the vertex is $(0, 1)$. Substituting in for y, we find that $k = 1$. You can also use the discriminant if you merge the two equations. Start by setting the equations equal to each other, then subtracting k so that you have: $0 = 5x^2 + 1 - k$. Use the a, b, and c-terms in the equation to fill in the discriminant: $a = 5$, $b = 0$, and $c = 1 - k$. The c-term is $1 - k$ because both are numbers that are not attached to an x. There's one solution when the discriminant equals 0. Plugging these values into the discriminant gives you $0 - 20(1 - k) = 0$, which simplifies to $-20 + 20k = 0$. Solve for k, which equals 1.

#12 — Answer = A

Memorize Formulas. The sum of the solutions is $\frac{-b}{a}$, which is $\frac{-6}{2} = -3$. If you do it the long way with quadratic formula, you'll eventually get the solutions as $x = \frac{-3 \pm \sqrt{29}}{2}$. Break the +/– into the two solutions, and break the fraction up while you're at it: $\frac{-3}{2} + \frac{\sqrt{29}}{2} + \frac{-3}{2} - \frac{\sqrt{29}}{2}$. Now you can see that the radical terms cancel each other out. Add the other two terms: $\frac{-3}{2} + \frac{-3}{2} = \frac{-6}{2}$. Reduce to –3.

#13 — Answer = B

Guess & Check. The projectile will hit the ground when the height is 0. Since the answer choices are approximations, you won't get 0 exactly, but only Choice B will be close when you plug it in for t. If you want to solve directly, you'll have to use a calculator. You can graph the quadratic and use the CALC button to find the zero, or you can use quadratic formula.

#14 — Answer = D

Get Back to Basics. This is a very twisted FOIL question, so start by FOILing the left side:

$6x^2 + 3bx + 2ax + ab$. You can match these terms up with the corresponding terms on the right side of the equation. The two terms without an x are going to give you important information: $ab = 28$. There are not very many possible values for a and b. Try the most obvious first: $a = 4$ and $b = 7$. You can test these numbers in the other equation: $4 = 11 - 7$. You can also match up the x-terms in the two quadratics: $3bx + 2ax = cx$. Plug in the values for a and b: $3(7)x + 2(4)x = cx$. Simplify, and you'll find that $c = 29$. Only Choice D includes that value. You can also get 26 by switching the values of a and b so that $a = 7$ and $b = 4$.

#15 — Answer = C

Arithmetize to Get Back to Basics. The choices make it clear that we need quadratic formula. But the fractions in the equation make it clear that the algebra is going to be a huge pain. Get rid of them! If we Arithmetize $m = 2$ and $n = 4$, the equation becomes much easier: $x^2 + 1 = x$. Get the equation into standard form: $x^2 - x + 1 = 0$. Plug into quadratic formula: $\frac{-(-1) \pm \sqrt{(-1)^2 - 4(1)(1)}}{2(1)}$. Eventually, you'll simplify everything down to $\frac{1 \pm \sqrt{-3}}{2}$. At this point, starting plugging into the answer choices and see if there's a match. Hopefully you'll start to notice some patterns that let you take shortcuts. Choices A and B will be wrong because the first part of the top won't simplify correctly with the denominator. Basically, we'd have $\frac{4 \pm \cdots}{2}$, which will become $\frac{2}{1}$. But our quadratic formula suggests that it should be $\frac{1}{2}$. That would happen with Choices C and D: $\frac{4 \pm \cdots}{8}$. When you simplify the portion under the radical, Choice D would give us a positive number ($\sqrt{12}$), when we want a negative. Choice C simplifies to $\sqrt{-48}$.

Function Properties

The Basics

Like most topics on the SAT, functions sound harder than they actually are. If you haven't taken Algebra 2, some of this may seem very advanced, but a lot of it is just definitions.

Example 1

The basics of Function Properties are very similar to the basics of Quadratic Properties. You know that x-intercepts, roots, and factors are all basically the same. If you had a quadratic with x-intercepts of 5 and –6, then it would be factored as:

$$y = (x - 5)(x + 6)$$

Notice that the factors have the opposite sign (+/–) as the x-intercept. The same rule applies to "higher order" functions and polynomials:

In this case, we would expect a function that has x-intercepts at –2, 1, and 4 to have factors:

$$y = (x + 2)(x - 1)(x - 4)$$

Only one of these is an answer choice. **The correct answer is Choice C.**

Example 2

As the text says, they ask the same question multiple ways, just like with quadratics. In Example 1, they asked about x-intercepts. Now they're asking about roots. It's the same thing!

A function with roots at 0, –2, and 2 would look like:

$$f(x) = x(x + 2)(x - 2)$$

Choice A is the correct answer. It's the same thing, but with the factors in a different order. Since these terms are being multiplied by each other, the order doesn't matter.

> **Function Properties — The Basics**
>
> Like quadratics, longer polynomials also have roots, x-intercepts, zeros, and factors. The same rules apply. A root of –2 will match with factor $x + 2$.

The Twists

Example 3

There's one extra thing you should know about roots and factors. It also applies to quadratics, but it's mostly tested with functions like this one.

As you can see, this function has x-intercepts at 3, 0, and –2. We would expect that the function would have factors that look like:

$$y = x(x + 2)(x - 3)$$

That's Choice B, but it's not quite right. The one extra twist is that functions "bounce" off the x-axis when they have the same factor twice. Notice that the function dips down to touch the axis at –2, but it barely touches it before going back up. That's a "bounce," and it means that –2 is a double root, so the factor is squared:

$$y = x(x + 2)^2(x - 3)$$

The correct answer is Choice D. In general, if the exponent is even (2, 4, 6…), then the function will bounce. If it's odd (1, 3, 5…), then the function will pass through the axis like it does on this graph at 0 and 3.

Example 4

It's unclear why the SAT likes to test this rule. It has almost no relation to anything else on the test. It's also extremely confusing, which can make it hard to memorize. Here's what helps me:

Function Properties

They don't tell us the equation for $g(x)$, but we can imagine a simple one that includes the point they give us: $(-2, 7)$. How about:

$$g(x) = x + 9$$

It includes the point:

$$g(-2) = -2 + 9 = 7$$

But is it a polynomial? Well, if we cheat a little, we can get it to have a lot more variables without affecting the value:

$$g(x) = 0x^3 + 0x^2 + x + 9$$

But let's just stick with the simple version:

$$g(x) = x + 9$$

Now go through the choices. Choices A and B are clearly not true. The only factor is $x + 9$. A longer polynomial might have those factors, but the question says, which "must" be true. We've shown a case where it's not true. Cross off Choices A and B.

For Choices C and D, we actually need to divide (see the Dividing Polynomials packet for more):

$$\begin{array}{r} 1 \\ x+2\overline{)x + 9} \\ -(x+2) \\ \hline 7 \end{array}$$

Which means that:

$$\frac{x+9}{x+2} = 1 + \frac{7}{x+2}$$

So Choice C is true. The remainder is 7. And that matches with the example versions of the rule:

If $f(a) = b$, then b is the remainder when $f(x)$ is divided by $(x - a)$.

If $f(3) = 5$, then 5 is the remainder when $f(x)$ is divided by $(x - 3)$.

If $g(-2) = 7$, then 7 is the remainder when $g(x)$ is divided by $(x + 2)$.

Choice C is the correct answer. But we could try D just to make sure:

$$\begin{array}{r} 1 \\ x-2\overline{)x + 9} \\ -(x-2) \\ \hline 11 \end{array}$$

Nope! Honestly, this rule is not very important. It comes up occasionally, so it's worth paying attention to if you're looking for a top score, but most people can ignore remainder theorem without worrying.

Function Properties — The Twists

A function "bounces" off the x-axis when it has an even number of the same root. Usually the factor is squared.

Remainder theorem doesn't come up often, but it states:

If $f(a) = b$, then b is the remainder when $f(x)$ is divided by $(x - a)$.

Exercise: Functions and Factors

#1 — Answer = C
Factors and x-intercepts are linked concepts. Since all x-intercepts have a y-coordinate of 0, we need to look at the right column of the chart to see where $f(x) = 0$. That happens when $x = -1$. But the factor itself will be $x + 1$ because that's what gives us a zero: $-1 + 1 = 0$.

#2 — Answer = A
Memorize Formulas. A function with zeros at -5, 1, and 5 will have factors $x + 5$, $x - 1$, and $x - 5$, respectively. Choice A has those factors.

Function Properties

#3 — Answer = C

Memorize the definition of "zeros". The question is asking for the graph that intersects the x-axis 4 times. Only Choice C has 4 x-intercepts.

#4 — Answer = B

The first expression in the question is the rare case where the SAT gives extra information that you don't need. Focus on the second expression, which gives the factors… almost. The $(p^2 - 4)$ term must be factored further using Difference of Two Squares: $(p - 2)(p + 2)$. The fully factored form of the expression is $(p + 1)^2(p - 2)(p + 2)$, which means the polynomial has x-intercepts at –1, 2, and –2, which is Choice B. If you picked anything else, you fell for a trap. Next time, try to sense the difficulty. Pay attention to where you are in the section. The later the question, the more likely there's a twist.

Function Values

If you're new to function notation, these questions can seem really hard. But even if you have used function notation before, it's very easy to make a careless mistake. These questions are all about the x- and y-axes. Which one are they asking about?

Example 5

In the Roman numerals, all of the values are in the x position, so we should go to those values on the x-axis. Then go up to where $y = 3$. Do we intersect the function at that point?

I. $f\left(-\dfrac{9}{2}\right) = 3$ ✓

II. $f(1) = 3$ ✗

III. $f(2) = 3$ ✓

Only I and III are true, so **Choice C is the correct answer.** The value of $f(1)$ is 5, not 3.

Example 6

This question is slightly more confusing. It's asking about the minimum, so let's find that first. According to the graph, the minimum occurs at (5, –3).

Of course, both numbers are answer choices. The SAT is trying to trick you. They want you to be confused about x versus y.

But go back to the question. It's clear if you just read: "For what value of x…" They're asking for the x-coordinate of the minimum, which is 5. **So Choice A is the correct answer.**

Function Values — Summary

These questions are entirely about x versus y. Pay attention to which value they give you and which value they ask for. Here are the two most common situations:

- If $f(3)$ is given, then $x = 3$. Find y.
- If $f(x) = 3$ is given, then $y = 3$. Find x.

Exercise: Function Values

#5 — Answer = C

The question is asking for the x-value when $y = 2$. The x-coordinate is 4.

#6 — Answer = B

Guess & Check. The question is really asking for the y-value that has exactly two x-values. In other words, draw a horizontal line at each of the numbers in the choices. Choice C is wrong because $y = 2$ only intersects the graph once. Choice D is wrong because $y = 4$ intersects the graph 3 times. Choice A is wrong because $y = -5$ intersects the flat line at the bottom of the graph. It may look like two points, but it's really an infinite number of intersections because you have to include all of the decimals in

Function Properties

between (–2, –5) and (–4, –5). Choice B is correct because $y = -3$ intersects the graph exactly twice.

#7 — Answer = D

Guess & Check. Go through each choice and find the value of $f(x)$ using the graph. Then find the $g(x)$ value using the equation. Only Choice D works because $f(-1) = -3$ and $g(-1) = 3$.

Undefined

You can't divide by 0. Just try it in your calculator. You'll get an error.

Example 7

The question is clear as long as you know what "undefined" means. Just set the denominator of the fraction equal to 0:

$$x^2 - 6x + 8 = 0$$

$$(x - 4)(x - 2) = 0$$

$$x = 4 \text{ and } x = 2$$

Choice C is the correct answer.

Undefined — Summary

A function is undefined when the denominator of the fraction is 0. Find the values that would make the denominator equal 0.

Translations

There are a few rules that dictate how functions "move" in the xy-plane. You could memorize them, but usually you can figure out the translation without the rules. One way is to graph the two functions and see how they compare. Another is to focus on a known point, which is basically our Plug Points Into Equations strategy.

Example 8

We have two equations. Do they remind you of anything? Hint — they both have a squared term...

$$f(x) = (x - 2)^2 + 13$$
$$y = (x + 5)^2 + 13$$

They're both quadratics! And they're both in vertex form. We know the vertex of each, and we can see how it changes.

Starting vertex: (2, 13)
Translated vertex: (−5, 13)

The difference is 7, so the correct answer is 7.

Translations — Summary

Instead of thinking about the entire function, focus on one point and see how it changes.

If you want, you can memorize the rules for translations of a function $f(x)$:
- $f(x) + 2$ = translation up 2
- $f(x) - 2$ = translation down 2
- $f(x + 2)$ = translation left 2
- $f(x - 2)$ = translation right 2

Exercise: Special Function Values

#8 — Answer = D

Ignore the numerator. The question wants the denominator equal to 0. You could easily Guess & Check, but it might be faster to solve algebraically. FOIL and distribute: $0 = x^2 + 4x + 4 - 8x - 16 + 16$. Combine like terms: $0 = x^2 - 4x + 4$. Factor and you'll find that the solution is $x = 2$.

#9 — Answer = A

Plug Points Into Equations. This question is very easy if you just focus on the easiest point, which is the y-intercept (0, 10). The new equation is the negative version of the graph, so it should include the point (0, –10). Only Choice A includes that point.

Circle Properties

The Basics

Just like lines and quadratics, circles have a standard equation. Memorize it.

Example 1

$$(x - 3)^2 + (y + 2)^2 = 4$$

center: $(3, -2)$

radius: 2

point on the circle: $(3, 0)$

Points that lie on the circle will fit the equation:

$$(3 - 3)^2 + (0 + 2)^2 = 4$$

$$0^2 + 2^2 = 4$$

$$4 = 4 \checkmark$$

We knew that (3, 0) would lie on the circle because the center is (3, –2) and the radius is 2. Just go 2 units in any direction. So (3, –4), (1, –2), and (5, –2) are all on the circle. Let's graph it:

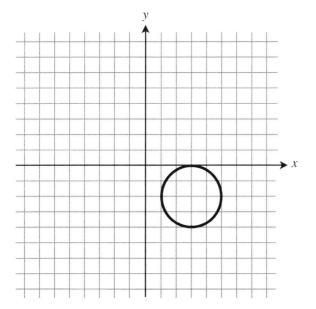

Circle Properties — The Basics

Memorize the standard circle equation:

$$(x - h)^2 + (y - k)^2 = r^2$$

The center is (h, k).

The radius is r.

Points that lie on the circle are (x, y).

The Twists

Example 2

The SAT twists the standard circle equation so that it's just a jumble of x's and y's. Completing the square is the only way back to Get Back to Basics:

$$x^2 + y^2 + 6x - 8y = 0$$

$$(x^2 + 6x) + (y^2 - 8y) = 0$$

$$(x^2 + 6x + 9) + (y^2 - 8y + 16) = 0 + 9 + 16$$

$$(x + 3)^2 + (y - 4)^2 = 25$$

The center is (–3, 4), and the radius is 5. For more practice completing the square, see Quadratic Properties. The only big difference is that, with circles, we maintain balance by adding the number to both sides of the equation instead of adding it and subtracting it to the same side. The point is that you have to keep things equal.

Circle Properties — The Twists

Get Back to Basics with weird circle equations by completing the square.

Circle Properties

Exercise: Circle Properties

#1 — Answer = C

Work backwards by starting with the equation of the circle described: $(x - 9)^2 + (y + 4)^2 = 25$. FOIL both terms to get the equation to look like the choices: $x^2 - 18x + 81 + y^2 + 8y + 16 = 25$. Combine like terms, and subtract the 25 to get Choice C (though, you kind of know C has to be right once you see that it's the only choice with $-18x$). You might be tempted to Plug Points Into Equations here, but the center of a circle is the <u>one time</u> when that strategy doesn't work. It's because the center is not actually <u>on</u> the outside of the circle.

#2 — Answer = A

Plug Points Into Equations. But first, eliminate Choices B and D because they do not have the right center point. The point $\left(1, -\frac{12}{5}\right)$ can be plugged into the two remaining choices to see if it's a point on the circle. The arithmetic is tricky because of all the fractions, but Choice A works.

#3 — Answer = C

Plug Points Into Equations. But this has a twist. Points that lie <u>on</u> the circle will work in the equation. Points that lie <u>inside</u> the circle will work in this inequality: $(x - 4)^2 + (y - 5)^2 < 9$. Think about it logically. This inequality is saying that the distance from the center is less than the radius. Only Choice C works in the inequality. You could also draw a graph of the circle and plot the choices as points.

#4 — Answer = A

Get Back to Basics. Group the terms, then complete the square twice:
$(x^2 - 2x + 1) + (y^2 - 12y + 36) = -12 + 1 + 36$.
Simplify and you'll get: $(x - 1)^2 + (y - 6)^2 = 25$.
Remember that 25 is not the radius. It's the radius squared, so take the square root to find that the radius is 5.

Linear Models

The Basics

If it looks like a line and moves like a line, then it probably _is_ a line.

Example 1

Ignore the story for a second. Look at the equation. It's very clearly a line:

$$y = mx + b$$
$$L = 2.1m + 0.6$$

In the Linear Properties packet, we focused on slopes and y-intercepts. The same is true here. But when we have a story, the parts of the line take on certain roles. The slope is usually a rate of some kind, like miles per hour or the price for each sandwich. The y-intercept is a starting point because most Models don't involve negative numbers, which restricts the graph to the first quadrant. (Look ahead to Example 3 to see a visual.)

In Example 1, the question asks for "the estimated increase, in centimeters, of the insect's length each month". That sounds like a rate — centimeters per month. They're asking for the slope of the line.

Don't get fooled by the m in the equation. The m is now the variable instead of x, and the slope is the number attached to the variable. **So the correct answer is Choice C.**

Example 2

The story is long. Is this a Math question or a Reading question? Ignore the story for now and focus on the end. This isn't all that different from the last example. Compare the equation to the standard line:

$$y = mx + b$$

$$n = 1{,}562 - 225d$$

Be careful. There's a slight twist here. The model does not line up exactly with the standard equation. Rearrange it to Get Back to Basics:

$$n = -225d + 1{,}562$$

The question asks for the meaning of 1,562. If this were a regular line, 1,562 would be the y-intercept. Since it's a model, it's probably something similar to a starting point.

Choices C and D are clearly rates, so both of those are wrong. **Choice B is the correct answer because it's literally the starting amount of wall space that Mark has to paint.** Choice A sounds more like an ending point.

Linear Models — The Basics

Even though there's a story, you should still think in terms of slopes and y-intercepts.

The slope is usually a rate (how much something increases or decreases) or a cost per unit.

The y-intercept is usually a starting point, initial value, or flat fee.

If the equation is slightly off, Get Back to Basics by using standard $y = mx + b$ form.

The Twists

Example 3

This is clearly a line, and the choices are clearly in $y = mx + b$ form. Most people start by looking at the y-intercept, which is 9. That eliminates Choices A and C.

Now look at the slope. It looks like we rise one box and run two boxes, so the slope is $\frac{1}{2}$ and the answer must be Choice D.

WRONG! The most common way the SAT twists graph questions is by messing with the scale on the axes. You're so used to just counting the boxes that you don't even bother to look at the scale. Such a common mistake, but also such an easy one to fix. Get in the habit of double checking the units every

Linear Models

time. I think you'll quickly start to see for yourself how often the SAT tries to trick you by changing the units.

You can find the slope by counting the boxes and knowing how much each box is worth. One box on the y-axis (the rise) is equal to 3 units, and one box on the x-axis (the run) is equal to $\frac{1}{2}$. The slope is really a rise of 3 and a run of 1, which is why **Choice B is the correct answer with the correct slope of 3.** To play it safe, Plug Points Into Equations. Test a point that the line passes through. For example $(1, 12)$ works in Choice B but fails in Choice D:

B) $12 = 3(1) + 9$ ✓
D) $12 = \frac{1}{2}(1) + 9$ ✗

Linear Models — The Twists

Check your units! The SAT loves to mess with the scale on the axes, so you have to actively check to see what each box represents when you're looking for the slope.

In general, there are a lot of ways that the SAT can twist Linear Models questions. The stories will be weird, but the equations will look like lines.

Exercise: Linear Models

#1 — Answer = A
Get Back to Basics. This is a line. Rearrange it to $y = mx + b$ form: $c = 1f + 3$. The question is clearly asking for a slope, and the slope of this line would be 1. If you picked Choice C, that's very bad! It's rare for an SAT question to be as easy as picking the only number that appears in the entire question. You should sense the difficulty and at least pause to prove your answer. If you're unsure, you could easily Arithmetize. What's the increase in flour from making 5 cupcakes to 6 cupcakes?

#2 — Answer = D
Turn the text into an equation: $L = GA$. The question gives you the age (A) and the chart gives you the growth constant (G). Substitute them into the equation: $L = (4.4)(3)$. Multiply to get 13.2.

#3 — Answer = C
Plug Points Into Equations. You have an equation from the first question: $L = GA$. The scatterplot is clearly a line, so pick a point that looks like it would be on the line. Both (8, 20) and (10, 25) look like they roughly lie on the line of best fit (not shown). If you test the first one, you're essentially finding the slope of the line, which is the growth constant: $20 = (G)(8)$. You'd find that G is 2.5, which is approximately the growth constant for the Toothless guppy.

#4 — Answer = C
You can solve this question without using the fact that the two fish are currently 8 centimeters long. This is a rare case where the SAT gives you information that you don't need. Instead, use the equation to calculate the length each fish would grow during 18 months. But first, you have to untwist the question by converting 18 months into 1.5 years. For the yellowback stickler, your equation would be: $L = (3.7)(1.5)$. For the blue snapper, your equation would be: $L = (3.4)(1.5)$. You should get that the yellowback grows 5.55 centimeters, and the blue snapper grows 5.1 centimeters. Subtract them to find the difference is 0.45 centimeters. If you did want to incorporate the 8 centimeters, you could include it as a y-intercept: $L = GA + 8$.

#5 — Answer = C
The twist is that they tell you that the model only works between 5 and 40 years. But that doesn't affect the estimated increase. That's still the slope of the line. The equation is already in $y = mx + b$ form, and 9 corresponds with the slope.

#6 — Answer = D
Create a $y = mx + b$ style equation. The starting amount (b) is 255,000, and the rate (m) is 120. Since the total weight can't exceed 340,000, you'll need to set up an inequality where the $mx + b$ part is less than or equal to 340,000. Putting all of this information into $y = mx + b$ gives you: $340,000 \geq 255,000 + 120n$. The slope and y-intercept have swapped positions, but it's still a line.

Linear Models

#7 — Answer = B

There's a really mean twist in this question! You might be tempted to put 100 in for w, but that is not correct. Devin wants to <u>increase</u> the total weight by 100, so you need to find the starting value first, then increase it by 100. Luckily, this model is already in $y = mx + b$ form, so the starting amount is 80. Adding 100 means that you need to find the value of t when $w = 180$. Solving for t, you should get 12.5, which is approximately 13.

#8 — Answer = C

This is basically a Rearrange Formulas question. Subtract 80 from both sides, then divide both sides by 8: $t = \frac{w - 80}{8}$. You can't simplify this any further because the terms on the top cannot both be divided by 8.

Exercise: Linear Models 2

#9 — Answer = B

Plug Points Into Equations. They give you the equation of the line of best fit. They want the y-value when $x = 3$. Use your calculator, and you'll get 38.54.

#10 — Answer = A

Plug Points Into Equations. The twist is that the x-values are <u>not</u> 2010 and 2015. The question specifies that t is years since 2010, so the first point is really $(0, 46)$, and the second point is really $(5, 52)$. Only Choice A includes both of those points.

#11 — Answer = A

The twist here is that there are two "x" variables. But this equation still matches up with $y = mx + b$. Choice A is correct because it describes the 2 as a rate, which makes sense since it's the slope. Choice B is incorrect because 35 would be the y-intercept. Choices C and D are incorrect because nothing in this equation suggests that there is a maximum or minimum.

Quantity & Value

The Basics

These models are essentially Point of Intersection questions with a story. You'll need to create two equations. They're called Quantity & Value because the two equations almost always represent the total quantity/number of items and the total value/cost of those items.

Example 1

The bolded headings are meant to keep you organized. You should follow a similar process when you encounter Quantity & Value questions on the SAT. Start by very clearly stating your variables (the SAT loves to twist these questions by matching the variable with the wrong value (see #2 in the Exercise).

Let d = dimes

Let q = quarters

The Quantity equation will give you the total number of coins:

$$d + q = 15$$

The Value equation will be a little more complex because you need to multiply each variable by the value of that item. In this case, dimes are worth $0.10 each and quarters are worth $0.25 each:

$$0.10d + 0.25q = 2.70$$

To find the point of intersection, either stack the equations and eliminate a variable or manipulate an equation so that you can substitute. Since the Quantity equation is usually very simple, it's probably easier to manipulate it and substitute:

$$\begin{array}{r} d + q = 15 \\ -d \qquad\quad -d \\ \hline q = 15 - d \end{array}$$

$$0.10d + 0.25q = 2.70$$
$$0.10d + 0.25(15 - d) = 2.70$$

Distribute:

$$0.10d + 3.75 - 0.25d = 2.70$$

Combine like terms:

$$3.75 - 0.15d = 2.70$$

Subtract:

$$\begin{array}{r} 3.75 - 0.15d = \quad 2.70 \\ -3.75 \qquad\qquad -3.75 \\ \hline -0.15d = -1.05 \end{array}$$

Divide:

$$\frac{-0.15d}{-0.15} = \frac{-1.05}{-0.15}$$

$$d = 7$$

The correct answer is Choice B. But one thing to point out is that the number of quarters is 8:

$$7 + q = 15$$

And of course, that's an answer too. The SAT will almost always give you answer choices that represent both of the variables. Get in the habit of rereading the question before you bubble so that you don't accidentally choose the wrong variable.

Quantity & Value — The Basics

Quantity & Value questions are really just Point of Intersection questions with a story. And you'll need to come up with the equations.

Take the time to write out what each variable represents.

Start with an equation that represents the Quantity of items.

Then make an equation that represents the Value of the items. This one will usually have coefficients in front of the variables.

Solve using the stack method or by substituting.

Double check to make sure that you've solved for the correct variable.

Quantity & Value

The Twists

Example 2

This is a Quantity & Value question that has been twisted into something that seems completely different. But we know that it's Quantity & Value because we have two items that have different values (6- and 10-person tables). Stay organized:

Let x = 6-person tables
Let y = 10-person tables

How many tables are there? (Quantity):

$$x + y = 18$$

How many people will be seated at these tables? (Value):

$$6x + 10y = 152$$

Manipulate the Quantity equation so that it's in terms of one variable:

$$y = 18 - x$$

Substitute into the Value equation:

$$6x + 10(18 - x) = 152$$

Solve:

$$6x + 180 - 10x = 152$$

$$180 - 4x = 152$$

$$-4x = -28$$

$$x = 7$$

Did we solve for the correct variable?

Let x = 6-person tables

$$x = 7$$

"how many of the tables are 10-person tables?"

No! Plug back in to find y:

$$7 + y = 18$$

$$y = 11$$

The correct answer is 11.

Example 3

This question has a little bit more going on, but at least we don't need to solve any of the equations. There are two main twists. First, we have inequalities to worry about. Second, we have these other two weird inequalities in addition to the normal Quantity & Value equations.

Start with the Quantity & Value parts. The question says that Mona "needs to order at least 12 pizzas", which sounds like the Quantity of pizzas needs to be greater than or equal to 12. We can eliminate Choices A and B because they have the wrong inequality sign in our Quantity equation. It should be:

$$x + y \geq 12$$

The Value equation should be:

$$14x + 16y \leq 180$$

Both of the remaining choices have this, so it doesn't affect our answer. Still, it's important to know why it needs to look like this. The question says that "her budget for the party is no more than $180", which means that the Value of the pizzas needs to be less than or equal to $180.

Quantity & Value

The remaining inequalities are strange, but just think about what they would be saying. The question tells us that "x is the number of regular pizzas". Turn the two remaining choices into words:

C) $x \geq 1$
The number of regular pizzas is greater than or equal to 1.

D) $x \leq 1$
The number of regular pizzas is less than or equal to 1.

Choice D makes no sense. Why are we limited to just one regular pizza? For that matter, the last inequality would say that we can only have 1 pepperoni pizza, which is just 2 pizzas total. Yet the question already said she needs at least 12 pizzas.

Choice C is the correct answer. The question actually says that Mona needs "at least one pizza of each type" which is why both of the extra inequalities need to be included in the set. She can't order only pepperoni pizzas. She needs at least one regular pizza.

Quantity & Value — The Twists

Quantity & Value models can take many forms, and have weird stories. But the process to solve them is very consistent. Look for clues, like two different items that have different values.

Pay attention to inequalities. Sometimes they're testing your knowledge of the symbols (< vs >) more than your knowledge of the equations.

Exercise: Quantity & Value

#1 — Answer = 8
Your Quantity equation should be: $h + s = 11$. Your Value equation should be: $5h + 3s = 39$. Since the question wants the number of screwdrivers (s), you should use the "stack" method to eliminate the h-terms. You'll find there are 8 screwdrivers.

#2 — Answer = C
Notice that the second equation in each choice (Quantity) is exactly the same. Focus on the Value equation. The question says that x represents the number of boxes, which weigh 50 pounds each. So Choices A and B are wrong because the variables are matched with the wrong values. Choice C is correct because the total weight must be less than or equal to the plane's capacity, which is 10,000 pounds.

#3 — Answer = 13
Your Quantity equation should be: $r + b = 19$. Your Value equation should be: $2r + 5b = 77$. Since the question wants the number of black cards, you should use the "stack" method to eliminate the r-terms. You should get that there are 13 black cards.

#4 — Answer = D
Choices A and B can be eliminated because they have the wrong Value equations, pairing the wrong cost to each variable. Choice C has the right pairings, but the Value equation should equal the total cost, not the total quantity. Choice D correctly sets up the Value and Quantity equations.

#5 — Answer = 2
Set your variables. You can make T the number of 12 petal flowers and F the number of 14 petal flowers. Your Quantity equation should be: $T + F = 16$. Your Value equation should be: $12T + 14F = 196$. Since the question wants the number of 14-petal flowers, you should solve for F. Use the "stack" method, and you'll get that $F = 2$.

Geometry Models

The Basics

Arithmetize. If they're talking about dimensions, give the shape actual dimensions. Draw pictures to help you visualize.

Example 1

This question is begging to be Arithmetized. Pick a value for the width:

Let $w = 10$

So the length is 5 feet shorter than twice the width? Twice the width is 20. Five feet shorter means:

$l = 15$

The perimeter is the sum of all the sides. That's two lengths and two widths:

$$p = 2l + 2w$$

$$p = 2(15) + 2(10)$$

$$p = 30 + 20$$

$$p = 50$$

Now just check the choices to see which one equals 50:

A) $5 - 2(10) = -15$ ✗

B) $4(10) - 10 = 30$ ✗

C) $6(10) - 10 = 50$ ✓

D) $2(10)^2 - 5(10) = 150$ ✗

Choice C is the correct answer. Just so you are aware, Choice D gives the value of the area. Another one of the SAT's tricks.

Example 2

This is another great Arithmetize question. When working with percentages, 10s and 100s are the best numbers to pick because the math will be much easier. Here's the rectangle:

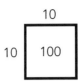

It's a 10 by 10 rectangle with an area of 100. "But isn't that a square?" Yes. But a square is just a rectangle with equal sides.

The question says that the length is increased by 20% and the area is decreased by 16%. Since we picked 10s and 100s, we can do this math in our heads:

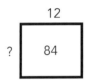

Just make an area equation to find the value of the missing side:

$$A = lw$$

$$84 = 12w$$

$$7 = w$$

Going from 10 to 7 would be a 30% decrease, **so Choice C is the answer.** You could solve this with equations, but you're just asking for trouble. There are so many more things to keep track of with equations. Plus, if you make a mistake, it will be harder to notice.

I've watched hundreds of students answer these two "Basic" examples, and 95% of the students who try to solve with algebra either make a mistake or never figure out what to do. Why set yourself up for failure? In real life, shapes don't measure w feet or A square meters. They have actual dimensions — numbers! Notice this problem on the SAT, and fix it by Arithmetizing.

Geometry Models

Geometry Models — The Basics

Know the basic area and perimeter formulas for a rectangle:

area = (length)(width)

perimeter = 2(length) + 2(width)

Very rarely, you also need to know the area formulas for parallelograms and trapezoids:

area of a parallelogram = (base)(height)

area of a trapezoid $= \left(\dfrac{b_1 + b_2}{2} \right) h$

Arithmetize so that you can more easily visualize the geometry. When working with percentages, pick 10s and 100s so the math is easier.

The Twists

Example 3

This question should remind you of something. Lines!

$$y = mx + b$$
$$A = 5p + 100$$

It sounds like they're asking about a rate, so you might be thinking that 5 is the answer because it's the slope. But be careful. They've twisted this question. The slope gives the increase in the area for each additional foot of the perimeter, but the question wants the increase in the perimeter for each additional square foot of the area. See the difference?

The simple solution is to rearrange the line so that it gives the perimeter in terms of the area:

$$A = 5p + 100$$

$$A - 100 = 5p$$

$$\frac{1}{5}A - 20 = p$$

Now it's easier to see that the answer is $\frac{1}{5}$, but you could have Arithmetized from the start:

Let $p = 10$

$$A = 5(10) + 100$$

$$A = 150$$

Now increase the area by 1 additional square foot, like the question says:

$$A = 151$$

$$151 = 5p + 100$$

$$51 = 5p$$

$$10.2 = p$$

Our value of p increased by 0.2, which is equal to $\frac{1}{5}$. **Choice B is the correct answer.**

Geometry Models — The Twists

Sometimes a Geometry Model isn't really about Geometry at all. Think about other question types, and solve accordingly.

Arithmetize to make things easier!

Exercise: Geometry Models

#1 — Answer = 25

Arithmetize. You'll have to be clever. If you make $BC = 100$, $AD = 200$, and the height = 1, then you'll have easier numbers to work with. The area of a trapezoid is given by $\left(\dfrac{b_1 + b_2}{2} \right) h$. Plugging in your values gives the original area as 150. If you reduce BC and AD by 25%, they become 75 and 150, respectively. The new area is 112.5. Find the percent

Geometry Models

decrease with the OPEN formula: $(150)(1 - P) = 112.5$. Solve for $P = 0.25$, but don't forget to convert it back into a percentage. (see the Percentages packet for more on OPEN formula)

#2 — Answer = B

You can find the original volume of water in the tank, or you can skip directly to the 1,800 cubic centimeters that are added. This volume of water will have a length of 30 and a width of 20 when it is poured into the tank. That's enough that you could find the height of just those 1,800 cubic centimeters: $1,800 = (30)(20)(h)$. Divide to find that the added height is 3 centimeters. That's in addition to the 10 centimeters that were already in the tank (because it was originally filled halfway), so the total height is now 13 centimeters.

#3 — Answer = 18

As instructed, set the two congruent sides equal to each other: $2x - 11 = x - 3$. Solve for x to find that $x = 8$. Use 8 to find the perimeter. The two congruent sides are 5, and the base is 8, which adds up to 18.

#4 — Answer = 9

Create an equation for the width: $w = l - 8$. Use this equation in the area formula, which is length times width: $153 = (l)(l - 8)$. You'll create a quadratic equation: $0 = l^2 - 8l - 153$. You can factor this into: $0 = (l - 17)(l + 9)$. Since you can only have a positive value, the length is 17, which makes the width 9. You could also have used Guess & Check from the start since the SAT tends to give easy-to-use numbers. Just keep multiplying numbers that are 8 apart until you get 153.

Exponential Models

The Basics

The SAT almost always tests exponential equations in the form of a model, or story. It's important to understand how Exponential Models differ from Linear Models. Notice that linear growth is constant. The line always has the same slope. But exponential growth is curved. As you increase x, you keep going up by larger and larger amounts.

Example 1

Some questions are only testing the definition. Let's go through the choices:

A) This is linear growth because the amount of the increase doesn't change. If Grover makes $100,000 in his first year (initial salary), then he'll get a $1,000 raise each year (1% of initial salary). That's a constant increase of $1,000 per year. Usually we associate percentages with exponential growth, but this time it was a twist to throw you off. And that's why you always read all of the answers!

B) This is more complicated, but it's basically the same as Choice A. This time, Grover would get a raise of $2,000 (2% of initial salary) plus the extra $500. That's a larger increase, but it's still the same amount each year. The constant rate is $2,500 per year, which is linear growth.

C) The key words in this choice are "1.2% of his previous year's salary". This tells us that his salary will increase by more and more as his salary grows each year. For example, he'd get a raise of $1,200 after the first year (1.2% of initial salary), but he'd get a raise of $1,214.40 after the second year (1.2% of his new salary of $101,200). After the third year, his raise would be $1,228.97 (1.2% of his second year salary of $102,414.40). **Since the growth itself is growing, this is an example of exponential growth.** Let's check D just to be sure.

D) This is very obviously linear growth. Grover's salary will increase by the same amount each year, so it's a constant rate.

Choice C is the correct answer. It's important that you learn to recognize exponential growth and decay. But it can be easier to notice linear growth, so you can often find exponential growth through Process of Elimination. You need to associate the phrase "constant rate" with linear relationships.

Exponential Models — The Basics

Exponential growth usually involves percentages.

But make sure that the percentage leads to larger and larger growth each year. If the rate of increase is constant, then that's linear growth.

If a model is decreasing exponentially, then it's called exponential decay.

The Twists

Example 2

There are many versions of the Exponential equation in the world, but I prefer to use the **OPEN** equation so that we're consistent with how we learned Percentages. But since the change takes place over time, we'll use a variable exponent on top of the percentage. Otherwise, it's the same equation!

It might be helpful to remember that anything raised to the 0 is 1. That's why the original amount is outside the exponent:

$$(\text{Original})(1+P)^0 = \text{New}$$

$$(\text{Original})(1) = \text{New}$$

$$\text{Original} = \text{New} \quad \text{(when zero time has passed)}$$

In this question, you can tell from the choices that the equation itself doesn't really matter. The only thing to decide is how you represent 2% growth. We'll always think of percentages as decimals when we're dealing with Exponential Models:

Exponential Models

$$2\% = 0.02$$

But we don't want to find 2% of the bacteria. We want to <u>add</u> 2% more bacteria. This is why the exponential OPEN formula has a 1 in the parentheses. We add or subtract our percentage, depending on whether we want growth or decay. In this case, we definitely want growth:

$$1 + 0.02 = 1.02$$

Choice B is correct because it shows the correct percentage. Since this is the most common twist, it's very important that you get in the habit of double checking that you've got the right percentage in the parentheses.

Example 3

In this example, we need to construct the Exponential Model from scratch. The original is clearly stated:

$$(O)(1 \pm P)^t = N$$

$$(800)(1 - 0.12)^3 = N$$

$$(800)(0.88)^3 = N$$

Notice that our percentage doesn't actually look like 12% of anything. That's because we're really saying that we want 88% of our value each hour. There's no difference between taking 88% of something and decreasing something by 12%.

Solve for N. Don't forget PEMDAS dictates that we need to deal with the exponent first, and then we multiply:

$$(800)(0.681472) = N$$

$$545.1776 = N$$

To the nearest whole number, the correct answer would be 545.

Exponential Models — The Twists

Use the OPEN formula to build exponential equations the same way you use $y = mx + b$ to build lines. It's the same formula as percent change, but with a variable as an exponent on the percentage.

$$(O)(1 \pm P)^t = N$$

Pay very close attention to the percentages. Percentages should be expressed as decimals. If growth, add the percentage to 1. If decay, subtract the percentage from 1.

If the twist affects the other parts of the equation, you can probably Arithmetize to better understand what's going on.

Exercise: Exponential Models 1

#1 — Answer = 116
Set up an exponential model using the exponential OPEN formula: $100(1 + 0.03)^5 = N$. Use your calculator, and you'll find that the value is approximately 115.92, which rounds to 116.

#2 — Answer = 12
Set up an exponential model using the OPEN formula, but take note that this time we know N and need to solve for the original: $(O)(1 + 0.80)^6 = 408$. Solve for O and you'll get that there were 12 wolves in 2005.

#3 — Answer = A
Arithmetize. If $x = 1$, then the grocery store would have 156 customers after 1 year. Since the choices model the number of customers in terms of months, you should find the equation that gives you 156 customers when $m = 12$ because 12 months is the same as 1 year. Only Choice A gives you 156. Almost everyone who gets this wrong picks Choice B. You can easily prevent this error by Arithmetizing! And you can even get away with just seeing the exponent and not solving: $150(1.04)^1 = 150(1.04)^{\frac{12}{12}}$.

Exponential Models

#4 — Answer = D

This is a mean question! Even though you're in the Exponential Models exercise, this question says that the cost of the contract increases at a constant rate, which is d dollars per year. A constant rate means linear growth, not exponential. So Choices A and B are wrong. Since the rate is given by d, Choice D is the answer because the rate needs to be the slope of the line.

#5 — Answer = C

Arithmetize. Even though the question is talking in terms of percents, 5% is <u>not</u> the percentage that goes in parentheses. If there were 100 gallons of water in the pool to start, then only 5 gallons would remain after 6 hours. In other words, the 5% tells you the new amount, not the percentage. Your equation should be: $(100)(1 - P)^6 = 5$. Divide by 100 to get $(1 - P)^6 = 0.05$. To get rid of the exponent, raise both sides to the $\frac{1}{6}$ power. You should get: $1 - P = 0.607$. Solving for P gets you $P = 0.393$, which is approximately 39%. If you have trouble getting rid of the exponent, then just Guess & Check with the answer choices by substituting them in for P.

#6 — Answer = B

First, create an exponential model to find the original amount of trees in the forest. Since the rate is given in terms of decades, the exponent will be 7 to represent the 70 years between 1940 and 2010. Your model should be: $(O)(1 - 0.04)^7 = 3,075$. You should get approximately $O = 4,092$. To find the number of trees in 1960, the exponent should be 2 for the 2 decades since 1940: $4,092(0.96)^2 = 3,771$. Do the same thing for 1980, where the exponent will be 4: $4,092(0.96)^4 = 3,476$. The difference is 295, which is closest to Choice B. It's a little off because you rounded along the way. This question has a lot of steps, but they're easy once you have the model.

Exercise: Exponential Models 2

#7 — Answer = C

Use the OPEN formula to structure your equation. Since the value is increasing, use plus: $(200)(1 + 0.03)^t = V$. Simplify to get Choice C.

#8 — Answer = C

It should be easy to eliminate Choices B and D because the question explicitly says that the stock increases in value. This situation is exponential growth because the percent increase is applied to the previous month. As time goes by, 0.9% will be worth more and more as the stock is worth more and more.

#9 — Answer = C

You should know from the OPEN formula that 1.14 is related to the percentage. Choice A sounds like a starting point, which would actually be 8. Choice B sounds like a constant rate, but this is not linear growth. Choice C is simply another way of talking about the percentage. Essentially, the original number of gulls is multiplied by 1.14 for every day after September 1st. Choice D is backwards because 8 is the starting point.

#10 — Answer = B

Plug Points Into Equations. Start with the easiest point, which is $(0, 4)$. Since anything raised to the 0 is 1, you should be able to eliminate Choices A and C. The next easiest point would be $(1, 7)$. This point only works in Choice B.

#11 — Answer = D

Use the OPEN formula. The original number of points is 70. The percent increase is 15, which will become 1.15 when substituted into the formula: $(70)(1 + 0.15)^x = y$.

Exercise: Exponential Models 3

#12 — Answer = D

Tricky question! The key phrases are "same rate" and "same volume". Even though the question starts with a percentage, these phrases tell us that water is leaving the tank at a constant rate. This is actually a linear model. And since they are asking for the volume remaining in the tank, we know that it's decreasing.

#13 — Answer = D

We know that 0.9 has something to do with the percentage. That should eliminate Choices A and B because the number of gallons that evaporate will

Exponential Models

change every week. Choice D is correct because the proportion left will always be 90%, which is 0.9 as a decimal. It's important that this happens every 12 weeks because the exponent includes a fraction. You can Arithmetize with $w = 12$ to confirm this.

#14 — Answer = C
Use the OPEN formula to build the equation. The original value is 36 dollars. The investment is growing, so we'll use $1 + P$. And the percentage will be 0.113 as a decimal: $(36)(1 + 0.113)^t = V$.

#15 — Answer = C
Eliminate Choices A and B because this situation is not linear growth. Use the OPEN formula to build the equation. The percentage should be 1.02 because the formula would involve $1 + 0.02$.

#16 — Answer = C
Get Back to Basics. We know that this situation should be represented by the OPEN formula. We'd expect it to look like this: $(x)(1 + p)^5 = N$. If you completely ignore the 100, you should still lean toward Choice C. The reason we need the 100 is that the wording of the question has the percentage as a regular number. For example, "the investment decreases by 8%" would make $p = 8$. Normally, we automatically convert the percentage into a decimal, making 8 into 0.08. Dividing by 100 does the same thing here.

Rearrange Formulas

The Basics

This is just Algebra! The story rarely matters. The answer choices will help you understand what you're supposed to do.

Example 1

This question doesn't give you an initial equation, but you should memorize the formula for speed:

$$\text{speed} = \frac{\text{distance}}{\text{time}}$$

$$s = \frac{d}{t}$$

Now you can rearrange the formula as asked. Multiply both sides by t.

$$\left(\frac{t}{1}\right) s = \frac{d}{\cancel{t}} \left(\frac{\cancel{t}}{1}\right)$$

$$st = d$$

Choice A is the correct answer.

Example 2

Here's a good example of a question where the story doesn't matter. The choices clearly want you to rearrange this formula to solve for v^2:

$$E_k = \frac{1}{2}mv^2$$

$$(2)\ E_k = \frac{1}{\cancel{2}}mv^2\ (\cancel{2})$$

$$2E_k = mv^2$$

$$\frac{2E_k}{m} = \frac{\cancel{m}v^2}{\cancel{m}}$$

$$\frac{2E_k}{m} = v^2$$

The correct answer is Choice C.

The Twists

Example 3

A common twist is to ask you to compare different values in the formula. You could do these algebraically, but the SAT knows the most common mistakes and will make those mistakes into answer choices. You're better off picking values and Arithmetizing.

In this question, the width is constant, so you can make it equal to 1 to keep things simple. Keep the areas simple too. The subscripts help you keep track of each Plot, since each one will have a length and a width:

$$\text{Let } w_A = w_B = 1$$
$$\text{Let } A_A = 3$$
$$\text{Let } A_B = 1$$

The question says that the area of Plot A is 3 times the area of Plot B, so we picked 3 and 1 because they're the easiest. Just make sure that you assign the values to the right plots.

Now use area formula to compare the lengths:

$$A = lw$$

$$3 = (l_A)(1)$$
$$3 = l_A$$

$$1 = (l_B)(1)$$
$$1 = l_B$$

Rearrange Formulas

So the length of Plot A is 3, and the length of Plot B is 1. **Since 1 is $\frac{1}{3}$ of 3, the correct answer is B.** You probably could have thought this one through logically, but it doesn't take long to Arithmetize and prove your hunch. The SAT is good at making you trust your instincts, even when they're wrong. Get in the habit of being careful and thorough, and you won't fall for as many traps.

Example 4

Things get complicated when there are squared terms in the formulas. It's very easy to make mistakes, so numbers help a lot. The cylinder formula is given in the Reference Chart: $V = \pi r^2 h$. Instead of working with a million variables, let's Arithmetize to better visualize what's going on.

Think ahead a little bit. Since the radius of A is 4 times the radius of B, we should pick numbers that reflect that relationship in the most simple way we can think of:

Let $r_A = 4$
Let $r_B = 1$

Next, pick a simple number for the height of A so that we can calculate the volume of A:

Let $h_A = 1$

$$V_A = \pi (4)^2 (1)$$
$$V_A = 16\pi$$

The question tells us that the two cylinders have the same volume. Instead of picking a number for the height of B, we'll solve for it using the values that we already know:

$$V_B = \pi (r_B)^2 (h_B)$$
$$16\pi = \pi (1)^2 (h_B)$$
$$16 = h_B$$

Now we have enough information to answer the original question: what is the ratio of the height of A to the height of B? Make a fraction:

$$\frac{h_A}{h_B} = \frac{1}{16}$$

So the ratio is 1:16, which is the same as Choice D.

Rearrange Formulas — The Twists

When they start asking about ratios or comparisons, Arithmetize. Pick simple numbers that will be easy to manipulate.

Just be careful that you put the right values in the right places. Using subscripts (the little A's and B's) helps you stay organized.

Exercise: Rearrange Formulas

#1 — Answer = C
Divide both sides by $5dm$ to get w by itself. You'll get $w = \frac{p}{5dm}$. The story is irrelevant.

#2 — Answer = B
Arithmetize. Normally you'd have to use the Reference Chart to find the formula, but it was given here for convenience. You should make the original dimensions of the pyramid a length of 3 (to cancel out the fraction), a width of 1, and a height of 1. This makes the original volume equal to 1. As instructed, multiply the height by 6, which makes it 6. The length and width stay the same, so the new volume is also 6, which is 6 times greater than 1.

#3 — Answer = B
Multiply both sides by v to start: $Lv = (c + s)^2$. Take the square root of both sides to get $\sqrt{Lv} = c + s$. That's all you need to do. Arithmetize if needed.

#4 — Answer = C
Arithmetize. Pick convenient numbers. Make $c = 0.5$ and $s = 0.5$ so that the top term becomes 1^2, which is just 1. The original velocity should also be $v = 1$ so that the original length is simply $L = 1$. Double the velocity so that $v = 2$. Now the overall length is $L = \frac{1}{2}$, which is a decrease of 50% from the original.

WTF Models

There's no real lesson for these. It's best to let you try the questions without much direction. All of the answers are given as one long Exercise. There aren't really that many patterns on these questions. Some will be similar to the "Value" half of the Quantity & Value models. Others will be like Ratios, so thinking in terms of units will help you stay organized.

Overall, Arithmetizing can help you on the questions where they just want you to generate an equation. When they want you to solve, you might be able to Guess & Check, but that's hard when there are no answer choices.

Most Multi-Part Models will include a variety of the other types of models that we've seen. Remember that you should treat multi-part stories as separate questions. You will almost never need the answer from one of the parts to answer the others. They're independent of each other, and just happen to rely on the same chart, graph, or equation.

Oh, and if you're wondering why they're called WTF Models, just wait until you try some of the hard ones. You'll probably get that "WTF?" feeling and understand.

```
┌─────────────────────────────────────────┐
│        WTF Models — Summary               │
│                                           │
│ Show your work. Stay organized. Read      │
│ carefully.                                │
│                                           │
│ Arithmetize to better understand what's   │
│ going on.                                 │
│                                           │
│ If you're completely lost, take your best │
│ guess and move on. But pay attention to   │
│ where you are in the test. If it's an     │
│ early question, it's probably easy, so    │
│ trust your gut. If it's later on in the   │
│ section, it's probably hard, so it's okay │
│ to guess and move on.                     │
└─────────────────────────────────────────┘
```

Exercise: WTF Models

#1 — Answer = B
This is essentially the Value equation. Match the volume to the correct variable: $16w + 20s$. You can't combine these terms.

#2 — Answer = C
The twist here is that you need to convert the percentages into decimals. That eliminates Choices A and B. Choice C is the answer because it matches the discounts with the correct variables. Technically this is a linear equation, but it doesn't match the $y = mx + b$ format that we're used to. We don't need to convert it because the values in the question are supposed to appear in the equation as is.

#3 — Answer = D
Arithmetize. If Luis rented the truck for 7 days, it would cost him $(7)(\$50) = \$350$. Since 7 days is equivalent to 1 week, you can plug $w = 1$ into all of the choices to see which one also gives you 350. Only Choice D works.

#4 — Answer = A
Arithmetize. You should assume that there were 100 hares originally, in January of 2010. A 10% increase would mean that there were 110 hares in December of 2010. A 6% decrease would mean that there were 103.4 hares at the end of 2011. Be careful here. The question says that h is the number of hares at the end of 2011, so your numbers make $h = 103.4$. Plug that into the answer choices to see which one gives you 100, which is the number of hares at the beginning of 2010. Only Choice A works.

#5 — Answer = 120
Create two equations: $J + L = 300$ and $L = J + 60$. Substitute the second equation in for L in the first equation: $J + J + 60 = 300$. Solve for J to get that $J = 120$.

#6 — Answer = 5
Create two equations, but be careful with the subtraction that represents the "less than". Your equations should be: $B = S - 3$ and $5B + 3S = 49$. Substitute the first equation in for B in the second: $5(S - 3) + 3S = 49$. Solve for S to get that $S = 8$. But since the question wants the value of a blerg, you need to plug back into the first equation: $B = 8 - 3$. So a blerg is worth 5 points.

WTF Models

#7 — Answer = 46

Create two equations. The first is easy: $x + y + n = 138$. The second should be: $n = \frac{1}{2}(x + y)$. Since the second equation is messy, you should multiply by 2 to eliminate the fraction: $2n = x + y$. Notice that $x + y$ is also in the first equation. You can substitute without ever finding the values of x and y: $2n + n = 138$. Solve for n and you'll get that $n = 46$.

#8 — Answer = 25

There are many ways to solve this question. The easiest is to focus on the green apples since you know both the percentage and the actual number. The question says that Ivy will pick a total of 11 green apples (6 in the morning and 5 in the afternoon). Those 11 green apples represent 20% of all the apples since it also says that 80% of the apples should be red. You can set up a proportion to find the total number of apples: $\frac{20\%}{100\%} = \frac{11 \text{ green}}{x \text{ total apples}}$. Cross-multiply and divide to find that Ivy picks a total of 55 apples. Subtract the 11 green apples and the 19 red apples that she has already picked to find that Ivy needs to pick an additional 25 red apples.

#9 — Answer = B

Since the right side of the inequality is the same for all of the answer choices, you should focus on the left side. The question says that the team will need to win x additional games, so you can eliminate Choices A and D because they're subtracting x. The question also says that the team won 55% of its first 120 games, so Choice B is the answer. There's no need to take 55% of x.

#10 — Answer = D

Subtract H. Subtract B. Divide the whole thing by n. The most common mistake is subtracting H and B at the same time and forgetting to distribute the negative to the B. This is really just a Rearrange Formulas question.

#11 — Answer = 39

Set up an inequality such that Venue A > Venue D, as stated in the question. Using the formula and the values from the chart, your inequality should be:

$(3,000 + 800) + 75n > (3,500 + 875) + 60n$. Simplify and solve for n to get that $n > 38.3$. You need to have a whole number of guests, so you <u>must</u> go up to the next highest whole number, which is 39. Even though you would normally round down to 38, you can't in this case because then n would not be large enough.

#12 — Answer = 122

First, take 30% off the cost of the band at Venue B by using the OPEN formula: $(650)(1 - 0.30) = 455$. Then put the values into the equation: $(5,500 + 455) + 85n = 16,325$. Solve for n, and you should get that $n = 122$.

#13 — Answer = D

Unfortunately, there's no quick way to solve this. You need to set the equation equal to $10,000 and solve for n for each venue. You should get that Venue $A = 82$, $B = 45$, $C = 60$, and $D = 93$, so Venue D allows the most guests for that budget.

#14 — Answer = C

This is essentially a Linear Model. Put the equation into $y = mx + b$ form: $y = Fx + (H + B)$. The y-intercept is the entire term in parentheses. This is a weird twist, but it should be more obvious that F is the slope because it's attached to our x-term. The total cost of the hosting fee and band would be the initial value if there were 0 guests.

#15 — Answer = B

First, eliminate Choices A and C. The cost needs to be less than or equal to $10,000, so the inequality sign in these choices is backwards. The real question is whether the a belongs in parentheses. Since 75 is the cost per plate, you need to multiply both g and a by 75 to determine the final cost for the people who attend. In other words, you need to subtract $75 for each guest who does not attend. Choice D is wrong because it simply subtracts the number of guests who do not attend without taking into account that each of them would save Lauren $75.

Angle Rules

The Basics

Use the Reference Chart when you can. The most important constant is that supplementary angles add up to 180°. That means angles that lie on the same line will always be equal to 180°.

Example 1

This question is all about constants. Fill in the angles as you find them. Start with the supplementary angles:

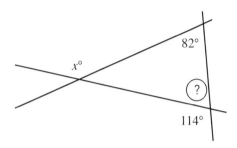

$$180 - 114 = 66$$

If you know two angles of a triangle, you can find the third:

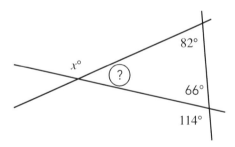

$$180 - 82 - 66 = 32$$

Now use supplementary angles to find x:

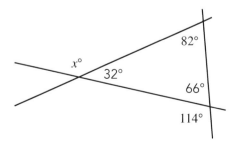

$$180 - 32 = 148$$

The correct answer is 148. Even if you don't see how you'll get to the final angle, you should keep adding whatever angles you can calculate to the picture. You'll eventually find your way to the right place.

Angle Rules — The Basics

Angles that lie on the same straight line add up to 180°. They are called supplementary angles.

If you're stuck, look for opportunities to use angle constants.

Figures are drawn to scale unless the question specifically says it's not. The angles that you get should roughly match the picture. Use that to check your work as you go.

The Twists

Example 2

There are a few other facts that can help you untwist the hard questions. In general, it's a good policy to check the question for unused information. It's very rare that the SAT gives you information that you don't end up using.

In this example, we are told that there are parallel lines. You might remember that two sets of parallel lines make a parallelogram, which has certain rules about congruent angles.

If not, that's okay! Try to make a picture that's similar to the parallel lines picture on the top of The Twists column.

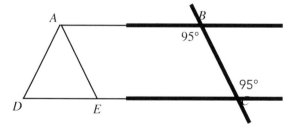

Angle Rules

If the top left angle is 95°, then the bottom right angle (which we just created) also has to be 95°. We can use the other set of parallel lines too:

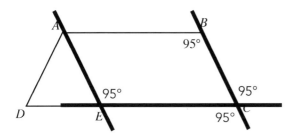

Use supplementary angles to start putting the triangle together:

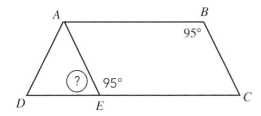

$$180 - 95 = 85$$

There's one more piece of information that we haven't used yet. The congruent sides AD and AE tell us that ADE is an isosceles triangle, which means that the angles opposite those sides are also congruent:

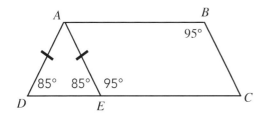

The correct answer is 85.

Angle Rules — The Twists

When two parallel lines are crossed by another line (a transversal), they form congruent angles (alternate interior angles) on opposite sides of the line.

Isosceles triangles have a pair of congruent angles opposite a pair of congruent sides.

Exercise: Angle Rules

#1 — Answer = C
If you extend the lines, you'll see the same image that is on the front of the packet. Angle b would also be the unmarked angle to the left of angle a, which means that a and b are supplementary (add to 180°). If $a + b = 180$, then $a = 180 - b$.

#2 — Answer = D
The angles in a triangle must add to 180°, so create an equation: $5x + 7x + 48 = 180$. Solve for x, which is 11 degrees. But be careful! The question doesn't want the value of x. It wants the measure of angle B, which is $7x$, or 77°.

#3 — Answer = 52
In this case, you need to know that the total number of degrees in a quadrilateral is 360. First, find the unmarked angle inside the shape, which is $360 - 156 = 204$. Now you can add all the angles together: $204 + x + x + x = 360$. Solve for x, which is 52. It's tempting to divide this picture into two triangles, but we don't know anything about the angles you'd create. They look like right angles, but they're not.

#4 — Answer = C
You need to know that the angles that are opposite each other are congruent, so $a = d$, $b = e$, and $c = f$. Since $b = e$, the equation in the question tells us that $c = d$ too. Substitute b in for e to see why: $\cancel{b} + c = d + \cancel{b}$. Since $a = d$ and $c = f$, then $a = c = d = f$. Choice C says this.

Similar & Congruent Triangles

The Basics

If you see two triangles and nothing else, you should instantly think of Similar Triangles. Set up ratios, and compare the correct sides.

Example 1

You should be able to set up ratios for this question, even if you have no idea why the triangles are similar. Just compare the sides of one triangle to the corresponding sides of the other triangle:

$$\frac{10}{12} = \frac{15}{AE}$$

Here's why this works. The question says that AB is parallel to CD, which means that these angles are the same (think back to the picture from the Angle Rules packet):

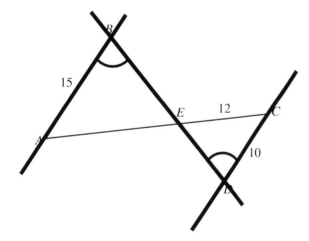

We also know that the angles near point E are congruent because they're vertical angles:

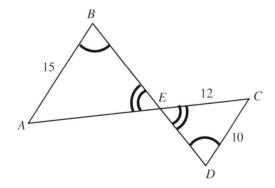

This is all we need to prove that two triangles are similar (AA). The remaining angles must also be congruent because there are always 180° in a triangle.

When you create your ratio, corresponding sides will be opposite the congruent angles. In other words, we know that AB and CD correspond because they're both opposite the congruent angles near point E. Sides AE and EC are both opposite the congruent angles at B and D.

$$\frac{10}{12} = \frac{15}{AE}$$

Cross-multiply and divide:

$$10(AE) = 180$$

$$AE = 18$$

But be careful! Choice A is wrong. Sometimes the SAT twists the question slightly by asking for a different side. In this case, they want the entire length of AC. Since we know AE and EC, we can find AC:

$$18 + 12 = 30$$

The correct answer is Choice D.

Similar & Congruent Triangles — The Basics

If you see two triangles, there's a good chance it's a Similar Triangles question.

Make sure that you compare corresponding sides in your ratio.

Reread the question, just in case the SAT is asking for something different.

The Twists

Example 2

If you have never seen the SSS, SAS, etc. list before, then congruent triangles might be more

Similar & Congruent Triangles

trouble than the topic is worth. It's a lot to understand for very little reward on the SAT. These questions don't show up very often.

For this example, we already know that two pairs of angles are congruent across the two triangles. Right now, we could say that these two triangles are <u>similar</u> because of AA (angle-angle).

Adding the third angle for Roman numeral I would not tell us anything new. That would be AAA, which is one of the congruent triangle exceptions. To show you why this doesn't work, here's a third triangle with the exact same angles, but notice that it's a different size — they're not congruent:

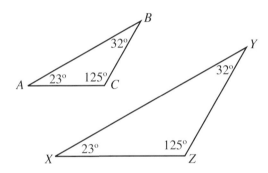

Roman numeral II would give us a congruent side in between the two congruent angles. That's what we mean by ASA (angle-side-angle). When we have this arrangement of congruent parts, we know that the rest of the pieces are also congruent — the two triangles are the same. We can visualize this with solid lines for the known congruent pairs and dashed lines for the unknown pieces. Notice that there's really only one way to extend the dotted lines to make a triangle:

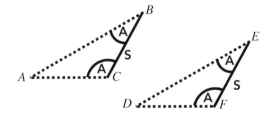

Similarly, Roman numeral III would also create a valid congruent triangle proof:

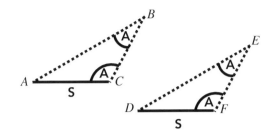

It's a little less visually obvious why this AAS (angle-angle-side) combination must produce congruent triangles, but it does. It's best not to think too hard about how all of this works. Full understanding is not necessary for the SAT points. You mostly need to be able to recognize the relationships between the given angles and sides:

    I.   AAA ✗
   II. ASA ✔
  III. AAS ✔

Therefore, Choice C is correct.

Similar & Congruent Triangles — The Twists

We only need two congruent angle pairs to prove that two triangles are <u>similar</u> (AA). Proving <u>congruent</u> triangles requires more information:
- SSS
- SAS
- ASA
- AAS
- HL (Hypotenuse-Leg)

There are two combinations that do <u>not</u> prove triangles congruent:
- AAA (we only know that they're similar)
- ASS (remember, "don't be an ASS!")

Hypotenuse-Leg is actually an exception to the "don't be an ASS" rule because we would know that two triangles share a right angle (A), the same leg (S), and the hypotenuse (S). However, once we get into right triangles, it's better to think in terms of trigonometry. Because of soh-cah-toa, if any two pieces of right triangles are congruent, then the triangles are fully congruent.

Similar & Congruent Triangles

Exercise: Similar & Congruent Triangles 1

#1 — Answer = C

You can use ratios to find the length of BC: $\frac{5}{13} = \frac{20}{BC}$. Cross-multiply and divide to find that $BC = 52$. Use Pythagorean Theorem to find the length of AC: $20^2 + AC^2 = 52^2$. You'll find that $AC = 48$. You can also reverse those steps too. Use Pythagorean Theorem with smaller numbers to get that EC is 12. Use it in a proportion to get AC.

#2 — Answer = 110

This question is twisted to give you the length of a side that you don't need. They're hoping that you get confused and don't know which side to use in the ratio. Since EC is next to angle C, you need to pick AE because it's next to the congruent angle A. Your ratio should be: $\frac{330}{540} = \frac{EC}{180}$. Cross-multiply and divide to find that $EC = 110$.

#3 — Answer = B

Fill in the unknown angles. Angle A is 37° and angle F is 53°. This helps you match the sides in your ratio. AC is opposite the 53° angle, so the correct answer should have DE in the numerator because it is also opposite the 53° angle. Since AB is opposite the right angle, the denominator should be EF because it is also opposite the right angle: $\frac{AC}{AB} = \frac{DE}{EF}$.

#4 — Answer = B

Choices C and D are both wrong because they aren't telling us anything new about the two triangles together. Learning a fact about just one triangle doesn't help us compare them. Choice A is wrong because it would give us the ASS arrangement, which does not prove congruence. Choice B would give us SAS, which proves that they're congruent.

Exercise: Similar & Congruent Triangles 2

#5 — Answer = C

The key is to ignore AB at first. Get Back to Basics. This is clearly about two similar triangles, so find a way to make ratios to compare them. The given side AC in the big triangle is comparable to BC in the smaller triangle. BD and AE are also comparable. You can make this ratio: $\frac{BD}{BC} = \frac{AE}{AC}$. We don't know the exact measurements of BD and AE, but it really doesn't matter as long as the proportion is preserved. The easiest thing is to just make BD be 2 and AE be 5. Solve this proportion for BC: $\frac{2}{BC} = \frac{5}{40}$. You'll get that $BC = 16$, but don't fall for the trap answer Choice B. We were asked for AB, so subtract the value of BC from the total of 40 for AC. In general, you should use the actual names of the lines in your proportions instead of x so that you don't forget what you're solving for.

#6 — Answer = 80

We could find the measures of all of the angles, but we don't need to. If $\angle A$ corresponds to $\angle D$ and $\angle B$ corresponds to $\angle E$, then the 100° must correspond to the remaining angle in the bottom triangle, which is $\angle EFD$. We're trying to find $\angle AFE$, which is supplementary to $\angle EFD$, so $180 - 100 = 80$.

#7 — Answer = C

The twist here is that there are actually 3 triangles: ABD, BCD, and the big triangle ABC. The ratio in the question is about the big triangle ABC, so you need to use sides from a triangle that is similar to ABC. Both of the small triangles have a 52° angle, just like the big triangle, so that's not much help. But only triangle ABD shares an additional angle with the big triangle. They both include angle A. When two triangles have two of the same angles, then they are similar (AA). Your answer should only use sides that are in triangle ABD. In the big triangle, AB is opposite the 52° angle at C, so your ratio should have AD in the numerator because it is also opposite a 52° angle. That's actually all you need to get the answer because Choice C is the only one that has AD in the numerator. Still, BC is opposite angle A in the big triangle, so BD should be the denominator of the ratio because it is opposite angle A in the small triangle. This is very confusing, but hopefully a picture helps. The triangles have been separated and rotated to show the corresponding sides:

Similar & Congruent Triangles

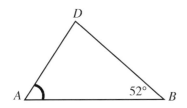

Exercise: Similar & Congruent Triangles 3

#8 — Answer = B

This is a twist on the normal similar triangle rules. Obviously, these aren't triangles, but the proportions work the same way. Parallel lines will divide intersecting lines into proportional segments. You can set up something like this: $\frac{AB}{BC} = \frac{FE}{ED}$. Plug in the correct values and solve for $AB = \frac{30}{4} = 7.5$.

#9 — Answer = C

The twist here is that they give you information that doesn't matter, which is rare on the SAT. The fact about the perimeters is irrelevant. The angles will not be affected by the difference in the triangles' sizes. Get Back to Basics by drawing triangle DEF. It should match up to ABC exactly as shown below. You will see that $\angle D$ is the same as $\angle A$. There are 180° in a triangle, so subtract the right angle and the 52° to find $\angle A = \angle D = 38°$.

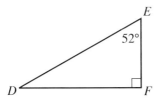

#10 — Answer = C

There are a lot of trap answers here. You could plot each of the points, connect the dots to see the full

triangle, and then see if it looks like a bigger version of ABC. The main complication is that DEF is reflected, so it might be hard to see the similarity. The most thorough way to figure out what's happening is to find the proportion between the two triangles. We can compare the distance between points A and B to the distance between points D and E. To get from A to B, we would go up 2 boxes and over 1 box. To get from D to E, though, we would go up 4 boxes and over 2 boxes. Ignore the difference in direction (left vs. right), and you can see that the relationship is the same: $\frac{2}{1} = \frac{4}{2}$. In other words, triangle DEF is twice as big as triangle ABC. We can follow this same "slope" logic to move from point D to F by doubling the "slope" from point A to C. To get from A to C, we'd go down 1 box and over 2 boxes. Doubling that, we'd get from D to F by going down 2 boxes and over 4 boxes. That would get us to the point $(-5, -1)$. We can confirm this by moving from point C to B and then F to E: $\frac{3}{1} = \frac{6}{2}$.

Cylinders & More

The Basics

They give you the formulas in the Reference Chart.

Example 1

Plug Points Into Equations! Just put the information into the formula:

$$V = \pi r^2 h$$

$$144\pi = \pi r^2 (9)$$

$$\frac{144\pi}{9\pi} = \frac{\pi r^2 (9)}{9\pi}$$

$$16 = r^2$$

$$4 = r$$

Be careful! The question asks for the diameter, not the radius. It's underlined! **The correct answer is 8 because the diameter is double the radius.**

Cylinders & More — The Basics

Use the formula. Keep π as a symbol.

Don't confuse radius and diameter. The diameter is twice the radius.

The Twists

Example 2

A common twist is to ask about two cylinders. Sometimes the volume is the same, like when they're pouring liquid from one container to another. Other times, they want you to compare two differently-sized cylinders. Regardless, you're still basing everything off of the standard cylinder formula.

Let's start this question by looking at the first cylinder:

$$256 = \pi r^2 h$$

Right away, I sense a problem. There are too many missing pieces of this formula. The question asks me to eventually build a cylinder that is "three times as tall and one half as wide", but I don't know how tall or wide <u>this</u> cylinder is. This question is begging to be Arithmetized. With a calculator, the numbers you choose wouldn't really matter, but I would try to pick numbers that would make the math as easy as possible, regardless:

For the original cylinder…
Let $r = 2$

I'll pick a number for r that will be very easy to divide in half later for the second cylinder. But first I need to figure out the height of the original cylinder using the formula:

$$256 = \pi (2)^2 h$$

$$\frac{256}{4\pi} = \frac{4\pi h}{4\pi}$$

$$\frac{64}{\pi} = h$$

This number looks scary, but it's really not. The π will cancel out when we start working with the second cylinder, but we could even get rid of it now if we were very confident in our Arithmetizing skills. This question is asking about cylinders where the radius and height change, but π is a constant, so it can't ever change. In other words, we could have ignored the π from the beginning because it remains constant between the two cylinders. We're only interested in how the changes in radius and height affect the volume. If this is confusing, don't worry about it for now. Keep practicing Arithmetize and you'll get better at knowing the nuances of the strategy.

Let's follow the instructions and change the values of our radius and height for the second cylinder:

"three times as tall" means:

$$h = 3\left(\frac{64}{\pi}\right) = \frac{192}{\pi}$$

Cylinders & More

"one half as wide" means:

$$r = \frac{1}{2}(2) = 1$$

Therefore, the volume of the second cylinder is:

$$V = \pi(1)^2\left(\frac{192}{\pi}\right)$$

$$V = 192$$

As promised, the π's canceled to leave us with a new volume of 192. And if you had used a calculator and chosen different values for the original radius and height, you still would have gotten 192 as the new volume.

Solving algebraically is easier <u>if and only if</u> you don't make any careless algebra mistakes along the way. Most students either get lost in all the variables or fail to square the new radius completely. To solve with traditional algebra, you'd start out the same way:

$$V_1 = \pi r^2 h$$
$$256 = \pi r^2 h$$

There's nothing else you can do with the first equation. But then you'd need to very carefully build the equation of the second cylinder:

$$V_2 = \pi \left(\frac{r}{2}\right)^2 (3h)$$

Simplify:

$$V = \pi \left(\frac{r^2}{4}\right)(3h)$$

$$V = \frac{3\pi r^2 h}{4}$$

Now what? Look back at the first equation that we mostly ignored. It actually tells us some very important information. When solving this with algebra, we don't know the values of the individual variables, so we need to be comfortable working with

groups of letters and numbers. Notice that the same group appears in both equations:

$$256 = \pi r^2 h$$

$$V_2 = \frac{3(\pi r^2 h)}{4}$$

The term $\pi r^2 h$ is in both of our equations. Since we based the second equation off of the values in the first, we can just substitute in 256 for $\pi r^2 h$:

$$V = \frac{3(256)}{4}$$

$$V = 192$$

Again, the correct answer is 192. As always with algebra solutions, they're faster and easier if you see the shortcut, but there's not much you could do if you didn't see it. Arithmetize should be your default move on a question like this, but at the least, it should be a strategy that you try if you can't find the shortcut within 10 seconds. Don't waste time staring at questions, hoping that the solution appears to you. Use a strategy and start working!

Cylinders & More — The Twists

The SAT can twist cylinder questions in lots of ways, but you're usually not straying too far from the standard cylinder formula.

Make sure that you're careful when you are working with the cylinder's radius. Since the term is squared, changes will also need to be squared. Use parentheses, and you should be fine.

Exercise: Cylinders & More

#1 — Answer = 151, 152, 153, 154, 155, 156, or 157
You should start with either the minimum or maximum value of the radius. If you assume the radius is 2.45 inches, then the volume formula will be: $V = \pi(2.45)^2(8)$. Use your calculator, multiplying with the π button to find that the volume is approximately 150.9. You need to round up to an integer, which is

Cylinders & More

151. If you had started with 2.50 as the radius, you would have gotten the volume as 157.1, which should be rounded down to 157 so that it falls within the range. Any integer in between is also acceptable.

#2 — Answer = 160

Instead of finding the volume of the whole cylinder with and without the rock, just find the volume of the 2 inch height change. Another twist is that they give you the area of the base, which is a circle. This means that you can replace the entire πr^2 portion of the cylinder formula: $V = (80)(2)$.

#3 — Answer = 10

If the radius is equal to the height, then the volume formula becomes: $125\pi = \pi r^2(r)$. The π's cancel, so the equation simplifies to: $125 = r^3$. The cube root of 125 is 5, but the question does not want the radius. Double the radius to find that the diameter is 10.

#4 — Answer = 109

Start by finding the volume of the cylinder portion: $V = \pi(2)^2(6)$. This simplifies to 24π. Next find the volume of the sphere. Since each end is half a sphere, you have one whole sphere. The formula is given in the Reference Chart: $V = \frac{4}{3}\pi(2)^3$. This simplifies to $\frac{32\pi}{3}$. Add the two values and use the π button on your calculator to find the actual numerical value, which is approximately 108.9. Round to the nearest cubic millimeter, which is 109.

Part Over Whole

The Basics

Part Over Whole questions are remarkably similar to each other. The process is almost always exactly the same. You'll create ratios that relate a value for part of the circle to the value for the whole circle. Let's take a simple example — a quarter of a circle:

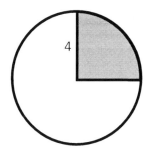

A quarter of a circle forms a 90° angle. If the radius of the circle is 4, then the shaded area is 4π. The arc length for the shaded region is 2π. And the angle could also be expressed as $\frac{\pi}{2}$ radians.

But we often don't have enough information to know all of these things at once. Or at least not immediately. But we can use the fact that all of these parts are the same fraction of the whole:

$$\frac{\text{part}}{\text{whole}} = \frac{90°}{360°} = \frac{4\pi}{16\pi} = \frac{2\pi}{8\pi} = \frac{\frac{\pi}{2}}{2\pi} = \frac{1}{4}$$

No matter what, the part is one fourth of the whole circle.

Example 1

Start with the pieces that we know. They give us part of an angle, so we should compare the angle of the shaded part to the whole number of degrees in a circle:

$$\frac{\text{part}}{\text{whole}} = \frac{67.5°}{360°}$$

Our ratio will be consistent when we talk about the area because it's still the same fraction of the circle. We don't know the area of the part, so that's our x. But we do know the whole area, so that's the denominator of the fraction:

$$\frac{\text{part}}{\text{whole}} = \frac{67.5^o}{360^o} = \frac{x}{64\pi}$$

Cross-multiply, but keep π as a symbol. You almost never have to use 3.14 to multiply it out.

$$360x = 4{,}320\pi$$

Divide to find x:

$$\frac{360x}{360} = \frac{4{,}320\pi}{360}$$

$$x = 12\pi$$

So the area of the shaded region is 12π. **Choice B is the correct answer.**

Part Over Whole — The Basics

A fraction of a circle will be consistent. It will have the same fraction of the degrees, radians, area, and circumference. You can use ratios to relate these different values.

Put the part over the whole. There are always 360° in a whole circle, so you'll often use the number of degrees as one of the ratios.

Do not multiply out π unless you absolutely have to. π either cancels out or stays as a symbol in the answer.

The Twists

Example 2

The twist here is that there are more steps, but the core of the question is still Part Over Whole because part of a circle is bolded. Start by setting up the ratio. They want the length of the bold arc, so one of our ratios will look like:

$$\frac{\text{bold arc}}{\text{whole circumference}}$$

Part Over Whole

The bold arc will be x, and we can find the whole circumference because they told us that the radius is 10. Use the Reference Chart if you forget the circumference formula:

$$C = 2\pi r$$

$$C = 2\pi(10)$$

$$C = 20\pi$$

So half our ratio is:

$$\frac{x}{20\pi}$$

We need to set that equal to something. Since there are degree measures in the picture, we probably will end up using degrees and the angle that opens up to the bold arc (the bigger angle JOK, which is right where the letter O is):

$$\frac{x}{20\pi} = \frac{\text{bold angle}}{360^o}$$

Looks like we need to find that bold angle. What do we know? That angle L is 36°. That's not enough to figure out the other angles. Is there anything in the question that we haven't used? Yes. The question tells us that JL and KL are tangent to the circle. The word "tangent" should pop out of the question. It's really important. A line that is tangent to a circle forms a right angle with the radius of the circle:

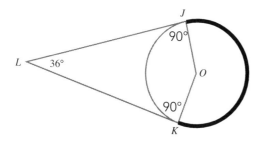

This helps a lot. JOKL is a quadrilateral (four-sided figure), and all quadrilaterals have 360°. We can figure out the smaller angle near center O:

$$360 - 90 - 90 - 36 = 144$$

If we put that angle on our figure, it's clear that we can now figure out the larger bold angle where the letter O is:

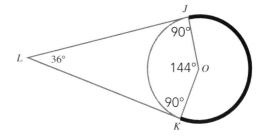

$$360 - 144 = 216$$

Put that into our Part Over Whole proportion:

$$\frac{x}{20\pi} = \frac{216°}{360°}$$

Cross-multiply and divide:

$$360x = 4{,}320\pi$$

$$x = 12\pi$$

The correct answer is Choice B. One thing to point out is that Choice A is a trick answer. That's the length of the unbolded part of the circle. Just a reminder to be careful!

Part Over Whole — The Twists

There might be other steps, but everything will come back to Part Over Whole ratios. Start there so that you know what to look for.

Use the Reference Chart for circumference and area formulas. It also reminds you that there are 360° and 2π radians in a whole circle.

Exercise: Part Over Whole

#1 — Answer = 135

You're given part of the circumference, so use the radius to find the whole circumference, which is 8π. Set up your Part Over Whole ratios: $\frac{3\pi}{8\pi} = \frac{x}{360}$. Cross-

Part Over Whole

multiply and divide to find that the angle is 135 degrees.

#2 — Answer = 7/16

You can still use a Part Over While ratio, but you don't need to set it equal to anything because they're asking for the entire fraction, not a part. You have part of the circle in terms of radians, so put that over the whole number of radians in a circle: $\dfrac{\frac{7\pi}{8}}{2\pi}$. You can simplify the fraction by multiplying the numerator by the reciprocal of the denominator: $\dfrac{7\pi}{8} \cdot \dfrac{1}{2\pi}$. This reduces to $\dfrac{7}{16}$.

#3 — Answer = 40

There's no need to figure out the angles of a pentagon. Since it's a regular pentagon, it divides the circle into 5 equal pieces. Arc BD is 2 of the 5 pieces. Set up the Part Over Whole ratios with this fraction and the whole circumference: $\dfrac{2}{5} = \dfrac{x}{100}$. Cross-multiply and divide to find that arc BD is 40.

#4 — Answer = 3

You have both the area and angle of the part, so you can find the whole area: $\dfrac{40}{360} = \dfrac{\pi}{x}$. Cross-multiply and divide to find that the whole area is 9π. The question asks for the radius, so use the area formula and solve for the radius: $9\pi = \pi r^2$. The radius is 3.

#5 — Answer = 46, 47, 48, 49, or 50

They give you the radius, so you should calculate the whole area, which is 25π. They give you a range of values for the area of the part, so the easiest thing to do is pick something in the middle, like 10.5. At least it gives you a starting point to set up your Part Over Whole ratios: $\dfrac{10.5}{25\pi} = \dfrac{x}{360}$. Cross-multiply and divide to find that $x = 48.128$. You actually need to use the π button on your calculator this time. But since the degree measure has to be an integer, you should round the decimal to 48 degrees even. If you had chosen a different value for the part of the area, you would have gotten other possible values for the degree measure. All of the values above are acceptable because they give a partial area that falls between 10 and 11.

Trigonometry

The Basics

This is where the SAT has a big advantage over the ACT. You do not need to memorize crazy trigonometry formulas for the SAT. In fact, the most common trigonometry questions require only knowledge of soh-cah-toa.

Example 1

Use soh-cah-toa to go through all of the choices.

A) $\sin B = \dfrac{\text{opposite}}{\text{hypotenuse}} = \dfrac{b}{c}$

B) $\cos B = \dfrac{\text{adjacent}}{\text{hypotenuse}} = \dfrac{a}{c}$

C) $\tan B = \dfrac{\text{opposite}}{\text{adjacent}} = \dfrac{b}{a}$

D) $\tan A = \dfrac{\text{opposite}}{\text{adjacent}} = \dfrac{a}{b}$

Choice B gives us exactly what the question wants, which makes it the answer.

Trigonometry — The Basics

Know the trigonometric ratios. Use soh-cah-toa to help you remember them.

The hypotenuse is the side across from the right angle. It is always the longest side.

The Twists

Example 2

A lot of people have trouble with trigonometry because they never really learned what sine, cosine, and tangent mean. They're ratios. They don't give the value of the sides of a triangle. They give a comparison. Just like with other Ratios, Part Over Whole, and Similar Triangle questions, the fractions that we make will be consistent, even as the values change.

In this question, we're given the value of sin B, so we should work backwards and think about what that means in terms of the sides:

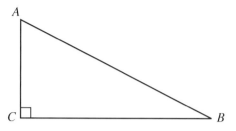

$$\sin B = \frac{3}{5} = \frac{\text{opposite}}{\text{hypotenuse}} = \frac{AC}{AB}$$

The question also gives us the value of AC, so let's put that in our ratio:

$$\frac{3}{5} = \frac{12}{AB}$$

Do what we always do with Ratios. Cross-multiply and divide:

$$3(AB) = 60$$

$$AB = 20$$

Put the side lengths on the picture:

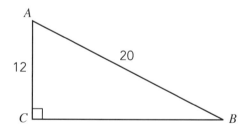

They want BC, and we can get it by using Pythagorean Theorem, which is given in the Reference Chart:

$$a^2 + b^2 = c^2$$

$$12^2 + (BC)^2 = 20^2$$

$$144 + (BC)^2 = 400$$

Trigonometry

$$(BC)^2 = 256$$

$$BC = 16$$

The correct answer is 16.

Trigonometry — The Twists

Soh-cah-toa describes different ratios between the sides of a triangle. When questions are twisted, you'll probably need to set up a proportion to compare the trigonometric ratio to the actual side lengths.

You'll almost never need to use the sine, cosine, or tangent buttons on your calculator.

If you have two sides of a right triangle, you can use Pythagorean Theorem to find the third.

Formulas

Example 3

If you can't use soh-cah-toa, then you probably need to use one of these two formulas. You have to memorize them because they're not in the Reference Chart, but they don't come up that often, so they're a low priority.

Understanding why they are true makes them easier to remember:

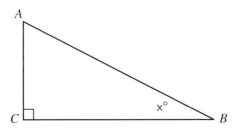

Let's start with $\sin x$. In this case:

$$\sin x = \frac{AC}{AB}$$

How does $\cos (90 - x)$ fit into this? Remember that there are 180° in a triangle. We already know that 90° are accounted for by the right angle. Angles A and B make up the other 90°. In other words:

$$A + B = 90$$

$$A + x = 90$$

$$A = 90 - x$$

Put that on the picture:

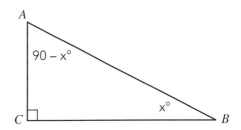

Now find the ratio for $\cos (90 - x)$:

$$\cos (90 - x) = \frac{AC}{AB}$$

It's the same as $\sin x$! That's because the opposite side for angle B is the adjacent side for angle A. The second version of the formula is true for the same reason.

Formulas — Summary

Memorize the extra trigonometry formulas:

$$\sin x = \cos (90 - x)$$

$$\cos x = \sin (90 - x)$$

The two small angles in a right triangle add up to 90°. That's why these formulas are true!

Trigonometry

right triangles, so that's my clue to use the other formula instead.

#1 — Answer = 5/13 or .384 or .385

Remember that trigonometry is all about similar triangles. The values are ratios, so the sine of angle A is the same as the sine of angle D. The sine of angle D is the opposite over the hypotenuse, which is $\frac{5}{13}$.

#2 — Answer = 4/3 or 1.33

The twist is that the cosine is given as a decimal. You always see trigonometry as fractions, so convert this to a fraction: $0.8 = \frac{4}{5}$. Now you can use these numbers as values for the side lengths. Since cosine is adjacent over hypotenuse, you can make side a equal to 4 and side c equal to 5. This is a 3-4-5 special right triangle, so side b is equal to 3. This is a common triangle on the SAT, so you should be comfortable filling in the third side without having to go through Pythagorean Theorem. Now find the tangent of A, which is the opposite side over the adjacent side: $\frac{4}{3}$.

#3 — Answer = 3/5 or .6

Use the formula on the front of the packet: $\cos a = \sin (90 - a)$.

#4 — Answer = A

Using ratios requires the least amount of memorization because the whole numbers of degrees and radians in a circle are given in the Reference Chart: $\frac{900}{360} = \frac{x}{2\pi}$. This is essentially Part Over Whole. Cross-multiply and divide to find that $x = 5\pi$.

#5 — Answer = 0

Draw point D somewhere along line AB, and draw CD, which should divide the 90° angle into two separate angles. You can label angle ACD as x, which means that angle DCB is $90 - x$. You can replace the angle names in the equation with your labels: $\sin (x) - \cos (90 - x)$. Since $\sin (x) = \cos (90 - x)$, your equation is really: $\sin (x) - \sin (x)$. This is equal to 0. Remember that if an SAT Trigonometry question seems really hard, it's probably going to use this rule in some way. We could try to use soh-cah-toa at first, but drawing line CD will likely create a problem — we no longer have right triangles. Soh-cah-toa requires

Advanced Geometry

The Basics

There are a lot of geometry rules, but each individual geometry question will use only 3 or 4 of the rules max. The Reference Chart can guide you to the right rule. Try to think in terms of the basic shapes: rectangles, triangles, and circles.

Example 1

This picture clearly involves right triangles. Normally, if we have two sides of a right triangle, we can use Pythagorean Theorem to get the third.

In this case, we only have one side. When that happens, we need to use the special right triangle proportions. These are given in the Reference Chart! Essentially, certain angle measures allow us to know all of the sides of a right triangle, even when we only have one side.

In this question, the 30° and 60° angles should jump out. Why are they telling us this? It probably matters. Sure enough, the Reference Chart shows us that 30-60-90 right triangles are special.

Let's match up the proportions on the Reference Chart to the 30-60-90 right triangle on the right side of our picture:

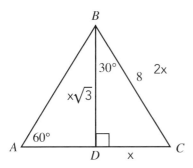

Create an equation using the one side that we know and the corresponding proportion:

$$2x = 8$$

That helps us get the value of DC:

$$x = 4$$

And the value of BD:

$$x\sqrt{3} = 4\sqrt{3}$$

That's what the question wants, so Choice C is the correct answer.

Advanced Geometry — The Basics

If you have <u>two</u> sides of a right triangle, use Pythagorean Theorem to find the third side.

If you have <u>one</u> side of a right triangle, look for 30°, 60°, and 45° angles so that you can use the special right triangle formulas in the Reference Chart.

The Twists

Example 2

Shaded region problems are common on the SAT. If there's a circle involved, it might be a Part Over Whole question. If not, use shapes that you know well to build the region, or subtract to get the region as a remainder.

In this question, we know that the area of the big square is 4 because each side is 2.

After that, you might be stuck. But remember that geometry questions rarely give you information that you don't use. The angle in the top right is split into $2x$ and x. What do we know about this angle? Since it's the corner of a square, it must equal 90°, so:

$$x + 2x = 90$$

$$3x = 90$$

$$x = 30$$

Put those angles on the picture, and you'll see that we've got 30° and 60° angles, not just in that corner, but in all of the triangles. Those should jump out. We're working with 30-60-90 right triangles. Use

Advanced Geometry

the Reference Chart to remind yourself of the formula. Here's one of the triangles removed from the main picture so that we can more easily see what's going on. I'm also using y so that we don't confuse the sides with the x's in the angles:

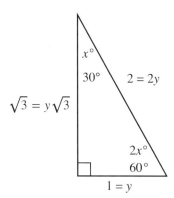

We can find the shaded area by starting with the big square and "chopping off" all of the triangles:

shaded area = big square − 4(triangles)

The area of one triangle is:

$$A = \frac{1}{2}bh$$

$$A = \frac{1}{2}(1)(\sqrt{3})$$

$$A = \frac{\sqrt{3}}{2}$$

So our shaded area equation becomes:

$$\text{shaded area} = 4 - 4\left(\frac{\sqrt{3}}{2}\right)$$

$$\text{shaded area} = 4 - 2\sqrt{3}$$

That's it. Choice D is the correct answer. You could also get this answer by building the small square itself. Notice how the shaded square lies along the big leg of the triangle, but only part of it. The rest of the big leg is matched up with the short leg, which had a measurement of 1. The entire big leg is $\sqrt{3}$, so we can do some subtraction to find the

portion of the big leg that is also the side of the shaded square:

side of shaded square = big leg − small leg

side of shaded square = $\sqrt{3} - 1$

The area of the shaded square will be the side squared:

$$(\sqrt{3} - 1)^2$$

$$(\sqrt{3} - 1)(\sqrt{3} - 1)$$

$$3 - \sqrt{3} - \sqrt{3} + 1$$

$$4 - 2\sqrt{3}$$

Advanced Geometry — The Twists

Be clever.

Solve shaded region problems by focusing on familiar shapes — rectangles, triangles, and circles.

You can build shaded regions by adding together other shapes.

You can also find shaded regions by subtracting away shapes until the shaded area is all that remains.

Three-dimensional shapes can be solved either by using the volume formulas in the Reference Chart, or by finding two-dimensional shapes hidden within the picture.

Exercise: Advanced Geometry 1

#1 — Answer = 1/3 or .333

This sounds like a Part Over Whole question, and it basically is. Draw in another radius from point O to point N. You've created an isosceles triangle. Since ON and OM are both radiuses of the circle, they are congruent, which also means that the angles opposite those sides are congruent. That makes angle N equal to 30°. You can subtract the two 30°

Advanced Geometry

angles to find that angle O is 120°. Set up a Part Over Whole ratio: $\frac{120}{360}$. This reduces to $\frac{1}{3}$.

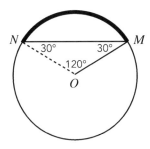

#2 — Answer = C

You can solve this by making two triangles. First, label the point directly below point P (the back bottom left corner) as point R. You can find the length of line QR, which is the diagonal of the base. You've made a right triangle with legs of length 2. Using Pythagorean Theorem or 45-45-90 triangles, you should find that QR is equal to $2\sqrt{2}$. Now you have a second triangle that cuts through the middle of the cube. It has one leg PR, another leg QR, and the hypotenuse is PQ, which is what the question wants you to find. The length of PR is 2, and the length of QR is $2\sqrt{2}$. You can use Pythagorean Theorem to find PQ: $(2)^2 + (2\sqrt{2})^2 = PQ^2$. You'll find that PQ is equal to $\sqrt{12}$, which simplifies to $2\sqrt{3}$. Many three-dimensional shape questions can be solved by making two-dimensional triangles.

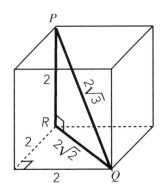

3 — Answer = D

Arithmetize. Let $a = 2$. A hexagon can be divided into 6 equilateral triangles, in this case with sides of length 2. Each of those equilateral triangle can be divided into 2 special 30-60-90 right triangles. In this

case, the hypotenuse is 2, which corresponds to the $2x$ side according to the Reference Chart. Because we picked $a = 2$, the value of x is 1, which makes the side opposite the 30° angle equal to 1 and the side opposite the 60° angle equal to $\sqrt{3}$. You can use these two sides to find the area of the equilateral triangle. The base is 2, and the height is $\sqrt{3}$: $A = \frac{1}{2}(2)(\sqrt{3})$. The area of one equilateral triangle is $\sqrt{3}$. Multiply this by 6 to find the area of the entire hexagon (since there are 6 of these equilateral triangles in the hexagon). The area of the entire hexagon is $6\sqrt{3}$. Choice D gives you this same value when you replace the a with 2.

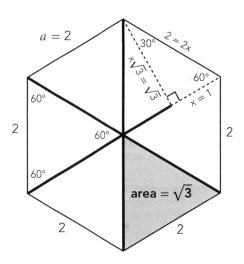

#4 — Answer = B

Very very rarely, the SAT tests the Unit Circle. You need to know which trigonometry functions are positive and negative in each quadrant. Use "All Students Take Calculus" to remember. The first letter of each word tells you the positive function in the quadrants as you cycle through:

Advanced Geometry

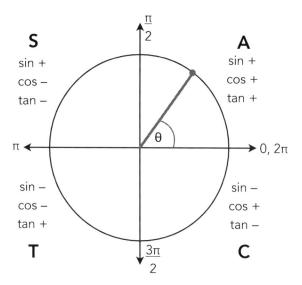

This question tells you that angle x is in the first quadrant, which means that a is positive to start. But $-a$ will need to be the cosine of an angle in either the 2nd or 3rd quadrants because those are the quadrants where cosine is negative. Choice C can be eliminated because it actually gives the exact same angle. Since 2π is a full circle, C is just going around the circle once and ending up where we started. Choice A would be in the 4th quadrant (bottom right), which can't be correct because cosine is positive in that quadrant. Choice D is similar in that we'd be starting at 0 radians, going around the circle a full time for the 2π radians, and then going below the x-axis for whatever angle that x is. Basically, this choice is identical to Choice A. That leaves Choice B, which is in the second quadrant, where cosine is negative. If this confuses you, don't worry. It is not commonly tested on the SAT. It only matters if you're shooting for a 750 or better.

Exercise: Advanced Geometry 2

#5 — Answer = B

Whenever you have circles involve with hard geometry, start by drawing radiuses. In this case, connect points A and O. We know that this is an isosceles triangle because the two radiuses must be equivalent. That means that the angles opposite the equal sides must also be equal ($\angle A$ and $\angle B$). And since $\angle B = 60°$, then $\angle A = 60°$, and $\angle AOB$ must also be 60° because that's all that's left to make 180°.

It turns out that this triangle is actually equilateral. This question ends up being like a Part Over Whole because we'll need to find the area of the sector and then subtract the area of the equilateral triangle. The area of the entire circle is $\pi(6)^2 = 36\pi$. Our ratio should be: $\frac{60}{360} = \frac{\text{sector}}{36\pi}$. Cross-multiply to find that the area of the sector is 6π. In order to find the area of the equilateral triangle, we'll need to divide it in half to find the height, which is part of a 30-60-90 right triangle. Use the Reference Chart to find that the height is $3\sqrt{3}$. The area of the triangle is $\frac{1}{2}(6)(3\sqrt{3}) = 9\sqrt{3}$. Subtract to find the shaded area: $6\pi - 9\sqrt{3}$. To help you visualize, here are separate drawings of the sector and the equilateral triangle:

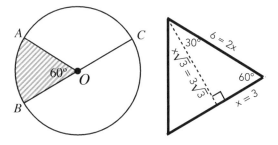

#6 — Answer = B

Get Back to Basics. It's fairly easy to split this shape into something more familiar — a triangle and a rectangle. You can fill in the missing dimensions of the triangle using the dimensions given. The area of the rectangle is $(8)(3) = 24$. The area of the triangle is $\frac{1}{2}(4)(3) = 6$. Add the two pieces to get the area of the whole.

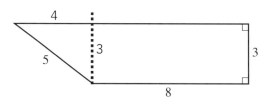

#7 — Answer = D

Draw a square inside a circle with each corner touching the outside edge of the circle. Draw a radius from the center to a corner of the square. Draw another radius from the center to one of the adjacent corners, forming a right triangle with the right angle on the center. This is also an isosceles

Advanced Geometry

triangle because both legs are radiuses, so we can use the 45-45-90 proportions to find that the side of the square is $4\sqrt{2}$. The area of a square is the side squared: $(4\sqrt{2}) = 16 \cdot 2 = 32$.

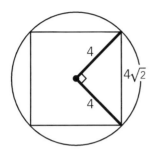

#8 — Answer = A

The SAT rarely tests circle rules, other than sectors (Part Over Whole). However, it does happen occasionally. For this question, you need to know that inscribed angles are equal to half of the inscribed arc. An inscribed angle has its vertex somewhere on the circumference of the circle. In this case, $\angle ABD$ is inscribed, so it has half the measure of the arc that it opens up to. Half of 70 is 35, so $\angle ABD = 35°$. Since we have parallel lines, we know that $\angle ABD$ and $\angle BDC$ are alternate interior angles, which means that they are congruent. (see the Angle Rules packet for more on parallel lines)

Exercise: Advanced Geometry 3

#9 — Answer = C

There are a lot of ways to get the correct answer, but Arithmetizing might make all of them easier, especially if you have a calculator so that the messy radicals and π's won't be an issue. For the sake of showing off the power of Arithmetize, I'm going to make $k = \sqrt{2}$, which is a very strange number to pick (don't we normally pick 0 and 1?). If you start by connecting point O to A or B, you'll see that you're building a 45-45-90 triangle with the radius. Knowing that k is the hypotenuse, which must follow the proportion $x\sqrt{2}$, I picked $k = \sqrt{2}$ so that the main x in the proportion is 1. That makes the short side of the rectangle 1 and the long side 2. The area of the rectangle is $(2)(1) = 2$. The area of the circle is $\pi(\sqrt{2})^2 = 2\pi$. Subtract the rectangle from the circle

to get $2\pi - 2$, which matches with C if we factor out the 2 and substitute for k. Yes, we could have still picked a simple number for k, but the rest of the solution would have been more difficult. Arithmetizing on hard questions sometimes comes down to a choice between annoying numbers to start or annoying numbers at the end. When you're first learning how to Arithmetize, always choose easy numbers to start. But as you gain experience, think ahead to plan out the Arithmetizing that will work best for each situation. Here's the picture with the un-Arithmetized expressions for the rectangle:

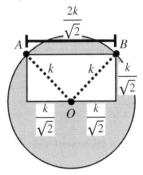

#10 — Answer = D

Like #4, this question tests the Unit Circle. Start with the "All Students Take Calculus" memorization helper to put the original angle and all of the choices into a positive/negative context. Cosine is positive in the 4th quadrant, so we need our answer choice to give a positive result as well. Choice A does not. The radian measure $\frac{\pi}{6}$ is an angle in the first quadrant (where cosine is positive), but the negative out front will make the entire value negative. Unfortunately, all of the other choices would produce positive results because $\frac{\pi}{3}$ is also in the 1st quadrant and $\frac{11\pi}{6}$ is in the 4th quadrant (where cosine is positive). The rest of the question is actually about 30-60-90 triangles. You need to be able to convert the radian measures to degrees: $\frac{\pi}{6} = 30°$, $\frac{\pi}{3} = 60°$, and $\frac{11\pi}{6} = 330°$. If you use the 30-60-90 proportions from the Reference Chart, you'll build a right triangle with a hypotenuse of 1 (which is the given radius in the question).

Advanced Geometry

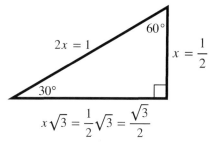

$$2x = 1 \qquad 60° \qquad x = \frac{1}{2}$$

$$30°$$

$$x\sqrt{3} = \frac{1}{2}\sqrt{3} = \frac{\sqrt{3}}{2}$$

We can compare this triangle to the one formed in the original picture. The cosine of $\angle AOB$ is $\frac{\sqrt{3}}{2}$, which is basically the adjacent side. The $\sin(30°) = \frac{1}{2}$, which proves Choice B wrong. The $\cos(60°) = \frac{1}{2}$, which proves Choice C wrong. That leaves Choice D, which is also correct because 330° is basically an angle of –30°. This question is absolutely insane. It's not a high priority, even for people shooting for an 800. This topic is unlikely to come up on the test. Your best bet to minimize the memorization and still give yourself a chance at the points on something like this is to use the "All Students Take Calculus" memory device to keep track of which trigonometric function is positive or negative in each quadrant. That's usually enough to eliminate some answers. From there, look for the familiar 45-45-90 and 30-60-90 triangles.

#11 — Answer = C

The twist here is that the height of the cone is not given. We can use the 10 as the hypotenuse of a right triangle that is inside the cone. Work backwards from the area of a circle formula to find the radius of the base: $36\pi = \pi r^2$. You can use Pythagorean Theorem or 3-4-5 triangle proportions to find that the height is 8. Plug the values into the formula for cones from the Reference Chart: $V = \frac{1}{3}\pi(6)^2(8)$.

#12 — Answer = C

The figure is extremely misleading. If arc AB and arc BC are congruent, then the angles that open to those arcs are also congruent, so $\angle A = \angle C$. Once you fill in $\angle A = 40$, you can subtract from 180 to find the remaining $\angle B$: $180 - 40 - 40 = 100$. As a reminder, when there's no "note", you can assume that the figure is drawn to scale. If there is a note, you might still be able to use the picture a little bit. But sometimes the picture is purposely drawn to make your life hard. The picture will make no sense with the actual values of the sides and angles. Trust the math, not your eyes.

If you found this book helpful, please review it on Amazon.

It helps others find this study guide, and the support is greatly appreciated!

Made in United States
Orlando, FL
01 March 2023

30547590R10180